BEING GOOD

BEING GOOD

*Women's Moral Values
in Early America*

Martha Saxton

ᵂ HILL AND WANG

A DIVISION OF FARRAR, STRAUS AND GIROUX

NEW YORK

Hill and Wang
A division of Farrar, Straus and Giroux

Printed in the United States of America
First edition, 2003

Library of Congress Cataloging-in-Publication Data
Saxton, Martha.
    Being good : women's moral values in early America / Martha Saxton.—
1st ed.
        p.   cm.
    Includes bibliographical references and index.
        ISBN: 978-0-8090-1633-4
    1. Ethics—United States—History.   2. Women—Conduct of life—History.
3. United States—Social life and customs.   I. Title.
BJ1610 .S39 2003
170'.82'0973—dc21
                                                                    2002032836

Designed by Jonathan D. Lippincott

www.fsgbooks.com

1   3   5   7   9   10   8   6   4   2

This is for
Francesco and Josephine Ferorelli, my children,
and Enrico Ferorelli, my foundation

CONTENTS

PART THREE

ACKNOWLEDGMENTS

The many, many people who deserve my thanks start with Jonathan Galassi, who thought the idea would make a book, and Eric Foner, an extraordinary teacher and historian, who supervised the thesis which became the first third of *Being Good*. Several other teachers and friends at Columbia, including Betsy Blackmar, Nancy Woloch, Alden Vaughan, Rosalind Rosenberg, and the late Eric McKitrick, gave me much help and encouragement. I am grateful to the Society of Fellows at Columbia for the chance to teach Lit. Hum. and to the Bunting Institute at Radcliffe for the wonderful year of 1995–96, teaching nothing. At Amherst College, my friends and colleagues have all been generous to a fault. My thanks to Rhea Cabin, Frederick Griffiths, Frank Couvares, Michele Barale, David Blight, Margaret Hunt, Rose Olver, and Kevin Sweeney for their help—intellectual, moral, and material. My editor, Thomas LeBien, helped give a draft, ramshackle from years of additions and partitions, shape and a new trim line. Kristina McGowan saw to its well-being in countless ways. My uncle, Alexander Saxton, is a continuing inspiration.

This project is twenty-two years old, the age of my oldest child, so I want to thank a lifetime of friends for seeing it and me through our formative years. My deep gratitude goes to Susan Moldow, Wendy Gimbel, Judith Thurman, Jean Strouse, Susan Galassi, Diane and Geoffrey Ward, Kate Wenner, Susan Hassler, Lindley and Dorothy Forsythe, Marina Warner, Diana Wylie, Richard D. Smith, Michael Beldoch, Peggy Davis, Margaret Higonnet, Dubravka Ugresic, Carolyn Eisenberg, Georges and Ann Borchardt, Ken Kusmer, Florence Ladd, Tina and Bill Reinhardt, Cynthia Vartan, Rollene Saal, Kathy Dalsimer and Peter Pouncey, and Eden Lipson.

My thanks to the Massachusetts Historical Society, the Boston Public Library, the New England Historic and Genealogical Society, the Houghton Library at Harvard, the Swem Library at the College of William and Mary, the Virginia Historical Society, Colonial Williamsburg, and the Missouri Historical Society for their help in using their rich collections.

BEING GOOD

INTRODUCTION

How did early American women think about trying to lead a good life? By what standards did they evaluate themselves and their efforts? Where did they come from morally, and how did their morals change over time? In the first decades of the United States' existence, many white women's moral ideas about themselves were truncated by the dependence and obedience expected of them as wives and by their enforced absence from the great debates concerning politics and the structure of the economy. Ironically, slave women had, whether they wanted it or not, more personal and moral autonomy within marriage than white women had, but far less in the wider social context.

Moral life is intimately connected with emotional life, and it is impossible to talk about one without implicating the other. Parents and other people in authority usually deliver moral prescriptions with emotional warnings that evil will be received with anger and punishment and good will be rewarded with love and encouragement. Children internalize the emotional messages as readily as, if not more so than, the ethical ones. As children grow up and absorb the moral code surrounding them, they will also be likely to be pleased with themselves when behaving as they should and worried, frightened, or perhaps defiant when behaving as they should not. Of course children and adults experience far more complex feelings than simple pleasure or self-dislike in making moral choices. Values have powerful, if not always predictable, effects on emotions, and vice versa. Furthermore, and particularly for women, societies moralize emotions themselves, emphasizing the virtue in sweetness and compassion, the vice in anger, or, for the early republic, the unalloyed good in the expression of motherly love.

Being Good looks at women in three communities in early America to see what moral values were prescribed for them and how they responded to these values. The book starts in Puritan Massachusetts, an obvious choice for a story about moral questions. Puritans famously wished to be an example of a community living out God's word both for themselves and to demonstrate to the corrupt in England what a pure life looked like. Boston and its environs were a relatively homogeneous community, established by people who argued interminably but who saw the world and their places in it with relative uniformity. Although many in Massachusetts were not Puritans or were not good ones, and although many disagreed on points of doctrine with the clergy and magistrates, no one seriously threatened their moral authority in the seventeenth century.

I

Part One is a discussion of moral standards for women in Boston from 1630 to 1700. It attempts to define the comprehensive moral system Puritan authorities devised to organize the lives of women in their familial and community relations. The discussion begins with childhood and shows how Puritans educated their girls to render them obedient, humble, and passive, their parents giving them such names as Chastity, Mercy, Silence, and Charity. Puritan ideas and laws about sex, including the sexuality of Native Americans and Africans, demonstrate Puritan efforts to instill in girls modesty and easily tapped wells of shame. Puritan habits of introspection and self-criticism led girls to search themselves for, and to find, wickedness.

They scrutinized themselves for moral information about what needed to be brought under control, instilling the discipline for their married lives. Men were expected to select agreeable and sexually attractive spouses while women were to find mates they could obey. Individual choice mattered for women, but its reward was to be found in deference more than in desire.

The discussion of marriage falls into two parts: its moral outlines and internal dynamics, as well as some of the ways wives enlarged its boundaries. The first part deals with the reach of obedience into the relation, the expectations surrounding sexuality, and the risks of melancholy. The second deals with divorce, separation, adultery, and aspects of wives' lives that were not necessarily related to marriage but occurred at the time of women's maturity. It suggests that some managed to achieve a substantial measure of moral authority as vigorous advocates of the moral system in which they lived. The last chapter treats motherhood. Mothers, like wives, had opportunities to experience the pleasures of achieving stature in the family and the neighborhood through rigorous observance of the moral code. But the isolation of life in the New World, the unremitting work, and the substantial risk of depression that accompanied the Puritans' system of strict emotional control could flatten mothers' energies and capabilities, leaving them and their children in a bleak, despondent landscape.

Another facet of Puritan maternity was mothers' relative emotional independence from their children, augmented by the imperative that they rescue their children from sin and place them on the road to salvation. Puritans' dour view of the moral condition of small children made motherly discipline an urgent task. The solitude of the search for salvation emphasized each Puritan's existential isolation. Thus Puritan culture was not particularly hospitable to excessive dependence or the kind of moral and emotional merging that characterized nineteenth-century middle-class white life.

Throughout the book I attempt to show the lifelong interrelationship among women's behavior, feelings, and the moral system designed to control them. Puritanism stressed self-distrust and trying to understand and fulfill God's desires. Authority proceeded from rationality. Women, who were considered imperfectly rational at best, could only proceed from obedience to a higher (male) rationality. However, being a foot soldier for Christ within a culture that does not value personal autonomy, as Puritans did not, was not itself inherently humiliating for women. Many women created strong identities and strong families despite the repressive culture and took pride in the belief that they were doing God's work as best they could. Most accepted the fundamental notion that men and women had different restrictions on them and different tasks in society.

Puritans in general saw potential significance in everything. This habit of mind made life a serious business for both sexes. Puritans could find God's blessings in another's disaster, even while they could discover harbingers of disaster in their own apparent blessings. I confess to having what John K. Nelson, historian of Anglicanism, has called dissenter bias: I admire the way Puritans examined the lives they led. I do not admire their self-serving interpretations but their imperative to interpret, which was an invitation, indeed a duty, for both sexes.

Sex is most frequently associated with women's moral values. This is probably because men have traditionally been most interested in controlling the sexual behavior of women to the exclusion of many other kinds of behavior. Puritans tried to regulate sexuality as a profoundly important appetite that could alienate one from God. They worked hard to associate independent sexuality, aggression, and self-assertion in women with shame as a central disciplinary strategy. But they were not Victorians, as historians have pointed out for decades. They were relatively practical and frank about sex, even as they wished to moderate its hold on the female imagination in particular. The installation of self-control was even more important to Puritans than controlling sex, and they tried to regulate love as well. The disproportionate emphasis on the sexual behavior of women became more pronounced in the nineteenth century, when it acquired significantly more symbolic weight than it had in the seventeenth and eighteenth centuries.

In addition to looking at the Puritans' overall ideas and behavior, I have tried to see how the moral systems for different groups chafed against one another, starting with male and female Puritans and including Puritans and Indians, and Puritans and Africans. Puritans sought to create harmony between men and women through complementary prescriptions for sexuality, emotional and familial responsibilities, and identical prescriptions for detachment from the world and devotion to God. These complementary prescriptions did not endure. Puritan men in the New World began to look less and less to religion and more to their callings, and after 1660 women increasingly dominated the church rolls. Women's piety and virtue came to be a central support on which the whole community could base its moral confidence. Puritans, who had once seen all community members as equally culpable and equally affected by one another's actions, came to believe both that God had ordained that women suffer more than men and that women were closer than men to God. The roots of a kind of implicit social bargain developed in the emerging distinctions of piety according to gender. Women's suffering and religiosity, if combined with an otherwise "godly carriage," began acquiring broadly redemptive potential.

Encounters with Native societies and with Africans challenged, reconfirmed, and in some ways altered the moral values of the English immigrants. Racist stereotypes about both Indians and Africans began to exaggerate the significance of the chastity of European womanhood in creating a virtuous (female) identity in the New World. Moreover, the heroic ethos of Native warriors gave Puritans an easy justification for self-interestedness and ruthlessness, a tradition that, like others, continued long after Puritan theology had been displaced.

II

The second third of the book is set in the mid to late eighteenth century in the eastern part of Virginia, with very occasional forays into Maryland. This was the oldest and wealthiest part of Virginia, a largely Anglican community. In 1790 all Virginia had about five hundred thousand residents, half largely of British descent and half West

African. In some counties in the eastern section Africans outnumbered whites. Half slave and half free, Virginia harbored at least two
major moral outlooks. The dominant moral outlook evolving among
white Virginians in their slave society—as opposed to a society with
slaves like Massachusetts—was to have determinative consequences
in shaping the values of the new republic.

If Puritans laid the groundwork for the elevation of women that
became dogma in the nineteenth century, eighteenth-century experience in Virginia taught white men and women how living in a slave
society offered a wealth of ready-made (if inaccurate) white-serving
contrasts in values between blacks and whites. Educated white girls
were reading novels and handbooks describing an emergent moral
ethos based not simply on obeisance to authority but also on feelings
of sympathy and empathy. They incorporated a vocabulary of delicacy, sentiment, and subtle emotional and moral distinctions that
supplemented but rarely overrode the injunction on women to obey
men. Elite white women did this in the shadow of a population of
250,000 enslaved Africans, who whites believed were defined by in-
delicacy and brutish feelings. The origins of the rule of sentiment
and sympathy that characterized the nineteenth century appeared in
eighteenth-century Virginia against a background of the presumed
incapacity of African Americans to feel and articulate refined sentiments and hence to recognize and act on the moral dictates of sympathy and empathy.

As the eighteenth century progressed, elite white mothers were
sometimes emboldened to defy their husbands on questions of family discipline, including corporal punishment for their sons. They,
too, were empowered by the substitution of gentleness and exemplary conduct for coercion, which was rapidly acquiring an unsavory
reputation. Lacking the spiritual independence and individual gravity of Puritan women, white women in Virginia imitated British
models of feminine gentility, cultivating dependence, empathy, and
refined sensibility, a kind of emotional and moral style that psychologist Carol Gilligan has termed *relatedness*. Their displays of sensibility and delicate feelings acquired social potency through racial
comparisons: In the Chesapeake the whip was associated with slave
discipline and with African feelings blunted by barbarism.

A slender bridge of emotions and morality that black and white Christians could sometimes traverse together had its origins in the First Great Awakening's revivals in the mid-eighteenth century in Virginia. There white parishioners noted the remarkable depth of feeling among newly converted black worshipers. Just as men had linked piety to suffering in women in Puritan Massachusetts, so most whites explicitly or implicitly linked suffering to slave piety. Demonstrative emotionalism quickly came to be associated with Christianized blacks in interracial congregations. Powerful testifiers to God, black Christians impressed and sometimes frightened whites, providing a standard for engaged piety. White constructions of the strong displays of feeling of black Christians first evident in this Awakening had become commonplace by the nineteenth century. Black emotionality and white female emotionality often overlapped, and their similarities, I believe, came to encourage a more repressed emotive and sexual style in white women than had been the case in eighteenth-century Virginia.

If there came to be an unspoken moral complementarity in Virginia underpinning society, it was between whites and blacks, not between men and women. Unlike women in Massachusetts, women in Virginia were not considered significantly more pious than men. Planter society valued white women's chastity, but it also valued the pleasures of flirtation, romance, and sex, and it offered many opportunities to the young to enjoy the pleasures of dalliance. Rising illegitimacy among white women may have heightened revolutionary and postrevolutionary anxiety about the role of women in a republic whose virtue needed all the support it could muster. Given the existent mythology about black women's willing promiscuity, anxiety over the republic and rising sentiment against slavery made it logical for its defenders to enlarge on the supposed natural differences between the sexual behavior of white and black women to answer the new demands for a supply of national virtue.

Unwilling participants in this bargain, first-, second-, and third-generation West African arrivals in mid- to late-eighteenth-century Virginia came from traditions that varied in regard to female chastity. Some ethnicities considered the ability to get along with a partner and the proved capacity to have children the significant determinants in marriage. Other communities insisted on virginity before matrimony. None of these variations mattered in white ascriptions of moral values to blacks. Black women's presumed lasciviousness made them acutely vulnerable to sexual predation, and this of course confirmed white assumptions about their sexual standards and behavior. Meanwhile women slaves struggled to hold on to traditional West African values elevating motherhood to the highest social importance. They fought with owners and overseers about their reproductive health and the care of their children. Their assigned moral status and their vulnerability made their fight to protect and preserve themselves and their children that much more urgent.

III

Missouri in the early nineteenth century brought emigrants from New England with strong Calvinist backgrounds together with large numbers of whites and blacks from Virginia and other parts of the South. Moral traditions from New England and the South came together, sometimes in conflict, and mixed with yet others. Anglo-Americans pouring into the territory were taking over an area, surrounded by Native Americans, that the French had settled lightly in the eighteenth century. Missouri in 1820 became a slave state at the edge of free territory. From the 1830s on, migrants from Germany and Ireland arrived. A substantial and growing Catholic population interspersed with Protestants, many of them awakened in the revivals of the early nineteenth century, offered possibilities for moral conflict and moral comparisons, as did slavery, Indian policy, cultural differences among ethnic groups, and the various ways that politics and the rapidly growing economy entered women's lives. St. Louis in the early republic brings into one focus a rapidly growing center of trade, a society at the border between European and Indian settlement, the largest religious groups then (and still now) dominant in the United States, and a border state where slavery was permitted but not completely ascendant.

The territorial and commercial expansion that was creating

wealth and leisure for some white Americans was dependent upon the continued displacement of Indians. The early European settlers' decision to adopt a more or less continual state of war with Native people had produced almost three hundred years of violence to resolve the mode of sharing the continent. White and black American women living near these conflicts usually had little say in where they lived or in the prosecution of Indian policy. In and around St. Louis, white women seem to have supported military conflict and removal of the local Indians. Frightened, often isolated, most white women were willing to accept the necessity of violence. Evangelical women understood a moral obligation to try to Christianize the Indians, and some worked to that end. All agreed that Indian culture was fast disappearing and that that was as it should be.

In the postrevolutionary years the sexually pure white woman had become the nation's hedge against its distressing commercialism and violent politics. The sexual purity that Puritans had assigned to women had acquired extra symbolic meaning in a multiracial society. Men ascribed to white women's chastity the difference between white civilization and black degradation. Middle-class white women had to demonstrate their purity through chaste language, severe standards for judging others, and carefully monitored behavior in and out of the home. Conscious of the less repressed style of African Americans, with whom they often worshiped, white women appreciated the dangers of losing control.

Chaste, white (Protestant) women reputedly influenced the country in myriad virtuous ways, but in practice the strictures of obedience in marriage, while downplayed by moralists, were strong. Obedience placed a barrier between perception and action that of necessity discouraged critical moral thinking. Society generally, but not always, encouraged women's submission to higher authority more than moral challenges. On the other hand, evangelical women increasingly used the touchstone of their own feelings to reason morally. Woman's individual conscience, originally activated in search of her own salvation, acquired more range in the early nineteenth century.

With the approval of their husbands and the cooperation of their ministers, Protestant women engaged in charity work, although overall reform activities in Missouri were circumscribed by violent pro-slavery sentiment. Meanwhile nuns, with financial support from local Catholics, tended the sick and elderly and took care of Catholic orphans, first girls and later boys. Working in favor of the Catholics was an established tradition of both community work and, of course, communities of dedicated celibate women. Protestant women, on the other hand, had to signal submission to men and invent a rationale for their own extradomestic behavior before getting down to the tasks at hand.

The conditions of early-nineteenth-century marriage for white women in Missouri made difficult the choice of marriage itself, much less that of a husband. The duties of wives began with obedience and included repeated childbirth, the responsibility for the health and happiness of family members, and the probability of leaving their birth families and moving several times. These moves often meant debilitating isolation. There were continuities with the previous centuries, but individual and family mobility had greatly increased, health was deteriorating, women's emotional responsibilities were greater, and the ideological climate in which marriage took place had changed. The Revolution and the spreading ideology of sympathy promised both greater autonomy and lives directed toward happiness. Yet marriage and motherhood were dangerous, confining, and predicated on women's subordination. Choosing a husband, an activity supposedly transformed by a new spirit of voluntarism, was particularly hard for women in rapidly changing communities, and one that usually required the advice of family and friends.

Marriage was increasingly affectionate. At the same time, it was increasingly penetrated by the ramifications of commerce. Although a wife had nothing to say about how her husband made his living, the demands of his work structured her life. Middle-class women sometimes judged their marital happiness according to their husbands' purchases for them, collapsing the vocabularies of domesticity and the marketplace. Wives devoted attention to the careful consumption of items for family use, while making an effort to desire little for themselves. Husbands included in their obligations the custodianship of their wives' material desires.

Feelings achieved new validity in moral and family life in the nineteenth century because of a growing emphasis on emotion in religion and the revolutionary-era insistence on an individual's pursuit of his own happiness. Wives presided over this developing culture of sentiment, deriving their domestic authority from their emotional piety. In middle-class and rural families, religious women often led their families to church, camp meetings, and conversion. The points in marriage when wives both manifested and acquired moral power were childbirth and death, that of others and their own. Their unofficial ministry at home made them not just makers of meaning but actual sources of meaning in a world otherwise given over to the violent and headlong pursuit of wealth and position. Increasingly a reasoned but emotional basis for moral choice was in tension with the obedience and self-suppression required in marriage.

Child rearing and the transmission of moral values from generation to generation were now predominantly a woman's task. The virtues women taught were largely personal. Sympathy and empathy, celebrated since the eighteenth century among the prosperous, were more and more middle-class guides to conduct—but only within the middle class. Thus one moral system and emotional style, based on respect for sentiment, the individual, and the encouragement of voluntary behavior, governed middle-class family life, while a more authoritarian and coercive system characterized extrafamilial life. The rapid elaboration of sentimental culture made it clearer and clearer who could participate in its pleasures and who could not. Within middle-class culture, women displayed their relatedness to their children and their husbands. The larger emphasis on emotion over strict principle in religion and family life had the effect of increasingly making moral decisions accord with feelings and simultaneously of overdetermining feelings with moral meaning.

African American wives did not benefit much, if at all, from the growing consumer culture, but they experienced the expanding market through its role in separating more slave families than ever before. In the absence of many close and uninterrupted generational ties, African American women experienced significant autonomy in

choosing their husbands. After marriage, obedience to their husbands was not their greatest moral challenge. This may have made
the institution of marriage more attractive to African American
women. On the other hand, one of the reasons that wifely obedience
could not be a constant of slave marriage was that marriage was always in danger of dissolution. Also, married couples not infrequently
lived apart from each other. The difficulties of survival in a slave society were simply too relentless for husbands to make many of their
wives' decisions for them. The possibility of freedom was another
spur to the self-reliance of African American women. The location of
Missouri on the Mississippi River across from the free state of Illinois made liberty more than a distant dream to many, but freedom
was likely to carry with it the imperative of abrupt and terrible independence from family and friends. Black mothers and daughters
thought about and prepared for separation, either involuntary or
chosen. The external submission required of slaves masked among
many a core of self-reliance that mothers cultivated in themselves
and their daughters.

This training for slave girls might be required as early as the age
of five or six since there was a thriving market in and around St.
Louis for a "girl" who would help white women with their housework. The presence of the "girl" meant the possibility of middle-class
status for white women and middle-class education for their daughters. Elite white girls' education in skills and emotional attitudes that
would mark them as members of the middle class depended upon
the presence in their homes of a slave or poor white girl who would
perform the labor that they and their mothers were no longer doing.
This symbiosis produced resilient black women—if it didn't kill
them—and white women trained for relatedness.

In the early nineteenth century, inhabitants of St. Louis, like
other white Americans, worried about their national moral stature.
Just as Puritans had imagined themselves as the exemplary City on a
Hill, so much more did Americans see themselves as an enormous
experiment in liberty, one gigantic petri dish in which economic freedom and democracy would blend to produce the model republic.
The virtues that would keep them models to the rest of the world did

not reside in economic strife or men's scramble for political office. It lay in the sexual purity and selflessness of women—white women, because blacks were impure by definition. Although white women were national hostages to both the double standard and self-sacrifice, many of them saw rewards in assuming these burdensome responsibilities. They desired the respected moral status and the rising tide of prosperity that carried with it—albeit with ups and downs—the growing middle class.

The moral system and its characteristic emotions that emerged dominant in the nineteenth century developed out of a variety of sources, including political and economic necessities. The idealized moral identity of white women grew out of Christian virtues such as humility, charity, and kindness but stopped at the pale enclosing "respectable" whites. Scriptural support for sexism and distrust of women's sexuality completed white women's moral imperatives. The enormous growth of slavery in the eighteenth century and accompanying racist associations about black women generated an anxiety to refine further moral ideas about white women. The eighteenth-century elite's retreat from moral engagement on any but a private plane provided the layout for the nineteenth century's inward, humid domesticity. A tender, apparently noncoercive emotional style identified its practitioners. It encouraged obedience and submission to authority rather than self-reliance and an independent mind. At the same time, sentimental culture encouraged women to assume a kindly moral and social imperialism over nonwhite and non-middle-class people.

The moral ideas of black women, judged deviant and inferior, prepared them for the realities of life as colonized people: hard work, endurance, independence, mutual aid. Sexual fidelity, not purity, was a central goal. Slavery constantly imposed sacrifices on mothers, and they imposed on themselves the belief that the freedom of family members, however distressing their absence would be, was worth the sacrifice. The condition of slavery did not encourage in slave women the same kind of emotional and moral dependence on men that marriage in middle-class culture did. Nor could slaves enclose themselves within hothouses for the cultivation of family life.

White assumptions about the impure sexual and domestic behavior of black women provided a perverse reflected moral glory for white people. But the black community saw achieving freedom, not the fetishizing of the sexual purity of its women, as most relevant to its own moral worth.

We still struggle with long-lived tendrils of nineteenth-century moral ideas and moralized feelings. The emotional individualism and its malignant deviations, narcissism and anomie, with which we live now are rooted in the revolutionary goal of pursuing private happiness. The Second Great Awakening stamped this enterprise with righteousness, and women's sentimental culture shaped feelings and a language for its practitioners. Paradoxically, white families now increasingly must adopt what developed initially as African American survival strategies and accompanying moral understandings. These help them cope with an economy that is reaching ever deeper into family life. The inexorably expanding market means that fewer and fewer women can display the self-sacrifice and dependence that once reassured the nation it was being good.

Part One

PROLOGUE

The Puritans brought to the forests of North America powerful ideas about how to live the good life, modes of thought and action to glorify God and contribute to the benefit of society. These assumptions reflected changes wrought by the Reformation and the Scientific Revolution and included particularly what the philosopher Charles Taylor has identified as radical reflexivity. It encouraged a thinking person to look within himself to analyze and understand the material world. Ideas like melancholy and pain were now intrinsic to the mind of man, and their contemplation was an aspect of contemplating the self.[1] The Reformation reinforced this worldview, making salvation a matter between man and God. A minister could guide a congregant, but he had no mystical access to the Lord. Puritan husbands and fathers became God's representatives in the family, transferring to laymen the potent dignity, but not the mystical power, once reserved for the clergy. Women as well as men could experience and ponder God's direct mercy, but men retained the final authority over His meanings.

The work of early modern scientists, particularly Francis Bacon, rendered this view of the world immeasurably stronger and more persuasive. Their instrumental understanding of the earth implied that man's relation to the world was one of potential control and sub-ordination. Man viewed his rationality as subordinating the environment and increasingly saw his reason as sovereign over his feelings. This growing emphasis on reason, however, was problematic for women. Defined as incapable of rationality and hence self-mastery, women needed the free will of rational men to guide and, if necessary, subdue them.[2]

This revolution in thinking also meant that the sources of moral behavior were no longer outside man, but within. God's special and inexplicable grace was necessary for man's salvation, but he had to commit freely to the strenuous, lifelong effort to lead a godly life, guided by reasoning and self-reflection. Man's ability to see himself as a subject to be reformed and improved was of world-changing importance.

Women occupied an ambiguous space among these disengaged subjects. Puritan men believed that women, not being rational, incompletely dominated their own passions and feelings. On the other hand, women shared spiritual equality with men. Like men, women engaged in intense self-scrutiny, working to overcome worldly attachments while detaching themselves from their objects of desire and maintaining their responsibilities. Women officially did not have reason yet were supposed to behave as if they had.

A Puritan girl was subject to her father's authority, as a wife was subject to her husband's. Yet women, like men, reasoned through the steps to their salvation. With the aid of ministers, they collected their thoughts in a narrative and sometimes kept journals of self-examination. That they were prosecuted in church and court for offenses and pressured to confess their sins suggests a belief in their ability to learn from punishment and edify others with their education. The exceptions were black women. They were prosecuted more severely than white women for similar misdemeanors, but no one sought their public confessions; authorities believed there was nothing that white Puritans could learn from black women's experiences.

Puritans particularly worried about women's failures of rationality in matters of sexuality and maternity. Even the presumably disengaged male could lose awareness of God in the delights of human sensation and the sweet affection children evoked. Puritan men assumed women were far more open than they to these urges and desires. By policing these experiences, Puritan men hoped to control women as well as their own incompletely subdued sexuality and nagging yearnings for love and indulgence.

Puritans not only viewed morality as deriving from rational choices but also saw the good life as consisting of the careful fulfillment of everyday activities. With the Scientific Revolution and the Reformation, God was recast to smile on marriage, sexuality, reproduction, and the vocations that contributed to the common good. Doctors, merchants, and shipwrights, for example, all did praiseworthy work, and His approval no longer accrued exclusively to contemplation. Women's primary calling, housewifery, changed little in practice, but pursued with dedication, it achieved new importance in the scale of human efforts, as did fulfilling family responsibilities with love and goodwill.

The new moral and religious significance given to marriage and family brought women's activities into the spotlight. A patriarch directed work and devotion within the family, but the proof of success was in a harmonious marriage and godly children. This increased valuation of marriage, child rearing, and other ordinary activities was part of a new emphasis on how things were done rather than on what they were. As one Puritan theologian wrote, "God loveth adverbs; and cares not how good, but how well." Women were to perform their tasks, loving God, loving their families, and maintaining a becoming deference to their husbands. Women who did so with commitment and care could be assured that God judged their labors kindly.[3]

In stressing ordinary labors that were for the common good over the older aristocratic values of display, personal heroism, and heroic generosity, the Reformation gave new significance to women's work and the emotions accompanying their activities. An important exception quickly emerged in response to the presence of Native Americans in the New World. Military glory was a value of the ancient world, one that Puritans had only intermittently emphasized, yet they rapidly came to believe that God wished them to kill Indians, even women and children, from time to time. Puritans obsessively focused on the cruelty of Indian practices, blinding themselves to their own more impersonal, distant, but nonetheless terrible brutality toward Native peoples. While Puritans did not precisely revive Homeric values in the New World, their encounters with Native peoples permitted Puritan men, and occasionally women, to behave with violent speech and action otherwise forbidden.[4]

1

CHILDREN AND ADOLESCENTS

Puritans, whose faith was born in criticism, came simultaneously to celebrate and to constitute women in a vocabulary emphasizing modesty, timidity, obedience to authority, and self-doubt. Within a moral system devised with many purposes in mind, from the glorification of God to the control and ordering of work and family life, men publicly assigned significance to behavior. The result was a complex of beliefs designed to restrain women in a number of areas, including the expression of aggression, the assertion of sexuality, the pursuit of advanced intellectual activity, the independent acquisition of wealth, and the attainment of secular authority. Although church and state enforcement varied over time, and much depended on the personalities of individual fathers and husbands, women grew up in a society that could be both repressive and punitive.[1]

Women's legitimate road to moral authority was to enforce the moral system on themselves, children, husbands, and neighbors. In this capacity some women confirmed the Reverend Cotton Mather's late-seventeenth-century observation that they were more spiritually inclined than men were. Saturated more thoroughly in Puritan logic, women were also likely to see themselves as more sinful in nature, not just in deed, and, in the deadly atmosphere of Salem in 1692, as

more in league with the devil and less capable of defending themselves against witchcraft charges than men were.[2]

In the best case, the culture produced strong, self-contained, emotionally subdued, literate, and sometimes well-educated women who
had real but restricted moral authority at home and in the community
and who considered themselves equal to men in the eyes of God and
in their chances for salvation. Those who imbibed their training deeply
might also be subject to gloomy introspection, self-doubt, and a close
acquaintance with guilt and shame, particularly as concomitants to acts
of self-assertion. Puritans pioneered and refined the installation of
conscience, one that turned out to be more punishing for women than
for men. Perhaps their most distinctive and in many ways long-lasting
achievement, this Puritan conscience became fundamental to middle-
class child rearing in the early nineteenth century.

Puritan Girls

Puritans welcomed their babies but regarded them as inherently evil.
They were born stained with original sin, and it was only through the
fervent ministrations of their parents and their own active cooperation that children stood a chance of being saved from the eternal
fires of damnation. Moreover, while all children were evil, girls, inheriting Eve's disgrace, were even more corrupt than boys. Eve's
transgression in Eden preceded Adam's and exceeded his in sinfulness. For a girl, original sin suggested more than the roster of Puritan character flaws, which would have included pride, deadness
toward God, greed, lust, and overattachment to the world, as well as
weakness, gullibility, curiosity, immodesty, carnality, and, above all,
disobedience.[3]

Anne Bradstreet, first-generation Puritan, poet, and wife of the
magistrate Simon Bradstreet, described her early childhood like this:

> I begin to sin as soon as act:
> A perverce will, a love to what's forbid,
> A serpents sting in pleasing face lay hid:
> A lying tongue as soon as it could speak.[4]

In part to keep the young from temptation, boys and girls were schooled separately, and the General Court declared that all unemployed children be set to tasks in order that "boyes and girles not be suffered to converse together, so as may occasion any wanton, dishonest, or immodest behavior." Schooling was not just to control disobedience. Famous for their insistence on at least passive literacy (reading, if not writing) for virtually all members of their community, Puritans expected girls to learn to read, while boys were to read and write. Children did their earliest learning at home, or in a dame school at the home of a woman who could teach them to read, and some girls from prosperous families also studied writing. Male education, however, was of the greatest moment. In 1647 Massachusetts mandated that all communities of fifty families or more establish a common school but restricted these schools to boys until 1789.[5]

Unusual learning was something of a moral embarrassment to women. As the English Puritan Elizabeth Joceline observed, women needed to learn housewifery and to read the Bible, but "Other learning a woman needs not though I admire it in those God has blest with discretion." Even when male moralists expanded the areas for female study to include music, languages, and housewifery, they emphasized that girls should study only for religious purposes. Judge Samuel Sewall wrote with satisfaction that his daughter Betty had used all her evenings for three months to read one volume of the *Book of Martyrs*. For those girls who learned to write, the private diary was the proper place for their literary efforts, primarily to record moments of self-examination, self-correction, and the corrections of God. The Reverend Cotton Mather published bits of his sister Jerusha's diary. She listed her hopes for salvation, her fears of sleeping too much or too often, and her afflictions, providing notes after each item on its helpfulness in teaching her some new service to God. She commented on her acquaintances' dealings with God. She listed many flaws, culminating in "that Sin of Sins, my original Sin, my Nature is Sinful."[6]

The diary and conversion narratives were expressive forms that demanded that Puritans reflect upon themselves with an intense and ruthless honesty. The diary trained girls in self-observation and the identification and analysis of their feelings as indicators of their moral condition. Puritans catechized girls and boys publicly until they were sixteen. After that, ministers called only upon unmarried males to answer catechism in public, preparing girls for silence in church. The year after Anne Hutchinson had been exiled for heresy in the antinomian crisis that shook Massachusetts in 1637, the Cambridge Synod ruled that although a woman might, after a sermon, ask a question in public for information, "Yet this ought to be very wisely and sparingly done, and that with leave of the elders." Ten years later the Reverend John Cotton wrote that there were only two conditions under which a woman might speak in church. One was "to give account of her offence," and the other was to sing praises to the Lord.[7]

Idleness, whether of the rich or poor, Puritans believed, gave the devil an opportunity. To teach girls the domestic arts and keep them busy, many families sent their daughters to other households to learn housekeeping. For girls from more prosperous families this was a short, informal arrangement that took place somewhere around the age of twelve or later. For poorer ones the arrangement was contractual, and the girls became indentured servants, often leaving home at age eight or nine. The experience of wealthier girls placed in prosperous families was likely to be continuous with that at home. In all probability there would be no formal contract between them. There would be no physical chastisement. Captain Lawrence Hammond recorded in his diary the apparently friendly verbal agreement between his wife and John Nevinson, the father of thirteen-year-old Elizabeth, who was coming to live with the Hammonds for six years as a servant to be "taught, instructed & provided for as shal be meet."[8]

Indentured servants, however, who may or may not have been religious, might encounter Puritan values in a benign setting, but they might also, and often did, find that physical and sexual abuse followed even from docility and obedience. Issues of survival and self-preservation sometimes conflicted with Puritan ideals of obedience and meekness. John Winthrop's contract with Mary Gore spelled out fully the restrictions under which a servant lived. She was to serve faithfully and gladly, keep the family secrets, not waste its goods or lend them to anyone unlawfully. She was not to commit fornication or contract a marriage during her term of service. She was not to gamble, drink, or "absent herselfe from her said service day or night." She was to be meek and well mannered. Her master and mistress, for their part, were to instruct her in religion and give her food, clothing, a place to live, and all the necessities of life. Indian children, like the thirty-one Daniel Gookin distributed in the aftermath of King Philip's War, faced yet harsher conditions, including even lifetime servitude.[9]

Contracts effectively put a girl servant at the complete disposition, night and day, of the family for which she worked. They also, in their judicious employment of adjectives, gave the family moral say over her demeanor as well as her work. She was to be willing, cheerful, discreet, and humble. She was, as far as the law could enforce, to be on her employer's side, a family member in everything but inheritance rights and, probably, affection. While Puritan families may have realized this ideal among members sharing the same social standing, they often failed to achieve it across lines of economic disparity.

Work enforcement for indentured servants was routinely harsh and physical. Employers did not expect their servants to have imbibed the lessons of submission and self-doubt or to be reachable through verbal suasion. Men usually handled discipline, but some women physically disciplined servant girls as well. The treatment could be violent. A neighbor testified that William Cheeny struck his servant Experience Holbrook with his hand, and when she fell to the ground, he kicked her. When she got up and went inside, he followed her with a "pretty big stick." Sarah Eaton, the seventeen-year-old servant of Mistress Dearing's, testified that her mistress beat her sister Martha, also a servant, "about the head till the blood cam out of her eares, & so remayneth for certaine dayes the blood Flying out of her eares, & shortly after the said Martha fell first into a great fitt o' sickness & never was well since." Thomas Crosswell, his wife, and their daughter defended themselves in court against charges that they had beaten to death their servant Rebecca Lee. Servants had the legal right to complain about their treatment in court, but many girls were too young, too frightened, or too ill informed to complain. The lucky ones had parents who did so for them.[10]

Although violence in the early modern world was hardly unusual,

within the Puritan world it signified that the recipient was insufficiently submissive and had failed to comport herself with a Puritan
conscience. Indians were at even greater risk than white servants.
When Puritans became masters of servants who were unsubmissive
and of another race, their behavior was less constrained.

Puritans brought a number of prejudices to bear on Indians apart
from the pity and contempt they felt for their lack of religion. The
seventeenth-century traveler John Josselyn painted Indian men as
lusty and sexually indulgent and Indian women as possessors of bodies inhumanly impervious to the pain of childbirth. Most Puritans believed Indians to be innately lewd and lawless in their family lives.
The combination of attraction to and repulsion from the presumably
unfettered sexuality of the Indians added a particular danger to servitude for Indian girls. Increasing their cultural vulnerability was the
legal fact that only blacks and Indians could be bought for life. When
John Winthrop disposed of Captain Israel Stoughton's captives after
the massacre that destroyed the Pequot Nation, Stoughton requested
as a servant "the fairest and largest." Another soldier wanted and
had given a coat to "a little Squa," and a junior officer wanted a tall
girl with "3 stroakes upon her stummach." In a letter from John
Winthrop to William Bradford, governor of the colony at Plymouth,
Winthrop mentioned the capture of a princess whose first requests
were that the English not violate her body or take her children from
her. The vast majority of surviving Pequots were transported into
slavery in the Caribbean or enslaved in New England.[11]

In the shadow of King Philip's War, the English again enslaved
and divvied up Native women. So Richard Way petitioned the court
in 1676 to keep for the rest of her life a Mohegan girl who had
proved to be "faithfull loving obedient pesabell [peaceable] & quiat."
The Reverend Peter Thacher bought an Indian girl named Margaret
at about the time his Puritan maid Lidia Chapin came to work for
him. He prayed that the Lord would make Margaret a blessing to his
family and that she might come to "know & fear the Lord her Master," thereby acknowledging his religious responsibilities toward the
girl, as he might have toward any servant. Three months later, however, he reported that she had let his child fall, "wherefore I took a

good walnut stick & beat the Indian to purpose till she promise never to doe soe any more." He never beat Lidia despite his repeated references to her faulty carriage toward them all. Instead he spent considerable care and time in trying to reason with and persuade her of the error of her ways.[12]

Obedience, Sexuality, and the Road to Conversion

The capstone of maturity for Puritans was conversion, which most girls experienced during adolescence. Men watched over and judged their waverings, terrors, and hopes; thus the conversion experience, the most meaningful event in a Puritan's life, was a process conducted in self-doubt, directed and evaluated by men.[13]

Cotton Mather attempted to hasten along the conversion of his daughter Katy by reminding her of his own mortality. He warned her that he would die someday and that she would have a much harder life without her tender father. He added that people would regard her behavior with special interest because she was the daughter of the author of a book on ungodly children. Thereupon both father and daughter cried. He then assured his daughter that he knew from God that she was one of the saved, but still he warned her that she had to seek God every day lest some "dreadful Afflictions must befall her." When Jerusha Mather converted at sixteen, it required her brother Cotton's judgment that it was genuine. But she continued for her whole (short) life to write in her journal, *"I hope I am a Believer! I hope I am Converted!"* Members of both sexes expressed uncertainty about their conversions, but the structure of authority was likely to intensify a girl's doubt.[14]

Uncertainty and silence were components of the most important virtue in the canon for girls, obedience. Puritans connected obedience with the fear of God. Obedience for a girl was a more inclusive proposition than for a boy. She would owe it to a wide variety of people all her life, including her superiors in the family, school, church, and commonwealth. Many subprescriptions, such as modesty, repression of anger, and timidity or "shamefacedness," fitted under the umbrella of obedience. Freedom of will interested seventeenth-century Puritans only to the degree to which they struggled to prepare themselves to be chosen by God for salvation. Their guiding principles were that no amount of preparation could assure them of a place in heaven and that men and women legitimately could experience autonomy only in the circumscribed endeavor of trying to determine God's will. Autonomy was not officially desirable, and to the extent that Puritans defined a "self" it was depraved and needed to be subdued. It represented indecent desires and wishes not in conformity with mindfulness of God. On the other hand, men unquestionably had more autonomy in their lives than women did, because God required them to make family and community decisions and to select callings in which to honor God with labor.[15]

The Puritans' goal for girls was the production of docile women. Hugh Peter counseled his daughter to be "loving to all . . . meekness will make smooth all your ways." Moralist Reverend Richard Allestree, twenty years later, wrote that anger was a repulsive form of madness, bad enough for men but far worse for women. Writing "Yet man for Choler is the proper seat," Anne Bradstreet specifically allocated anger to males and prohibited it to females. Moralists also excoriated pride, a form of self-assertion, in girls. Elizabeth Joceline wrote that she would fear the vice of pride more in a girl than in a boy.[16]

In the most limited sense of the word, girls were extremely obedient to their parents—that is, girls almost never appeared in the court records accused of physically assaulting their parents. Adolescent female disobedience usually took the form of sexual rebellion, often accompanied, when exposed in court, by the transgressor's lamentations over her failure to obey her parents. Another form of female disobedience was more disguised, even from the rebellious girl herself: possession by the devil.[17]

Some girls, particularly poor ones in service to the prosperous, who had difficulty with the endless demands of obedience found in bewitchment an unconscious route for expressing their rebelliousness. Teenage Mercy Short blamed the devil for her internal warfare, but the practical consequence was that she was free to revile and tease Cotton Mather. Bewitched, she could express, but disown, great resentment against the authority of mothers—and ministers. Mercy Short's life as a rebel was brief; exorcised of the devil, she also lost her license to be outspoken, aggressive, and demanding. The possessed Elizabeth Knapp announced that the devil had offered her a husband, elegant clothes, and a lightened workload, pointing to the frustrations inherent in her lowly status. It is a measure of the disproportionate emphasis society placed on obedience for girls that boys never needed this unconscious outlet for their rebellious drives.[18]

We have seen that girls could not speak in church after the age of sixteen. Moral writers made it clear that girls were to be quiet out of church as well. Hugh Peter cautioned his daughter against being the "Busie Body who is but a Pedler to carry up and down, and vend the Devils Wares. How few lose anything by quietness, and doing their own work." Perhaps the most widespread Puritan citation on the subject of women talking was St. Paul (I Timothy: 2, 11–12), who said, "But I suffer not a woman to teach, nor to usurp authority over the man, but to be in silence." Males outnumbered females by a ratio of six to one in court cases of slander, but New Englanders believed that women were more talkative and more likely to speak offensively than men. Men felt particularly vulnerable to women's talk, which often consisted of social assessments of community members rather than male topics like agriculture and politics. Girls trained to moral criticism, however, were equipped with a potentially dangerous tool. Jerusha Mather wrote about how God dealt with town inhabitants, friends, and family, and what she thought about those dealings, her journal becoming a written—and silent—form of moral gossip, bracketed and justified by reflections and hopes for improvement.[19]

During adolescence girls agonized over the emergence of an unwonted outcropping of self-assertion, usually taking the relatively safer form of vanity rather than sexual activity. Anne Bradstreet at fourteen or fifteen found to her disgust that she was thinking vain and worldly thoughts and turning away from God as "the follyes of youth [took] hold of me." At sixteen she contracted smallpox, which caused her to repent but not, as she saw it, sufficiently, since it was only the beginning of a life of afflictions: imperfectly learned lessons and inadequate repentance. As a young woman Jerusha Mather struggled desperately against her willful flesh and spirit and regularly accused herself of pride, ungratefulness, disobedience, gluttony, and vanity. She spent days fasting in her closet, where, as her brother said approvingly, children grow old. Repetition of these self-accusations was part of the rugged discipline involved in subduing herself.[20]

Clergymen tried to abolish vanity because it contaminated modesty. And chastity formed the foundation of male Puritan control of females. Small girls were trained to avoid any behavior that might encourage the growth of an independent sexuality. Moralists urged parents to control the influences and activities in a girl's life that might stimulate the development of a sexual imagination. Listening to "wanton discourse" would violate a girl's ears; "every immodest glance vitiates her eyes."[21]

Puritans included fornication among the handful of examples used to illustrate words of five (for ni ca ti on) syllables in the *New England Primer.* Moralists' thoughts about it help explain their attitudes toward female sexuality. A document dated approximately 1640 in the hand of the Reverend Thomas Shepard evaluates fornication and weighs punishments for it. Fornication combined a wrong against the woman as well as a wrong against society because knowledge of it "hardened" those who shared it and because the commonwealth's honor suffered from the "unchastity and wantonness of men." In 1642 the court ruled that fornicators were to marry and were to be punished by a fine, corporal punishment, or some combination of the two.[22]

Shepard's is a clear statement of the Puritan principle that individuals were responsible to the whole community for their comportment. Men and women were equally affected by and responsible for the moral level of the whole group, although in this particular crime the authors clearly placed the onus of active sexual sin upon the man. The fornicator might have to pay the woman's father because his daughter's value had depreciated, but the authors thought a whipping would "do the man as much good & cleare up the repute & honor of the commonwealth." The woman sinned in gullibility and weakness, not from her lust.

A communal view of sexual sin and its effects did not survive into the next century. Older views of the danger inherent in women's sexuality persistently appeared alongside newer legal practices tending to treat the sexes equally. So Cotton Mather exhorted girls to hide their sexuality and reproach themselves for their innate ability to tempt men. He ruminated on the "weighty" question of whether a Christian was obliged to "pay his whore or no." He concluded it was not necessary because "no man thinks himself bound to pay a witch that has enchanted him; and this business is pretty much akin to that." Puritans associated many aspects of female sexuality with filth, corruption, and sin. Magistrates prosecuted women for such crimes as "merriment," talking privately with a man, being "light and lewd," and "walking abroad in the night."[23]

A number of instances of the sexual abuse of girls suggest that Puritans could be persuaded that females were the victims of male lust but that they viewed even girls with suspicion and fear—as much for their potential effect on men as for any inherent female lustfulness. This fear came into play in seventeenth-century child abuse cases in and around Boston, as did children's assumed unreliability as witnesses. A girl who accused a man of sexual abuse had to establish that she had made the attacker aware of her refusal and had resisted. Her case was improved by her reporting the crime quickly. Midwives examined the girl to make sure that she had been violated. If she had not been visibly injured, two witnesses had to testify to the crime.[24]

Daniel Fairfield and at least two other men abused Dorcas Humphrey, the daughter of one of the magistrates. Fairfield, one of Mr. Humphrey's servants, evidently abused both of Humphrey's daughters regularly in the peace and quiet provided by Sundays and lecture days. Next, Humphrey, a widower, put the girls out to board and be schooled at the house of Jenkin Davis of Lynn, a former servant of his. Davis's wife being pregnant, Davis turned to Dorcas. The girl subsequently went back to her father's house, where a household servant named John Hudson slept in bed with her because "she had no woman to lodge with." The result was, not surprisingly, that "he did abuse her many times," and John Winthrop concluded in his detailed narrative of the event that "she was grown capable of a man's fellowship, and took pleasure in it." Dorcas concealed all this until her father went to England; she then told a just-married sister about Fairfield. When the girl came before Governor Winthrop, she mentioned the others and also implicated her own two brothers. Everyone confessed partially, but all denied entering her, which would have been a capital crime. Fairfield, who had deflowered Dorcas, was whipped and had a nostril slit "so high as may well bee & then sewed." He remained in prison in Boston until he was well enough to have the procedure repeated at Salem. He was to pay Dorcas's father forty pounds and to spend the rest of his life in Boston with a rope around his neck. The unusual severity of this punishment probably reflected Humphrey's high status in the community. Davis and Hudson were whipped and ordered to pay Humphrey twenty pounds each. As for Dorcas, the court insisted that she be "privately and severely corrected." Although the girl had been under ten at the time of the first of these events, the magistrates did not see her as a victim. She had not reported Fairfield's crime quickly enough, and the magistrates believed she had come to enjoy sex.[25]

The General Court ruled, in the aftermath of the case against Fairfield, that rape of a child under ten should be punished by death whether or not the child had consented. But the Puritans later substituted for death "other grievous punishment."[26]

Ten-year-old Ruth Richards had been a better victim than Dorcas Humphrey. She had resisted the efforts of a nineteen-year-old fellow servant to rape her because, according to the trial records, she had constantly kept the fear of God in her heart. Nine-year-old Ruth Parson explained one reason why little girls were afraid to report their troubles to the magistrates. She reported that Edward Saunders had raped her four times and that she had feared to speak out because he had "threatened her and whipped her and pinched her on her back." Sarah Bugly had to combat both her fear and her inculcated deference to the wishes of men in reporting her rape by John Simple, who "begd of hir that she not tell her aunt & he would doe anything for hir." These exemplary victims were examined by a group of women to make sure that they indeed had been raped and were questioned closely to be certain they had been virgins at the time of the attacks.[27]

Despite the fact that child rape was a capital offense, the magistrates sentenced only two men to death or banishment for this crime. One was black; the other, an Indian. It seems significant that although black women appeared as the accused in the court records with disproportionate frequency compared with their percentage in the population, there were no black victims of child abuse in the records of either Middlesex or Suffolk County. If it was difficult for a white girl to establish victim credentials, it was impossible for one who was black. The court convicted a black man, Basto Negro, of raping the three-year-old daughter of his master, Robert Coxe. Coxe petitioned the court that since the slave had cost him a lot of money and since, as he testified, his little girl was not harmed, his servant not be executed. The court obliged, commuting the sentence to thirty-nine lashes and a rope around the rapist's neck.[28]

The Indian, called Twenty Rod, was convicted of so "violently forcing an Indian child of about 9 years" that he had endangered her life and her capacity to bear children. Despite the fact that the child had been torn so badly that she cried out when the midwives approached her, they examined her to verify that she had been hurt. In 1662 the court sentenced Twenty Rod to be "sold for his life to some of the Carib Islands & if he returne into this jurisdiction again to be put to death."[29]

The court's relative leniency toward child rapists—especially white ones—reinforces the notion that Puritans never could see females, even children, as entirely blameless in sexual matters. They started very young instilling in girls a disproportionate sense of responsibility for the control and repression of their own and men's sexuality. Puritan women accepted a legal code that increasingly penalized only them for expressions of sexuality outside marriage, their consciences trained to accept this injustice through an ideology that stressed the connections among women, sin, and sexual shame. Central to this training were self-doubt and modesty, which rendered aggressive behavior like accusing a man of assault as well as an aggressive defense of one's self shameful.

2

MASSACHUSETTS:
CULTURAL PERSPECTIVES
ON SEX, LAW, AND FEELING

Puritans anticipated a wide variety of catastrophes, individual and societal, resulting from uncontrolled sexuality. Within marriage, Puritans believed sex could contribute to domestic happiness and the
larger purpose of loving God. But because sexual misconduct attacked the well-being of the whole community, they were at pains to
root out sinners and punish members of both sexes. Increasingly,
however, they punished more women than men. In the seventeenth
century they prosecuted fornication with vigor, and it accounted for
almost 38 percent of all female crime. Indeed the state prosecuted
females at a rate that was three times higher than that at which it
prosecuted males. In some colonies, like Plymouth, the proportion of
female to male prosecutions was even higher.[1]

Puritans' efforts to repress various forms of expressivity and aggression as well as sex significantly enlarged the field of female cul-
pability, both legally and psychologically, and linked nonsexual but
unrestrained behavior with sex. For example, when Sarah Bushman
testified to defend her husband against the accusations by nine
women that he had made sexual advances toward them, she listed
the aggressive teasing of Elizabeth Payne, whom she considered the
instigator of the accusations. She recounted that Payne had pulled

the chair from under her husband, that she had pulled meat out of his hands as he ate, and that she had called him "old black beard." These "bold carriages" convinced Mrs. Bushman that Payne had "been Instrumentall to Intice" her husband to whatever advances he had made toward her. Mary Hawthorne accused Moses Hudson of raping her. The court would not convict him because of testimony that the two had smoked together. Society's extremely inclusive notion of female sexual provocation resulted in restraint and hyperactive consciences for many religious women, particularly those in elite families, where the moral training was careful and extensive. For others, the whole question of sexual responsibility was moot. Puritan society was eager to assign responsibility, and through their confessions many women proved willing to shoulder it.[2]

The striking number of women's confessions in the court records relates, I believe, to the Puritans' vigorous prosecution of sexual crimes and their effective child-rearing techniques, as well as to society's view of female expressions of aggression, pleasure, and sociability as aspects of sexuality requiring restraint. Women had to come to grips with this view either by internalizing it or by denying it. The array of confessions that the legal records offer, usually couched in the Puritan rhetoric of disobedience, hard-heartedness, and corruption, confirms not only the reserves of guilt that accusations could activate in Puritan women but also the effectiveness of the Puritans' inclusive view of what constituted forbidden sexual behavior in females.[3]

Apart from ideology and psychology, there was one important structural reason for the large number of confessions in Massachusetts. Defendants had to request jury trials in order not to be tried, prosecuted, and sentenced by magistrates. However, by the 1680s requesting a jury trial was hazardous for a defendant. Denial of guilt itself suggested a spirit in need of humbling. Thus Sarah Snell, who denied charges that she had behaved wantonly, demanded a jury, which then sentenced her to twenty lashes, double the usual penalty.[4]

The authorities needed confessions to confirm the inherent justice of their laws. Women's penitent admissions of guilt reinforced Puritan values and might, of course, help absolve the sinner. A confessing woman who appeared to experience the fear of God could often find reacceptance in her church, although she might still be fined or whipped.

It is extremely hard to evaluate sincerity at all, much less at a distance of three hundred years, but a significant number of women who confessed seem to have been motivated by a genuine belief in their own wrongdoing and a fear of God's wrath. Public shame proved a sufficient catalyst for many women, while others were obviously prompted by fear of the secular authorities, although this fear easily merged with that of God and could blend into and be construed as religiously inspired. For example, Elizabeth Healy made the standard, comprehensive confession, pointing to all the sins she committed growing up and assuming the blame for her disobedience to God, parents, and community. She claimed that her lover had overwhelmed her resistance and that they had had sex only once. Nevertheless, despite the exonerating circumstances, she confessed that she had "sinned openly befor God an the world so it is my hearty desire to confes and bewaill my sin befor God and his peopell."[5]

Some young men in Middlesex County openly rejected Puritan sexual values. In one case a group of young men—and perhaps women, although the evidence is contradictory—read a midwifery manual to find out about sex, partied, drank, and engaged in various sexual activities. A similar group existed in Ipswich. But I found no single woman's testimony that defied conventional views on sexuality. Women reviled ministers and the church, blasphemed, and committed other seemingly unredeemable offenses, but testifying to the pleasure of sex seems to have been too scandalous to risk.[6]

Many confessions were coupled with accusations against partners for forcing them to have sex. As with children, the magistrates found some confessed victims more victimized than others. The court determined Mary Phips had been raped because she was "so lame and weak" that she could not possibly be compliant. Similarly, George Brain had seduced the servant of a friend. The court decided that the servant was "void of the Common reason" and so could not understand what a sin was.[7]

Indentured servants were more susceptible to sexual harassment because they were supposed to obey orders and often had no nearby protectors. Thomas Langhorne, who was married, tried to seduce Elizabeth Holmes by citing Scripture, promising various explicit sexual pleasures, and exposing himself. He said that King David was "a good man and yet committed adultery." He retaliated to Holmes's complaint against him with charges of her aggression, stating that she was a "scandalmonger" and that her father complained that he could not control her.[8]

If women had not tried to fight off their suitors, they usually claimed that they had given in because of a promise of marriage. This did not exonerate them, but it could result in marriage. Of the few women who admitted to complicity in fornication, most cited an overwhelming desire to escape hardship at home or indicated some other aberration in their upbringings. What little testimony remains suggests that girls sought to get away from domestic brutality through sex. Elizabeth Healy confessed she had fornicated with Samuel Reynolds because he had told her he would take her away from her abusive mother. Phoebe Page, who apparently had several sexual encounters with different men, recounted great conflict with her father, whom she said she could not love. Sooner than go back to his house she would "goe into the wilderness as far as I can & ly downe and dy." The intensity of her aversion and despair in a society that insisted on the obedience of children, especially girls, and on familial harmony appears to point to a very abusive parent.[9]

The moral condemnations of single women intensified when fornication across social lines incurred the potential of marriage, revealing the secondary moral system within Puritanism. The contestants' moral repute, tied up with their social and economic status, became the central issue in a culture in which the authorities prescribed marriage as a treatment for premarital pregnancy. Hannah Stevenson became pregnant, she claimed, by Samuel Gookin, the son of Major General Daniel Gookin. She said Samuel had promised to marry her, and that was why she had given in to him. When she became pregnant, however, he pleaded with her to ingest savin, a poisonous shrub, considered an abortifacient. The Gookin family testified to Samuel's good character, stating that young women of "good report

& quality, & more desirable" than Hannah, "acquit him from any lascivious cariag or unruly behavior." Samuel himself called Hannah a
known liar and "strumpet" who had brought shame upon his name
and grieved him and afflicted his parents. She was accused of keeping company day and night with young men, of being disobedient to
her parents, and of exceeding her rank in the clothes she wore. The
court accepted Stevenson's charge that Gookin fathered her child,
ordered him to pay for it, but was unwilling to force a marriage of
such economically disparate people, a disparity that the Gookin family argued, successfully, was equal to moral disparity.[10]

Hannah Brackett, a servant of Major General Daniel Gookin
(Samuel's father), accused his grandson John Eliot of making her
pregnant. Eliot testified that Brackett had confessed to making love
with another man, whom a friend of Eliot's testified to seeing leave
her room at night. Brackett made such a penitent confession to the
midwives attending her during her "very hard labour" that they were
convinced by her sincerity in naming Eliot. Still, the court sentenced
her to ten stripes and refused to convict Eliot.[11]

The moral credibility of a poor female, dependent on the community, was even lower than that of a servant. If she abandoned a
submissive demeanor, she could expect no mercy. When admonished, Abigail Day, resident at the almshouse, complained about the
food and defamed "the man who keeps the Alms-house as if hee had
several times made Attempts upon her chastity." Cotton Mather was
amazed at the destitute woman's gall. Mather accepted the man's
oath that he was innocent and noted that she had no proof against
him. The few black and Indian servants appear to have been even
more vulnerable to physical and sexual abuse and even less capable
of getting redress.[12]

There were relatively few blacks in Massachusetts. One historian
estimates that there were two hundred slaves by 1676, four hundred
by 1700, and two thousand by 1720. Others have estimated one thousand by 1700. Although Boston had few slaves, it was deeply implicated in the trade. The first blacks arrived in 1638, and the first
English-American slave ship from the colonies left Boston in 1644.
After 1680 the traffic increased dramatically when Caribbean rum

turned out to sell well in Africa. Boston's slaves, however, did not come directly from Africa but were probably from Barbados and other locations in the Caribbean.[13]

Puritans were divided over the justice of slavery. Some, like John Winthrop's brother-in-law in England, hoped to see the traffic increase because white settlers needed laborers, and it was cheaper to keep twenty "Moores" than one servant. Some were horrified, though largely out of concern for slavery's effect on Puritan society. Samuel Sewall was sympathetic to the plight of blacks and published his antislavery tract *The Selling of Joseph* in 1700. He based his argument for abolition on his assumption that blacks could never live happily with whites. He granted that no one wished them to be free and that they themselves were ill equipped for freedom. He predicted that they could not have orderly families and that their physical appearance would keep them always as "a kind of extravasat [outside of its proper vessel] Blood." John Saffin's reply to Sewall's tract in 1701 was probably closer to the general opinion of black character circulating among Europeans in that epoch. He rejected the comparison with Joseph and wrote that blacks were cruel, deceitful, rude, libidinous, and ungrateful.[14]

Blacks show up accused of crime much more often than their percentage in the population would predict. Courts convicted black women of infanticide in higher numbers than whites. Black servants represented an unusually high proportion of offenders in general, and female blacks were especially vulnerable to prosecution.[15]

With few exceptions, Puritan authorities expressed a fundamental moral disinterest in blacks, and but for a handful of black church members, very few Africans adopted Puritan values. By excluding most blacks from moral membership in the community, Puritans created a group that had only negative reasons—i.e., evasion of punishment—to observe community standards of behavior. The main tenets of Puritan moral training for women were meaningless for Africans. Those Africans whose culture prescribed chastity now lived in a society that determined for them if, who, and when they would marry.[16]

White Massachusetts attitudes toward blacks ranged from distance to disgust. Jonathan Farnum and his wife refused to help "Joseph Neagro" when he came to beg assistance because he was afraid his wife would kill herself. Farnum's wife said that Joseph had "Better git som of his cuntry" to help the suicidal woman. When Christopher Good heard his neighbor beating her white servant, he tried to persuade her to stop, saying she was just a girl, "not a horse or a Negro." The comparison of Indians and Negroes with beasts had its parallel in the law. In 1716 Samuel Sewall hoped to overturn the law that taxed slaves of both races equally "with Horses and Hogs; but could not prevail." And he was almost alone in indicting slavery and slaveowners for the sexual behavior of their slaves: "It is too well known what Temptations Masters are under to contrive at the Fornication of their Slaves; lest they should be obliged to find them Wives, or pay their Fines."[17]

Black women who violated the sexual code encountered hazards that whites did not. Most Massachusetts blacks were slaves whose fates were entirely up to their owners. So pregnant black women who named their babies' fathers had little chance of marrying if the fathers were black and no chance if they were white. The testimony of Johanna "Black" is illustrative. She accused Joseph Carter, who was white, of making her pregnant. But when the midwives examined her during labor, she told them the child was by Carter's father's black servant Samson. Later Johanna changed her story again because, as she testified, Carter's wife had been one of her midwives, and Johanna was afraid Mrs. Carter "might hurt har." She claimed Carter had forced her to have sex one night in a ditch when most of the other men were in Boston at military training and Mrs. Carter was away. When it seemed Johanna might be pregnant, he told her to take savin. He suggested that she also do strenuous activity and, if that failed, that she murder the child in labor. He threatened to "sett the divels to worke upon har and that she shold never have a quiet life againe" if she accused him. Carter's wife and daughter testified that they had heard Samson's wife say that if Johanna had a baby, it was certainly Samson's; others testified that they had seen Samson at Johanna's master's house giving her "2 apples and a bottle of wine to drink." The baby, however, appeared to be white. One witness said it was "a white child," although somewhat "tawny" with brown, straight hair.[18]

At the same time that Puritans began to worry about interracial sex, they were losing interest in fornication. They no longer viewed the family as absolutely critical to the survival of the state. Illicit sexual practices no longer threatened to ruin the whole community. Hence fornication had become a private, not a public, offense. Simultaneously, Puritans had ceased to prosecute extramarital sex with much vigor and had ceased to evaluate men and women as equally culpable sexually. Without the active interference of the state, women came to be more and more victimized by a morality based increasingly on nonlegal sanctions that paid lip service to Puritan ideas about what constituted sexual sin but that, in reality, judged them much more severely than men for sexual infractions.[19]

At the same time, more and more men implicitly ceased assenting to the church's authority over their "private" behavior. Women, on the other hand, confined to privacy, continued in large numbers to be swayed by the spiritual and moral leadership of the church. The ministry paid increased attention to women at the very time that family and state were becoming more independent of each other because the church was faced with an increasingly female congregation and a drastic decline in its secular authority. The colony had come under crown rule, and the clergy no longer influenced politics as it had in the days of John Winthrop. Under the new government, for example, men did not need to be members of the church to vote in Massachusetts.[20]

While it is all but impossible to generalize about the moral meaning women gave to sexuality outside marriage, it appears that women who had absorbed Puritan theology tended to collapse together sexuality and various forms of expression like sociability, disobedience, and aggression. These women appear in the court records as penitent sinners, midwives acting as inquisitors, and female witnesses accusing other females. They lived in an environment where female sexuality was regarded with fear and ambivalence outside marriage and where authorities might discern female expressions of sexuality in many nonsexual activities. Even women who did not take Puritan teaching seriously had to operate in a world in which this apprehensive view of female nature predominated. No woman articulated defiance in the face of punishment. Puritans seem to have been successful in instilling attitudes of shame and guilt about sex in women, particularly in those from religious households, which, in Massachusetts, was a substantial number. These women functioned successfully in the Puritan world and were included in its moral purview.

Another group of women—often, but not always, made up of poor whites and blacks—would have been aware of negative moral assumptions about them and their sexuality. They might also have expected harsher punishments for infractions. Certainly, giving a choice to a slave or indentured servant between paying a fine and taking stripes would have seemed to the defendant cruel humor. Most of the growing black community, Indians, and many poor whites were in this way deeply alienated from a social, legal, and economic system that often made them vulnerable to sexual and social "crime" and blamed them as it victimized them.

The success Puritans had defining female sexuality as inherently shameful and in need of repression in single women and containment among wives in the long run was a remarkably effective tool in controlling women. Puritan ideas hardly prevented all women from experimenting with sexual pleasure, but they did promulgate a widespread definition of what constituted morally acceptable womanhood. A broad array of New England women internalized the belief that chastity was the fundamental moral criterion for female goodness. Moreover, Puritans managed to link aggression with the same experience of shame that sexual guilt could elicit. These triumphs, enshrined in the consciences of "good women," long outlived Puritan theology.

3

PURITAN MARRIAGES:

VIEWS FROM THE INSIDE

The family was the rock upon which Puritan society rested. Marrying and remaining married were moral imperatives for men and women. The general purposes of marriage were procreation, a means for men and women to avoid the sin of fornication, companionship, and an orderly, hierarchical model for social relations outside the family. Puritans saw marriage in a new, hopeful light, an institution indispensable to creating godly societies. To that end, Massachusetts criticized single women in print and discouraged them legally. Puritans' views of black and Indian marriages provide a useful insight not only into the experience of those groups but also as context for the marriages of the white majority.[1]

Though slaves were supposed to marry, it is unclear from the records how many of them actually were able to. One of the legal and practical problems confronting slave couples not owned by the same person was which master would support the children. It was simpler for the authorities to relax their insistence on marriage in the case of a pregnant black servant, just as it was easier to doubt the moral character of blacks. When Bess, the "negro woman . . . of Widow Howe," accused "Israel Reed's Negro man," Thomas Black, of fathering her child, the court believed Black guilty, assessed him for money to support the child and pay the midwife's fees, but did not force him to marry her. When Hagar went to court to accuse her master's son of fathering her baby, she told the court that she was a married woman with a husband and three-year-old child living in Africa. In the eyes of white people, shattered African marriages probably had little reality, but as the backdrop against which a sexual "crime" came to light these sundered unions must have contributed to a general sense of black people as incontinent and feckless. Black women, on the other hand, must have seen Puritan moral values as self-serving and ruthless.[2]

Since Puritans did not insist upon marriage for blacks, the result was that Puritans kept a pool of unmarried black women in a moral limbo. These women were prosecuted disproportionately to their numbers for fornication and infanticide. Conversely, they never appeared in court as rape victims. Puritans simply attributed to blacks a preference for disorder in their sexual relations that they themselves imposed on them.[3]

The marriages of Indians, on the other hand, interested Puritan authorities more. They saw these marriages as foils to their own cultural and moral virtues. Throughout the seventeenth century Puritans evaluated Christianized Indians' hybrid marriages not only to rate the converts' moral progress but also to check on their own.[4]

Southern New England Indians did not practice what Europeans considered marriage. Indians condoned premarital sexual experience and formed long-term relationships in various ways, sometimes to link lineages for economic and diplomatic reasons, sometimes for companionship and sex, sometimes with great formality, sometimes with little ceremony. The wealthiest men occasionally took more than one wife. Divorce was not difficult to obtain and lifelong fidelity not necessarily a goal. Coupling provided for procreation, pleasure, economic partnerships, and group stability. It did not carry with it the economic and political submersion of the wife in her husband's identity. Nor did it mean that husbands provided spiritual leadership to their wives. The English brought with them and imposed on Indian converts a relationship between man and wife that, in principle, subordinated the importance of their respective clans and elevated the authority of the husband over his wife.[5]

Puritans viewed with genuine horror the idea of race mixing. In this they established a precedent for racially based segregation, justified in part by their ascription of inferior morals to Indians and their consequent need for guidance. Despite their presumption of superiority, Puritans sometimes worried that these new Christians were in fact purer and more sincere than the English. This revealed an insecurity that plagued later white Christians with regard to African American converts. It also revealed the competitive aspect of Puritan moral culture, its need to check on and distinguish itself from others. Because of the Indians' declining population and visibility, Puritans lost interest in them over time, but the years after settlement reveal their anxiety to control Indian family life and their need to shine in comparison.[6]

Puritan writers traced the purpose of their own marriages back to God's creation of Eve as a companion and assistant to Adam. A woman was also supposed to be "the worthiest mercy, that a man may have in this worlde." She should be dear to her husband even beyond parents and siblings, their love binding them into one. This elevation of marriage meant a new emphasis on emotional and sexual pleasure in marriage. It also underlay Puritan thinking about spouses' economic interests. Puritans rejected the notion of any possible economic division between man and wife and gave Massachusetts husbands legal powers that English husbands did not have. Husbands in the Bay colony could dispose of any land their wives might have brought to the marriage, whereas under English law, authorities consulted wives as well as husbands on questions concerning wives' property.[7]

A young Puritan man had two major decisions in his life, selections of a calling and a wife. A female, however, had one major life decision, and it was not entirely her own. She waited to be approached. She also made her decision with her parents' assistance, based on whether or not she felt she could learn to obey and love.[8]

Although Puritans believed in mutual sexual pleasure in marriage, Puritan writers wrote of men's sexual desire, not women's. Temptation inhered in the female, but active sexuality was male. Puritans insisted on the prerogatives of men to make a sexual selection pleasing to them. In the commonplace book that John Cotton the elder and his son Seaborn Cotton shared, there is a recipe titled "For to Make a Hand som Woman." She was to have light brown hair, a high, straight brow, narrow black eyebrows, round hazel eyes, pure vermilion cheeks, a small mouth and coral lips, the underlip a little fuller than the upper, a pretty long white neck, a small waist, middle-sized hips, small legs and feet, and long hands, and "to be rather taller than shorter."[9]

On the other hand, Puritan men officially discouraged females from acting on their sexual preferences. Hugh Peter advised his daughter that she should marry only "In and for the Lord. The sensual part of that condition can never answer the incumbrances that attend it. Let Christ be your Husband, and He will provide you one to His own Liking."[10]

Girls could refuse suitors, but their guardians did not countenance long uncertainty in matters of marriage. Mary Downing soon transgressed what should have been a brief process of selection by encouraging a Mr. Norton, while seeming to love a Mr. Eyers, but in the end preferring one John Harwood. Her mother wrote John Winthrop that she thought neither Harwood nor her daughter was "to be excused or trusted." A very few parents forced their daughters to marry when they did not love. A female friend testified that on the day Mrs. Clements married her husband, William, she pulled her hand away from him and fell into tears. When the friend tried to persuade her to act lovingly to her husband, she answered: "[H]ang him hang him I canot abide him." She later petitioned unsuccessfully for a divorce, saying that she had been forced to marry against her will and that she "could never love him nor ever should."[11]

Some girls, raised in a culture that educated them to modesty, timidity, and doubt, had trouble making choices. They were taught to obey, not to choose. Selecting a husband smacked of self-assertion and refusing a suitor, of disobedience. Shy, troubled Elizabeth Sewall ran and hid herself in the family coach until one young man gave up paying court to her. When another came along, she demurred again. Her father, Judge Samuel Sewall, warned her that "your drawing back from him after all that has passed between you . . . will tend to discourage persons of worth from making their Court to you." He went on to assure her, however, that if she had an "immovable, incurable Aversion for him, and cannot love, and honour, and obey him, I shall say no more nor give you any further trouble in this matter." Not too long after, Betty Sewall married the young man in question. But it is unclear where her feelings fell along the lengthy continuum between an incurable aversion and love.[12]

Samuel Sewall's sway over his daughter also derived from God and was supported in law, but it was combined with affection. The power of religion and the daily exchange of approval for obedience or, conversely, cold disapproval for the opposite was much more effective than force or legislation could ever be. Puritans knew this very well, and for this reason they insisted on grouping everyone in households under "family government" in the hope that paternal authority would preside effectively over servants as well as children. But the reproduction of the Puritan moral system occurred with most reliability among the biological members, not in the extended Puritan family group.

Fellow Travelers

Moralists stressed that once married, a couple was to stay together. John Wing wrote that separation opened the door for Satan to tempt a wandering man to sin. For Roger Williams, even harboring the desire to separate from one's mate was a deadly sin. He wrote to Winthrop with satisfaction that a woman who "had made a passionate wish that God would part" her and her husband had died. "It pleased his Jealousy to hear her, and to take away a Child in her womb also."[13]

The trip to America strained—sometimes to the breaking point—the ability of some first-generation women to fulfill that most serious obligation of remaining together. Puritan men bound for Massachusetts with Winthrop often evaluated their wives' moral worth according to how they had reacted to the decision to emigrate. An arduous and perilous trip to an unknown and unsettled land meant leaving family, friends, and familiarity behind for wilderness, unending work, isolation, crude accommodations, Indians, the threat of famine, and imaginary terrors perhaps more frightening than everything else. It could not have been a very pleasing prospect to any but the most committed. Passion in the name of religion belonged to men and women equally, but wives were to express their passion by supporting the decisions of their husbands.[14]

Winthrop pressured women to follow their husbands to the New World. He wrote an associate in England that he could not understand one wife's unwillingness to emigrate and her preference for living in poverty in England when she could be comfortable here. He asked his correspondent to work on her to come over "by all meanes."[15]

Puritan men of the generation of the Great Migration (1630–1640), when more than thirteen thousand people came to Massachusetts from England, believed that a good Puritan wife did not linger on the sinful shores of Britain but encouraged her husband in his great service to God. The typical migrant to New England came as part of a family: a husband and wife in their thirties and some children. This pattern was different from those of other colonies, where young, unattached men were in the overwhelming majority. The Reverend Thomas Shepard wrote that he came to America in part at his wife's suggestion. During the preparations for departure to the New World, Winthrop wrote his spouse, "[B]lessed be God, who hath given me a wife, who is such a helpe and incouragement to me in this great worke, wherein so many wives are so great an hinderance to theirs."[16]

Less praiseworthy wives used health, finances, and even their interpretations of God's will to subvert the demand that they follow their husbands. They incurred criticism and pressure. Mrs. Winthrop wrote of the Reverend Wilson's wife, who was balking at the trip, that she "marvelled at what mettle she is made of."[17]

Lucy Downing, John Winthrop's sister, agonized over the decision for years, eventually deciding, against her husband's and brother's wishes, that she would remain in England. Aware of the great impropriety in her assuming command, however, she larded letters to her brother with expressions of general obedience to her husband's wishes and the desire that God would state His objectives for her a little louder. In July 1636 she wrote that the religious climate in England was improving for Puritans and that she was inclined to stay. It also emerged that she hated sea travel and change and that she anticipated a difficult life in New England. In another letter she claimed she would be "far nimbler to new eng: if god should call me to it." Her husband thought she would be nimbler if her brother would call her to it, so he wrote to Winthrop and asked him to encourage his sister to make the journey. Downing apologized for exercising too much sway over her husband. "Now you may saye," she wrote Winthrop, "I take too much apon me, I, but a wife, and therfor it is sufficient for me to follow me husban." She had expressed these same self-criticisms to her husband, she said, but had assured him that if he desired to go, she would not hinder him. Scripture and moralists, however, stood firm against marital separations, and Emmanuel Downing was unwilling to go alone.[18]

Bridget Usher, after quickly sampling Massachusetts, left her husband, Hezekial, for London. In his vitriolic will Hezekial put the man's case against female separation. He called it an "implicit Divorce" that gave "Into the hands of women to usurp the power . . . of their Husband's rather than in a way of humility to seek their Husband's good." They were happy to live without them "& so become separate; which is far worse than the Doctrine of Devils which forbid to marry." Usher concluded that he was not entirely blameless in his relations with his wife. But—and here he reasoned himself into a novel ambivalence about women's virtue—her "gentele carriage had given her tyrannical power over him."[19]

Obedient wives, who crossed the Atlantic with their husbands, were morally admirable Puritan women. But they may also have been more available to melancholy and hence to Satan than some who stayed home.

Obedience, Affection, Sexuality

Perhaps the most important treasure a Puritan girl was to have in her dowry was an obedient nature. Hugh Peter told his daughter that while a husband's duty was to love, teach, and provide for his wife, her duty was "subjection." John Wing, William Whately, and Thomas Gataker urged wives to fear and reverence their husbands, whom God had placed over them to guide their spirits and intellects and protect them from their numerous physical and moral infirmities. Whately wrote that a woman should be convinced that she was not her husband's equal, "yea that her husband is her better by farre; else there can bee no contentment, either in her heart or in her house." She was to repeat a catechism that concluded: "Though my sinne hath made my place tedious, yet I will confesse the truth, *Mine husband is my superiour, my better.*"[20]

Colonial Puritans employed Whately's equation of husband with God's deputy. Governor John Winthrop, who was happily married to a succession of submissive women, put the ideal case: "A true wife accounts her subjection her honor and freedom and would not think her condition safe and free but in her subjection to her husband's authority. Such is the liberty of the church under the authority of Christ, her king and husband . . . and whether her lord smiles upon her and embraceth her in his arms, or whether he . . . smites her, she comprehends the sweetness of his love in all, and is refreshed, and instructed by every such dispensation of his authority over her." Not all American Puritans saw female obedience in the cheerful light Winthrop did, but all agreed that it was essential to marital satisfaction and should exist regardless of the husband's comportment.[21]

Writers extolled the quiet wife. William Whately advised women to learn in silence and moderate their speech. He also strongly enjoined wives from talking with anyone else about the "faults and frailties" of their husbands. Mather concurred that wives, if they talked at all about their husbands, should do so with respect and not "in such Terms as the *Harlot* uses in *Proverbs*." Speech in early Massachusetts, as Puritans quickly learned, was often a dangerous weapon. They started early to control it, especially from potentially rebellious sources. The influential English theologian William Ames wrote that "the frequent use of obscene speeches seemeth to be more hurtful to piety, than the simple act of fornication." In 1682 the Reverend Allin linked the devil's ease in tempting David to lust with his corrupt conversation: "A chast conversation coupled with fear, is the best security against those *lusts* of the Flesh that war against our Souls."[22]

Through conversation wives arbitrated family behavior and evaluated the morality of their neighbors and friends. While Puritans expected females to do this and praised the wisdom and speech of the virtuous wife, they wished them to speak and judge with great discretion. Infractions against "conversation" (which included comportment as well as speech) were more worrisome in women than among men. As the subordinate sex women were automatically rebellious if they spoke out of turn to a man. When women appeared in court for abusive speech, it was usually against men, although sometimes it was simply for swearing and angry, rebellious behavior. Depending on the degree of repentance and the social standing of the speaker, punishments for abusive speech could be as severe as those for fornication, usually ten stripes. Men who spoke abusively usually had to recant in public, whereas Puritans thought it more seemly for women to refrain from such public displays.[23]

Women who refused to remain silent about their husbands or the authorities could expect little sympathy from the magistrates. A witness reported that Mary Holten spoke scandalously of the Reverend Stoddard "in a verry high handed manner, to the greate dishonour of God . . . and undervallueing Gods Messenger." She also tried to "disparrige & disgrace her husband" and "was resolved to geld him."[24]

Although the laws enjoined husbands from striking their wives to enforce obedience, most writers admitted the occurrence and told wives that they must endure such treatment. Winthrop instructed wives to find in husbands' blows God's love and correction. Mather declared that it was to the husband's dishonor if he beat his wife. But he promised patient wives "*Rewards* hereafter for it, as well as *Praises* here."[25]

Women who remained with husbands who were violent, cruel, and unfaithful drew praise. Mrs. Lyford, of Plymouth, endured, and sometimes witnessed, her husband's infidelities for years in silence. Eventually she testified against him. But, wrote Governor William Bradford approvingly, "being a grave matron, and of good carriage . . . she . . . spoake of those things out of the sorrow of her harte, sparingly." The wife of Jared Davis submitted to years of her husband's cruelty, drunkenness, lies, scandalous behavior, and indolence. He had, according to Winthrop, neither compassion nor humanity toward his wife, insisted on sex with her when she was pregnant (which Puritans regarded as dangerous), and did not provide for her. Worst of all, in Winthrop's eyes, he did not "put honour upon her as the weaker vessell." The governor admired Mrs. Davis, who, under all these provocations, continued to try to help her husband.[26]

Massachusetts Bay outlawed wife beating in 1641 and in 1650 levied a fine of ten pounds on violent spouses of either sex. Courts preferred to have husbands handle pugnacious wives humanely than to intervene. They paid attention to extenuating circumstances like insanity. However, when there was no suspicion of insanity, courts punished wives severely for violence against their husbands. Mrs. Brown threatened to kill her husband, Hugh, threw stones at him, hit him on the head, and called him a beast. The court ordered her to be severely whipped. While the Roxbury Church excommunicated Mrs. Martin Stebbins for violence toward her husband, the Dorchester Church returned Joseph Leeds to full communion once he confessed that he had bloodied his wife and thrown her out of the house. And even though 20 percent of males' homicide victims were their wives, while no wife was ever convicted of murdering her husband, the court was likely to chide violent husbands, telling them to treat their wives better. Sometimes they fined these men.[27]

Historians of marital violence and serious crime find that by the beginning of the eighteenth century, figures for men and women had begun to diverge markedly. This correlates with changes in the economy that diminished the role of women as economic producers and their control of property. Wives became more passive and less violent, while husbands' violence remained at the same level. Women's economic status declined over the period that their penchant for piety presumably increased. Mather's moral rehabilitation of women and his observation of their numerical superiority in church therefore corresponded to actual changes in female behavior, not just an accelerating clerical need of women.[28]

Moral teachings sanctioned male discipline of wives, even if the law prohibited the use of violence. Implicit in the moralists' teachings on jealousy, for example, was a justification for keeping errant wives in line. Charles Salter's testimony displays this understanding. He admitted that he beat his wife but said he thought she was seeing another man. By way of evidence, he said that when they had visited their child at the wet nurse's, he had gone right home, but his wife had not. She returned home somewhat later and refused to tell him where she had gone. He assumed it was to visit a man. A number of women testified for Salter's wife, Elizabeth, who had been beaten so badly she had visible wounds. One said that Elizabeth had often brought work to her house because she was "trembling for fear of her husband." Salter told the judges that he desired God would keep him from "the like passions and folly."[29]

Mid-century Puritans saw sexual union as supremely important in marital love. Because of the Puritan emphasis on female obedience and sexual passivity, the sexual relationship had different connotations for men and women. Husbands were expected to choose wives who appealed to them sexually. On the other hand, some Puritan men worried that they would lose sight of God in an orgy of marital sensuality. William Whately endeavored to spell out the rules for godly sex: It should be cheerful, sanctified, and lawful. By cheerful he meant "they must lovingly, willingly and familiarly communicate themselves unto themselves." As for sanctity, he stressed that men and women not come together as beasts in heat but should keep God in mind at all times and He would bless their union. God's presence would keep a couple's sexual interest in each other from burning out and "make it moderate," thereby preventing it from turning into unholy concupiscence. Finally, "lawful" sex occurred only during the woman's fruitful time. This corresponded to any time except menstruation, pregnancy, and the six to eight weeks following childbirth when she might lose blood.[30]

Although Puritans preferred subdued sexual expression in women, the sexual rights of spouses in principle were regarded as reciprocal. James Davis blamed his wife for denying him her body, and although his allegations proved false, it would have been a serious charge if true. According to the First Parish Church (Dorchester, Massachusetts) records, James Mattock was thrown out of the church because of a number of scandalous acts, among them denying "Coniugall fellowship unto his wife for the space of two years together upon pretence of taking Revenge upon himself for his abusing of her before marryage, and also for the avoyding of Charge by Children of her."[31]

On the other hand, husbands were believed to control their wives through sexuality. Captain John Underhill, a notorious rake, confessed to seducing the young wife of a rope maker. She resisted him, Underhill related with incredulity, for six long months. "But," recorded Winthrop, "being once overcome, she was wholly at his will." Through sexual activity, marital or extra, men acquired control of their sexual partners.[32]

A Puritan woman's love was to be informed by affection, compliance, and helpfulness. Puritans expected their wives to be as students to their husband-teachers and protectors. Without husbands, wives were incomplete emotionally and in their comprehension of God, which required the rationality they lacked. At the same time that Puritanism called for spiritually independent women, Puritan marriage called for dependent wives. As Margaret Winthrop (who usually closed her letters "your loving and obedient wife") wrote touchingly to her husband, "I can not expres my love to you as I desire in theese poore . . . [lifeless] lines, . . . and how much I doe desire to be allwayes with you to injoy the sweet comfort of your presence and those helps from you in spirituall and temperall dutyes which I am so unfite to performe without you." In another letter she thanked him for his words, which, she said, were like a sermon to her.[33]

Anne Bradstreet expressed the Puritan notion of female love as the experience of incompletion in her affecting "Letter to Her Husband, Absent upon Publick Employment": "My head, my heart, mine Eyes, my life, nay more, / My joy, my Magazine of earthly store." She begged him to come home, to return warmth and life to her, for in his absence she was worthless, lifeless, poor, stupid, and blind. (These are words Puritans used to describe their experience of the absence of God as well.) This touching poem represents a description of love as merging. The merging she described, however, embodied not reciprocity but the impairment of the female partner's integrity. As such it made wives more vulnerable than their husbands to grief and depression.[34]

Melancholy

All writers but John Winthrop admitted that permanent subjection was hard to bear. They also tried to protect husbands and marriage itself from the unhappiness of wives. Although Scripture did not demand it, Cotton Mather urged women to convert before marriage. Thus they would be better prepared for the difficulties ahead. Trying to buffer families from wifely discontent, Puritans insisted that women be cheerful in their subjection. A wife, according to John Wing, was to be "as a musician to cheere [her husband] up in his heavinesse." The cheer of a woman was a solace to a man but also a hedge against melancholia, which Puritans greatly feared, especially in women. John Winthrop, Jr., described it as Satan's instrument to "disturb the peace and comfort of the soule."[35]

Increase Mather, Cotton's father, recorded that a "godly woman" had begged his help, telling him that she was "troubled" by not being as cheerful as God wished: "I am dejected, and my soul disquieted, and when I meet with the afflictions I lay them too much to heart." Mary Cole wrote to John Winthrop that she desperately needed advice and encouragement because she was in miserable doubt about her salvation: "I still find such a corupt hart, and strong inclinations to sine, and weaknesse to resist temptation that upon every new assault I have new fears." She thought God had been very merciful with her, and that made her "abhore myselfe for my unthankfulness and deadnesse of hart and unbelefe." These were standard phrases of Puritans in the throes of the conversion crisis, but they also invited melancholy. Cole hated herself, and when she did not, she hated herself for not hating herself. She believed herself corrupt, dead in spirit, and ungrateful. She was fearful. She was lonely. She was not so isolated that she did not ask for help, but in the end she believed no one could help her except God, and she was unable in this period to feel His love.[36]

Prolonged doubt such as Mary Cole and many other Puritans experienced was melancholy or depression. It combined feelings of
helplessness, self-loathing, and alienation. Most frightening to the
Puritan imagination, it alienated desperate believers from God, leaving them to suffer the piercing anxiety and existential despair that
such separations produced. It could also heighten one's sense of
degradation and worthlessness through the striving of the imperfectly submerged self to express its desires or the inability to resist
carnal pleasure. Depending on the intensity and duration of the experience, it could result in severe personal and family problems and
even suicide.

Both men and women of the first generation seem to have suffered heavily from depression, fear, and uneasiness as a result of
their migration. Patricia Caldwell's study of conversion narratives
documents widespread feelings of irresolution, "voiced in a haunting
tone of muted, almost imperceptible anguish. . . . [They speak of]
the struggle against inward sadness, bewilderment, depression, and
especially spiritual paralysis." These lonely settlers, disappointed that
triumphant feelings did not attend their heroic odyssey, looked to
themselves and their new environment to explain their confusion and
misery. Men could and did bury themselves in their colony-building
tasks. But they were also implicated in their wives' dilemma. Since
they believed they had enacted God's plan, the only solution was to
go on. But repeatedly along the way they tried to make sure that
women did not fall into despair.[37]

The burden of the first generation was transformed by their children, through the jeremiad, into a ritualized expression of failure to
live up to their heroic progenitors. Influential mid-century Puritans
enunciated a preoccupation with inadequacy and doubt that probably resonated more with women than with men. There was no letup
for women in life's demands on them to be selfless. Whereas men
could be both aggressive and self-assertive, doing God's work in their
callings and homes, wives had many fewer opportunities, and the
poorer they were, the more this was true. They remained inside a
moral framework that constrained them to regard all choice, all action, and all thought as finally a question of obedience or disobedi-

ence: being good or being bad. Puritans believed that any activity or event could be seen as a lesson from God. Thus there was little morally neutral in the landscape where a doubtful soul could rest reassured—or simply rest. In a culture in which women and children were dependent upon men, this thinking translated the experience of "wives and children, indeed their very lives, [into] mere signs of an adult male's personal success or failure." Wives might see themselves as existentially alone with their uncertainty and simultaneously in an endless struggle to reflect well on their husbands' efforts.[38]

Puritanism attempted to limit female desires to those prescribed by its morality and to numb those proscribed. Moral writers and ministers usually connected melancholy to pride and willfulness. The good woman fought against it. Margaret Chearny lived for ten or eleven years "bound by Satan under a melancholick distemper . . . which made her wholly neglect her Calling and live mopishly." She took responsibility for succumbing to Satan's temptation to suffer for a decade, and she credited God with her recovery. Not all recovered. Mary Onion's first child was stillborn. She bewailed her past life, her worthlessness, her stubbornness and died. John Marshall recorded the suicides of three godly and pious women who died "through the malice of Satan, and the Righteous permission of God." Samuel Sewall recorded the 1688 suicides of two wives.[39]

Black wives as well as white suffered from melancholy. Certainly their journeys to the New World far outstripped those of the Puritans in fear, loss, and confusion. Sewall recorded in his diary the suicide of a black couple in November 1680. In the absence of evidence surrounding the bald facts, it is impossible to know if these two had adopted Puritan moral values. Sewall recorded the double suicide without comment and then proceeded to detail the suicide of a Cambridge man who despaired of God's mercy. Sewall did not probe black despair.[40]

While melancholy was the work of the devil and could strike the pious or the wicked, moralists generally assumed a collaboration between Satan and the woman if her state persisted or degenerated into suicide. The relation of melancholy to witchcraft was close. As in witchcraft, Satan found a way to enter the spirit or the body. In the case of melancholia, the orifice was figurative—i.e., sadness itself—whereas in witchcraft it was often a literal bodily opening. In both cases the woman failed by not resisting Satan's temptation to aggression either against others in the case of witchcraft or against oneself in the case of melancholy. While all women could be afflicted with melancholy, wholly giving in to it implicated a woman in a pact with Satan.[41]

Puritans stigmatized suicides by burying them in highly visible, quarantined spots so all could learn a lesson from their interments. When Mary Buss killed herself in October 1685, the Middlesex court specified that the "deceased was not buried in the common burying place, and though not in, yet very near to the highway, which is the greatest Road in the said town, and in a place very obvious to all that passe by, and also near unto one who formerly murdered himselfe." Some towns covered the graves of suicides with cartloads of stones, "a Brand of Infamy."[42]

Both male and female Puritans succumbed to depression. Wives, however, were more susceptible to melancholy than were husbands. The first generation's traumatic travels cut them off not only from English corruption but also from all that was familiar and comforting. Their response frequently was numbness, confusion, a sense of disappointment, and self-blame. This mood did not disappear suddenly. The next generation seems to have reconfigured its parents' depression as its own failing. Meanwhile life in the New World continued to be hard, lonely, and filled with anxiety. It was particularly so for women because of the absence of sanctioned outlets for female aggression and its link with shame, their emotional and increasing economic dependence as wives, the self-doubt they were trained to feel, and the anxiety the question of salvation provoked. Puritan men praised gravity, sobriety, and mildness in women and frowned upon merriment, a light carriage, and levity. But probably both sexes often felt the gravity and precariousness of their situation and instinctively felt that frivolity was a hollow response. Respected wives were measured and careful and had few lawful avenues but hard work and dutifulness through which to express or discharge their feelings of isolation, subjection, and self-doubt.

4

PURITAN MARRIAGES:

VIEWS FROM THE OUTSIDE

Intellect and Goodness

Puritans favored education in both men and women, but intelligent women could not always be trusted to remain deferential to male authority. Although moralists admitted that intelligent women sometimes married less intelligent men, this was not to alter the arrangements of authority between husband and wife. The Reverend Robinson wrote that "experience teacheth how inconvenient it is if a woman have but a little more understanding . . . than the husband hath." The inconvenience lay in the extra difficulty wives might have in offering subservience to their husbands, and subservience was a proof not only of excellence but also of wisdom.[1]

Intelligence and goodness were not, for Puritans, separate entities. Even if a wife seemed to be intelligent, she was more given to sin and therefore, as John Cotton wrote, "more subject to error than a man." Thus in principle the more intelligent a woman was, the more she would see the need to follow her husband's direction. Nor would an intelligent woman display her intellectual production. The Reverend Thomas Parker of Newbury, Massachusetts, published a letter to his sister in England on the publication of her volume of poetry: "Your printing of a book, beyond the custom of your sex, doth rankly smell." Puritan men believed that such behavior could initiate

an avalanche of sins that might very well demolish the moral arma-
ture giving society its shape.[2]

Anne Hutchinson's comportment showed how easily an intelligent woman could err. Hugh Peter identified her error as stepping
out of her ordained place. He lamented that she had *"rather bine a
Husband than a Wife, and a preacher than a Hearer; and a Magistrate than a Subject."* John Winthrop criticized Hutchinson's husband for the error of weakness, saying contemptuously that he was
"wholly guided by his wife." Anne Hutchinson's sin in attempting to
exercise the male prerogative of leadership through her brilliant verbal displays caused both Winthrop and John Cotton to imagine that
her doctrines would lead to sexual license and a general breakdown
of family structure and moral order. According to Cotton, her denial
of the resurrection of the body would lead her to the "promiscuus
and filthie cominge togeather of men and Weomen without Distinction or Relation of Marriage. . . . And though I have not herd,
nayther do I thinke, you have bine unfaythfull to yor Husband . . . *yet
that will follow upon it."*[3]

A glimpse at England in the years leading up to the Civil War and
the Interregnum (1640–1655), by comparison, shows parallel fears
as well as the success of Massachusetts Puritans in reining in the resistance, protest, and spontaneous prophesying that had characterized women on both sides of the Atlantic. Some women in England
cross-dressed to have male privileges. Others gave prophetic sermons in public places. Women widely objected to the law denying
married women property rights. As the historian of English women
religious radicals in this period writes, "those most concerned with
political order . . . were also those whose genuine respect for the
rights of all women and men came to be articulated in terms of an
exclusively male authority." During the Civil War the visibility of
prophetic women in radical sects like the Levelers and the Ranters
demonstrated how hard it was for male leaders to suppress voluble
female dissent. The violently repressive reception of Quakers in
Massachusetts is an example of how troubling Puritans found the disorder of these years, particularly the blurring of distinctions according to gender.[4]

In addition to sexual license, Puritans thought strenuous female intellectual activity might produce madness. Governor Winthrop wrote in 1645 that Ann Hopkins lost her wits because of "giving herself wholly to reading and writing, and had written many books." Had she not taken on men's activities, "she had kept her wits, and might have improved them usefully and honorably in the place God had set her." Winthrop associated Hopkins's intellectual activities with her inability to live in peace with her husband, in-laws, and minister.[5]

Women daring enough to challenge these conventions knew they were tampering with a powerful taboo. Anne Bradstreet's conciliatory introduction to her first book of poems included the lines:

> Men have precedency and still excell,
> It is but vain unjustly to wage warre;
> Men can do best, and women know it well
> Prehemininence in all and each is yours;
> Yet grant some small acknowledgement of ours.[6]

She continued by addressing men as the greatest writers, with "quills that soar the skies," and said that if they should ever happen to condescend to read her poems, she asked not for a wreath of laurel but for one of leaves of much humbler plants and vowed that her "mean and unrefined" work would serve only to enhance "men's glory." Perhaps she was ironic, but it is hard to be sure. Women continued to use this formula well into the nineteenth century to accompany other forays onto male ground.[7]

Late in the century Cotton Mather offered ambivalent praise to the writing women of New England, comparing them with soldiers and Amazons. He reserved his unmixed praise for women who read the Bible and encouraged men to write. Mather encouraged female intellectual activity, provided it contained no challenge to the dominant views on religion and the relation of the sexes. He supplanted the mid-century equation of reading and intelligence with sexual and moral breakdown with a less apocalyptic desire to harness women's intelligence and make it serve the work of godly men.[8]

Some Puritan women took the religious standards that surrounded them and converted them into active principles to live by, thereby commanding the respect of their husbands, giving them some measure of moral authority, and, incidentally, opening an outlet for aggression as well. These women channeled their powerful energies, intellectual and otherwise, within the constraints of Puritan morality and provided a model to subsequent generations of women wishing to wield moral force.[9]

Women's prayer groups persisted long after the exile of Anne Hutchinson, on into the eighteenth century. Women led these groups, and men were not usually welcome. Certainly Cotton Mather thought so. Such groups offered women a special opportunity to exercise their intellects and consciences in an atmosphere that was neither strictly private nor fully public. What's more, the greater opportunities and significance of female piety were matters of public record. The clergy was increasingly insecure because of the separation of church membership from voting and the continuing decline in men's attendance. The virtuous woman had existed before, of course, but the clergy's needs as well as the changing church demography were to give her growing prominence in the eighteenth century.[10]

The Helpmeet

A wife was to be her husband's helpmeet. She was to take care of the household and to do whatever else her husband wished. William Whately noted that the wife was her husband's deputy in the world and that each had a realm over which to rule. The younger Reverend John Cotton preached that a good wife was to "[keep] and [improve] what is got by the industry of the man." Cotton Mather went considerably further. The virtuous wife would manage her husband's profits so well that he would find it advantageous to give her the keys to everything and let her manage it all. Extensions of the helpmeet role took women into remunerative work. They baked, ran boarding-houses, sewed, taught, delivered babies, ran taverns, and much more. Women's labor raised moral questions. Women who participated in the market, trading and bartering locally, were more likely to be successful to the degree that they were obedient wives and "friendly neighbors." Their worldly ventures depended on a solid domestic foundation of being good.[11]

Women who provided food and drink came under regular scrutiny. The lady innkeeper was an extremely suspicious figure for Puritans. She not only served the public and was therefore exposed to all sorts of temptations moralists normally associated with men but dispensed that deadly combination: liquor and beds. The English Puritan John Dane's memories are instructive. Dane left home and found himself at an inn where the hostess was sitting in "her naked shift houlding her breasts open." She invited Dane to drink with her, but he pleaded weariness and hurried upstairs away from sin. At another inn he drank with a young woman, and when he went to his room, he found her waiting in bed for him. His hostess showed him to an empty chamber. In the morning he went to retrieve his clothes and had to elude the same young woman's tempting welcome. Dane concluded these episodes with sober relief that he never "knew any but thos two wifes that god gave me," and he praised the "wonderful unspeakable . . . marseys [mercies] of a god that taketh care of us when we take no care of ourselves."[12]

Henry Dunster, president of Harvard, had to write a petition to the Middlesex County court in 1654 defending the bread, beer, and morals of a Mrs. Bradish. He commended the quality of her products and denied parental charges that she was enticing the students to spend too much money and—doubtless more volatile an issue—time on her. In fact, she had asked Dunster more than once to prohibit his students from coming unless they were in great need of her products. Mrs. Webb also was a baker. The magistrates who admonished her many times for making bread that was too light, rebuked her in particular for her "covetous mind" and for "grossely" denying that she was taking bits off the dough after it was weighed. The church excommunicated her for her "grosse sins . . . her ways having bene long a grief of heart to her Godly neighbors."[13]

Puritans regarded alcohol as they did sex, anger, and other potentially explosive elements: lawful, but needing containment. In the early days of the colony Winthrop and the magistrates tried with little success to curtail the practice of drinking toasts because it led to drunkenness and possibly violence, in addition to wasting a lot of wine and beer. English moralists particularly excoriated drinking in women because it could lead to uninhibited sexual behavior. But colonial Puritans did not single out drunken women. They worried about drink's contributing to other scandalous behavior—waste, violence, adultery, lewdness, and impenitence—more than they worried about drunkenness itself.[14]

As a young minister Cotton Mather investigated the drinking of Ruth Fuller. He scrupulously collected two pages of evidence against her, documenting her slurred speech and her unsteady "gate." The church warned her that she would be excommunicated if she did not show up for her admonishment. She replied that she would be "hanged on the gallows" rather than do so. The church duly excommunicated her. The church received back repentant drinkers like Sister Hix of Dorchester and Jane Dence, also of the Mathers' congregation.[15]

Puritans officially allowed each drinker only half a pint and half an hour at an ale shop in which to drink it. Compared with men, women seem to have imbibed relatively little. Officials worried more about women as the brewers and particularly the dispensers of beer than they did about women as drinkers. Court records from Middlesex and Suffolk contain numerous presentments against women for selling drink to Indians, selling drink without a license, selling drink at improper times of the day, or simply selling too much drink. Goody Draper of Concord had to pay the costs of the Indian witnesses against her who charged her with selling them "strong water." Mary Bartlett was indicted for selling liquor without a license. "Sister George," after repeated accusations, confessed to the Dorchester congregation that she had let "some have drinke which made them drunke" and then had denied it. In addition, she had left the church in a disorderly manner, linking her disobedience in supplying liquor with a disrespect for authority.[16]

Midwifery was another common occupation for wives whose role as helpmeet went beyond the home. Puritans were suspicious of midwives and women with medical knowledge. For one thing, the differences between witchcraft and medicine were often indistinct. Also, the activities that forwarded a healer's profession often conflicted with traits prescribed for women. The proceedings of a church meeting concerning an old woman in Lynn with "good skill in chirigirry" demonstrates this. A onetime neighbor noted that she was a good Christian although she had "propounded herself" several times. She also kept her professional secrets, for which members of the congregation accused her of having a "proud and unbrotherlike spirit" and would not let her join the church. Finally, when she refused to try to treat people, she was "proud."[17]

In 1650 Alice Tilly, a midwife, became the center of a controversy in which the magistrates wished her censored and deprived of her right to practice. But a very large number of petitioners, more than two hundred women in six different petitions, wished to have Mrs. Tilly restored to her work, which they asserted she did very well. They feared that her husband would move the family out of town if his wife, whose income was crucial to them, could not establish her innocence. The magistrates saw it as a battle between their authority and hers. On the basis of her "cariage & speaches, & her urginge" others thus to petition for her, they argued, "nothinge but a compleat victory over magistracy will satisfy her excessive pride." That is, since she had gone so far as to defend herself actively, the magistrates had no choice but to humble her. The issue was no longer her skill but her self-will.[18]

Childbirth was a mortal struggle for mothers; they desired experienced help. But midwives had unusual authority that could make male leaders uncomfortable. They were the only women to participate in the administration of justice, attempting to extract the names of the fathers in bastardy cases. They had to give their expert opinions on the veracity of girls' allegations of rape. They testified on the likelihood of a pregnant woman's suffering from corporal punishment and whether or not a woman had recently borne a child. Anne Hutchinson had been a midwife, and her authority over numerous Boston women derived from her skill and aid, which had created a circle of trusting friends. The Reverend John Cotton wrote that in the beginning "she did much good in our town in woman's meeting at childbirth-travails, wherein she was not only skillful and helpful but readily fell into good discourse with the women about their spiritual estates." In the end, however, her ability to create a large and trusting acquaintanceship had helped call down the wrath of the magistrates upon her.[19]

The magistrates' deep fear of the midwife's power over birth is revealed in the repelled fascination with which Winthrop discussed the miscarriages of Hutchinson and one of her followers, the Quaker Mary Dyer. Winthrop linked Dyer's "monster" with the midwife, "one *Hawkins* . . . notorious for familiarity with the devill, and now a prime Familist." Winthrop read demonic and brutish characteristics onto the miscarried infant girl. "The eyes stood farre out, so did the mouth, the nose was hooking upward, the brest and back was full of sharp prickles, like a Thornback, the navell and all the belly with the distinction of the sex, were, where the lower part of the back and the hips should have been, and those back parts were on the side the face stood.[20]

In 1638 the court ordered that Jane Hawkins could no longer "meddle in surgery, in phisick, drinks, plaisters, or oyles" or, they added, "question matters of religion, except with the elders for satisfaction." Here again female knowledge had produced a questioner of authority. Four years later the court ordered Mrs. Hawkins's sons to remove her from the colony or she would be whipped or otherwise severely punished. The daughters of Eve conceived in sin and labored in sorrow. Comfort for mothers in labor—in itself a contradiction of Scripture—could easily be the devil's work.[21]

Wives as Disciplinarians

Wives were supposed to act as deputy husbands but often failed in the task of discipline. The wife of the Reverend Peter Thacher had a hard time dealing with her maid Lidia. She believed Lidia abused her, but she could not bear to discipline her or even to confront her about her behavior. When wives did use physical coercion, some seemed to do so out of fear of their husbands. In 1692 Mrs. Lee brought suit against the Crosswells for beating her daughter Rebecca to death. Rebecca, before her death, had told her mother that one time because she had come out of the barn and neglected to fasten the door, a lamb had been killed by a cow left outside. Thomas Crosswell beat her with a stick "untill she almost thought she was dead." Another witness found Mrs. Crosswell beating Rebecca because she had baked bread improperly. When the neighbor protested that Rebecca was only a girl, Mrs. Crosswell replied that she did not know what to do, "my husban will be soe angry." Mrs. Crosswell also permitted her daughter Silence to beat the girl "as long as she wold; so that she had butt breath or life to sturr."[22]

Adultery

A small group of women responded to marriage by breaking the Seventh Commandment. Adultery was, according to Puritan thinking, one of the worst transgressions a married woman could commit. Massachusetts made it a capital offense in 1631 and promulgated the law several times to make sure everyone was aware of it and could therefore be prosecuted under it. The colony departed from English practice by making adultery a felony, punishable by the state, whereas in England ecclesiastical courts tried such crimes. Adultery was defined by the marital status of the woman, not the man. The Massachusetts authorities executed only one couple for adultery. The usual punishment became forty lashes and standing for a time on a ladder by the gallows with a rope around one's neck. Plymouth colony attached the celebrated scarlet A to adulterers.[23]

There is the suggestion that the severity of adultery was defined not only by the marital status of the woman but also by her race. Cross-race adultery was less significant for Englishmen than for Englishwomen. In the 1631 case of an Englishman convicted of adultery with an Indian woman, he was sentenced to a severe whipping, as the magistrates considered but rejected execution. In an extremely unusual case in 1639 in Plymouth, a married Englishwoman was whipped while being pulled through the streets behind a cart and was forced to wear a badge for the rest of her time in the colony for having had sex with an Indian man. Her partner was punished less severely because she was adjudged to be at fault. One historian has determined that of the thirty-eight English people convicted of adultery between 1673 and 1774, thirty were women.[24]

Moralists considered women's adultery worse than both men's adultery and fornication. It contained within itself, in addition to unlawful carnality, the sins of wifely disobedience and self-will. The female partner of the only couple executed for adultery had problems conforming to Puritan marriage conventions. Mary Latham, eighteen years old, had been rejected by a young man "whom she had an affection unto." She then, against advice, married an ungodly man much older than she was, of whom she was not sufficiently fond to obey. Soon a number of men "solicited her chastity." Among them was James Britten, who fed her wine and "easily prevailed with her." Britten, who died with her, had been a scholar in England, but when he came to Massachusetts, reported Winthrop, he opposed "church government, etc." Britten confessed because he had been stricken with a palsy and feared further evidences of God's wrath. When Latham was convicted, she named several other sexual partners. In the end, Latham's godly upbringing reasserted itself, and she willingly edified Boston with her distress at her disobedience. The determining "sins" in her downfall were disobedience to her parents and, more crucial, the assertion of her sexual preference and affection for a young man. His rejection apparently filled her with such despair and humiliation that to punish herself and express her anger, she married a man who repelled her physically and, because of his irreligion, was impossible for her to obey. Adultery was the final step in her program of self-humiliation.[25]

The church commonly excommunicated members for adultery. Of the adultery of Mary Cooly, Cotton Mather wrote that she was far from repenting, and although she was absent, he censured her with a ringing incantation that ran in part: "I do declare her to belong visibly unto the doleful and woful kingdome of Satan, the ruler of Darkness of the world."[26]

As with children and single women, it was possible, although difficult, for married women to prove themselves the victims of attempted rape by showing that they had fought off their attackers and called for help. Sarah Higgins, who, with the fortuitous aid of her husband, managed to escape the attentions of John Bond, demonstrated how a virtuous wife should behave to a would-be adulterer. Once when Bond asked her to have him, she spit at him. On another occasion he forced her into a loft and attempted to rape her; she got away and elicited help from her returning husband. He reprimanded Bond with the odd exhortation that "[t]his must not bee soe on a Lord's day." Sarah Higgins had the good fortune to have a witness who was also physically capable of rescuing her.[27]

Fewer cases of adultery than of fornication reached the courts, probably because punishment was much more severe and because marriage and motherhood were more confining than single life. According to one historian, in the decade 1630–1640, adultery was twelfth in frequency after drunkenness, vilifying the authorities, lewd behavior, stealing, fornication, liquor law violations, avoiding jury duty, swearing, running away from servitude, extortion, and assault and battery. Women do not appear to have confessed to adultery often. A few women did take lovers, one can only assume, for the pleasure of it, in defiance of Puritan standards. Some took lovers, as in the case of Mary Latham, for more complicated motives. Such wives briefly defied Puritan morals but did not attempt to redefine those morals for themselves. Most Puritan wives did not challenge the sexual boundaries of Puritan marriage.[28]

Divorce

Puritans believed that God commanded marriage, yet unlike Anglicans, they saw it as a civil contract, not a sacrament. It could therefore be sundered. Women could obtain divorces if they could prove desertion. They could also win their freedom if they could prove adultery and some other sin. (For men, adultery alone was a sufficient reason.) Women obtained divorces more often than men, and they petitioned for them almost four times as often as men did on the grounds of desertion. From 1639 to 1692 there were forty divorce petitions before the courts, mostly on the grounds of desertion coupled with adultery and bigamy. Most were successful.[29]

Most Massachusetts divorces occurred because of the relative ease with which spouses could disappear. Sarah Helvis, for example, petitioned for a divorce in 1664 because her husband, a "serjant to a foote Company in Ireland," had remarried and had a child in Ireland. The court gave a divorce to Anne Clarke, whose husband, Denis, had deserted her and refused to return and "accompany with hir." In the meantime he had taken another companion and had two children in addition to the two he had had with Anne. Mary Bachiler, who had two sick children, petitioned the governor and deputies that her husband, a minister, had gone to England, where, she discovered, he had taken another wife several years before. She wanted to be free to find a "Meete helpe to assist hir."[30]

The courts also granted women divorces for husbands' sexual insufficiency. After fourteen months of marriage Anna Lane successfully petitioned the General Court to grant her a divorce because her husband, Edward, was impotent. He had been under a physician's care for seven months. She said she hoped her patient silence would not make the magistrates think that she should "remaine under the power of a pretended husband." In a diverting aftermath the couple appeared in court later pleading to be remarried. The judges informed them that their first marriage was still good. On leaving the court, officers bade them both good night, and Mrs. Lane amended that to "as good a Night as any woman in Boston."[31]

Impotence acquired after some years of marriage was grounds for a divorce, as Mary Holten knew when she plotted to give her husband, Samuel, something that would make him "shrinke up." While Mary had thought to obtain a divorce by rendering her husband sexually insufficient, he took the more traditional route of calling his wife an adulterer. In Holten's summation paragraph to the court, his words carry that assurance and conviction that Puritan moral rhetoric provided men in condemning women.

The Covenant has been notoriously violated on her part, & therefore ceases to bind me: her unfaithfulnesse has made my promise voide; by my marriage covenant I was bound unto a wife, not to a whore: by her adulterous practices she has cut of[f] her selfe from all claims to marriage society with me: . . . I have born with abundance from her, but now looke on it as my duty to urge the liberty of the law; as expecting nothing but a heart breaking sorrow from her of which I have had large experience: I can't satisfy my selfe without seeking to be freed from her from whom none of those ends that marriage was instituted for can be expected.

The outcome of Holten's petition is unknown, but if his claims were validated, he stood every chance of success.[32]

It is worth comparing this simple one-page petition with the massive documentation put together by Katherine Nailor, who seems to have had considerably more evidence at hand and infinitely less assurance of being rewarded. Mrs. Nailor had statements from four women testifying to her husband Edward's sexual incontinence, in addition to the deposition of a woman who had had an illegitimate child by him. She had testimony from Nailor's landlady that Nailor said he "would lye with any woman that would let him." A witness testified that one of Nailor's lovers had poisoned Mrs. Nailor's beer; another testified that when Mrs. Nailor had her last child, her husband left for several days in disgust and said when he returned, "What, art thou not dead yet. I have done what I can to kille you, and yet I can not." Another servant testified that Nailor usually came home drunk after midnight and would then try to make love to the maid. That failing, he would get his wife out of bed and make her wait on him. One winter evening he roused a daughter who was sick, had her strip, and made her stand in the cold for several hours. He insisted that she be silent and, when she sobbed, he beat her. On another occasion he threw his youngest child on the floor. He also kicked a third child down some stairs, although a witness broke its fall. The amount of evidence that Mrs. Nailor had to marshal to make her case is a testament to her frail chances at winning a divorce. Multiple adultery was not necessarily sufficient grounds, nor was abusive behavior toward her or her children. But, when they were taken all together, she did win her case.[33]

In the case of a divorce in which the woman was at fault, she could expect no support from her husband or the court. If, on the other hand, a woman became divorced and the husband was found to be at fault, regardless of who initiated the suit, it appears that the court restored to her those things that she had brought to the marriage and provided her with the house she and her husband had shared. In the case of Christopher and Elizabeth Lawson, he sued for divorce after they had been living separately for some time. The court ordered him to give her back her clothing, jewelry, and linens and to pay her the value of her livestock, which he had sold. He was also ordered to give her their house, all this so that "shee may have to live honestly without charge to the place."[34]

While divorce was hard to get, the fact that Puritan women believed that marriage under certain conditions could be dissolved suggested the moral accountability of husbands to wives. That handful of women who braved the courts to complain of adultery or desertion were rejecting the notion of obedience under all conditions and indicating that there was behavior in husbands that they and the community might agree was morally intolerable. On the other hand, the standards for moral accountability were higher and more arduous for women than for men.

Anglo Women and Native Americans

The Reformation was giving new significance to the family, women's work, and ordinary labors for the common good instead of older, aristocratic values of display, personal heroism, and heroic generosity. But in conflict with Native Americans, Puritans distinguished themselves as brutal and thorough, so much so that they appalled their Narragansett allies. Puritan women watched and sometimes participated in these battles and were cheered on for their own military feats. Ministers praised women who abandoned meekness and deference in favor of defiance and violence against Native people.[35]

The culture from which Puritan Massachusetts emerged was increasingly militant. For many years before the civil war in England

Puritan preachers emphasized the metaphoric spiritual war against Satan and urged military training on young men to avoid the "effeminateness" of the aristocracy. As Michael Walzer has written, "Puritanism . . . trained [seventeeth-century Englishmen] to think of the struggle with Satan and his allies as an extension and duplicate of their internal spiritual conflicts, and also as a difficult and continuous war, requiring methodical, organized activity, military exercise, and discipline . . . [P]ermanent warfare was the central myth of Puritan radicalism. The preachers made warfare appear a particularly vivid and significant expression of the disorder of the age. Here, moral confusion and social strain were turned into systematic enmity." The martial imagination of the arriving saints and the rigid emotional habits that accompanied their vision of the world, divided into the saved and the damned, contributed to the causes of Puritan-Indian conflict and help explain the combativeness of some Puritan women as well.[36]

Before the settlers arrived, Native people had attempted to establish reciprocal relationships with English adventurers, fishermen, and traders, but the English propensity "toward violence and kidnapping and their refusal to enter into and maintain reciprocal relationships finally succeeded in arousing the hostility of most coastal Indians." Between 1616 and 1618 horrifying epidemics wiped out enormous numbers of Indians along the southern coast. Puritans in 1630 found southern New England populated by about 10 to 25 percent of the precontact population of 120,000 Native people. The Puritans arriving saw the massive dying as God's special favor to them. They justified further claims through the fiction that Indians did not cultivate and improve the land.[37]

Within seven years of settlement, Puritans engaged in war with Connecticut Pequots, behaving with a violence hard even for the English to justify. During the 1637 massacre about four hundred Pequot men, women, and children were burned alive or shot trying to escape. Ongoing sporadic violence, and another, uniquely bloody war with the Wampanoags and Narragansetts in 1676 meant that Puritans lived with violence in the background virtually all the time. Puritan women, for the most part nonparties to the behavior and decisions that initiated the violence, were nevertheless observers and sometimes participants in this continual war. Some women exhibited extraordinary self-assertion and aggression, finding in the dominant Puritan portrait of Indians as godless savages permission to unleash some of the anger that English gender customs called on them to repress. In 1697 Hannah Duston killed and scalped four adults and six Indian children while escaping capture. Her husband, Thomas, successfully petitioned the court for twenty-five pounds in scalp bounties. Both Joseph Sewall and Cotton Mather entertained and honored her. Mary Rowlandson's best-selling narrative about her captivity among King Philip's army marketed her sensational odyssey and homecoming as a story of God's protection to His unworthy subject. It was only the first in what was a two-hundred-year-long string of stories celebrating varieties of Euro-American heroism when faced with an enemy popularly constructed as vicious, bloodthirsty, proud, and bestial.[38]

In having enemies so different from them and so easy to characterize as demonic, Puritans also found a target for the aggression that they usually tried hard to monitor and control. Puritans seemed to be purposeful, energetic, and confident in their pursuit of livelihoods and individual godliness. But this masked a discomfort about "their wishes to intrude, to encroach, to dominate, to attack—their whole assertive side. As frequently happens in such situations, they dealt with their conflict by externalizing it." Attributing to Indians the traits they despised in themselves, they found emotional release in punishing Native people for these projected failings. Many women, whose outlets for aggression were fewer than men's, must have found unthinking racism and even, for some, violence welcome outlets as well.[39]

Married women were to display and feel deference to their husbands and other male authorities in Massachusetts. When they worked outside the home, this demand was often in conflict with behavior required for the marketplace, and women developed two styles of behavior. They could shed deference very dramatically in dealing with Indians, and their culture encouraged routine verbal and imaginative hostility against Native people. Thus Puritan women employed at least two emotional and moral modes. One was in principle subdued and deferential, for dealing with their husbands and other Puritan men. The second, authoritarian and aggressive, was for dealing with others, who, in seventeenth-century Massachusetts, were primarily Indians but also included Africans and some poor whites.

5

MOTHERS

A principal social purpose of marriage was procreation. Estimates of the number of children in the average white household in colonial New England were likely to vary between six and eight, although families with ten to twelve were not uncommon. Colonial women survived childbirth at a higher rate than Englishwomen, but childbirth was nevertheless life-threatening. For seventeenth-century Massachusetts estimates vary; thirteen mothers' deaths for one thousand first babies is a recent average. After the first child a mother's chances improved; ten died per thousand for the next nine deliveries. Hence childbirth occasioned as much thought about death as about life.[1]

For Puritans, mortal crises were, by definition, moral crises. A woman securely converted and at peace with her Lord would confront her own demise with equanimity and at the same time communicate peace and courage to the living. Women, considered naturally fearful, were especially useful as witnesses to the belief that death was a triumph for the redeemed. Jerusha Mather, when she was five months pregnant, vowed that if God gave her an easy and short labor, she would dedicate herself to bringing up her child in fear of Him. As her labor approached, she prayed to be delivered from the sin of fear. As it happened, her labor was easy, but she and her baby died a short time later.[2]

If Puritan husbands absorbed their wives economically and polit-
ically in marriage, pregnancy and labor encouraged some husbands
to become one with their wives psychologically and morally as well.
The soul of the Reverend Joseph Tomson of Billerica profited mightily from the anxieties raised by his wife's pregnancies and deliveries.
When God visited upon his wife such a weakness as made the couple
fear her pregnancy might end badly, Tomson was grateful that the
Lord let him see that he had not been sufficiently grateful for her
health, companionship, and work. He prayed that God would restore
his wife's health and vowed perpetual gratitude, but when his wife
recovered, he charged himself with a return to indifference toward
his blessings and a "vile hart." At his wife's next pregnancy he went
through the same cycle: perceiving his ingratitude for his wife, the
fear that he might lose her, and, when she survived, an all too brief
sense of the glory and omnipotence of God. By his wife's third pregnancy his mortal fears for her seem to have abated somewhat, as did
his spiritual arousal resulting from her condition.[3]

The Reverend Michael Wigglesworth participated vicariously in
his wife's labor as well. When she had pain, he "lay sighing, sweating,
praying, almost fainting through weakness before morning. The next
day, the spleen much enfeebled me, and setting in with grief took
away my strength, my heart was smitten within me, and as sleep departed from myne eyes my stomach abhored meat, I was brought
very low and knew not how to pass away another night." His wife's
(or his) exertions prompted him to compare the bitterness of the
pains of childbirth with the "pangs of eternal death" and the awe-
some power of God.[4]

While many husbands experienced heightened religiosity at the
deliveries and deliverances of their wives, women, who spent most of
their childbearing years pregnant or nursing, seem to have regarded
these experiences as unworthy of mention and perhaps shameful.
Anne Bradstreet, writing on her own origins, describes herself:

> . . . conceived in sin and born with sorrow,
> Whose mean beginning blushing can't reveal,
> But night and darkness must with shame conceal.
> My mother's breeding sicknes I will spare,

Her nine moneths weary burden not declare.
To shew her bearing pains, I should do wrong,
To tell those pangs which can't be told by tongue . . .

Bradstreet associated pregnancy and childbirth with original sin and made clear that discussion of women's reproductive problems was indecent.[5]

Maternal Love

Puritans regarded maternal love, like sexuality, as a blessing, but one that came with moral danger. Puritans expected mothers to be tender and zealous in the care of their small children. But it was perilously easy for mothers to dote on their children to the exclusion of God. The inherent irrationality of women made their attachments to their children suspect, so that husbands were required to supervise them. Puritan men understood, however, the yearning for a loving mother. Although a mother might be too fond and therefore irrational, it was an irrationality that many Puritans tolerated and some even longed for. A true mother, like Thomas Shepard's wife, would give up her own life to save her child. Shepard, explaining to his son his mother's death, wrote: "Thy dear mother died in the Lord, . . . who did lose her life by being careful to preserve thine, for in the ship thou wert so feeble and froward both in the day and night that hereby she lost her strength and at last her life."[6]

Puritans associated goodness, happiness, and spiritual nurturance with breast feeding. Of all imagery pertaining to females, Puritans had the most positive associations to the lactating breast. The saints "collectively . . . suckled at spiritual milk." Both the word and the law became spiritual milk. In Puritan sermons ministers used metaphors giving God, the Father, the feminine capacity to nurse his children.

If Puritans worried that women were too fond, moralists also worried from time to time that perhaps mothers were not as fond as they were supposed to be.[7] For example, moralists like Richard Allestree insisted that mothers nurse their babies. Cotton Mather too in the New World had to instruct mothers to nurse their babies: "If God have granted her Bottles of Milk on her Breast, she thinks that her Children have a claim unto them. It shall not be her *Niceness*, but her *Necessity* and *Calamity*, if she do not suckle her own Offspring." Mather's words voiced the fear underlying the reassuring assumption of excessive maternal fondness: that such fondness might be neither deep nor reliable and could be curtailed by putting oneself first.[8]

Because Puritans wished mothers to be nurturing and affectionate, moralists frequently had to remind women not to be too lenient with their young for fear that the children would grow up godless. Ministers exhorted women, described as fearful and humble by nature and ruled by their emotions, to save their children from the sins of pride, self-indulgence, willfulness, and complacency. Mather advised mothers not to spare "*Corrections* where their Miscarriages do call for the *Rod:* [or to] *overlay* them with her sinful Fondness, lest God make them Crosses to her."[9]

Mothers, according to Mather, additionally could infect their children with original sin. The only way a woman could save her children was to "travail for her children more than once." A mother was to work as hard as she could, instilling the principles of religion in her babies, teaching them about God, and catechizing them as soon as they could speak. She had to make them fear as well as love her so that they would learn the habit of obedience. Her job was laborious and full-time. She would not, however, be granted full authority with which to do this job. In the courts, when mothers fought to preserve their influence over their young, magistrates placed husbands over wives and, in the absence of husbands, placed town officials over children.[10]

Puritan mothering could be exceptionally effective moral training because it combined strong but contingent love with an all-inclusive ethical system. While Puritans used public shaming, like the scarlet A in Plymouth, their most effective tool was the guilt that powerful mothers could impart, because it tended to inhibit incipient infractions rather than punish them after the fact. Puritan men, particularly ministers, witnessed to the power of pious mothers, but they also wanted her authority, especially over boys, to remain bounded by one of their own sex. When the father's moral authority failed, the court substituted other men over his children.[11]

Widows who wished to place out their children consulted with the selectmen in the absence of husbands. Elizabeth Brailbrook of Watertown apprenticed her daughter, "with the consent of the selectmen," to an Ipswich rope maker who would teach her to read and "instruct her in the knowledge of God and his ways." Ruth Lockwood's husband died in 1635, and the court ordered the Watertown church to "dispose of the children . . . to such persons as they thinke meete." If they did not do so in two weeks, the governor and deputy governor would dispose of them.[12]

The love that Puritan mothers offered their children was founded in an intense moral identification with their children. This kind of maternal attachment was merely the intimate, personal version of the Puritan view of the community as an interwoven moral network, in which the sin of one person stained everyone. Mothers believed that their children's behavior reflected directly back on them. This made their connection with their children close, sometimes to the point of discomfort.

Puritan mother love bore a special anxiety because it was often mixed with the fear of separation. The omnipresent threat of separation for Puritan children included not only illness and death and physical distance but also the terrifying possibility of eternal damnation. Some loving mothers made known their preference for seeing their children dead rather than sinning. This could give maternal affection and discipline a special urgency.[13]

Intimacy and separation from the maternal figure were particularly freighted issues for boys. They were forced to start separating from their mothers at six or seven, before the benefits of maleness were fully evident. They began wearing clothing that officially differentiated them from girls and started to come under their fathers' less "fond" tutelage. Meanwhile their sisters' attachments to their mothers would probably be untroubled until puberty, when they might go off to live and work with other families. Fierce anxieties about love seem to inform the contradictory attitudes some men later expressed about maternal care.[14]

In sermons, men idealized this potent maternal mix of love and law and yearned for bonding with an omnipotent mother, whom they sometimes transformed into God, the Father. In memoirs, men lauded individual mothers, often their own, as pious lawgivers. But in advice literature they were likely to denounce mothers as overfond spoilers of children and recommend that they either use the rod or bow to their husbands' use of it. In legal practice they consistently limited the authority of mothers, even when fathers proved dissolute and irreligious.[15]

Perhaps men limited women's temporal power in part because as children they had often found it so crucial to their own spiritual development. Increase Mather said his mother, "a very Holy, praying woman," desired for him grace and learning. She taught him to read and, according to her grandson, Cotton, increase "all that was Good." On her deathbed she exhorted her fifteen-year-old son to go into the ministry.[16]

Good mothers would rather see their children dead than live outside the grace of God. In Michael Wigglesworth's relentless jingle "The Day of Doom," "The tender mother will own no other / of all her numerous brood / But such as stand at Christ's right hand / acquitted through his blood." Thomas Shepard recalled that his wife repeatedly cried and prayed in secret for her son, requesting that "if the Lord did not intend to glorify himself by thee, that he would cut thee off by death rather than to live to dishonour him by sin."[17]

The powerful Puritan mother seems less fond than righteous, unwaveringly committed to religious principles. Mary Rowlandson, author of the first captivity narrative, published after the conclusion of King Philip's War, planted the tough English Puritan mother in the heart of the New World enterprise. She defined an important part of her identity through her concern and grievous suffering over her children. The Wampanoags wounded her six-year-old daughter, Sarah, who died in her arms after grueling forced marches. She recalled the love for her son through the hours spent combing the lice out of his hair. The fate of her son and her daughter who were still prisoners greatly diminished her joy upon her release from captivity.[18]

Yet outside the circle of her own children Rowlandson exhibited little sympathy—not for Indian babies or English babies or animal babies. She was pleased when her mistress's "papoose" died, because it meant more room for her to sleep in the tent. She refused to make another Indian baby a trinket. When Indians grieved for a dead child, she wrote of their coming "to howl," a verb that matched her use of "wolves" and "beasts" for the Indians. She even took food out of the mouth of an English baby who was failing to eat it as thoroughly as she knew she could.[19]

These repeated failures to extend her sympathy beyond her own family portray Puritan mothering in the New World as a mixture of tenderness and ruthlessness. Good mothers would sacrifice anything to see their children behave in a godly fashion. Their own salvation, unlike that of their husbands, depended upon the observable goodness of their children. This worried, critical, doubting, moral interdependence characterized good Puritan mothering. In the crucible of the mother-child relationship, "good" children emerged convinced that their mothers' spiritual fate rested as much in the child's hands as in the mother's. Such mothers emerged fortified in their moral practices, convinced of the efficacy and justice of their educational methods and the accuracy of their moral judgments. Motherhood provided some Puritan women with an arena in which they administered, advocated, and interpreted morality. In these home schools boys learned to respect and even fear their actively righteous mothers. This gave the mothers an outlet for intellect, energy, and (within limits) creativity; and it promised a substantial measure of domestic moral authority as its reward.[20]

John Wing specifically allocated to mothers the raising of daughters so that they might be "ornaments to the men who would marry them." A girl remained longer under her mother's tutelage than a boy because she had to learn housekeeping from her mother. Inasmuch as moral conditions prescribed for mothers and daughters were identical, distinct from those prescribed for men, and uniquely rigorous, the intense relation between the former continued into adolescence and beyond. It contained an inborn tension bred from the fact that mothers and daughters, unlike mothers and sons, would continue to reflect each other's social inferiority and moral constraint for their whole lives.[21]

Elizabeth Saltonstall's communication to her daughter underlined their moral interdependence. She wrote: "Were it not that I arrive at your good I should not be willing to deny myself as I do." If one thinks of mother and daughter as the same moral entity, the sentence loses its negative veneer of guilt and merely states a fact that would have been obvious to both of them. The mother's physical comfort or happiness was irrelevant when a question of her daughter's good arose. She asked her daughter to "be a peace and comfort to your parents and not a grief and shame."[22]

A form of moral bonding prevailed whether the mothers and daughters were virtuous and religious or not. Elizabeth Martin and her two daughters, for example, lived an irregular life. One neighbor testified that they pretended to go to church to pray but actually went to backbite. One witness testified that Mrs. Martin called her daughters "young whores" and that one of them replied, "Mother, you are as much talked of as we . . . why mother you were talked of bad before we were borne and will be when you are dead." When Mrs. Martin discovered that her daughter Margaret was pregnant, she slapped her and told her that "[i]f she had beaten her brains out when shee was young that she should not have that sin for to answer for that she hath now." Margaret countered that if she were going to hell, so was her mother, but she wished they would not have to go together because they would fight the whole way.[23]

In families in which religion was weak or nonexistent, the moral identification between mother and child lacked the effective blend of the judicious giving and withholding of love, combined with childhood terror about one's immortal soul. Mothers in these families used the relatively inefficacious tools of verbal abuse and violence to punish bad behavior, rather than exemplify selflessness, use pious love, and emphasize moral interdependence to instill values.

The pattern of moral reproduction was constantly in danger from the death of a mother. Fathers of motherless children tried to remarry as fast as they could, in large part to give their young new mothers. The bond of moral identity between generations was at risk. When the Reverend Michael Wigglesworth wrote to a widow named Avery, trying to convince her to marry him, she balked at the size of his family. He assured her that if the number of his children and "the diffi-

culty to guiding such a family" be her main objection, "the number
may be lessened if ther be need of it," by which he meant (one hopes)
that some of the children could be put out to other families, thus sev-
ering those children's intimate moral ties to the family. The younger
children, whose moral code may not yet have been fully formed, were
especially in danger from a new alignment.[24]

Poverty often disrupted the bond between mother and child. In
families that did not experience great want, Puritan mothering effectively produced self-critical, cautious young women who were likely
to work hard. They would try to curb their aggression and sexuality
and would probably be watchful over their expression of feelings.
Religion would be a central source of guidance and solace as well as
a legitimate target of strong feeling.

Infanticide

A very few women for whom moral considerations were a luxury became pregnant and could not rear their babies. These women, un-
prepared for motherhood and unwilling to be publicly shamed,
destroyed their children. While there were very few women who
committed infanticide, they loomed large in the imagination of
Puritan men and, at least during the seventeenth century, were vigorously prosecuted. The violence of infanticide annihilated the
happiest Puritan fantasy, nursing, which in its various incarnations integrated male and female, infant and parent, Puritan and God. In its
place the murderous mother substituted an image of female power
at its most malevolent, exercised at the expense of mankind at its
most vulnerable. Although the number of infanticides was small,
their evocative moral and emotional potential was great.

Before convicting a woman of infanticide, Puritans had to establish that she had concealed her deed and had a history of lewd behavior. The reputation of the accused was almost as important an
element in conviction as proving the commission of the crime itself.
In thirty-three cases between 1638 and 1730 Puritans convicted disproportionately high numbers of black women.[25]

Ministers worked very hard with women to confess and repent their infanticides unless they were black or Indian. I found no sermons preached upon the execution of a black convicted of infanticide. Cotton Mather commented upon two women who were executed in 1693 for the crime, identifying the white one as "young" and the other as "black." He referred to both convicts together until a certain point. "Many . . . a weary hour did I spend . . . to serve the souls of those miserable wretches. . . . I had . . . opportunities . . . to speak to them." But when he started to write about exacting a confession, the black woman disappeared, and he began referring to the convicts in the singular: "I had obtained from the young woman a pathetical *Instrument* in writing wherein she own'd *her own* miscariages & warned the *Rising Generacon* of *theirs*." "She" again became plural when Mather "accompany'd the wretches to their execution."[26]

In Mather's view, the black woman's confession had no public significance. The redemption in death of a black female from her evil life would neither motivate a sinner of the "rising generation" nor propitiate God. Black women were incapable of representing to white Puritans the triumph of God's merciful salvation over sin. On the other hand, they received the harshest expressions of Puritan punishment. Puritans burned at the stake a black woman accused of torching her master's house. Mather mentions this event only because its singular brutality failed to produce fear or repentance in a white criminal awaiting his execution.[27]

But in the hands of a successful minister the odious and feared (white) female victimizer became the ideal sacrificial victim, exhorting others with her last breaths to learn from her example, do as she did not, heed all authorities, love God, and submit willingly and fearlessly to His commands. If the female was uniquely hateful as an aggressive malefactress, she was uniquely powerful as a public penitent.[28]

This was especially true in the 1690s. In this period of increased convictions for infanticide, preachers strove diligently to offer their listeners sincere restatements of community morals from repentant women sinners. The Bay colony, recently deprived of its original charter and hence its moral and legal autonomy from England, turned both its confused anger and its hopes for redemption on women, both witches and infanticides, when the community seemed in jeopardy. Puritan spokesmen hoped that examples of profound repentance might help appease the Lord and convince Him of the willingness of His people to mend their ways. Convicted women who had taken Puritanism seriously went to their deaths willingly, affirming God's justice and the community's judgment upon them. They often cited their disobedience as children, their disregard for religion, and their lascivious behavior as reasons for their later sins.

Women indifferent to Puritanism died without applauding its justice. Their silence implied that men and their morals sometimes trapped women unjustly in situations from which there was no decent exit. Some acted defiantly, rejecting the Puritan view of death as redemption for the repentant sinner, by denying any crime. Others rejected the idea implicitly by confessing but dying fearfully.

At the turn of the century the Ipswich hangman executed a young woman named Esther Rogers, whose cheerful death testified to her belief in repentance and redemption. Rogers had killed two bastard infants, both fathered by black men. The minister in charge of her last weeks recorded that although Rogers had grown up in a godly family, she had given no thought to religion herself. At seventeen she lost her virginity to a black boy living in the same house. She strangled the resulting child and buried it in the garden. She said she soon "got over and rid of all my Fears, and even all thoughts thereof, giving myself up to other wicked company and ways of Evil." She later had an affair with the black servant of a neighbor and left his infant in the snow by a pond. Neighbors confronted her with it. Her minister convinced her to loathe and repent of her sins. With her dying words she told others to be obedient: "Run not out a Night, especially on Sabbath Nights, refrain from bad Company for the lords sake. . . . Improve time, you do not know what a Comfort it is to be . . . in Gods Ways; If you do not love God, he will not love you." Four or five thousand people watched this model penitent go to her death cheerfully crying out to the Lord.[29]

Some women convicted of infanticide believed that the fathers should bear responsibility along with them, although in most cases

women alone incurred the entire punishment. Sarah Smith of Deer-
field, Massachusetts, was the wife of Martin Smith, who had been held
captive by the Indians for three years. She had formed a liaison with
one Joseph Clesson and had become pregnant. When she told Clesson, he offered her money to conceal the child and begged her not to
name him as the father. Smith had few options. If she confessed, she
could be charged with adultery and suffer the consequences. She had
the baby alone, strangled it, and attempted to conceal the body. When
some of Smith's neighbors discovered the dead baby and asked who
the father was, Smith charged Clesson. He denied everything, and
without evidence or a confession there was little the authorities could
do to him. Smith was hanged in August 1698.[30]

Since the minister's concern with a woman charged with infanticide was to make moral use of her, we get from clerical accounts of
convicts little sense of the domestic conditions of their lives. Occasionally the court records offer us a more intimate glimpse of these
tragedies. Mary Flood told her neighbors over and over that she had
to murder her child because her husband would not work to get food
for it. She said she had to go out three days in succession to bring
home a little something for the family to eat, and such absences were
bad for the baby. One time Mary Flood drank too much. Her daughter said Flood had hit the baby in the stomach repeatedly with her
fist. The baby cried a great deal that evening, and at some point
Flood called out in desperation that she would have to kill either the
child or herself. Neighbors heard her shout to the baby that it should
cry and be damned. In the morning she and her husband told the
neighbors their baby had died. The thirteen-week-old baby was severely bruised on the right side.

Flood did not confess. She did admit to drinking too much and to
"giveing two [sic] much Liberty to her passion." Enervating poverty,
marital discord, and the constant problem of hunger combined to
push the inebriated Flood beyond her ability to imagine anything but
despair. With an unimpaired capacity for anger and aggression, she
would not embrace punishment and recast her circumstances in
moral terms not her own.[31]

Few women with Puritan backgrounds remained defiant when

convicted of infanticide. One who did formulated her aggression as a manifestation of a spiritual struggle. Dorothy Talbye of Salem had a troubled marriage. Her husband, who was evidently hard on her, was later excommunicated for "much pride and unnaturalness" toward his second wife. At least in part because there was no socially acceptable outlet for her fury at her husband and the confines of marriage, Talbye fell into a depression and began to ascribe her frighteningly aggressive impulses to revelations. She once attempted to starve herself and her whole family to death because she believed the Lord had told her to do so. Her behavior grew more challenging, and the church excommunicated her. The town had her whipped, causing her to be more "dutiful" toward her husband. The improvement, however, was brief and illusory. Not very long after, acting on what she described as a command of God, she broke the neck of her three-year-old daughter Difficulty so that, she later explained, the child would never have to suffer.

At her trial Talbye refused to confess until Governor John Winthrop told her that she would be "pressed" to death, a technique of interrogation usually reserved for unrepentant witches. She then made her confession and asked to be beheaded because it was "less painful and less shameful" than hanging. She was ceaselessly rebellious. When the Reverend Hugh Peter read the announcement of her excommunication, she tried to run away. On the gallows she took off the cloth that was to cover her face and put it between her neck and the rope. And she grabbed at the ladder after she had been suspended from the gallows, trying to save herself. The Reverend Peter, deprived of a repentant mouthpiece, warned the onlookers to beware of revelations and not to despise the words of excommunication as Talbye had done.[32]

Puritan juries and magistrates maintained a consistently higher conviction rate for women who committed infanticide than for any other kind of killer. The female baby killer, rare as she was, held a power over the Puritan imagination disproportionate to her numbers. She was the evil counterpart to the loving, fond, nurturing, self-sacrificing mother who was essential to the reformation of society.[33]

6

AGING AND DEATH

Puritans offered a public role that carried a modicum of moral authority to widows over sixty years old. The Reverend John Davenport wrote that virtuous widows were to be unofficial deaconesses, and the Reverend John Cotton added that these women were "fit assistants to the Deacons." Henry Dunster specified in his notebook in 1631 that aged widows had the responsibility to minister to the "sick, lame, weary, & diseased." Initially, few widows were strong enough to carry out the job assigned to them, and as time went on, the church's commitment to alleviating the distress of the poor and infirm diminished so that fewer and fewer women were asked to perform in this honorable capacity. But the fact that mid-century Puritans carved out a place of honor for some females is noteworthy.[1]

Cotton Mather, writing at the end of the century, argued that old women should provide a "good example to the younger women in sober modest & godly conversation avoiding idlenesse, vaine talke, & light behavior." He also spent considerable time elaborating the morally correct behavior of a marriageable widow, discussing if and in what spirit a widow might remarry, the tone and quality of her grief, and her behavior as a stepmother and second wife. Finally, Mather defined the job of the late-seventeenth-century elderly widow: She was to focus her energies on longing for the "Day when the Lord Jesus will send his Angels to fetch her unto the Regions of everlasting Light and Life." There is, to my knowledge, no such corresponding advice to widowers.[2]

The main job of unmarriageable widows then, in the absence of much deacon's work, was to die well. A good widow might fear death, but in the end she should welcome it. Cotton Mather recorded of his mother-in-law's demise that although she had been all her life of a *"Fearful Temper,"* she was especially "in her lifetime under some slavish fear of *Death,*" but as her death drew close, "she comfortably gott over it." Puritans had sympathy and respect for an excellent female death. Judge Samuel Sewall several times visited his neighbor Dame Walker on her deathbed in 1695 and recorded her last days with approval, omitting her final frightening delusions. Puritans very much wanted the deaths of fearful but virtuous old women to be peaceful and godly to reassure both the dying and her survivors that the end for the saved was a joyful herald of eternal bliss. The labors of ministers and others could produce a well-shaped moral finish, but they could also distort the experience of the dying woman. The deaths of Dame Walker and Mather's mother-in-law are examples of the use to which Puritan men put female suffering, for both individual and society-wide lessons.[3]

Dead Puritan women often evoked lists of their excellent characteristics. John Winthrop buried a wife whom he described as a woman of "singular virtue, prudence, modesty, and piety." In 1725 Cotton Mather eulogized Abigail Brown for having been "sincere, cheerful, humble, modest, meek, gentle, peaceable, tender-hearted, patient and full of goodness." In death Puritans routinely transformed women, but not men, into a list of moral qualities, allotting virtues in the place of achievement. With this attention came the desire, both poignant and suffocating, to interpret, to control, and, when possible, to profit spiritually by women's behavior. The more symbolically important women's behavior became, the less room there was for variation—or missteps.[4]

Women's behavior, symbolic and actual, became ever more significant as men fell away from the church and focused on secular concerns. By the end of the seventeenth century it was only for women that religious and social purposes remained identical. "Puritan women, then, subscribed to a Christian role developed out of male needs to pursue social goals no longer validated by religion, out of ministerial determination to control doctrine and governance. . . . Perhaps a new role was created too, as members of the church, women became the keepers of the covenant and protectors of the idea of mission."[5]

Puritan habits of thought, inquiry, criticism, and logic would benefit women and men, particularly as Puritans ceased reading Scripture as literal truth. Puritan cultural habits, such as a desperately honest pursuit of self-knowledge, persisted long after New England Calvinism had been defanged. The installation of consciences and the powerful experiences of loving empathy some Puritan couples felt for each other were emotional innovations of great importance in the moral growth of Americans. If Puritan women's consciences were often overactive and husbands' empathy could cannibalize rather than share spouses' experiences, nevertheless the pattern of the former came to underlie mainstream child rearing. Moreover, spouses' capacity of empathy for each other came to define a central, perhaps *the* central, component of nineteenth-century romantic love. Puritan culture, with its emphasis on self-examination and the strict accounting for one's feelings in addition to one's deeds, was at the center of nineteenth-century evangelical experience, which women in turn placed at the heart of middle-class family life.[6]

Finally, the belief in women's moral superiority that was so fundamental to nineteenth-century reform movements and that energized as well strands of twentieth-century politics, including Progressivism, the Second Wave of Feminism, and the Moral Majority, was born in the evolution of New England Puritanism. But before the idea of women's moral superiority congealed in the nineteenth century, it became modified over the eighteenth century and restricted to white women.

Part Two

7

VIRGINIA GIRLS

In 1690 the population of Virginia was about fifty-three thousand, 88 percent of it white. By 1780 the population had grown to some 538,000, approximately half of whom were black, and of these, all but a few were slaves. By the middle of the eighteenth century Native Americans made up only 1 or 2 percent of Virginia's population. The majority of the population was living in the Tidewater, the flat coastal plain irrigated by several rivers and bounded on the west by rising hills, the urban center of which was Williamsburg, between the York and James Rivers. A town of about one thousand in 1760, Williamsburg had been established in 1633 and was Virginia's capital for eighty-one years until Richmond superseded it after the American Revolution.

Williamsburg was the center for the commercial, cultural, and political life of the largest and one of the most prosperous colonies in eighteenth-century America. Every month the town held a court of common pleas and two other courts. One dealt with slave crimes, the other with all cases concerning amounts above twenty pounds as well as with appeals from all the lower courts holding sessions in April and October. Williamsburg was also home to the College of William and Mary, founded in 1693 primarily to provide ministers for the An-

glican Church during a period when the church was vigorously prop-
agating its brand of Christianity and combating dissenters of all
stripes. William and Mary secondarily proposed to propagate the
faith among the Indians.

Williamsburg published the colony's newspaper, the *Virginia
Gazette*. It was usually a weekly, sometimes a biweekly, that included
stories of local and colonial interest and items picked up from London newspapers often detailing scandals, sexual misbehavior, and the
loose morals of the English aristocracy. It also provided a place to advertise the sale of goods and services and notify the surrounding
countryside about runaway slaves, wives, and horses. As the list suggests, runaway slaves predominated, then wives, then horses. The
Gazette, in addition, gave notice of the arrival of merchant and slav-
ing ships.[1]

The Virginia gentry were and were not British. Virginians, unlike
Puritans, did not come over rejecting important aspects of English
life. They admired British fashions, education, and liberties. At the
same time, they were defensive about their provincialism and critical
of their admiration for the mother country. They mimicked British
styles and attitudes while enduring the uneasiness, self-doubt, and
rebelliousness such "self-colonizing" provoked. It was an unease that
proved particularly hurtful to women. Since much of the anti-British
rhetoric of the revolutionary period associated femininity with the
corruption of British society and its rulers, feminine morality was an
important subject in the complex relation between the colonies and
the mother country. A kind of reflexive antagonism against women
appeared against a wider background of middle-class revulsion
against a voluptuous, self-indulgent, and licentious aristocracy. The
Virginia Gazette's focus on the corruption and feminization of the
British aristocracy gave Virginians a titillating critique of Britain
while reinforcing their shared culture.[2]

In the mid-eighteenth century, newspapers like the *Gazette* had
a maximum circulation of about six hundred and a readership of
considerably more. Directed at the colony's influential men and reflecting their attitudes, these papers were of significant cultural
importance in the prerevolutionary world, enlarging its boundaries to

include Europe—about 65 percent of their material was lifted from London sources—and simultaneously Anglicizing and Americanizing colonial culture. They did the latter by disseminating a relatively homogeneous body of information throughout the upper echelons of the colonial world. These sources of information diminished somewhat the cultural gap between those widely educated and the simply literate. After the 1730s American papers added fiction, poetry, and "remarkable" stories, brief narratives of ridiculous, horrific, or exemplary incidents that may or may not have accurately represented real events. The purposes of these accounts were moralistic and didactic.[3]

The genteel of Virginia, increasingly in debt to British merchants because of low tobacco prices and expensive tastes, were anxious about issues of luxury, extravagance, and effeminacy. The *Gazette* kept these questions sharply in focus, encouraging the colonials to ascribe their problems to the moral decay of the British ruling class. Such tales helped convince Virginians of their own moral health. The prominence of titled participants and ranking clerics in sordid dramas made clear that these did not reflect homegrown troubles. Occasionally an editor inserted a local version of a remarkable story, but always with a wholesome twist that furthered the distinction between mother country and colony.[4]

Aristocratic Englishwomen were often at the center of these stories. They were either the deluded victims of corrupt men or simply vain, luxurious, and salacious. Once in a great while the *Gazette* printed an anecdote about the amusing foibles of a wealthy colonial woman, usually an elderly widow—a woman without male guidance—but for the most part the Virginian women whom the paper noticed in print were poor whites and slaves who appeared as criminals, sexual miscreants, or runaways—from slavery or marriage.

Individual stories about the effeminate English aristocracy exemplified the whole country's decadence; those who should be moral exemplars were instead England's most licentious. Virginians could take satisfaction in their own relative innocence and in the absence of a sexually immoral, spendthrift class of wealthy women. At home, Virginia gentry men were primarily concerned that female disorder from the lower ranks might threaten slavery and the dominion of the wealthy. The restrictions on colonial gentry women, the isolation of rural life, and the perquisites of being elite seem to have precluded much deviant female behavior. But the ubiquitous theme of the feminine viper in the bosom of the English upper classes betrays the power these images had with elite Virginians. Virginian men comfortably shared a variety of assumptions with British men on the English origins of virtue, the necessity of maintaining patriarchal order, the threat of the unruly poor, and the place of noblesse oblige in maintaining the social order.

Girls' Education and Work

The goal of all white parents, whether of the gentry or not, was to produce daughters who would be obedient and make good wives. There were virtually no opportunities for a girl to support herself outside marriage. Anne Matthews of Virginia decided that her motherless grandchild Nancy needed to be sent to an aunt in England, where there were "Many prittey traids there that she might put her to, that is Not in my power to doe here." There a single woman with some education might become a governess, schoolmistress, or seamstress. Nancy lacked the resources—or, in the language of the day, was not interesting enough—to acquire a gentry husband.[5]

As for education beyond the management of a house, Virginians reserved it to ornament the lives of gentry girls who would have the leisure to display it. Gentry boys received a classical education, including mathematics, Latin, and philosophy, to equip them to engage in debate and action in the public world. Gentry girls were taught to read and write, to embroider, to play an instrument, to dance, and possibly to speak a little French or Italian. Their accomplishments represented their privileged social station the same way that fine clothes did, and were intended to make young women attractive companions to well-off men. Although the learning was likely to be superficial, literacy was, as we shall see, of great value to adolescent girls.[6]

Virginia's leaders historically distrusted education for any but the wealthy, believing it encouraged unrest among the poor. In 1620 Governor William Berkeley infamously announced that he thanked God that Virginia "had no free schools nor printing, and I hope we shall not have." Eighteenth-century Virginia's ruling gentry desired minimal government and the lowest possible tax rate, and not surprisingly the colony had no comprehensive system of public education and would not have until after the Civil War. In this period 14 percent of white girls of low social status learned to read while 45 percent of boys from the same background did.[7]

Virginia required all white families to educate their children to a trade and give them the fundamentals of Anglicanism. About half the women in the Chesapeake in the eighteenth century were literate, and about two-thirds of the men. Indenture contracts sometimes specified that girls who were bound out should be taught to read. One stipulated that such a girl learn to read "in her Mother tongue," another that she learn to "Read sew spin and knitt," while a third required a year's schooling. An equivalent indenture for a boy would specify writing as well. In the indenture of the brother of the girl who was to read and sew, spin, and knit, he was to learn to read, "write and cypher perfectly." In this, Virginia resembled Massachusetts, where it was not uncommon for girls to learn to read but not write and usual for boys to learn both.[8]

Indentured children could solicit the help of a justice of the peace if their education proved inadequate or violated moral standards. Elizabeth Wright, a "poor orphan," made a complaint against Barnard Eliot for "miscarriages," which were most likely of a sexual, not an educational, kind. The York County court ordered her freed from his service and instructed the church wardens to find her a new master. But her action was rare. In 1770, of 1969 actions in the York County records, there was only one in which an apprentice complained of his or her master. When indentured girls were mulatto, the term of service was generally much longer than the average ten- or twelve-year contract for a white child, and there were no provisions for education.[9]

For slaves and very poor whites, acquiring any education at all was a matter of the rarest good luck. One source estimates a 0.01

percent literacy level among slaves in the early to middle eighteenth century, up to 7.6 percent by the last decade. This upsurge parallels the spurt in manumissions that accompanied the revolutionary enthusiasm for freedom. Though literacy had a moral and religious function, its immediate cost and potential for destabilizing the social system weighed more heavily upon the minds of lawmakers.[10]

Young white and black girls grasped their respective positions in the world from planter parents' earliest efforts to separate the two races. In the seventeenth and very early eighteenth centuries some parents had sent their children to England to be educated. The William Byrds sent their daughter Ursula to England around 1684 because "shee could learn nothing good here, in a great family of Negro's." By the later part of the eighteenth century this custom had stopped, but the problem of black company for white children on rural plantations persisted. Landon Carter worried that he had no one but blacks with whom to leave his young children and grandchildren.[11]

If education was a privilege granted according to status, then work was its opposite, a burden that the elite bore lightly while the less fortunate bent under its weight. From the earliest days in the colony white Virginians had been loath to engage in manual labor and had sought ways to get rich without doing any. Early in the seventeenth century, when tobacco provided a salable product, first indentured servitude, then slavery provided the labor. The plantation owner took pride in his judicious agricultural management but not in work per se. Virginians, white and black, viewed physical labor with distaste. Hard work was for the poor and identified them as different in a way it did not in Massachusetts.[12]

Wealthy Virginians valued leisure and filled it with pleasure. When Thomas Jefferson was at home in Virginia, he made time to play the violin, ride horseback, tinker and invent, think, write, and socialize. To his daughters he preached that "of all the cankers of human happiness none corrodes with so silent, yet so baneful an influence, as indolence." John Harrower, a Virginia tutor from the Shetland Isles, had a blunter view of empty time for girls. He wrote his wife to keep their daughter "tight to her seam & stockin" because "[i]dleness or play or going about from house to house . . . is the first inlet in any of the sex to laziness and vice."[13]

Gentry Virginians kept their young daughters as busy as possible. Little as most Virginians valued education for girls, it provided a way to pass time harmlessly.[14] Young slave girls, however, grew up learning that their role was to work hard in a society where work was devalued. At age six or seven they began with chores that old women also did, such as taking care of the poultry, ewes, lambs, and pigs. They might also weed the vegetable gardens and help out in the big house. Girls learned about the distribution of power among adults and could observe their mothers' authority diminish when their small daughters started to work under their white mistresses' supervision.[15]

Consumption and Individuality: Clothing

Gentry girls who had finished their formal education but were not yet married had few compelling functions to perform beyond finding mates. In theory, they were expected to learn the role of plantation mistress and prepare by supervising younger female slaves. They often took leave from this to traverse the plantation circuit, looking for available young men while keeping decorously busy. Lucinda Lee Orr wrote that she had been "working a little screene, to hold in my hand to prevent the fire from burning my face." In this period the growing market made it possible for girls from planter families to represent their families in society by spending money and time on appearances. Girls who could bought books and clothes and looked to both to help define themselves.[16]

Virginia planters placed great importance on physical appearance, and this fact could not have been lost on poor whites or blacks. This emphasis encouraged the gentry to extravagance in dress and ensured that there would be great contrasts in apparel between rich and poor. Moralists agreed, up to a point. The Reverend James Fordyce, in *Sermons to Young Women*, which, along with *The Ladies Library*, was one of the most popular books of advice for girls in the

colonies, wrote that women had an obligation to make themselves attractive. Thomas Jefferson admonished his daughter Martha that she
had a duty to her family and friends to make herself clean and attractive. Landon Carter criticized his neighbor's wife for her "towering
aparel" and two waiting maids but added, forgivingly, that he supposed she had done it to "shew her respect."[17]

Gentry girls had to try to make a good appearance inside and out.
Into this world of appearances, moralists taught that the display of
girls' moods and concerns should be modulated to captivate men.
This kind of message, which mixed moral pronouncements with the
business of attracting men and marrying, best displays the blend of
principle and manipulation in elite moral female education.

Moralists like Fordyce, the novelist and satirist François Fénelon, and the Reverend Richard Allestree promulgated the idea that
to be attractive to men, females should cultivate the appearance of
certain moods and jettison others. In particular, "briskness and levity
of deportment . . . can never be pleasing to a man of sentiment." A
man in search of a wife, said Fordyce, will look for "women well-bred
and sober-minded at the same time; of a cheerful temper with sedate
manners."[18]

According to Fordyce, girls were more appealing when they were
exhibiting their capacity for empathy, particularly their ability to feel
sorrow. "Never, my fair auditory, never do your eyes shine with a
more delightful effulgence, than when suffused with all the trembling softness of grief for virtue in distress, or of solicitude for friendship in danger." Girls were also attractive as listeners. Since they
were trained to display the tones of sympathy and empathy, a certain
alienation from their actual feelings would seem inevitable.[19]

Society as theater made expensive demands on costuming. Guardians without money worried that without the right clothes their
charges might not find mates. Anne Matthew wrote an English relative that her ward Nancy was fifteen and a "pritey girl I think. If she
had but Cloths to appear in decently. If her poor aunt Davenport had
not left her some of her Cloths when she dyed, Nancey would have
been very poorly off indeed." Nancy's beauty needed a stylish frame
for her to find a husband of some means. If the poor were tempted

to compete with the rich in matters of dress, moralists cautioned them "never to go beyond their circumstances, nor aspire above their station." Thus dress was, as it had been in Massachusetts in the seventeenth century, supposed to identify a woman's circumstances, with the difference that among the rich elaborate clothing conveyed respect, while among the poor it betrayed improper ambition.[20]

The rich often imported their clothes from England. Colonel Randolph, a planter, gave his daughter two barrels of tobacco every year "to purchase dresses and ornaments." By way of contrast, Landon Carter paid one hogshead of tobacco for brown linen and cotton from England to clothe all five hundred of his slaves. Cloth was the nexus between the slave or poor woman and the rich. Fabric represented the labor of the have-nots in a very concrete way, for West African women brought with them a rich knowledge of textile production. Plants hoed and weeded, food cooked, children looked after, laundry washed: None of these labors resulted in any lasting *thing* that so clearly represented women's work as did the production of fabric.[21]

Because of the female craftsmanship and effort that went into the making of fabric and clothes, the appropriation and distribution of these items was a complex, tension-filled process. On his plantation Carter allowed his slaves enough "Virginia cloth" for one suit of clothes a year. He became angry when he discovered that through his daughters' lack of supervision, his "house wenches" were managing to get two suits per year out of the material. His spinners and he struggled over when and how long they were going to work and what their reward should be. The women who made cloth sometimes fled from the control of Carter's daughters and sometimes took bits of the material they had made.[22]

For whites, the inadequate clothing of slaves symbolized their social worthlessness. In the early eighteenth century there was wide variation in the clothing of slaves, but over time it became more uniform. The repetitive style and fabrics of slave clothing aimed at effacing signs of individuality, although slaves' ingenuity and the gifts of some planters constantly announced the wearer's uniqueness. (In 1735 in South Carolina, where blacks outnumbered whites, a law decreed that a constable or any other person could take from a slave any item of clothing deemed "above" his or her condition.) When white or black serving women ran away, they usually stole extra clothes. A typical advertisement for an indentured servant read that she had run away with "Two chintz gowns, one dark, the other light, with sprigs and branches, and a coat of the same, one . . . white callico gown, one blue India persian quilted coat, lined with light brown shalloom [a closely woven wool], almost new, one pair of stays, not half worn, one black . . . bonnet, trimmed with the same."[23]

In West Africa people wore many different colors and patterns together, according to what pleased the wearer. The quantity of cloth a person wore indicated social status; more clothing indicated greater power. Thus nakedness carried social humiliation. Decoration and ornamentation were extremely important in West Africa and not only indicated individual taste but also communicated information. A certain style of bracelet identified a parent of boy twins, another a parent of girl twins, and a necklace of a particular substance announced that a mother had just given birth. These are only a few expressions of an abundant aesthetic and language of adornment that slavery could not completely stifle.[24]

Thus Virginia women of different races and classes struggled with one another over their appearance, each implicitly invoking a certain moral view of her actions. Planters' daughters believed that they were supposed to dress as well as they could to demonstrate their esteem for others of their social world. This belief was consonant with their parents' view of them not just as members of the family but as their ambassadors to the gentry social world, where their clothing reflected the resources and status of their parents. The historian and philosopher Charles Taylor has described men in this period as adopting an increasingly instrumental attitude toward the world and toward themselves as projects for development and self-control. They looked inside themselves for the rational and ethical processes by which to evaluate their actions and decisions in the world. Eighteenth-century polite society was about performance, and both men and women were on display. But young women passed much more time than men learning to evaluate responses to their outward appearance. The growth of their interior resources, moral and intellectual, was repeatedly interrupted by the need to monitor the impact of their looks.[25]

Consumption and Individuality: Fiction and Friendship

Eighteenth-century gentry girls, invited to participate in local polite society, tentatively searched for suitable identities. They examined their feelings in the security of close friendships. They judged one another's behavior and evaluated the moral ideas that had governed their education. They did this in letters and journals, imitating the intimate, friendly tone of English novelists, who, after mid-century, had begun to be an important part of their imaginative world.[26]

From the mid-eighteenth century on, the Virginia gentry was altering its ideas about what constituted satisfaction. The individualistic search for emotional self-fulfillment that we associate with introspection, intimate friendships, and romantic love gradually displaced earlier ideas that emphasized the harmonious playing of roles to achieve peace and accord within the family and society. Earlier in the century Virginians had tried to exercise restraint and care in the expression of emotions in order to ensure domestic harmony, although of course ruder, wilder feelings did sometimes break through. But at the same time, impelled by the expanding consumer culture, including the reading of novels emphasizing the significance of personal desire and choice, some began to look inside themselves for their authentic feelings.[27]

The people most restrained by the code of emotional restraint were gentry girls, for whom educators, moralists, and parents insisted on chastity, self-denial, deference, and the ability to please men. Moralists warned girls against their jealousy, irrationality, vanity, loquacity, suggestibility, and incapacity for real friendship. Girls should not talk much, and they should organize well what little they did say. Criticism was worse than talking. Moralists argued that girls almost never formed friendships of any value among themselves because they were universally too envious and spiteful to be able to endure hearing others praised. Only one moralist, and it is not coincidental that she was a woman, disagreed. Sarah Pennington advocated a style of friendship in which the partners improved from each other's scrutiny. Out of step with her fellow moralists, Pennington was in accord with gentry girls and numerous female novelists like Sarah Fielding, Helen Maria Williams, and, later, Jane Austen, who wrote about girls' friendships based on deep mutual understanding and learning in the context of moral self-improvement.[28]

To motivate girls to undertake their many duties, moralists and novelists promised beauty as a reward for good behavior, whereas anger, peevishness, and obstinacy would make them ugly. "An enraged woman is one of the most disgusting sights in nature," Hester Chapone wrote, and went on to say that "complacency and love" were the expressions that belonged on women's faces. *The Matrimonial Preceptor* states it succinctly: "[T]hose who wish to be lovely, must learn to be Good." Virginians overwhelmingly agreed. Robert Bolling, planter, member of the House of Burgesses, and satiric poet, wrote of a fifteen-year-old cousin who rejected his marriage proposal as having a "haughtiness . . . a Fierceness in her Countenance; which, on any little Emotion, destroyed . . . that pretty softness, which is so amiable in a young lady."[29]

Manipulating the promise of beauty, moralists undercut the play of girls' curiosity and any confidence they might have had in their mental capabilities. They encouraged empathy but questioned the capacity of girls to share with and learn from one another. Hungry for ways to find out more about their world and themselves, many girls turned to novels.

Until Samuel Richardson's *Pamela* was published, works of fiction received an unenthusiastic welcome from moral writers. Fiction had generally displayed its Restoration roots in bawdiness and loose morals. But Pamela, the pretty chambermaid who manages to fend off the increasingly diabolical sexual advances of the gentleman she will one day marry, convinced many of the beneficial moral influence a novel could wield. Virginians, although they worried about the moral effects of individual novels from time to time, soon accepted the practice of reading fiction, and wealthier planters began buying volumes of Samuel Richardson, Oliver Goldsmith, Tobias Smollett, Henry Fielding, Laurence Sterne, and Daniel Defoe. The novel, read aloud, soon joined poetry and plays to become part of an evening's entertainment.[30]

Fiction offered girls a new way to think about themselves. The values novelists espoused (chastity, modesty, self-denial, and the discreet pleasing of worthy others) were indistinguishable from those of the moral writers. But their heroines were intelligent and displayed good judgment, rationality, and a superior ability to discern vice from virtue and refinement from vulgarity. Reading this pleasurable genre also equipped young women for polite conversation. Novelists represented heroines as rational, effective, and sensitive, a view more in line with those of the Scottish moral philosophers like David Hume and Adam Smith, whose thinking underlay much of liberalism, rather than the clerical authors of conduct books. Novelists also validated sensitivity and virtuous emotions as the moral bases of choice and conduct. This notion would come to characterize and justify a point of view identified with nineteenth-century women's fiction and women's reform.[31]

Girls read novels eagerly but with guilt. They were sensitive to the moral ambiguities of the new form: the ease and pleasure in consumption, the unfamiliar narcissistic thrill of finding girls like themselves at the center of attention, and the novelists' dangerous flirtations with the subjects of romance and sexuality. The moral landscape was reassuringly familiar, but the medium was strangely free of authoritarian voices, and the lessons were illustrated with titillating scenes that contrasted provocatively with their moral purposes. Indeed the form seemed deliciously free and freeing.

Adolescent Lucinda Lee Orr confessed in her 1782 journal that she had too large an appetite for fiction and advised her friend Polly, for whom her journal was written, to eschew it and "read something improving. Books of instruction will be a thousand times more pleasing . . . than all the novels in the World." Nevertheless, in their correspondences the girls repeatedly refer to imaginative works, and the self-consciously literary style of their letters and journals, including the assigning of fictional names to each other, suggests their familiarity with a variety of literary works, particularly epistolary novels like Samuel Richardson's *Pamela*, Rousseau's *La Nouvelle Héloïse*, and Fanny Burney's *Evelina* (1778).[32]

Letters and diaries, informed by novel reading, supported and structured the intimate friendships of gentry girls. Eliza Ambler and Mildred Dudley wrote each other detailed letters, in deliberately literary ways; they also preached, cajoled, narrated, advised, and entertained. They did so by differentiating each other, illustrating a repeating theme in their correspondence: the oppositions they developed to individuate themselves. Mildred and Eliza agreed that Mildred had a rational, cool, detached character, in contrast with Eliza's lighter, romantic spirit, which allowed her to flirt with men she did not intend to marry and enjoy extravagant entertainments. Eliza, unlike Mildred, was susceptible to the flattery and insinuations of people whose characters she might not judge accurately.[33]

Lucinda Lee Orr made an analogous distinction between herself, a romantic, and a new friend: "a truly good Girl, but nothing of the romance in her. . . . I wish to heaven I had as little." The possession of a romantic nature qualified Lucinda to be a heroine but meant that she had a susceptible nature, insufficiently under the control of her rationality. Whereas the girls were never at any real risk of failing to observe society's rules, their juxtaposition of these alternative temperaments conveys their understanding of the contrasts between the old restrained emotional life of the Virginia elite and the emerging search for emotional expression and fulfillment. Asserting emotional needs was a hallmark of a newer sensibility.[34]

Some heroines were simply too dangerous to identify with. Lucinda Lee Orr criticized Alexander Pope's *Eloisa* for having parts that were "too Amarous for a female."[35] She thought that exposure to such passionate expressions would undermine a woman's rationality, which was all she had to protect her from seducers. Also, the threat and promise of moralists and novelists that goodness would produce beauty endured. Girls living in the Chesapeake knew that this equation was flawed but could not come up with a better one. Lucinda tried to measure the women she met according to both standards:

"very clever, though not handsome," "very agreeable, though not handsome," "very handsome, though appears to be a little proud," "homely, though right agreeable," "homely but very polite and hospitable," "not a handsome face, but is a genteel person," "truly Amiable, but not handsome," "[i]s a thousand times prettier than I thought her at first, and very agreeable." She concluded one of these assessments with the homily "But how preferable is good sense and affability to beauty: more pleasing a thousand times." These repetitive ruminations rejected the moralists' formulation, but they indicate the relentlessly intrusive concern with appearance that accompanied girls' self-study.[36]

Chesapeake girls saw learning through reciprocal moral examination as the aim of friendship. Mildred and Eliza discussed in detail their own and others' acts, refining as they did so their ideas about proper and improper curiosity. Mildred, in recounting to Eliza the story of their friend Rachel and the birth of her illegitimate baby, asked her friend to "write me soon and let me know how he [your father] will act." (Eliza's father was the executor of the estate of Rachel's deceased father.) As soon as Mildred had let the expression of curiosity escape her, however, she snatched it back, saying, "[B]ut why need I doubt; In this as in everything else he will Do exactly as he ought to do." Her rhetorical retraction suggests her discomfort with seeking information, especially about a respected man. Another pair of friends condemned a mutual acquaintance's curiosity as an unwholesome eagerness to consume and circulate information about others. In doing so, the correspondents implicitly excused more discreet and concerned curiosity stemming from intimacy. Girls approved of curiosity when it came from a sympathetic party who would not abuse a confidence. They implicitly blessed this form of curiosity by founding their own intimacies upon it. This ensured that the learning they did about themselves took place in the context of attachment. Curiosity was unacceptable when it was disrespectful or solicited for unfeeling purposes.[37]

Similarly, girls studied the practice of criticism. Eliza and Mildred accepted, indeed solicited, criticism of each other and of others for their moral improvement. They focused on living up to their part of the double standard, however, not on challenging its inequities. Eliza mentioned hating the French when commenting upon the seduction of Rachel by a French officer. Mildred assented to the formulaic gibe at French licentiousness but concentrated her attack on Rachel for failing to "keep in view the dignity of her Sex." If Rachel had had a mother's care "and been taught the heinousness of such a departure from female rectitude all might yet have been Well." In Mildred, prohibitions on criticism and injunctions to defer to men inhibited her critical appraisal of them, while her impulse to take moral action facilitated her critiques of Rachel. Though Mildred was morally active, she was actively engaged in wielding the double standard.[38]

Mildred censured Rachel's behavior but did not abandon her. She felt sympathy for her and wished to ease her distress. She empathized with the romantic temperament through novel reading and her friendship with Eliza. She urged Eliza to call on Rachel when she passed through town. She visited the young mother, saw her child, and commiserated with Rachel's guardian more than once. Her sympathy and understanding of the contradictions implicit in the desires of romantic girls led her to a complex moral position, combining criticism with sorrow and the ongoing responsibility of friendship. She was acutely sensitive to her culture's values, yet through a friendship of mutual exploration she had experienced the compatibility of censure and ongoing attachment, an aspect of the "different voice" that psychologist Carol Gilligan identifies as a moral view congenial to women. Gilligan notes that women tend to elevate the importance of sustaining a relationship to equality with unchanging abstract principles of universal justice that men are more likely to espouse. She offers the "different voice" as another, valid moral orientation, not one necessarily inferior because of its flexibility. Mildred's moral judgments are firm, but she holds on to them while maintaining her relation with the fallen Rachel.[39]

Virginia girls explored friendship, reading, and writing as part of their ongoing education for marriage and maturity. Friends exercised reciprocal moral authority under the shelter of mutual affection. They eagerly searched themselves for differences from their friends to help them understand themselves better. The search for a unique

self was a relatively new concern for the upper class. Girls, almost all
of whom were to become wives and mothers, explored individuality
through their emotions, fine moral judgments, and likes and dislikes,
not, as men might, through higher education and professional training. Moral essayists since the seventeenth century had seen women
as a function of the men they were to serve. Thus the road to individuality for women would be considerably longer than that for men,
whose search for self would be based in their activities and profes-
sions and be aligned with liberalism and economic individualism.
Women, on the other hand, began to look for the self in a swamp of
family roles, overgrown with repression and moralist-recommended
feelings.[40]

The likelihood was that a Virginia girl might discover in herself
a flaw or two, but on the whole she would find someone agreeable.
The scope of her moral explorations, however, were bound by a society that valued external appearances very highly, that unquestion-
ingly supported the double standard, and that subordinated women
to men and black to white. Virginia girls' groping toward an authentic identity in a culture that had little or no use for female authentic-
ity was often less a journey of self-discovery than an exercise in
inspecting moral minutiae. Still, it was pleasurable and indicated the
direction that female individualism was to take. While men would
pursue economic success, women would explore their sentimental
and moral characters.

Obedience

As in Massachusetts a century before, obedience was the key to
moral training for women in Virginia. Children owed it to their parents, particularly to their fathers. Moral writers insisted that obedience to parents was to be blind and unquestioning except in the case
"where the command is unlawful." Girls needed to have "a great reverence of their parents' judgments, and distrust of their own," all the
while linking obedience to their chances of finding husbands.[41]

Gentry girls seem to have been relatively obedient within the family, certainly more so than their brothers. On the other hand, they expressed more aggression than Puritan girls of the previous century. Virginia parents focused on external behavior and only cursorily scrutinized their girls' interior life and actions. The Puritan style of implanting self-control was more effective.

The daughters of Robert Carter got into fights among themselves, plucked their eyebrows (a forbidden activity), and provoked and sometimes cursed their brothers. Their level of disobedience seems high in comparison to that of seventeenth-century Massachusetts girls, although never high enough to challenge seriously society's assumptions about what kind of young women they were to be. The Carter brothers meanwhile stole rum, seduced slave girls, and ran away from home, providing a good example of the difference in tolerated behavior between the sexes.[42]

The absence of the Puritan habit of severe repression seems to have produced women who had easier access to their feelings and more comfort in expressing them. Gentry girls were somewhat more likely to accept their desires, likes, and dislikes than Puritan girls had been. The presence of a large slave population also offered a legitimate object for expressions of white violence from both sexes. Sally Fairfax, as a young girl, for example, asserted that the male slave she deemed responsible for her cat's death should be "cut to pieces . . . he should be killed himself."[43]

8

THREE PERSPECTIVES ON GENDER AND SEXUALITY: ANGLO-AMERICAN, AFRICAN AMERICAN, AND NATIVE AMERICAN

Anglo-Virginians insisted that gentry girls observe the demand for chastity before marriage, but they did so in the context of a pleasure-loving society. Young women probably observed the letter but not the spirit of that law. They responded ambiguously to moralists' mixed messages advising girls to be at the same time modest and attractive to men. The influential moralist James Fordyce used the morally ambiguous example of Mme Maintenon's relationship with Louis XIV to illustrate that submission was sexually attractive. The king's interest was due in part to Mme Maintenon's "attention, and her submission." The resulting tension was obvious but rarely discussed: Gentry girls were to be flirtatious but remain virgins. The tension was greatly heightened by the fact that gentry men, unlike Massachusetts Puritans, had few scruples about expressing their sexuality. Although they subscribed to the double standard when it came to gentry women, the culture emphasized flirtation and sexual attraction. The consequence was that adolescent girls had significant opportunities for sexual play—at the peril of their reputations.[1]

Gentry males believed that their prerogatives overrode the duty of nongentry girls to disobey an unlawful command from a superior male. Ben Carter's family was amused when it seemed he was having sexual relations with a pretty slave named Sukey. Richard Randolph had an affair with a girl of low rank, a dalliance that he defended to his mother as foolish but "natural." With differing degrees of risk, Virginians of both sexes played openly with sexual temptation. Whereas Puritans tried to enjoy food, sex, and drink while never losing sight of God's transcendence, Virginians believed that a good time was its own justification.[2]

Planters prepared their sons and daughters to be entertaining in society. Moralists debated the virtues of dancing, and ministers remained on the sidelines at dancing parties, while planters employed dancing masters for their children to equip them for the countless balls they would attend. Even during the Revolution a young army officer recorded twelve balls and dances from January to May in 1777. Lucinda Lee Orr filled her diary with accounts of impromptu all-night parties with men. She wrote of an incident in which she and her friend Hannah wanted to take an evening walk, "but were prevented by the two horred Mortals, Mr. Pinkard and Mr. Washington, who seized me and kissed me a dozen times in spite of all the resistance I could make." Philip Fithian, who was engaged to a woman in the North, reported that after dancing at a neighboring plantation, he played a game called Button, during which he had had "several kisses of the Ladies."[3]

Robert Bolling recounted several instances in wooing Anne Miller in 1760, in which they were alone or on a bed together. Once he found her "pensive on a *Bed*. I could no longer withhold, but overcome by an Excess of passion, I threw myself *thereon*, and pressed her to my bosom." They had time and opportunity for more than a little foreplay, nor was their behavior unusual.[4]

Relations between marriageable young men and women had a pronounced theatricality, echoing the eighteenth-century gentry's emphasis on performance. The wealthy displayed their power and authority through clothing, posture, gesture, and speech. Young men were to enact their passion for a young woman as if it rendered them helpless puppets. Young women played out a contrived ignorance of the intentions and shock at the very mention of passion. These performances supported the myth that women were the source of men's aggressive sexuality. Logic therefore demanded that they should bear responsibility for it.

Within limits—the exclusive nature of elite society altogether and hence women's restricted choice of mates and the financial motives for many marriages—courtship momentarily reversed the power of the sexes. Eighteenth-century elite culture gave new significance to the primacy of feelings in selecting a mate, and this increased women's bargaining position in matrimony. Some gentry women clearly enjoyed their brief moments of authority. Eliza wrote her friend Mildred that she was feeling just a little vain because she had a pair of handsome gentlemen at her feet. Her friend accused her of coquetry, and Eliza said she thought she would let them dangle a bit while she made up her mind. She savored controlling the destinies of two men even as her friend reminded her that she must not strut her attractions at the expense of male pride.[5]

The power of women extended to their refusing to marry where they did not love as well as to their putting off a desired proposal with protestations about its suddenness, unexpectedness, or undesirability. Words and gestures were prescribed for the occasion. Demurral suggested the frailty of woman's constitution—incapable of sustaining sudden shocks—and her innocence: too great to think of sex or marriage. A delicate woman considering marriage was no longer a flirting, sexy adolescent; she was a trembling virgin stunned to have the fate of a man in her hands. While the ideology of sensibility and fiction exaggerated the extent of her power, she was nevertheless not just a pawn in an interfamily business deal.

Departures from Obedience

Since girls' most intensely felt social goals were to please men and to wed, their disobedience usually lay in distorting these duties. Rebellions, usually directed against fathers, ranged from secrecy and passive defiance to aberrant sexual behavior and unsanctioned liaisons and marriages.

Polly, Thomas Jefferson's youngest daughter, was passively non-compliant. She delayed answering her father's letters and then wrote brief, unsatisfactory ones. Many of her father's letters begin with variations on "I did not write to you, my dear Poll, the last week, because I was really angry at receiving no letter." When Polly, at seventeen, decided to marry, she settled on her first cousin John Eppes. She was so afraid of her father's disapproval that she got her sister Martha to tell their father of her desire. As it happened, Jefferson claimed to welcome her choice, but her anticipation of disapproval suggests the accumulated guilt she lived with for her habits of passive disobedience.[6]

Landon Carter was another father unusually involved in the lives of his children. But his difficult temperament complicated his desire to control those around him. He was a misogynist who once said he did not think "there can be a more treacherous, interprising, Perverse, and hellish Genius than is to be met with in A Woman." In 1766 he complained that his daughter Judy had gone off to the races when she was menstruating. He kept track of the periods of all his daughters because of his two passions: medicine and control. He also complained about what Judy ate, her use of the carriage, and the hours she kept. Judy repeatedly defied her father. She pursued an active social life away from the Carter plantation, visited a family of whom her father disapproved, and eventually married a man he had proscribed. Her rebellion exacted its price. Initially Carter was so outraged by Judy's act that he refused to see her. From the evidence it seems that Judy's marriage caused her as much pain as it caused her father. Rebellions against tyrannical fathers sometimes cost the rebel's happiness as well.[7]

The greatest disobedience of course was illegitimacy. Rachel, a friend of Mildred Dudley's and Eliza Ambler's, had an illegitimate baby by a French viscount, an officer stationed in Yorktown. Rachel was one of a very large number of young women who, during the revolutionary years, had babies before they married. In her case, it would be a mistake to read her behavior as a defiant challenge to the sexual status quo. She clearly hoped that her Frenchman would marry her, and she remained abjectly at her guardian's through the tense and difficult confinement and postpartum months. Although

Rachel experienced considerable discomfort, she did marry eventually, but not the viscount. Moreover, although Rachel's son did not live with her and her husband, he did go on to study at William and Mary.[8]

Virginian men and women shared a measure of tolerance for extramarital sex that is reflected in anecdotes and poems in the *Virginia Gazette* and by the attitudes of observers. Young white women took the blame and bore the responsibility for bastardy, but society did not ostracize them, nor did they sacrifice the chance to marry.[9]

A poem in the *Virginia Gazette* in June 1775 suggests that the gentry regarded premarital adventures of members of other classes—even those that produced mulatto children—less with moral horror than with knowing amusement as long as the mother was black and the father white. Virginians tolerated interracial sex when it conformed to this formula.

Many of the gentry families of eighteenth-century Virginia lived with illegitimate mulatto offspring, some of whom were recognized, like John Custis's son Jack and George Wythe's son Michael, while others, like Thomas Jefferson's putative children by Sally Hemings, were not. The children of slaveowners and slave women were living testimony to the ambivalence elite Virginians displayed about sex. On the one hand, illicit sex was disapproved of, so masters usually did not recognize their children and, in denying them, of course made them slaves. On the other hand, men would be men. These offspring represented their fathers' virility in a culture that gave virtually free rein to the desires of elite males. Men projected onto black women a general sexual willingness that justified their status as prey. This encouraged men who did not pursue black women to condone it among their acquaintances.[10]

Although in the seventeenth century Virginians had used moral language to excoriate sexual sinners, by the eighteenth century the questions that interracial sexuality raised for Virginians had little to do with the morality of sex itself and much to do with the perceived evil in upsetting the social and racial hierarchy. The proper sexual relation was one in which a white man dominated all women. Consequently Virginia brought its heaviest legal disapproval to bear on marriage between the races. A 1691 law fulminated against that "abominable mixture and spurious issue" of black and white and outlawed interracial marriage on threat of banishment from Virginia. This was one of a number of bills passed to prevent any possible alliance of blacks and whites against the rich. The legal degradation of blacks offered poor whites a sense of superiority and powerful association with the white gentry.[11]

By the eighteenth century men had disappeared entirely from laws governing sex, but women remained "lewd." Legislators described women as the source of illegitimacy and the sole bearers of its responsibility and punishment. Only unmarried mothers paid the standard fine of five hundred pounds of tobacco or fifty shillings plus the cost of their prosecutions. Infrequently they also received twenty-five lashes. Legislators tried to keep track of all births occurring within the parishes and ruled that the owner of the house in which any woman delivered was obliged to report that birth to the church wardens. But parishes demonstrated limited interest in pursuing errant women. If a woman up and moved from a given parish, as opposed to simply not showing up at her trial, no one tracked her down. There are no records suggesting that parishes communicated with one another to find unmarried mothers. Lawmakers tried to prevent women from leaving temporarily to avoid paying their fines, but if a woman was gone, no one sought her to teach her the responsibility for her sin.[12]

The Anglican Church functioned less as a moral arbiter than as an agent of both mercy and control. Bearing a bastard did not sever a churchgoer from her church or result in her being publicly shamed. To the contrary, the church often provided her with charity. Mothers of illegitimate children had to pay their fines to the church wardens of the parishes in which they lived. The wardens in turn provided some care for indigent parishioners, so there was a certain reciprocity between church and sinner. Indeed the church aided single mothers to raise their children, illegitimate or not, binding them out as soon as possible. In an effort to relieve parishes of this burden, the House of Burgesses passed a law in 1769 guaranteeing relief to a parish's illegitimate children. With meager success, it sought to force fathers to shoulder this cost, enacting a law requiring men identified by mothers as the fathers of bastards to pay ten pounds or go to jail. I found only one such action between 1770 and 1790.[13]

Slave women mothering mulatto children caused only private, not institutional, commotion. But indentured white mothers of illegitimate children fathered by men other than their masters were to pay twenty shillings. Indentured servants who became pregnant were sold to other masters for one more year after completing their original terms. However, if a free white woman had an illegitimate child by a black or mulatto, she had to pay fifteen pounds or be "disposed of for five yeares" by the church wardens. Her child was bound out until it arrived at the age of thirty. If she were an indentured servant, she would be sold for an additional five years after completing her original term.[14]

The courts were staffed almost exclusively by the gentry, who were not likely to prosecute one of their own for an activity most did not consider a crime. Thus white men rarely faced any punishment for sexually exploiting women. Virginia laws and their pattern of enforcement, or nonenforcement, were structured to keep white men dominant and white women from black men.

West African Women

Estimates vary on the number of slaves imported into Virginia, but the most reliable figure seems to be forty-three thousand from 1700 to 1740, of whom almost all but four thousand were imported directly from Africa. After mid-century the larger importations of Africans tended to go to the Piedmont, with fewer than 10 percent of the new arrivals staying in the Tidewater counties. Recent scholarship suggests that these importations were more or less equal in terms of males and females and included a relatively high number of children, unlike importations of slaves into wealthier colonies.[15]

West African culture therefore played a vital role in mid- to late-eighteenth-century slave life in Virginia. African values, revivified by the frequent replenishment of "outlandish" people, informed the way slaves conceived of their obligations to themselves and their community. And women's cultures had strong representation. Between one-third and one-half of the incoming slaves in the early eighteenth century were Igbos from what is now Nigeria. They were the largest ethnic group from the Bight of Biafra (now middle-west Nigeria).[16]

The Igbos were (and are) a sprawling and complex group, encompassing Muslims and people of other religions. Nevertheless, they demonstrated an aspect of West African culture that seems to have transcended many tribal and religious particulars, the deep and powerful bond between mother and child.

Olaudah Equiano, a Muslim Igbo, arrived in Virginia in 1756. He became free in 1767 and wrote a memoir describing his early life in West Africa from which we can catch glimpses of Igbo women. He recalled being "very fond" of his mother and with her almost constantly. Equiano's remembrance points to the special feeling between mother and child that Mungo Park observed in his eighteenth-century travels among the Mandingos in present-day Mali. "Accordingly, the maternal affection . . . is everywhere conspicuous among them; and creates a correspondent return of tenderness in the child. . . . The same sentiment I have found universally to prevail, and observed in all parts of Africa, that the greatest affront which could be offered to a Negro, was to reflect on her who gave him birth." While Park's claim for the universality of his observation is exaggerated, travelers' accounts almost always comment on the strength of the bonds between mothers and children. Among the Igbos in particular a wide variety of rituals and social structures emphasized the solidarity and power of women. For example, female authority, the *omu* who presided over a female cabinet, ruled on a wide variety of issues of importance to women in particular and the community as a whole.[17]

More convincing than European men's comments were the cultural arrangements of West African families that supported mothering. Most West Africans were polygamous, and wives therefore had marital relationships that were attenuated by sharing their husbands with other wives and by observing periods of two to three years' sexual abstinence during pregnancy and lactation. West African children usually spent their first years exclusively with their mothers, so the bonds between mother and child had an intensity and uninterrupt-edness that did not exist between husband and wife. A second aspect of the lives of women in West Africa that bore on their values and de-rived from the first was the unusually strong bond between women. The mother-daughter tie initiated this link, and it extended to the larger female community.[18]

The Gold Coast (now Ghana) supplied 16 percent of Virginia's slaves. Among the Ashantis, one of the coast's main ethnic groups, young wives in the early years of marriage often lived with their mothers rather than with their husbands. Births took place in the home of the mother's mother. The Ashantis believed that the mother was a child's most important adviser and protector. The Ashantis demonstrated the strength of the mother-child tie as well as the even stronger bond between mother and daughter.[19]

Angola sent Virginia 15.7 percent of its slaves. In the mid-seventeenth century Father Jerome Merolla da Sorrento recorded his observations while trying to convert to Catholicism the Sogno people south of the Zaire River. He encountered difficulties in im-pressing upon them the importance of the sacrament of marriage. To the Sognos marriage meant reproduction and a way to organize work. Mothers arranged their daughters' marriages to begin with a long trial period in which the couple discovered whether or not they could have children and live peaceably together. If either partner proved deficient, the other returned his or her nuptial gifts. At pu-berty these same Sogno women spent two or three months in a spe-cial house where they spoke to no men, washed a specified number of times daily, and anointed themselves with a particular dust of a red tree mixed with water and other things. The culture afforded females special, separate rites that emphasized their importance as bearers of children and suggested the Sognos' protective attitude toward this essential function. Women in such societies, who shared similar ritu-als, were likely to form their strongest bonds with one another.[20]

Although Virginia received fewer slaves from the Senegambia region than from the Bight of Biafra, it received a substantial share, 15 percent, approximately 10 percent more than most other regions in the South. These were the slaves the South Carolinians most desired. They included the Mandingos, Serers, Wolofs, Lebous, Bambaras, and Fulbes as well as a large number from farther east who cannot be identified. The eighteenth-century religious wars between the Muslims and their non-Muslim foes in the region of present-day Senegal and Mali provided both Muslim and non-Muslim prisoners of war as slaves for British, French, and American ships from 1726 to 1807.[21]

The memoirs of Ayuba Suleiman, a Muslim nobleman enslaved and taken to Virginia in the early nineteenth century, described the marriage arrangements of the Mandingos. Fathers paired off their children, exchanged gifts and goods, and had the priest complete the preparations. "But now comes the great difficulty . . . for the women, cousins and relations, take on mightily, and guard the door of the house to prevent her [the bride] being carried away; but at the last the young man's presents and generosity to them, make them abate their grief." At that point the groom tried to carry the bride off, but as soon as she mounted the horse, the women began to cry out and protest and tried to take her off the horse. "However," Suleiman concluded, "the man is generally successful, and rides off with his prize." The women's ritual attempt to prevent the abduction of the intended bride underscores dramatically the strength of female ties.[22]

The matter of West African women's ideas about sexuality is far too complex to reduce to any formula. Some societies, such as Equiano's people and Muslims in general, tried to contain sex by inhibiting the sexuality of women. Some in Sierra Leone and on the Windward coast seem to have practiced female circumcision. Among the Wolofs, virginity in unmarried women was expected. However, for the Sognos, compatibility and the proved ability to reproduce were more important than chastity.[23]

In short, Africans arrived with an extremely broad range of cultural backgrounds: Some did not include ideas of sexual pleasure for women at all, others thought it should be contained within marriage, and still others believed it might precede marriage. All came from worlds where women's communities were strong.

Virginia men displayed a complete lack of interest in the varied sexual beliefs, practices, and moral injunctions that African women brought with them into Virginia. Instead they superimposed onto them their own desires and fears, recognizing no distinctions among black women and characterizing them all as passionately sexual. The Anglican Church supplied ideological support to slaveowners for their wholesale ascription of untrammeled sexuality to black women. The Reverend Thomas Bacon, for example, preaching to slaves in Maryland, implied that it was black women's lasciviousness that was responsible for interracial sexual contact.[24]

White owners' descriptions of their runaway female slaves were often lists of sexual characteristics and assignments to them of passionate appetites. "Wench" was the noun inevitably used synonymously with slave women. By this period it connoted "sexually loose" as well as its earlier meaning of "common." Many runaways were "comely" or "likely" (as in to have children) while more were "lusty." "Bold" was another adjective with sexual overtones that planters used persistently. In addition, advertisements for runaways often detailed the sizes and shapes of women's sexual features. Moll had "very large breasts." Another had "some scars on her Breast." Aggie was a "fair straight made lusty Mulatto and has small breasts," and Edith, who was "fullbreasted, . . . has remarkable black lips." Indentured white runaways, however, were usually described according to their national origins, accents, clothing, and whatever property they might have.[25]

Black women arriving in Virginia in the eighteenth century came with dramatically varying definitions of their moral obligations as women in the cultures from which they came. Faced with exploitation, incomprehension, and violence, they did the best they could to protect themselves, their children, and the relationships they formed that gave meaning to their lives.

Anglo-Virginian Thoughts on Native Americans

How eighteenth-century Virginians imagined seventeenth-century Indians explains little about the Powhatans but rather something about Anglo-Virginian men's concerns about gender and race. Virginians looked to the Pocahontas story in particular to rewrite Virginia's history in the mid-eighteenth century as the colony filled with rebellious Africans, and westward-moving settlers detonated ferocious violence with Indians. Eighteenth-century white women's fears of Africans and Indians became part of Virginia's moral imperative to escalate the violence, not defuse its sources.

At the time of Virginia's settlement there had been about fourteen thousand Algonquian-speaking Powhatans, a designation that included a host of subgroups, many of whose names still adorn Virginia in one form or another, such as Rappahannock, Potomac, Nansemond, Chickahominy, and Appamattuck. In 1790 the federal census gave the population of all Virginia as five hundred thousand, approximately half of whom were black. By then Native Americans made up no more than 1 or 2 percent of Virginia's population.

When the English arrived, the Powhatans lived in a culture that was unusually hierarchical and unusually militaristic, compared with other eastern woodland Indians. The Powhatans loosely dominated a recently organized confederacy joining most Tidewater villages. Men and women divided the work, women doing most of the farming, curing of hides, home construction, cooking, and child care, men hunting and fighting, building canoes and weapons, clearing land, and doing some of the agricultural work that their ruler, Powhatan, demanded as tribute.

From the standpoint of English observers, Powhatan women, who did the majority of the work in the fields, were degraded. Englishwomen in theory did not do agricultural work, and hence their labor was not taxable. Women who did agricultural labor in Virginia were taxable because they were field hands. As the seventeenth century went on, this set up a sharp distinction between African and English women. Furthermore, early Virginians thought that Powhatan women exhibited unwonted sexual license. Powhatan's wives either sexually offered themselves or were offered by him to English visitors, who consequently viewed the women as depraved.[26]

Before the end of the seventeenth century English raids, settlement, and diseases had reduced the Indian population drastically, so that by the early eighteenth century only remnants were left. By 1691 the English had forbidden intermarriage between Indians and

whites, and in 1705 lawmakers subjected Indians to the same code as
that applied to the rapidly growing population of Africans. They denied them the right to carry guns, hunt on English lands, hold office
in civil, religious, or military institutions, bear witness in court, sue
for freedom from masters, and own Christian servants. Only three
marriages between whites and Indians (including that of John Rolfe
and Pocahontas) had been recorded before the inclusion of Indians
in the code of 1705.[27]

Because the numbers of Indians remaining in the East by the
mid-eighteenth century were so small and there was no local inter-
cultural violence, influential Tidewater inhabitants, like the planter
William Byrd and his contemporaries, were safe to ruminate on
how the English might have handled Anglo-Indian relations better.
Byrd and the Reverend Peter Fontaine, a Huguenot immigrant
who achieved prominence, both dreamed of a Virginia past in which
sexual conquest replaced military conquest. Using Pocahontas as a
moral paragon, they wishfully refashioned the Powhatans' meaning
and virtue to reflect their anxiety about contemporary sexual relations between blacks and whites.[28]

In Byrd's and Fontaine's reinvented Virginia, Indian women, the
industrious victims of male Indian laziness, would have made good
wives for the first English planters. They would have populated the
whole of Virginia with children who were free, passably white, and
the legitimate heirs to the land. Also, the men would have had the
"Merit of saving [the Indians'] Soul[s]." Byrd added that the French
intelligently had encouraged such marriages, while the English had
lost a good opportunity to "civilize and convert these Gentiles." The
Indians could not have complained of losing their lands if they had
given it away as dowries with their daughters. Such marriages, he believed, would have saved bloodshed and populated Virginia with
progeny who would have been white by then, "for if a Moor may be
washt white in three Generations, Surely an Indian might have been
blancht in two." He did not speculate on why young Indian women
would have wanted English husbands or on what Indian warriors
would have done while a generation of Powhatan women married
English planters.[29]

The Reverend Fontaine made some of the same points twenty-five years later. Like Byrd, Fontaine held intermarriage with Indians greatly preferable to the "abominable practice" of sex with blacks, which had produced a country that "swarms with mulatto bastards." The Indians, he argued, were at least as white as Spaniards and Portuguese, and their children would be white if they could be persuaded to stop smearing themselves with bear grease and staying out in the sun without clothes.

Fontaine as a minister emphasized conversion, Byrd as a planter emphasized the acquisition of land, but both imagined Englishmen sexually possessing Indian women as the peaceful route to replacing Indian culture and landholding with English culture and English landlords. Their thinking reflects not only a wishful stroll down a path not taken but also their concern over a growing population of children of white fathers and slave mothers, as well as a preoccupation with inheritance. A white man with mulatto children as heirs was betraying Virginia's commitment to keeping land in the hands of white males. Indian women would have served as receptive vessels for English religion, culture, and sperm, while transmitting their fathers' claims to Virginia to its new owners. The sons of these unions would have become Thomas Jefferson's yeomen, legitimate heirs of Virginia, instead of bastards inheriting slave status or free mulattoes challenging the claims of white men to control of the land.[30]

In the revolutionary period Pocahontas became useful as a symbol of the nobility of Native Americans and, by extension, of colonists. The symbol had use, but it did not affect actual policy toward Indians. The Tidewater gentry might take the Revolution as an occasion to use stories of Pocahontas as republican propaganda, but Virginians were simultaneously aware of ferocious ongoing border warfare. In 1774 Lord Dunmore, governor of Virginia, had begun to issue patents to land on both sides of the Ohio River despite the fact that the British had prohibited the settlement of the land west of the river. Drunken Virginians crossed the Ohio and murdered thirteen Shawnee women and children, causing even Dunmore to say the slaughter was "marked with an extraordinary degree of cruelty and inhumanity." No one prosecuted the killers, so John Logan, an Iroquois whose family had been wiped out, went into Virginia and took thirteen scalps. Governor Dunmore declared war on the Shawnees and raised three thousand men to destroy their communities in Ohio, territory then claimed by Virginia. After one battle in which Dunmore lost 222 men and the Shawnees sustained fewer but significant losses, the two made a sort of peace. Still, whites continued to encroach on Indian land, and Shawnees continued to make sporadic raids against them. When the Revolution began, the British allied with the Shawnees, Delawares, Miamis, and Wyandots, raiding as far east as the Shenandoah Valley, and managed to push white settlement back from Kentucky.[31]

Virginia women were not invited to comment on colonial policies or politics. A notice that ran several times in the *Virginia Gazette* counseled women to believe what their men told them about the patriot cause and eschew tea. "We propose not, ladies, to enter too much into the much agitated subject of American grievances. . . . Your husbands, your fathers, and all your dearest friends of the other sex, have no doubt frequently discussed, in your presence, this momentous point; on the determination of such friends we may all safely rely." *The Ladies Library* advised women that their virtues were domestic, that political enthusiasm did not become them. "If they must show zeal it should be against those who were not of their own religion and nation." The moral imperative for women's politics, then, was to hate those who were different from them.[32]

Women throughout the colonies did of course discuss politics and revolution, and most adopted the loyalties of their male relatives. Unlike Byrd and Fontaine, who imagined friendly and profitable interracial sex, women focused on nightmarish fears of interracial violence. They feared the personal consequences of slavery and unremitting white and Indian conflict, and some understood their duty to hate "those not of their own religion or nation." In Virginia white men were preoccupied with preserving their power over Africans and Indians, and their methods frightened the white women who depended upon them.[33]

In a letter to the *Virginia Gazette*, Anne Terrel of Bedford, a western county, wrote about the reasons why she could sustain her husband's absence during the Revolution. She cited the "wickedness of a cruel and abandoned Ministry . . . forging chains to bind . . . us [and our] posterity into a lasting state of slavery." From the slavery the English would impose on Americans and their children she immediately shifted to England's conspiring with Virginian slaves to "cut our throats" and to its "instigating the savage Indians to fall on our frontiers . . . whole families inhumanly butchered by those savages, without regard to age or sex; the infant torn from its mother's arms; the milk in its innocent mouth; its brains dashed out against the next post."[34]

Reflecting the limited sphere for women's patriotic involvement, Terrel asserted that women could be most helpful by applying their virtues of "frugality and industry at home." She evoked the domestic morality of self-restraint and careful management that men had long touted in Virginia, particularly in the debt-ridden decade before the Revolution. She encouraged other women to join her in "laying aside our visiting and fashions, and earnestly [to] attend to carding, spinning, and weaving, and brown our fair arms in our bleach yards . . . and although [homespun] may not be so very fine, yet we may say we paid nothing for it to Great Britain, and that we are free women." Freedom from economic enslavement to Britain was feasible if women would sacrifice ease and vanity and honor the call to thrifty housewifery. In so doing, Terrel exhorted the genteel to take up the work of servants and slave women, to "brown [their] fair arms" and wear the garb of the poor. Virginia women did in fact produce increased quantities of homespun during the Revolution, but while Terrel's republican rhetoric implied inclusiveness, even a visible blurring of racial differences in the pursuit of freedom, in reality the homespun producers continued to be the poor, slaves, and servants, not women of the gentry.[35]

As women faced the crucial moral choices and problems of the revolutionary era, both moralists and their daily circumstances urged them to agree with their husbands. Regardless of their views on the Revolution, elite Virginian women were vulnerable to terrifying consequences if the systems of exploitation from which they benefited ruptured. Of course the risks from continuation of this exploitation were also great, but as wealthy whites they had much to gain from the labor of Africans and the continued displacement and slaughter of Indians. Thus their political support of their husbands' views was strongly determined by their subordination to their husbands and their social and economic position. It was not until the nineteenth century, in any case, that the growing importance given to feeling and empathy supplied women with a vocabulary of their own in which to express effective political opposition. While a very few women like Abigail Adams and Mercy Otis Warren employed the language of justice and the rights of man, nineteenth-century women reformers were to make themselves widely heard in the newly moralized domestic values of sentiment.

9

MATRIMONY: INSIDE VIEWS

Virginians married early—at about twenty—compared with their New England counterparts, who married at around twenty-four. Inexperience and youth contributed to making bad choices, but both rich and poor women married young, some as young as twelve, because they had little else to do. Wealthy parents had interests in controlling marriages because their property and the production of potential heirs were at stake. For poorer farmers the labor of their daughters could be a serious loss. A series of laws from the late seventeenth through the mid-eighteenth century aimed at preventing early elopements. Girls from twelve to sixteen were automatically disinherited if they married without their fathers' consent. Legally fathers could prevent minor daughters from marrying, but practically it was hard to thwart a strong-willed girl.[1]

Virginians did not share Puritans' idealism about marriage. White men were likely to see it in economic terms, a tendency that increased in the mid-eighteenth century as tobacco prices fell and planters found themselves more and more indebted to British merchants. Virginia men's thinking about marriage took place during debates over women and commerce. One side, deriving its ideas from the Scottish moral philosophers, assigned women refinement, modesty, sensibility, and the power to improve men and society. The other associated women with indolence, sensuality, and greed. In this latter view, women were insatiable consumers who drew men into lechery and vice. This model also provided many of the commonest metaphors patriots used to describe the corruption of the British administration.[2]

With these debates as a backdrop, young men and women balanced attraction and finance. Gentry men were frank about the pecuniary aspect of their marriage decisions. John Page wrote to St. George Tucker that he had not yet found a wife although he was "attracted to Miss Lowther but it is a mistake" because she was a mild-tempered, pretty "poetess but has not what would justify my marrying." For Page, beauty was a requirement, but only a dowry would "justify" marriage. Some men were not so scrupulous about beauty. In 1771 William Carter, twenty-three years old, married an eighty-five-year-old widow with three thousand pounds.[3]

While gentry men seem unconflicted about the necessity of marrying for money or at least thrift, women expressed a variety of views on the subject. Mildred Dudley agreed in principle to the notion that marrying a poor man was a mistake that would lead to dependence but expressed sorrow about curtailing her relationship with a moneyless admirer. She wrote her friend Eliza Ambler that she was breaking off with a young Englishman who had enlisted with the American troops. "My own weak heart," she concluded, "reluctantly consents to the truth of the observation" that rationality should prohibit her from marrying a penniless young man.[4]

Eighteenth-century financial dependence was linked to political dependence and consequently to corruption and the tyranny of a wealthy few over a large, unrepresented body politic. According to this formulation, the poor were easily corrupted. Dependent upon richer people for their livelihoods, they gave their political allegiance in return. The virtuous citizen was a man with enough property to depend on no one; his vote was his own.

Mildred's invocation of the specter of dependence was inapplicable. Women had no civic identity, and Mildred would be dependent upon her husband whether he were rich or poor. What dependence upon a poor man would have meant to Mildred was a life of some labor, and if she shared the assumptions of most elite Virginians, she would have viewed such a life as shameful, not to mention unpleasant. The moral opprobrium gentry men and women attached to "dependence" in both its senses helped ensure a continuity of membership in the elite of Virginia.

A Virginia woman understood that the husband she would take would define the limits of her world and that she would need his good temper and affection to smooth over the obligatory nature of her "rigid duties." Unlike a Puritan woman, a Virginia wife would not see her husband as God's representative on earth, although he would in most cases be the family judge and jury. She understood that maintaining her own emotional equilibrium would be key to her marital happiness, and therefore some women strove to make sensible, not impassioned, choices. Proceeding rationally, in the sense of assessing character, not necessarily fortune, a woman could hope to make an accurate appraisal of the man she would marry. If she also felt desire, so much the better, but desire alone would cloud her judgment. Her life would be considerably more tolerable if she felt some respect for the man in whose service she would be.[5]

Some Virginia women openly criticized the economic basis of marriage, hoping to produce happier unions. The growing emphasis on the sanctity and rightness of virtuous feeling supported the arguments some young women made against loveless marriages. They argued for respect and affection rather than passion in selecting mates. They were careful to show that sexual attraction would not inform their choice of husband. Thus women criticized marriages based on finance as prostitution, deftly reversing the gentry claim that women who married for sexual desire rather than rational reasons were whores. One young woman wrote to her parents, via the *Gazette*, announcing her elopement with a man lacking the requisite fortune. She castigated her parents for upholding a system of "prostitution," thereby forcing her into a secret engagement. Another wrote that she would rather be the "affectionate wife of private Mr. M———, than the legal prostitute of some Right Honorable Lord."[6]

The slowly changing basis for marriage constituted a significant moral and emotional transformation for white women, designed to free them from a system in which marriage was merely a reconfiguration of men's property. Unions in which there was no mutual love affected wives, who were economically and emotionally dependent and legally subordinate, far more than they did the husbands on whom they depended. The increased value gentry society placed on emotional satisfaction, as distinct from sexual satisfaction, gave some wives an informal leverage they had previously not possessed.

In a proper engagement a man located an appropriate young woman and asked her father if it was all right for him to declare himself to her. If the suitor was socially and financially acceptable, the father gave his approval and let his daughter make the next decision. A daughter was, as in Massachusetts, to refuse to marry when "her heart could not go with it." The families of Virginia women exerted a strong influence on them, however, and fathers, uncles, and brothers all counseled and advised their female relatives. Still, young Virginia women were active participants in choosing a husband—most often but not always within the limits of an economically and socially approved circle. By silently acquiescing to the demands of financial parity while speaking publicly about love and respect, gentry women could appear untouched by the economic aspects of marriage, all the time being well aware of and compliant in such arrangements.[7]

Most young women of the gentry married within their circle, ensuring that they would remain economically privileged. It was a matter of public discussion that gentry marriages concerned money. When the *Virginia Gazette* reported on marriages, it often included a reference to the amount involved. Indeed "interesting" to describe a bride meant "wealthy." By articulating a critique of marriage, women were insisting on their rights to choose men who would not abuse their power, but most women were unlikely to sacrifice the rank to which they had been born. By assenting to unions, they were aware that negotiations would begin between prospective in-laws regarding how much each would settle on the young pairs and when.[8]

Obedience, Friendship, and Their Discontents

As with Puritans, obedience was the most important of the virtues a Virginia wife could possess. She was not to be "mistress of herself, nor have any desire satisfied but what is approved of by her husband." This subjection was comprehensive; once a woman was married, her central concern was to please and defer to her husband. *The Ladies Library* traced the need for woman's obedience to the "penalty" that was laid upon her "disobedience to God, that she, and all derived from her, should be subject to the husband." For their part, husbands were to rule their wives gently, invoking reciprocal affection, but they were to rule. The *Preceptor* stated that the husband, as the ruling soul, was not subject to the desires and urgencies of the body. The wife, as the ruled body, was enslaved by weakness, passion, and the voluptuousness of submission.[9]

Men of the Chesapeake gentry criticized wives for displaying physical affection for their husbands. Whereas Puritan men had worried about their own sensuality, Virginians worried about their wives'. Landon Carter wrote about an "agreeable" wife who was "more fond of her husband perhaps than the Politeness of the day allows of." Advice givers counseled religion as a wife's most reliable companion. But it was not the transformative religion of the Puritans in which a wife struggled for her husband's soul; it was a meditative, solace-giving kind. Women were to try to make their husbands more pious with gentle persuasion, but if that did not work, they were to put a good face on what they could not change, especially infidelity. The most a wife with an errant husband could hope for was a faith that would sustain her. Writers argued that contention was useless and counterproductive except for the gentlest, most infrequent remonstrances. No matter what the problem in the marriage, "a patient submission, and a conscious propriety of behavior is [*sic*] the only attainable good." Virtuous—i.e., compliant—behavior was its own reward.[10]

Records of Virginia wives who evinced a deep and pervasive faith that provided them with a frame of reference separate from that of their husbands are relatively rare.[11] Indeed religion occupied a very different place in the lives of eighteenth-century Virginians from those of Puritans in Massachusetts or the Virginia evangelicals, Baptists and Methodists, to the west. Puritanism effectively controlled social behavior, but it also sparked intellectual labor and gave importance to individual struggles with selfishness, complacency, and appetite. It encouraged women to observe their own and others' behavior and judge it. It asked women to fight furiously for their own salvation and that of their families. Unlike Anglicans in Virginia, Puritans never doubted for a moment that women had souls or that those souls were in every way equal to the souls of men. The mandate of Puritanism for women was complex, but it unequivocally prescribed intensity of faith, self-doubt linked with self-exploration, close observation, and vigorous combat against sin. In these ways it emphasized woman's individual moral capacity and her accountability to God.[12]

The Anglican mandate in Virginia stressed obedience to all authority, as did Puritanism, but it did not mitigate this with any call to active spiritual struggle or deep scrutiny of self and other. It did not encourage girls to think but simply to remain composed during church services and pleasant while performing their duties. Anglicanism in eighteenth-century Virginia emphasized woman's inferiority because it emphasized man's superiority—in a hierarchical world, where religious ritual ideally bound rich and poor together across wide and clearly defined social boundaries. Rather than foster moral struggle and reckoning, Anglicanism spotlighted women's dependence and contingent existence. While the radical dependence that Puritans acknowledged could become, paradoxically, the road to worldly and morally charged activism, the dependence that Anglicanism praised defined women's role as obedience and passive acquiescence to male familial and clerical authority.

Despite its progress through western Virginia, the Great Awakening left the Tidewater relatively untouched. Traditional Anglicanism still controlled much of the area despite inroads by the earnest, ascetic Baptists and Methodists elsewhere in the state. Anglican sermons rarely exceeded twenty minutes, and church services were social as well as religious experiences intended to bring rich and poor together in harmony while emphasizing the preeminence of gentry men. The elite often entered services later than other congregants and left ahead of the women and men of lesser rank.[13]

For their part, the gentry of eastern Virginia abhorred evangelical intensity and piety. The enthusiasms of the Great Awakening meant questioning and the possibility of change; it could upset the hierarchical order of society and create spiritual leaders out of poor men, blacks, and even women. Moralists particularly disliked extreme piety in women because it made them contentious and dictatorial.[14]

While women were to be punctilious in their observances, they were to "practice" religion, not to argue about it. "Enjoy your faith in modest silence," advised Fordyce, "and think well of those who differ from you in opinions, if they agree in morals." Behavior, not the spiritual journey, counted for women. The obituary of Elizabeth Steptoe commended her for possessing "in an eminent degree the happy talent of being religious without enthusiasm." The inscription on the tomb of Lettice Turberville (d. 1732) read that she was a child whose religion had been "pure, Fervent, Cheerful and of the Church of England." Her virtue was "steadfast, easy and natural." These adjectives underscore the unworried, equable quality that eighteenth-century Anglican men desired in the women they worshiped with.[15]

Religion did help some married women through life. Ann R. Page, who lived on a large plantation in Frederick County, began to withdraw from society shortly after her marriage. She underwent a deep religious experience and shared her new faith with numerous slaves on her estate. She drew inspiration from the slaves' faith and devotion and eventually freed them. From her son's memoir, it is clear that her spiritual life provided her with direction, strength, and solace.[16] That this highly devout Christian was led to free her slaves suggests that the deepest religious experiences that white people underwent carried the threat of destabilizing conventional life. In the Tidewater, however, the waves of evangelical fervor had little effect. The Anglican Church resisted the enthusiasm and moral rigor that the Baptists and Methodists encouraged. The Anglicans' embrace of slavery completely undercut its potential for critical approaches to the status quo. This was true not only for slavery but also for the subordination of women that was ever more tied to the defense of slavery. Anglican disdain for religious enthusiasm tried to hold at bay inquiry into the moral underpinnings of slavery. For these reasons the piety of white women in the Chesapeake was likely to be private, although sometimes mistresses shared it with their slaves.[17]

While religion helped wives cope within the limits imposed on them, women commented on the transformation that marriage effected with ruefulness, surprise, or sardonic acceptance. Lucinda Lee Orr noted how changed her friend Hannah was. "Matrimony alters us mightely," she wrote. "I am afraid it alienates us from everyone else."[18] Some women hoped to find companions in their spouses, as the culture of sensibility based on the positive assessment of women by the Scottish moral philosophers had opened the way for women to become friends with men. John Adams addressed Abigail as "friend," as French Americans did in the early nineteenth century. In a perfect sentimental world, marriage should include friendship. It is significant, however, that most Chesapeake husbands did not aspire to the egalitarian and voluntaristic kind of marriage that "friend" would signify. An elite man's commitment to dominating his household and slaves generally ruled out the possibility of making his wife much of a friend.[19]

Barred from friendships with men, women made friendships with one another to sustain themselves through the demands of marriages. Indeed women expected a form of female solidarity and took offense when other women did not express interest in one another or orbited exclusively around men. Male moralists, in spite of evidence of female solidarity, predicted that wives' jealousy and competition for men other than their husbands would cut them off from one another. They warned troubled wives not to share their difficulties with anyone, impressing on women who ended up with unfriendly, unfaithful mates that they had no one to turn to and only religion to solace them.[20]

Marriage was necessary to "the support, order, and comfort of society," the Reverend James Fordyce wrote, but he admitted it "subject[ed] the women to a great variety of solicitude and pain." He thought that marriage was such a difficult condition for women that if it were not for the strong personal bonds they formed, they could never endure it. Fordyce was probably thinking about the ties of motherhood, but friendship served this purpose too.[21]

Women, for their part, expected other women to express interest in female intimacy. However, they offered it with discrimination.

They needed to talk intimately but were alert to differentiate concern in others from gossip gathering. Chesapeake society prized entertainment and charm, and possession of intimate information about others could provide much unkind, even dangerous amusement.

Elite Virginia girls, raised to self-consciousness, theatricality, and a fairly frivolous round of activities, were poorly prepared for the life of gracious acceptance of subordination that marriage meant. They would have to run complex households in a culture in which many disdained work. They often had little but artificial contact with young men who in turn were raised to willfulness and domination. Women rarely had as much education as their husbands, and the couples shared few interests beyond family. Girls raised to "sensibility" and sympathy, as elite culture demanded, learned to read the moods and feelings of others but did not thereby acquire emotional strength or resources for the isolation and subjugation marriage would mean. Anglicanism did not provide to most women the spiritual independence of the Puritan faith. Women's best hopes lay in the transformation of marriage from their sexual and social subordination in an economic alliance to a companionable partnership. There was a model nearby for such marriages in the slave community.

Afro-Virginian Marriages

White Virginians did not officially recognize slave marriages, but they saw them all the time. Planters generally gave male slaves permission to marry but were also responsible for breaking up couples when selling slaves. One historian has found that in the Chesapeake male slaves often took considerably younger wives, and some took more than one wife, in continuation of West African practices. When sales loomed, men petitioned their owners in hopes of averting separation. Charles Ball, of Maryland, sold and sent south on the same day, was denied the chance to see his family for the last time. He later wrote, "My heart died away within me."[22]

Owners' notices of runaways provide poignant testimony about

the numbers of slave women fleeing to join their husbands. A
twenty-year-old Virginia-born pregnant woman named Grace ran
away, her owner speculated, to return to "Mr. Collier," with whom
she had lived at Hampton before she had been taken away. Hannah
left in October 1775 to go to one of two places where her owner
thought she had a "Husband at each." Phillis, who was sixteen years
old, had lived with "one Free Harry," to whom her owner thought
she had run. A large number of runaway notices did not specify
where slaves may have gone, but many women probably ran to relations or husbands of whom their owners were unaware. These marriages provided a model of partnerships in which the accumulation of
property was necessarily beside the point and the subordination of
slavery was shared.[23]

10

MARRIAGES:

MORAL AND FINANCIAL ECONOMIES

The *Virginia Gazette* reprinted in the latter half of the eighteenth century a steady stream of anecdotes about the decadent, effeminate British aristocracy. Virginia readers took satisfaction in their own relative innocence and in the absence of a sexually immoral, spendthrift class of wealthy women. But the ubiquitous theme of the feminine enemy within the English upper classes betrays the power these images had with elite Virginians. Virginian men comfortably shared a variety of assumptions with British men on the English origins of virtue, the necessity of maintaining patriarchal order, the threat of the unruly poor, and the place of noblesse oblige in maintaining the social order.

Within this prerevolutionary colonial culture the woman was a suspicious, ambivalent figure. On the one hand, she could assume a morally upgraded role of the indispensable private supervisor of children's and men's characters. On the other hand, upper-class corruption, excess, and greed were associated with femininity. For Virginians, accustomed to making distinctions between black and white, rich and poor, it was easy to apply these contrasting assessments to two different groups.[1]

A wife's virtue in Virginia was intimately connected to looking out for her husband's fortune. A marriage guide described the world as divided into two realms: his world of the accumulation of wealth and her world of morals. Men should busy themselves enlarging the couple's fortune, while wives should be increasing their "virtue." In their old age the couple would retire to a country estate that his "profession" and her "oeconomy" had purchased. For men, wifely frugality represented virtue, love, and, as hostilities with Great Britain grew more intense, independence. As tobacco planters saw their debts increasing, a wife's rejection of luxury contributed not only to her husband's comfort but also to his manhood. Growing debt more and more associated him, in the revolutionary rhetoric of republicanism, with the effeminate, parasitical aristocracy of the mother country.[2]

Struggles between men and women over money and management intensified during the revolutionary years. The symbolic identification of femininity with self-indulgence made women the natural targets of distrust. Thomas Jefferson routinely lived beyond his means and was happier curbing his daughters' luxuries than his own. When Martha asked him to pay for a dress she had already bought, he wrote her a little sermon to the effect that he would do it, but he also asked her if she could not "see . . . how imprudent it is to lay out in one moment what should accommodate you for five weeks? That this is a departure from that rule which I wish to see you governed by, thro' your whole life, of never buying anything which you have not money in your pocket to pay for. Be assured that it gives much more pain to the mind to be in debt, than to do without any article whatever which we may seem to want." He spoke from firsthand experience.[3]

While men expected thrift from their wives, society also expected wives of the wealthy to be indulgent, humane mistresses and praised them for those qualities in managing families, households, and slaves. Rachel Williams, who died in 1746, for example, was "to her servants not at all severe." Another was "to her servants, the best of mistresses"; still another, characterized by "an unbounded share of humanity and indulgence." At the same time, the wife of a wealthy man was to see that the plantation women's work was done well and without waste. A mistress was to supervise the tending of the poultry and the kitchen and see that the spinning, weaving, sewing, food preparation, and preservation all were done with care.[4]

Thrift and indulgence were often incompatible. The logic of the plantation required impersonal, harsh rule, while the logic of sensibility required that women empathize and forgive. Women did not view frugality as an unqualified virtue. Mary Maury judged her sister-in-law a "mighty housewife, but a cruel woman." Winifred Beale Carter, a daughter-in-law of the irascible Landon Carter, never interfered or took an interest in his frequent "corrections" of field and dairy hands, spinners, weavers, and poultry tenders, but she did struggle to protect her favorite slaves from his dangerous and violent medical interventions. She and others tried to protect an elderly slave called Mulatto Betty from Carter's ministrations. Betty agreed to and then refused various treatments of Carter's, trying to pick her way among his sometimes lethal dosing. Carter, frustrated by her refusals, complained, "She has too much encouragement from with in doors to be thus obstinate." However, where Landon Carter saw waste and undisciplined behavior, Winifred saw an opening for her sensibility.[5]

A good mistress was to extract obedience and good—i.e., economically rational—behavior from slaves without resorting to physical abuse. Her tool was supposed to be the awe and respect she inspired. But wives rarely could lay claim to much respect, much less awe, for themselves. A few used religious faith, linking awe for God and slaves' desires to get to heaven with obedience here on earth. As more and more slaves became Christians in the latter part of the eighteenth century, mistresses could use many biblical messages to exhort them to work. Wives, for the most part, relied on their whiteness and their proximity to unindulgent masters to convince slaves to take their orders.[6] If in theory the "good mistress" never indulged in violence, the mistress in fact lived in a society resting on the white population's violent suppression of the black.

William Byrd's first marriage, chronicled in astonishing detail in his *Secret Diary*, gives us an insight into the pressures that could obliterate a mistress's "unbounded share of humanity and indulgence." At issue was Mrs. Byrd's unwillingness to submit to her husband's repeated, humiliating expressions of mastery over her. Inevitably the pair dragged their slaves into their skirmishing. In one case Mrs. Byrd "caused Prue to be whipped violently" against Byrd's wishes. As a result, Byrd had his wife's favorite, Anaka, whipped, noting that Anaka "had deserved it much more, on which my wife flew into such a passion that she hoped she would be revenged of me."[7]

It would be too simple to say that Mrs. Byrd took out on the slaves the anger she felt toward her husband. She had few scruples against violent behavior toward subordinates. But the empathy that the culture of sensibility lauded, especially for women, usually remained contained within and defined by class privilege. It was not assumed to apply to poor whites and certainly not to African Americans. The power that slaveholding women exercised over the lives of blacks tempered the sense of their oppression as women and gave some a taste for the violence usually monopolized by men. Indeed the power that Mrs. Byrd used toward her servants may have intensified her feelings of fury toward her husband. If a slaveholding man had a unique understanding of freedom because of his experience with slavery, a slaveholding woman encountered an acute ambiguity in slavery. On the one hand, she wielded naked power over slaves and could express at their expense her rage at the constraints of marriage in general and her husband in particular. On the other hand, her power over slaves was largely dependent upon his authority. She might pass along fury and frustration, but her own authority was always circumscribed. She tasted both the liberty of the slaveholding planter and the subjection of his subordinates.

Women experienced simultaneous power and subjection differently. Those who resolved the issue of their own submission in religious devotion were more likely to regard slaves with some measure of identification. Others like Mrs. Byrd, achingly aware of their own subordination, rejected identification in favor of the familiar, comforting myths of superiority and radical difference.

In what seems like a contradiction, men wished Virginia wives to be frugal, but they did not want to see them earning money. As a general rule, Virginia society paid women so little for whatever work they did outside the home that all but a handful depended upon men economically. Yet married and single women persisted in trying to supplement their incomes and broaden the scope of their lives with various types of work. The almost exclusively agricultural character of the Virginia economy meant that for women there was little even low-paying work outside the domestic context. Thus, with the exception of the employment of some widows, who had inherited their husbands' businesses or properties, most women in Virginia could not support themselves other than through family farming. If they did not marry, their steadiest prospects were to work as housekeepers or to hire out for domestic work. The *Gazette* frequently ran advertisements for such women.

A few women worked as midwives, although they were soon forced out of this profession by male doctors. Wives occasionally owned taverns or, more frequently, because liquor licenses were expensive, provided hospitality from their homes. They fed and lodged travelers and received some gratuity. Others sold liquor. Women who were caught retailing drink without permits were fined ten pounds. Women also acquired (very) small amounts of money through work for the church. Married women or widows did laundry, took care of the sick, cleaned the church, buried the dead, and performed the job of sexton, which entailed gravedigging and bell ringing.[8]

One lucrative economic activity some women engaged in was to provide for troops, during both the Seven Years' War and the Revolution. In most cases, however, wives were acting for absent husbands, who would collect the profits later. In the records of King and Queen County, Virginia, twenty women appear as providers of beef and brandy to the revolutionary armies. Brandy was by far the more rewarding product, bringing twenty-five pounds for a gallon, while a sterling pound bought something over eighty pounds of meat. Wartime traditionally offers women unusual autonomy and freedom from the gender-based morality normally constricting them. However, wars are followed by conservative periods emphatically reestablishing the dominance of men and the subordination of women in the home. The Revolution was no exception.[9]

During the Revolution some men extended their anxiety about

parasitical women to the poor laundresses following the Continental army. Captain Robert Gamble of Virginia wrote in his orderly book that his men were not getting the proper amount of washing from the three women attached to his company, despite the fact that the women were drawing rations. He delegated a sergeant to divide his men up into three groups and assign one to each woman. She would receive soap from the soldiers, but when it was not sufficient, she would have to buy extra. "But on no pretence whatever is she on average to exceed two Dollars P Dozen. The Woman's Just Accounts shall be punctually paid at the End of every month." He went on to say that if any woman refused to comply with this "reasonable Order," her rations would be stopped, and for a second offense she would be "dismissed with disgrace as a useless charge & Expence to the Continent."[10]

White men wanted their wives, and women in general, to save, not spend, to hoard, not earn. They also wanted them to soften the jagged realities of slave society, but they did not want them to change these realities. A woman was to be the provident custodian of her husband's valuables. Christianity and society demanded that wives be sympathetic and humane toward the poor as well as toward immediate dependents, but thrift was clearly to dominate indulgence. (Slaves were not considered poor. Indeed, if a slave owned, for example, cattle, anyone could legally remove them so that the church wardens could sell them and distribute the profits among the *real* poor.) Wealthy women were sometimes conflicted about the violence of slavery, but few renounced its privileges. Nongentry women tried to participate in the market, especially when it expanded in wartime. It is in the struggles of separating couples that we see how strongly women resented their economic subjection.[11]

Marriages Made and Broken

Evidence about happy unions comes mainly from husbands. Undoubtedly there were numerous marriages in which mutual contentment prevailed. Moreover, the fact that men's voices predominate in testifying to marital happiness is partly explained by differences in literacy and by the higher societal value placed on men's letters. But it is also likely that men were more contented with the shape of eighteenth-century marriage than women. A man could be happy with a wife who was "dutiful" or "obedient" or who possessed "condescending, sweet humility" and maintained "conjugal fidelity," or who simply led a life of "Innocence and piety." These descriptions come from obituaries in the *Virginia Gazette* and point out the obvious: that a "good" wife could make a husband comfortable without experiencing pleasure herself.[12]

At their worst, marital obligations to submit and to provide labor and sex could put wives into a hellish servitude. Many husbands of course did not exercise their authority harshly. Nevertheless, that such authority had the community's blessing meant that wives were thrown legally on their husbands' mercy. Although faced with few economic options beyond marriage, women left their husbands in significant numbers.[13]

Wives effected the overwhelming majority of separations in the Tidewater. Most achieved de facto separations and did not pursue matters further. A legal separation required proof of adultery, and prior to the Revolution a divorce in the modern sense would have required an act of Parliament (or possibly of the House of Burgesses, but no one attempted the feat). After the Revolution, in the enthusiasm it created for individual choice and voluntary relationships, spouses could get divorces for adultery in Virginia, and at least three did so. But since the legal machinery was so cumbersome, expensive, and intimidating, particularly to women, desertion was by far the wives' preferred method in terminating marriages.[14]

Husbands reacted immediately to their wives' disappearance as the economic problem it was. A wife's desertion raised the specter of debt, never too distant from the minds of Tidewater men, because a husband was legally responsible for his wife's debts. When marriages dissolved, husbands were prompt and adamant about cutting their losses. Creditors sued husbands to acquire payment of wives' debts, and husbands used the publication of runaway notices to acquit themselves of this financial responsibility. The issue was who deserted whom and for what cause. If the husband was blameless, as he almost invariably presented himself, then the wife had no further claim upon him.

The numerous advertisements concerning runaway wives in the *Virginia Gazette* bear a strong resemblance to runaway slave notices. In both cases white men assumed their entitlement to domination over other human beings, as an extension of their ability to own and control property. Men used their economic power to maintain their property and withdrew it when the property rebelled. Like incantations, the same words and phrases appear over and over: "run away from the subscriber." Sometimes men added personal details describing the wives or slaves (or horses—the language is the same) or attached grievances detailing how those persons had ill-treated the deserted husbands. In both cases, financial loss occasioned moral outrage, which in turn transformed women, slaves, and servants into scheming, lascivious, deceitful, greedy malefactors.

The majority of separated husbands accused their wives of desertion and some of marital transgression. George Galaspie said he doubted his wife's "attachment to [his] interest,"—i.e., his economic self-interest. The phrase generally describes the impasse that inspired wives to leave their husbands and husbands to misunderstand their wives' motives. Men saw marriage as an agreement whereby man and woman should see the husband's interest as a shared goal. But the way power was distributed and wielded in eighteenth-century marriages made some women unable to adopt their husbands' interests as their own, whether from their inability to suppress their own individual desires and differences, from their husbands' intemperate exercise of authority, or simply from anger at their own subordination.[15]

Men charged deserting wives with various misdeeds, including profligacy, disobedience, immodesty, defiance, indiscretion, and withholding sex. Sarah Russell's husband claimed that she "behaved very indecent" to him and would not "live with me." Another husband complained that his wife had been "very unfriendly," and yet another that his wife had been a "naughty and furious Housewife." Husbands often accused their wives of putting them in debt and of stealing their possessions. John Stacey announced that he would not pay the debts of his wife, Anne, who he said had already run him into debt before eloping on February 22, 1752. Some men simply notified the public that they would no longer be responsible for their wives' debts. Husbands were happy to claim their eloping wives' debts if their estates were worth more than their debts. William Green advertised that no one who owed money to Sarah Green should settle with George Pitt, with whom she appeared to have been living at the time of her death. William Green claimed the right to sell off Sarah's properties, houses, and slaves and to receive her outstanding debts.[16]

In rare cases we can hear women's voices. Wives talked about their husbands' misuse of power and preoccupation with money. Margaret Bannerman placed a lengthy advertisement detailing how her husband, Benjamin, had married her and then progressively denuded her of her possessions. He moved her out of her own house and into a house in town: "His policy . . . was to get the sole management of my cellar where there was to the value of 1500 pounds in liquors." He also seized fifteen hundred pounds in cash. "In a few weeks we parted beds; after that he moved me upstairs where he kept me a prisoner, under three locks with very little provision, until he forced me to make over to him three houses in town which he rented." He also took five slaves. Eventually he took her clothing.[17]

A few notices suggest that the decision to separate was mutual. These disarming no-fault confessions were rare and seem to have happened only when husband and wife had properties of their own. Husbands with some property treated with greater respect the relatively few women who came to marriage with dowries than they did the majority of women, who had nothing of their own besides their ability to work and have children.

A number of announcements show that couples could manage to separate amicably without the benefit of the courts. George Jones advertised that he was not to be further responsible for his wife's debts, but he prefaced this by saying, "Whereas my wife *Anne* and myself cannot agree in the management of our Affairs . . ." When, in 1774, Coleman Theeds and his wife, Elizabeth, decided to separate, each gave bond to the other and agreed that "they will not interfere with any Estate which shall hereafter accrue to either party . . . no Person, after this Date, may credit the Wife on the Husband's Account, or the Husband upon that of the Wife's." Similarly William Sowell and his wife, Sarah, "who for some time past lived separately and apart from each other," agreed to continue to live this way. They each planned to enjoy their separate properties and not to interfere with each other's estates.[18]

Some women—it is impossible to tell how many—ran from violence at home. Husbands could beat their wives legally, although the practice was frowned upon. Wives could protest, but it could be dangerous to do so. Elisabeth Coltart was married to a doctor who beat her so frequently that she often had to seek refuge in other people's houses. Four years went by before she reported her husband to the authorities. The day before he was to go to court, he promised her in front of the "gentleman and lady" with whom she was staying that he would never hit her again. She moved back with him, and he kept his word for about three weeks. Then he asked her to draft a statement to the effect that she had falsely accused him of violence toward her. When she refused, he "fell to beating [her] and swore he would never stop till he had the last drop of blood of [her] body." She reported him again to the justice of the peace and wrote to her cousin St. George Tucker, asking for help to return to her father and mother. Coltart went to jail. Tucker sent enough money for Elisabeth to get a separation and promised to send her 150 to 200 pounds annually for as long as she should need it. Elisabeth Coltart was courageous to bring charges against her husband. She was also lucky to have friends and a powerful relative to turn to for help. Flight without legal redress, a safe place to go, or a future source of support was the fate of most poor, illiterate women.[19]

Desertion did not always free a wife of her husband. John Newdall did not let things go with a debt disclaimer. He had lived with his wife, Martha, in Maryland until she ran away with Abraham Hannison to Virginia, where John caught up with them. Martha unsuccessfully tried to stab John, illustrating her intention not to return to him, but he refused to go away. He established himself nearby at a landing on the Rappahannock River. A neighbor told Martha that she "Ledd a bad Course of life to keep Company with another man," but Martha replied that she had never loved her husband and never would.

John Newdall stalked his wife but feared her lover. He confided to neighbors that he was afraid that the first time he got drunk his wife and lover would kill him. He was not mistaken. One day all three shared a pint and a half of rum punch with some sailors. John passed out. When the sailors deposited him onshore, he revived enough to ask Martha to cover him with a rug. The next day he was discovered dead. Martha and her lover were subsequently arrested for John's murder.[20]

Murder was a rare remedy, but its existence underscores the fact that marriage among whites in the eighteenth-century Chesapeake was less egalitarian than it had been even in seventeenth-century Massachusetts. The Virginia gentry slowly began shifting its marital ideals to incorporate sensibility, sympathy, and companionability. Still, while slaveowners might speak softly in their parlors, they carried very big sticks. Masculinity among planters was, as one historian noted, defined by "contentiousness, combativeness, and martial language," not the best combination for domestic harmony. The need for husbands to be capable of routine brutality placed Chesapeake wives in a very different relation to them from that which Puritan wives had occupied toward "God's deputies" in their households. Virginia's gentry men exercised ungodly power from which wives of sensibility had to avert their eyes.[21]

The religious culture of the Chesapeake offered women little independence or moral prestige and no welcome, even as passive observers, to a critical, exegetical tradition of thought and scriptural interpretation. Instead of a double standard for sexual behavior, there was a confusing multiplicity of standards. A key piece of Chesapeake sexual ideology victimized black women by associating them with licentious behavior. This served to exonerate white and black men from any sexual crimes against black women. White Virginia men assumed and protected the chastity of elite white women at the same time that they enjoyed flirtatious femininity, arch chat, and theatrical emotionality. Ideology neither defamed nor protected poor white women but left them to fend for themselves in a culture in which powerful men found it easy to get their way.

In prerevolutionary Virginia, British and colonial ideas about women were in conflict as commerce penetrated deeper into British society and made itself felt in the colonies as well. This turmoil contributed to the unsteadiness of marriage in the Chesapeake as women fought to ameliorate a system that, at its worst, confiscated whatever goods they had and forced labor, not to mention children, out of them. After the dust of the Revolution had settled, white wives were to have a new, elevated role in building the nation even if their economic status was not, for the time being, improved.

11

FOND MOTHERS

Virginia men, unlike Puritans in Massachusetts, wrote few paeans to their mothers. They took motherhood for granted. The inimitable Landon Carter remarked that women had nothing on their minds but the "breeding contests at home." Certainly women spent a great deal of time pregnant and nursing. Martha Jefferson Randolph had twelve children, Mrs. Robert Carter mothered thirteen, and John Marshall's mother had fifteen. The average for the period was about eight. Given the high rates of miscarriage and infant and maternal mortality, white women were interested in limiting their pregnancies. By the end of the eighteenth century they began to appeal to their husbands to cooperate—that is, to abstain from sex. Some eighteenth-century women hoped nursing would provide contraception. Moralists encouraged nursing as good for babies and a good way to keep mothers at home and away from dissipation.[1]

Nevertheless, many gentry women availed themselves of slave mothers to nurse their infants. The tutor Philip Fithian was shocked to discover that the family's doctor's first child was being nursed by a slave and that Mrs. Carter had wet nurses feed many of her thirteen children. While slave mothers frequently had to fight for the right to nurse their own infants adequately, poorer white women, whose material contributions to the family were essential, simply had to fit nursing into an already burdened day.[2]

The slave population began to rise through natural increase in the 1720s. African women arrived believing that having and taking care of children were sacred obligations for which they would need a helpful female community. They also believed that they must take care of their bodies for their role as producers of children. Historians have noted that female slaves attempted to avoid work during menstruation. Since most West African women came from cultures that taught them they would defile anything they touched during menstruation and must separate themselves from their community during that time, something more than evading tasks was motivating their menstrual complaints. Women probably lost four to eight workdays a month to menstrual complaints. Slaveowners saw this as malingering, and it undoubtedly contributed to their general assessment of slave women as "deceitful" and "artful."[3]

The same kinds of dissonances occurred around pregnancy. Masters wanted slaves to reproduce, and some went so far as to offer prizes for exceptional fertility—a Faustian bargain, to be sure. Moreover, involuntary pregnancies were not infrequent. One young black slave woman had a black husband but was also subject to the sexual desires of the white overseer. She had a black child by her husband and subsequently delivered fraternal twins: a black boy, named Austin, and a blue-eyed mulatto girl, named Sarah, presumably from separate conceptions with her husband and the overseer. Black women could also be sexual victims of men of their own race. On Robert Carter's plantation his slave Christopher raped another slave. Christopher was convicted of the charge, but Carter successfully interceded for his pardon rather than have him executed. In 1769 the House of Burgesses repealed the law whereby the state had castrated male slaves for a variety of crimes, including absenting themselves from work. The only crime thereafter for which a slave could be castrated was the rape of a white woman. In the eyes of white planters, black women were to be available for both races.[4]

In the absence of marriages respected by law and given the high incidence of sexual abuse of black women by white men, and also sometimes by black men, slave women did not always rejoice at the births of children. Whites sometimes suspected slave mothers of infanticide. In 1775 Stephen Ham petitioned the House of Burgesses for compensation for his slave Jude, who had killed her son Caesar and then set fire to the house she had lived in. Jude was burned as well and died a few days later. Just after the turn of the nineteenth century an unmarried slave named Fanny attempted to kill her sixth child at its birth. Her owner cited religious scruples as her reason. These cases of despair are remarkable for their rarity given the conditions under which slave women bore children. Planters identified several runaways between the mid-eighteenth century and the Revolution as pregnant, and there may have been many others whose pregnancies planters could not yet recognize. Despite their condition, these women were determined to reach a safe spot to deliver their children.[5]

Many mishaps occurred to pregnant slave women who were not allowed to take care of themselves. They were prey to malnutrition and related illnesses. They could be subject to brutal discipline if their owners did not know or believe that they were pregnant. They also suffered from the complementary problems of inadequate care or, just as bad, heroic medical care. According to sketchy nineteenth-century figures, the death rate for slave mothers was slightly lower than for whites, though by modern standards high for both. Slave mothers had an advantage in being relatively immune to malaria (compared to white women), and slave women usually had fewer children than white women. Their children, who tended to be smaller because of hard work and poor nutrition, were also easier to deliver. The death rate of slave children under one year old was twice that of white children.[6]

It is only one of the countless tragic ironies of Chesapeake slave society that a culture that was pressuring its white women to nurse was fighting to keep its black women from doing the same thing. Slave women working in the fields fought valiantly to nurse their babies as often as they could. On Landon Carter's plantation they told the overseer that Carter had allowed them five breaks a day to nurse their children. When Carter discovered what they were doing, he had a number of them whipped and reduced the times to half an hour before starting work, half an hour before breakfast, and half an hour before they finished at night.[7]

When black women acted to protect their own children, they often called punishment upon themselves. Mary Campbell at mid-century wanted to have her slave Mrs. Jenny whipped because she had taken her sick child to live with a free black and nursed the child there.[8]

Most historians agree that the white Western European family changed over the course of the eighteenth century. Childhood emerged as a special time in the life cycle, and children began to be treated not as miniature adults but as creatures with special needs. These changes also implied a more egalitarian relation between husbands and wives. While this is usually tied to the growth of a middle class, the changes in the Chesapeake occurred in a colony that had rapidly changed from a society with slaves to a slave society. Elite whites in the Chesapeake, in addition to following the patterns of their British counterparts, may have wanted to develop strategies that distinguished them from the brutality and chaos that they were inflicting upon Africans. Sometime in the mid-eighteenth century in the Chesapeake the family became more child-centered, and affectionate child rearing began to replace a more authoritarian style. Although marriages became slightly more egalitarian, husbands' and wives' attitudes toward family life did not change in step with one another. Instead an ongoing disagreement between fathers and mothers over the treatment of children characterized Chesapeake gentry parenting.[9]

While the tone and intent of family life seem to have changed, educators' notions of child rearing also underwent a major alteration at the time of the American Revolution. Ideally, respectful persuasion obviated the need for severe punishment, and flexibility and kindness were to replace the harsh discipline characteristic of the early eighteenth century. Men began accepting empathy and sympathy as desirable parental qualities, no longer seeing them as corrupting, effeminate influences leading to a boy's ruin. Among the reasons for this transformation was the diffusion of John Locke's educational thinking advocating the abandonment of coercion in favor of persuasion. Locke's *Essay Concerning Human Understanding*, published in 1690, posited an infant's mind as the famous tabula rasa, waiting for impressions to be registered upon it, rather than as a womb filled with embryonic patterns for all subsequent ideas. Three years later Locke published his immensely influential *Some Thoughts Concerning Education*, in which he developed the notion that teaching should be done by example, not by imposing rules on children. He insisted that a child should obey and accept instruction from his parents because of the respect he bore them, and he rejected harsh discipline and coercion as being obstacles to achieving that essential affection and respect. Novel reading, too, helped spread genteel culture stressing the truth and innocence of emotion, particularly female emotion, guided by right reason.[10]

The changes in family life that occurred over the course of the eighteenth century had mixed results for women, on the one hand elevating their status and on the other restricting them to supportive roles and further widening the gap between the sexes that was characteristic of the nineteenth century. Thus a mixture of benefits and liabilities resulted from the reevaluation of motherhood in the Chesapeake. Gentry mothers, to a significant extent, softened the patriarchs' tone and contributed to a gentler handling of their children. While there were undoubtedly a number of reasons for this change, gentry mothers' efforts, rooted in and reinforcing the culture of sensibility, helped bring about the changes in the family that were noticeable by the early nineteenth century.[11]

In endorsing affection and tenderness as a basis for parental respect, men were giving their approval to Whig ideas of sensibility about the innate sympathy in all humans and women's civilizing effects on society that originated in the Scottish Enlightenment. Gentry men were partly imitating the British elite and partly distancing themselves and their families from the slaves and poor whites around them. Empathy stopped with the near and dear and was not to lead to questioning the wider social and economic system. On the contrary, displays of refined emotion reinforced class and racial distinctions.[12]

By the later years of the eighteenth century displays of male sensibility were thought to enhance gentry public life, both economic and political. Patriarchs more and more adopted a paternalistic patina as they grew more experienced in methods needed to control almost a quarter of a million enslaved Africans. On the other hand, fondness increasingly gave mothers a modicum of moral authority.[13]

These mothers' struggles and desires correspond closely to the recently articulated morality of relatedness, which begins from an understanding of the dramatic "limits of autonomy and control." Women, as both children and mothers, start from the assumption of the interconnections among humans and experience the self as inextricably created and understood in relationships with others. From this it follows that women's moral ideals entail a primary concern to maintain and sustain relationships. Hence mothers may be expected to fight against separation from their children and for leniency in discipline since ideally no one in a woman's circle of care should be made to feel pain or be left out.[14]

Relatedness appeared as an express aspect of gentry mothering at the beginning of the eighteenth century and became more insistent over time in the Chesapeake. It showed up at the time that family life stabilized in the Chesapeake, in the early eighteenth century, after the extremely high death rates of the seventeenth century had come down, and children were no longer so likely to lose a parent or two before maturity. Research confirms that when mothering is largely done by women, as was true for mothers of young children among the Chesapeake gentry, girls will develop "mothering" characteristics—i.e., relatedness characteristics, including dependence and emotional expressivity—while boys, on the other hand, will be likely to develop emotional restraint and independence.[15]

Gentry fathers valued independence as the sine qua non of manhood and the evolving concept of republican virtue. An independent man made decisions for those without independence—namely, women, servants, children, and social inferiors. A white man's independence, particularly in a slave culture, was crucial to his membership in the gentry. A mother's fondness particularly perturbed men when it was directed at boys. If mothers made tender alliances with their sons, their sons might not struggle to retain their full range of patriarchal rights but relinquish some to the fond mother or, later, the seductive wife. The nightmarish prospect of domestic power shared with women animated gentry men to struggle to overcome maternal fondness toward their sons.[16]

Fondness in the early eighteenth century brought into question woman's rationality and hence her ability to exercise proper authority over slaves and children. Late-seventeenth- and early-eighteenth-century advice books usually focused on the dangers of mothers' being unable to control their weakness for their children. Puritans and Anglicans alike expressed great anxiety over fond women. Thomas Cobbett had written in 1656, in *A Fruitfull and Usefull Discourse Touching the Honour Due from Children to Parents*, that "fondness and familiarity breeds and causeth contempt and irreverence in children." Richard Allestree's immensely popular *The Ladies Calling* warned mothers that their love "often needs a bridle." Moralists warned mothers not to dote on their children or make them idols. The British moral philosopher Bernard Mandeville wrote in 1714 that "the weakest minds have generally the greatest share of [pity], for which reason none are more compassionate than women and children." Mandeville's explication displays the ambiguity of fondness, simultaneously compliment and accusation.[17]

Over the years the Byrd family patriarchs, however unwillingly, had to learn to adapt to fond mothering. In the early eighteenth century Colonel William Byrd II praised his wife for allowing their son to be sent to school in England and for hearing of his being whipped without a protest. In letters Byrd presented himself as helpfully containing the destabilizing effects of fondness on his overwrought wife. His confident irony emphasized his imperturbability and her hyper-emotionalism. As a disciplinarian Byrd took no prisoners. He had both his niece and nephew beaten for not learning their lessons. Twice he remarked in his journal that he made the indentured Eugene "drink a pint of piss to cure his bedwetting." Byrd wished to assume his wife's acquiescence in his disciplinary methods, but she tried to protect their children from his heroic dosing and refused to stop mourning for her dead son when Byrd urged stoicism.[18]

Thirty years later Elizabeth Byrd defied her absent husband's wish to send her son to Great Britain and refused his request for money. Marshaling the language of the sentimental fiction that informed her ideas, Elizabeth insisted on her status as the fond—and suffering—mother.

> Ah little did I think once, of ever being parted from my dearest Mr. Byrd. . . . My prayers and best wishes always shall attend you, and our blessed babes. If ever it is in my power to be of service to my children, I shall take all occasions in letting my comforts know they may depende on haveing the affectionate mother in me, for I had as leave want as they should.[19]

In the Dangerfield family a mother tried unsuccessfully to end the tutor's nighttime whippings of her son. Gentry men and women fought over girls and slaves but most bitterly over the treatment of the boys. Men feared that fondness directed toward boys would emasculate them, render them unfit for the role of patriarch, and compromise the autonomy they needed for political participation. The Reverend Peter Fontaine worried that his sister-in-law's fondness might merely spoil her daughter but would completely "crush" her young son.[20]

If fondness increasingly justified the softhearted interventions of white mothers, it was to have nothing to do with slave discipline. The mother-child bond among slaves became at a certain point, as far as planters were concerned, a discipline problem. It was easier for planters to conceive of slave mothers as having dull feelings for their children than to imagine them suffering over their pain and absence. In the nineteenth century with the growth of the internal slave trade the presumably more numb feelings of slaves was an article of faith among slaveowners. Slave mothers often ran to their children, and the children even more often to their mothers, and both were routinely punished for actions that would have been attributed to fondness among whites. I found only one slaveowner who identified fondness in a slave mother. He told his overseer to make "a proper allowance for the feelings of a Mother" in disciplining her two sons.

Robert Carter's rare ability to imagine maternal fondness in a slave woman compelled him morally to acknowledge her as a fellow human being. So powerful was this recognition that he emancipated his slaves in the wake of the Revolution.[21]

Over the eighteenth century some elite white mothers tried to convince their husbands to soften their methods of discipline. Their job was both harder and easier because it took place in a slave society characterized by brutal discipline. It was harder because violence was central to the planters' world; without force the whole system would have fallen apart. Hence it was at the heart of planter philosophy of how things got done. On the other hand, just as slavery produced in planters a desperate desire for freedom, so violence must have produced in them a great yearning for the noncoercive, voluntary relations Locke and others wrote about. While almost no planters would permit themselves to recognize the depth of feeling between slave mother and child, European visitors to West Africa had extolled it in their forebears. But the white slaveholders did come to accept and even to admire the maternal love of their wives, cousins, and neighbors. Its tender manifestations were ornaments to family life and demonstrated at the same time how different planters were from their brutish servants. By mid-century "fondness" was rapidly losing its shadings of credulous, foolish, and irrational. Maternal tenderness, for white women, was commencing its journey to nineteenth-century sanctification as unambiguous, pure, and redemptive. Men in their turn began exercising a vocabulary of fondness and connection that suggested a new view of themselves as virtuous partners in, rather than overlords of, family life.

While fondness gave mothers a certain moral stature, it carried no real authority with it. As shrewd boys quickly came to see, relatedness offered the possibility of extensive negotiations on disciplinary matters that once might have ended quickly in whippings. A postrevolutionary letter from the adolescent Richard Randolph to his mother, Frances Bland Randolph Tucker, offers a glimpse of an exchange between a fond mother and her disobedient son. It demonstrates the pervasive reach of fondness as an idea as well as the ease with which it could be manipulated. Randolph was in Princeton, where he and his brother spent a few months studying in 1787. His letter attempts to explain and justify a series of his rebellious acts, all documented in letters that his mother had found and that had included his attending a forbidden party, spending money without permission, reading sexy stories, having an illicit sexual relationship, and finding the maternal bond constricting. The letter shows a privileged boy, on the brink of manhood, who has learned the language of mutuality, sensibility, and relatedness while exercising his male prerogative to violate those ideals.[22]

In phrases typical of sentimental fiction, Richard designed his defense to stress his love and connection to his mother, the satisfaction he got from her happiness, and his misery in her unhappiness. He never dealt directly with his actual misdeeds but painted his infractions and sexual escapades as "natural," hence inevitable and, consequently, not worthy of much notice. He repeatedly emphasized his sensitivity to his mother's feelings in place of any ethical principles. "I was afraid of making you uneasy—this was the motive which actuated me alone. . . . It was not because I was really afraid of you—you had been too kind & tender to admit of such a thought. But I assure you it was my fear of making you unhappy." His invocation of his intimacy with his mother obscured the reality that mothers were not permitted to adjudicate questions touching traditional male prerogatives. Richard asked his mother to be less concerned with abstract justice than with the eighteenth-century southern gentry's view of male nature with all its limitations. "I have been unfortunate in having passions which I had never resolution to govern or resist," wrote the young man. ". . . Was not this Natural Mama."

Richard defended his friends by saying that they had opposed his sexual liaison as "imprudent." She could rest assured, in other words, that his friends stood in loco parentis and were giving him a mother's advice. He honored his mother as a friend and legitimated his friends as surrogate mothers. Mother and son, however, both perceived the dangerous role of Richard's male friends. While they, like him, might employ the language of sensibility, care, and equality, they actually wielded male privilege and autonomy.

Richard invoked his mother's fondness to overlook his missteps.

In concluding, he referred appreciatively to her "great partiality for [her] children & [that she] always [made] as many allowances as are consistent with their welfare. You have overlooked my misconduct perhaps too much. . . . I hope it ends here!" In this ambiguous conclusion, he expressed not only the desire that he would reform so that she might not have occasion to go on forgiving him but also the contrary and more likely possibility that given his nature, he might need her fond forgiveness again and again.[23]

Richard Randolph sculpted his plea to fit his understanding of his mother's love for him, her need for connection, and his own desires. He believed that her pleasure in their ongoing connection, however compromised by his peccadilloes, outweighed her desire for moral authority over him. His words honored his mother's wish for mutual love, while his actions indicated that other urgent and conflicting needs, approved by the male world, pressed on him, overruling his mother's wishes for his behavior. Maternal fondness was losing its negative connotation over the course of the century, but it was also proving useful in preventing women from exercising moral authority over men.

12

THE LOGIC OF LUXURY

However, though she was grown an old woman, yet she was one
of those absolute rarities, a very good old woman.
—William Byrd[1]

The eighteenth-century Chesapeake widow found herself in a difficult dilemma. The moral prescriptions for her behavior—passivity,
selflessness, and a fatalistic outlook—had little relevance for her material struggle to survive. As the eighteenth century progressed, a
number of factors (demographic, political, and economic) underlay
changes in social practice that created an increasingly restricted
sphere for widows and produced poisonous caricatures about them.
English authors of moral advice books wrote to convince women to
retire from the world when they became widows, encouraging them
to shun even innocent pleasures.[2]

Remarrying was considered a bad idea. Some believed it dishon-
ored the dead husband; others frankly warned women that it would
be foolish to give up their recently acquired freedom and property.[3]

The Chesapeake formula for the successful older woman appears
in countless eulogies in the *Virginia Gazette*. These positive descrip-

tions, based on selflessness, emphasized the cheerful acceptance of what destiny might bring. The editors praised affection, obedience to authority, thrift, undemonstrative piety, contentment with little, and mildness with dependents. Seventy-six-year-old Amey Eppes had been an obedient and affectionate wife, "a kind and forgiving mistress," and never had an enemy "so inoffensive was her conduct." Sarah Winfrey had been "affable" as a wife and "read[y] to oblige," "tender and affectionate" as a parent, a mistress of "humanity and indulgence." Eulogists also praised women who appeared unafraid of death and looked to it with peace and contentment. Being uncomplaining in death spared the emotions and fears of survivors.[4]

Old women, a category that often included widows, were also to display the familiar virtues of selfless caring for family and friends; they were to exercise only gentle moral authority over slaves, to bear suffering stoically, and to be religious without enthusiasm. Against these good, inoffensive, homegrown widows and dowagers was the by now familiar figure of the Whig nightmare, the luxury woman, sapping some man of his wealth so she could satisfy her lust for clothes, gaming, and lovers. The older she got, the more repulsive her desires and her inability to control them. As a widow, of course, she also existed dangerously outside the institutional restraints of marriage. Political metaphor, stand-in for the corruption rife in Great Britain, this figure offered an easy target for resentment, fear, and blame. A rich misogynist vocabulary was ready to describe the origins of colonial men's problems.[5]

Marriage to a virtuous man was the only established way a woman might be saved from her passionate self. Satirists sometimes urged young men to marry rich old ladies.[6] But they reserved the cruelest satire for the sexually rapacious older woman.

William Byrd wrote his cousin Mrs. Taylor a lengthy and purportedly true account of an Italian woman whom he called Bona Roba (or Good Stuff). A no-longer-young widow, visiting Virginia from Italy, Bona Roba fails in the most humiliating way to use her sexuality to acquire a Virginia husband. Byrd began by speculating as a man of the world that she was probably a Venetian whore because of her mastery of the arts of pleasing men. He continued that because she was a little elderly, her breasts had lost their firmness, so she had her chambermaid blow air into them with a tiny pipe through her nipples. She placed a sort of wax over her nipples to hold the air in them. On a hot day it happened that the wax melted and the air came out "as fast as it well coud do, thro' so narrow a channel & produced a sound that was a little unseemly, and that too not in separate notes but with a longwinded blast." The signora "slunk away . . . & has never appeard out of her Doors since."[7]

Moralists' advice about preserving and enhancing a dead husband's memory, taking God before another earthly mate, and teaching young wives and mothers to carry out their duties faithfully never could carry much weight in the colonial Chesapeake. Until the middle of the eighteenth century women were scarce, and a widow in such a world was very likely to remarry. A widow with property was a particularly attractive prospect. The colony gave to a widow of an intestate man one-third of his movable goods and the use of one-third of his land while she remained alive, or—if he stipulated, as he often did—while she remained his widow. The land was usually kept for sons, while daughters traditionally received personal property and slaves if there were any. In the seventeenth century, when land was plentiful, daughters sometimes received some, and widows often received more than their thirds. In the seventeenth century husbands had been very likely to appoint their widows executrices of their estates, but these practices had all but ceased by the 1750s. Often a wife was merely receiving back the land, or some portion of it, that she had brought with her into the marriage. A widow who possessed slaves could not send them out of state or permit a slave or slaves or any child of slaves to leave Virginia without the approval of her heirs. Her ownership of property and slaves was temporary and not hers to alienate. A larger number of surviving children, less land to go around, and more children mature enough to manage an estate made husbands considerably less willing to give control of property to widows. Husbands were also less willing to give them control "of the children's upbringing and education."[8]

After mid-century, when the sex ratio was closer to equal, widows did not automatically remarry. The economic insecurity these widows experienced did not produce the requisite tranquillity and selflessness to earn them eulogies. Instead of a life of retirement and religious devotion, widows were often trying to hold their own financially in a world where self-interest was something men, not women, were socialized to pursue. A woman who suddenly had to take care of her financial interests not only made nonsense of the notions of the public male and domestic female but also challenged the sexual division of labor that kept women out of production for the cash market and in family production.[9]

During the latter half of the eighteenth century the products of rapidly increasing wealth began to be in evidence throughout the colonies. Chesapeake planters, in addition to living more and more luxuriously, were also increasingly in debt and anxious about it. Up through the beginning of the Seven Years' War the great planters speculated very profitably in western lands. After the war, however, this market disappeared, and tobacco profits simultaneously began to fall. Wealthy and not-so-wealthy planters who had created enviable estates found themselves in a cycle of debt that angered and frightened them. Planters considered falling prices and debt a matter of shame and a criticism of their abilities as masters of the tobacco crop.[10]

While they took market forces personally, many also blamed women for making the kinds of expenditures that identified them as members of the elite. Worries about wifely frugality and economically advantageous marriages preceded concerns about controlling widows' access to land, money, and slaves. The ambivalence and discomfort that planters experienced from increasing debt on top of high investments in luxuries help explain men's growing unwillingness to allow their widows to manage their husbands' estates and the animosity of some sons to their widowed mothers. In a world of men anxious over the linked issues of their income and their freedom, older women and widows were a focus of male ambivalence.

In 1748 the House of Burgesses passed a law allowing widows to express dissatisfaction with their inheritances within nine months of the deaths of their husbands and renounce the portions willed to them in the expectation of receiving a larger share of slaves and "other personal estate," other than land, that is. In the York County court records there are numerous such renunciations. Sarah Waters, widow of William Waters, had to sue in court twice, in the winter of 1768 and in the following winter, to refuse her husband's will and challenge the execution of his estate.[11]

Widows, suddenly made heads of households, often failed to report themselves, their working dependents, or their possessions to the parish officials, putting themselves in legal jeopardy. White widows who failed to report their slaves and black and Indian women who failed to report their children or themselves were deemed complicit in evading the tithe.[12]

Wealthy and poor widows both were suddenly at the mercy of forces that had been in the control of their husbands. Elizabeth Jones's deceased husband's creditors sued her and attached her estate because she did not show up in court for the trial. Women often did not have male relatives or friends to help them out and lacked the experience, and sometimes the literacy, to defend their interests in court. In some cases, their dead husbands' debts forced widows to sell off parcels of land to creditors of their husbands.[13]

Widowhood became calamitous for mothers in conflict with their sons.[14] Mary Campbell, who had lived well during her husband's lifetime, found herself in widowhood cold, hungry, and at war with one of her sons. She had gotten help and advice from one daughter and one son. But she bitterly criticized the son who offered no aid and behaved as if he were entitled to her possessions. She had sent a slave to him to work, and when she asked for payment, he had become angry and said he owed her nothing. When the weather was cold, he would not send wood. Mary concluded, "It is of no use to ask anything of him."[15]

Campbell did not turn to God or attempt to keep vivid and shining her husband's name. Far from displaying the widow's virtues of withdrawal from the fray and passive acceptance of what fate handed her, she relied on her own strength: "I have bless God a spirit, that can support me in adversity as well as prosperity." But she was painfully aware that her dependency on and relations with her children dictated the terms of her survival: "Nothing ever affects me so much as your brothers cruel[ty]." To continue to lead the style of life that was familiar to her put her aggressively at odds with her son, and a lifetime of obedience to her husband availed her nothing. In addition, ongoing litigation or simple disagreement inevitably cast her in the role of an irrational woman: at best foible-ridden, at worst rapacious.[16]

Other Chesapeake widows and sons fought over land, money, and autonomy. Mary Byrd's struggle with her son William Byrd III was protracted and ended with his suicide in 1777. The dark picture we have received of the widow Mary Ball Washington, mother of the first president, emerges from a similar struggle. George Washington painted his mother as grasping and overwhelmingly burdensome although the evidence merely shows that she was relatively poor. However, in the Chesapeake, when widows had control over their own lives and exercised even limited control over the lives of their sons, those sons were very likely to see them as having wrongly usurped goods and influence that they themselves properly deserved. By and large, men could usually overcome or limit the processes that gave widows such unusual sovereignty. However, the moral judgment upon widows trying to live out their lives independently has been harsh. As widows they were vulnerable to stereotypes like increased irrationality and the possession of repulsive and rampant sexuality. Such stereotypes supported the desires of Virginia men to keep property out of the hands of women. The majority of long-forgotten widows in this period experienced the painful double bind of having to look out for themselves while being held to standards of modesty, self-sacrifice, and humanity from which men were exempt.[17]

Coda

The absence of records makes it all but impossible to identify the ages and marital statuses of eighteenth-century enslaved and free black women. It is clear, however, that mature free black women faced the same problems as white widows except, of course, that they had little property and no slaves to struggle over. Men fought no rhetorical symbolic battles over the moral character of these women. What little the women accumulated through their hard labor, they shared with others in need. At least one out of every six female runaways from the Tidewater went to Williamsburg to hide. The four free black families there that assisted runaways all were headed by women—a laundress, a seamstress, a cook, and a spinner.[18]

Part Three

13

EARLY ST. LOUIS: AN INTRODUCTION

American travelers to St. Louis in the early nineteenth century all remarked on the manners of the French inhabitants. For many, the French, particularly Frenchwomen, were immensely charming, gracious, and warm. Others, especially evangelical converts, were appalled at the Sabbath breaking, dancing, and love of pleasure evident all around them. Steeped in distinct ideas of status and leisure, the French (Creoles) brought a special flavor to elite St. Louis culture at sharp variance from the worldview of Anglo-American evangelicals, who were a growing part of St. Louis's new middle class. The French lived by a code that did not derive from conditions of uncertainty, whether financial, social, or religious. Pleasure and predictability were central to their confident worldview.[1]

Yet a third group silently influenced both the French and Anglo-Americans. It was a group without a prescriptive literature, whose ideas about the good life, pleasure, and morality were largely obscure to the first two. African Americans were nevertheless a vivid presence against whom people of European descent defined themselves inversely, or so they imagined, since they were so often mistaken in the values they ascribed or projected onto slaves and free people of color.[2]

French merchant fur traders founded St. Louis in 1764, and a few Creole families, dominated by the Chouteaus and the Gratiots, presided over the settlement. When, in 1803, the United States took possession of the city through the Louisiana Purchase, the French elite worried about the American takeover and what republican rule might mean. Their first act as Americans indicated their fears: enforcement of a new code of tight discipline over their restive slaves, who were dreaming that an American takeover might mean emancipation.[3]

After securing slave control, most French merchants worked to firm up their claims and acquire more land in anticipation of the speculation that would start once settlers began arriving. Even this competition for wealth, however, was restrained by the existence of a provincial aristocracy, by centralized control of the economy, and by a belief in the organic, interdependent nature of hierarchical society. In the French view, virtue resided in behaving correctly within one's social sphere. Correct behavior required reciprocal responsibilities, industriousness, and the cultivation of mutual pleasure in connections with others. This unusually democratic, egalitarian social structure and the economic freedom and general prosperity it encouraged produced independent, peaceable colonists, unused to restraint or great stratification.[4]

In the young United States, by contrast, order, virtue, and morality were believed to depend upon the survival of disinterestedness within an expanding market economy, in which men of unfixed rank aggressively pursued their fortunes. Disinterestedness was less and less expected of them. Among the Americans who came to St. Louis, violence in service of economic and political interests was common. Rufus Easton, a member of the emerging American elite, burst into an 1806 meeting of the land board and clubbed the commissioner brutally. Judge John Smith, of Tennessee, wealthy and well educated, had killed at least fourteen men in duels by the end of his career. As one St. Louis historian puts it, "eye-gouging fights, cursing and shouting, political arguments and generally churlish behavior became commonplace on the streets." Moralists did not necessarily have in mind the ferocity of Missouri men struggling for power when they exhorted women to improve themselves and their children, but these men on the make *were* excellent examples of the poisoned passions of self-interest.[5]

As the work of American men increasingly determined their status and identity and consumed all their time, the fate of American virtue seemed to depend more and more upon mothers and their ability to remain uninterested in their own material advancement, pleasure, or self-cultivation. Whereas the French believed pleasure accompanied and rewarded benevolent behavior, Americans thought pleasure distracted men from making livings and women from upholding the virtue of the republic. The French salon had few counterparts in America, and Jefferson discontinued the levees over which George and Martha Washington had presided, closing off a unique public space in which genteel, educated women could share the pleasures of polite exchange with political leaders. The Second Great Awakening, beginning around 1800, which reinforced patriarchal life while elevating community respect for women's moral endeavors, emphasized the formal relegation of American women to domestic life.[6]

Whatever differences emerged between privileged Anglo-American and French girls were not due to the quality of their formal education. Anglo-Americans generally sent their girls to the convent schools Philippine Duchesne had founded before St. Louis provided non-Catholic schools. Although there were short-lived academies run by Protestants, it was not until 1833 that Mary Sibley founded Linden Wood, a school for girls, "the first," its founder wrote, "that lifted up the standard of opposition to convent Education in the West . . . of sufficient importance in the eyes of the Arch enemy, to make the Jesuits its traducers." But even when non-Catholic education was available, many Anglo-Americans still wanted their girls to learn French both as an ornament and as an entrée to the elite French social world.[7]

In the period 1803–1835, French and American families had similar aims in educating their daughters—i.e., to obtain those characteristics that would aid them in marrying well and becoming virtuous mothers. They differed, however, in important ways on what constituted a good life. Hence their moral emphases differed, and so in turn did the texture of their daughters' emotional and psychological lives. These differences emerged primarily in family and religious life. French Catholic parents communicated a greater acceptance of physicality, emotional expressivity, and pleasure as a normal part of life than did the Anglo-Americans, whereas Protestant evangelical education was shaped to teach girls to monitor the Christian acceptability of their own and others' behavior.[8]

The records of Mother Philippine Duchesne's convent school reveal a religious atmosphere in which all were tolerated and very few were chosen. A key distinction between the evangelical Protestants and Catholics was that the latter did not expect many to have a vocation for the religious life and judged girls accordingly. The nuns had two different scales for youthful behavior. They tried to influence girls without a vocation to lead chaste, useful lives, but they did not expect them to be capable of great self-discipline and sacrifice. Those who demonstrated the beginnings of a calling for religious life had to live up to higher standards. Many fell out along the way. It was widely assumed that the religious life was not for most, and this two-tiered system incorporated all in the same church. Evangelical converts, on the other hand, were likely to associate comfortably only with other converts; their relations with the unconverted were either as missionaries or as strangers. The converted viewed the unconverted as wanting persuasion and internal strength, not simply as ordinary mortals with ordinary human weaknesses.

The French also enjoyed far greater assurance of attaining heaven than did evangelical Americans. The French presumed a rational relationship between the here and the hereafter: "[O]ne is recompensed in another life for the good which one does in this one." They believed that God understands our acts as we do. This suggests an important difference between the conscience of a pious French Catholic and the sweeping, all-revealing spotlight of evangelical conscience, which warned against taking satisfaction in good deeds. In evangelical culture, children could not be sure of God's interpretation of events. Human worthlessness and utter dependency on God hampered evangelicals from drawing concrete conclusions about the relationship between act and recompense. Salvation in the evangelical system was a single event, an epiphany, a moment of glorious certitude following usually dreadful suffering and doubt. But like Puritans, evangelical converts could fall back into uncertainty and be wrong in their assumptions altogether. For Catholics the matter of salvation had predictability and a cumulative logic, resulting from a final balancing out of good and bad deeds as one might measure grain or sugar. The evangelical temperament hindered Christians from enjoying their worthy acts and from the solid assurance of achieving heaven.[9]

French writers, unlike Anglo-American moralists, stressed pleasure as a motivation for good conduct, the pleasure of self-satisfaction, generosity, fulfilling one's noblest desires, and industry. Perhaps most important of all, they stressed the pleasure of communication. There was little emphasis on restraint between the sexes, on closing off the family from the social and natural world, or on the vital necessity of woman's suppression of self and sacrifice of pleasure. Self-sacrifice was built into women's lives as chaste daughters and devoted mothers, but French writers focused repeatedly on the pleasures inherent in the tasks womanhood assigned the female sex. Writers' evocations of the pursuit of noble causes—philanthropy, kindness to the needy (and small animals), and human communication—all constituted avenues to a pleasure that strikes the reader accustomed to evangelical prescriptive literature as positively voluptuous. American moral writers agreed there was a certain pleasure in behaving correctly, but they usually concentrated on being sure the motives for the behavior were pure. In other words, the reward for self-reform was the chance to perform more self-reform. To be a good adult, the child must learn to inspect ruthlessly her or his conscience for impure motives. The scope for virtue was narrow and confined largely to the family. Its pursuit was freighted with self-doubt, and for evangelicals, its heavenly rewards were by no means assured. By contrast, French moralists promised good children the pleasures of happy participation in their social world and a heightened sense of self-satisfaction.[10]

Another important difference between the two systems of

thought is that French writers encouraged a wide-ranging, if superficial, empathy that included members of all classes, provided they were white. Moralists conceived of the relevant social world as an organic whole in which white people were joined by bonds of humanity, and cultivating those bonds gave pleasure and meaning to life. An underlying appreciation for nature and human nature was a touchstone for all. A badly lived life was one that failed to cultivate wholesome connections with others of all social levels.

The assumption underpinning this empathy was that people might lose their money, but they never lost their status in society. A lady remained a lady even in straitened circumstances. Similarly, a peasant who had made considerable money remained a peasant, if a wealthy one. This element of social predictability gave French Americans, particularly in St. Louis, a confident platform on which to advocate widespread empathy and benevolence. African slaves, however, were not included in the idealized world of the French moralists. While sharing common religious bonds—record books note numerous baptisms and marriages celebrated by slaves and free blacks in the Catholic Church—they were constrained by the French belief that the circumstances of one's birth in society were by far the most important determinant in shaping a French life. Being born black, in the French view, determined one's intellectual and moral capacities. Blackness brought with it the possibility, as the influential Abbé Raynal wrote in 1770, to "corrupt and destroy our people." Hence, separation of the races was required.[11]

In the United States the Catholic Church deferred to what it regarded as the rabid race prejudice of Americans and tried to include blacks in worship and education when possible. Although church officials were often racists and even slaveowners, many would have preferred the convenience and lower cost of integrated institutions. St. Louis Catholic officials looked to the largest diocese in America—Baltimore—for guidance on this moral and social issue, although St. Louis never went as far as did the Baltimore church in reaching out to free and enslaved blacks. Like St. Louis, Baltimore had both a well-established Catholic population and an influx of San Domingans in the first decade of the nineteenth century. Jacques Joubert, a

Sulpician priest, who had helped women escape from slavery, established an order of black nuns, some of them San Domingans. The
first members based this order on a vision of a kind of holy slavery
that emphasized service to the black community and the virtues of
charity, patience, meekness, and humility. The pope in 1831 approved the new order, which wanted black sisters to educate "young
women of color."[12]

Madame Duchesne, in deference to local prejudice, offered separate one-day-a-week education to those African American girls and
women who were able to avail themselves of it. "[O]therwise he
[Bishop Du Bourg] says, we should not hold the white children in
school. He told us how difficult it is to overcome race-prejudice in
this country." Bishop Du Bourg, who himself owned slaves, expressed interest in starting a "kind of Third Order of the Sacred
Heart for colored women, whom he wished the nuns to train for mission work . . . among the Negroes of Missouri and Louisiana."
Madame Duchesne wrote of a "mulatto," who "long[s] with her
whole heart to enter with us, but we may not accept her as a religious
[nun]." She speculated on a way to maintain separateness, recalling a
house in Paris for girls whom their parents had "complained of." "A
very edifying community was established for them, having its own
rule, but occupying a separate building. . . . Could not we, too, gather
together colored girls who want to leave their world and set aside for
them one or two of our own nuns until they would be able to continue on their own as a community or congregation according to
their own special calling?" As it stood, the place of African Americans
in the St. Louis Catholic world was to serve the nuns and priests but
not to be able to take orders.[13]

The French found it comfortable to regard Americans as more
racist than they were, but this may have been less evident to slaves.
Certainly, Catholicism was more inclusive than the Protestant de-
nominations, and its benefits included an implicit shared humanity.
Furthermore, some French refused to separate slave families. Also, a
more widespread ideal of empathy characterized most French Creoles and may have ameliorated conditions for some French slaves
compared with those owned by Anglo-Americans. On the other

hand, most French and Americans believed in the necessity of slavery and its attendant discipline. In light of this fundamental commitment, differences in style and attitude have only limited significance.

Americans trained their children in an even narrower empathy than that of the French, one that extended not much further than the family. Its goals were to bring pleasure to increasingly private life and to cement the blood family together against the strains of ambition, competition, and public temptations. Writers saw the family as the only bulwark against the chaos of the institutionalized instability of fortune and status that characterized the early United States. Family members were to be guarded against familiarity with strangers and friends alike. Corruption, temptation, misrepresentation, and danger were everywhere. Only in the bosom of the family could mothers teach and children learn the virtues that were essential to keeping America "safe." Moreover, in evangelical families the doubt surrounding salvation echoed and intensified social and economic uncertainties. For the French, society was already safe because positions in it were largely fixed and salvation relatively secure.[14]

In prescriptive French literature sudden reversals of fortune figured importantly, but these stories, unlike American ones, did not comment on economic or social instability so much as on the persistence of status in spite of bad luck. Writers like Arnaud Berquin, Jean François Marmontel, and the Comtesse de Genlis suggested that unlucky events might affect anyone at any time but that the social order itself was stable. Often stories hinged on restoring impoverished aristocrats to their fortunes. Occasionally, immoral individuals were punished by being replaced in their families by poor but worthy relatives or acquaintances. But the family and society remained intact, and true nobility was recognizable through poverty's disguises.[15]

American moral literature discussed reversals of fortune as well but assumed that they completely altered the status of the woman or family affected. If individual family members dramatically changed their economic status for the better, the family was threatened. Such changes might well indicate the abandonment of moral principles and the uncontrolled triumph of greed. In French stories, rising fortunes usually connoted the good management and good character of an already noble wife or child. They confirmed goodness; they did not threaten it. For American moralists the possibility of financial reversals was the reason why mistresses should treat their servants well; they might exchange places. Treating servants well, however, was a strategic precaution, not requiring empathy so much as diplomacy. And in Missouri, many servants were slaves, who required neither. Only family members merited the effort of empathy.[16]

Subsequent chapters will continue to compare French and Anglo-American moral and emotional styles and will explore, as far as possible, how these groups morally situated themselves relative to one another and to black women, free and slave. The experiences of German immigrant women who poured into Missouri after the 1830s provide another perspective on developments in the state. Because they arrived significantly after the Americans, they play a more peripheral role in this history and will appear in the text only as adult women. Their well-reinforced robust class divisions contrast with the more permeable barriers separating and identifying Anglo-Americans.

This section will also discuss the emergence and significance of two emotional and moral modes that developed with the growth of a middle class. The first of these I call sentimental individualism, a belief that spread rapidly after the American Revolution and embraced the right of white Americans to pursue their destinies and companions. Parental input in their children's choice of marriage partners had been diminishing since the first settlements and melted away most rapidly in the years after the Revolution. Though passion and the lack of restraint that it implied still carried the negative connotations of irrationality from the eighteenth century, men and women increasingly looked to marriage to be sustained by love, candor, and intimacy.[17]

The other important emotional and moral development in the early republic emerged as the complex of feelings and activities psychologist Carol Gilligan identified thirty years ago as relatedness. In Gilligan's research, women define their own moral worth on the basis of their ability to care for and respond to the needs of others. Thus they see their identities as interdependent with the identities of those for whom they care. This interdependent sense of self is in sharp distinction to that of white males, who see themselves as separate and independent rights-bearing economic and political individuals. These opposing senses of identity produce differing worldviews and distinct ideas about how to arrive at moral choices and behavior. Whereas a man will typically seek to answer a moral question by applying an inexorable or a universal rule, a woman will desire to settle things so that responsibilities are met and no one suffers. This reluctance to pronounce judgment on others, which has been traditionally seen as a sign of a weak conscience, derives from women's dependence on men for their material support and therefore encourages deference to their point of view. Women's choice is limited by their dependence, precisely as Whig political theorists argued when opposing political corruption that would occur because of economic dependence. In the Whig formulation male independence, based on land ownership, would free men to vote in their own interests. In this model, the dependence of the rich on the labor of poor and slaves was obscured, while the political and moral dilemma of dependent white workers was spotlighted. In Gilligan's formulation, women's dependence on men prevented them from ascribing to universal moral rules. In this configuration, male dependence on the physical and emotional work of women was obscured while many expressed ambivalence toward or disapproval of women's moral accommodations.[18]

Middle-class women dealt with the tension their dependence on their husbands created in a variety of ways, including elaborating a sentimental culture within their homes. This culture described and confined the white middle class within a landscape of sweet feelings, coziness, and sensitivity and excluded all others from its trust and intimacies. As one critic has written, sentimental culture "[encourages] depersonalization of those outside its complex specifications . . . [while] it elaborately personalizes, magnifies, and flatters those who can accommodate its image."[19]

GIRLS AND FREEDOM

Black girls in St. Louis and its hinterlands had abbreviated girlhoods. The great majority were slaves; most of them would not live with their mothers beyond fourteen, and a substantial number would be sold away much earlier. White people generally imagined for their girls a life of marriage, child rearing, religion, and domesticity. To the extent that slave parents indulged in hopes for theirs, it was for decent and humane owners, work that would not harm them, and loving connections not arbitrarily ended. Slave mothers also dreamed of freedom for their children, a dream that by its very nature put them outside American law and prevailing morality. In St. Louis freedom was a livelier hope than in many parts of the South. Illinois, a free state, was just across the Mississippi River, and St. Louis was filled with people moving in and moving on. Many parents did more than hope, seeking liberty in as many ways as possible, through self-purchase, the legal system, and running away. The problem with these, but most of all with escape, was that they imposed separations on families as abrupt, if not exactly as painful, as being sold away. Unfinished childhoods and brutal separations punctuated the lives of most African American girls, and mothers dreamed of freedom that would not impose more losses on their daughters. The mother-daughter relationship was often the closest tie in the African American complex of relations.[1]

Samuel Ringgold Ward, a fugitive slave, wrote, "The fugitive exercises patience, fortitude, and perseverance, connected with and fed by an ardent and unrestrained and resistless love of liberty, such as cause men to be admired everywhere." Ward's formulation has to be rethought for women. The "resistless love of liberty" did not cause women, white or black, to be admired everywhere or indeed anywhere in the early republic. African American women's appreciation of liberty was likely to be both more complicated and contingent than men's. Relatively few women ran, compared with men, and when they did, they sometimes ran with children.[2]

In West African societies being part of a web of kin and community connections defined identity and shaped labor, behavior, and obligations. Hence slavery, which tore people from their homes, extended families, and social worlds gave Africans an extra ration of pain and psychic trauma. African women's lives involved contact with numerous people, as well as rituals that affirmed their significance and maturity and expressed their connection with the natural and spiritual worlds. The social meaning of West African women's lives came in the context of their relationships with their own mothers, women's social groups, their children's husbands, and extended kin. The pleasures experienced in these relationships were the fundamental elements of human life. In West African societies, ties of blood were deeper and more valued than conjugal ties. Thus a woman's relationship to her children and her parents preceded in responsibility and emotional import her relationship with her husband.[3]

Slaves in the Upper South in the antebellum period had about a 30 percent chance of being sold away throughout their lifetimes, most likely when they were between twelve and twenty-five. In a new western state such as Missouri the chances that a slave had been transported, hence enduring some family breakup, or would be sold away were even higher. With the exception of observant Catholics in Perry County, there is little evidence that Missouri slaveowners took any particular notice of the family circumstances of slaves in transacting deals. In Boone County, 30 percent of children under fifteen years of age were sold off. In 1834 in Marion County, north of St. Louis, a slave trader bought three small children from an owner, but the children's mother killed them all and herself rather than let them be taken away. A St. Louis trader took a crying baby from its mother, both on their way to be sold, and made a gift of it to a white woman standing nearby because its noise was bothering him. In Callaway County little girls were sold away from their mothers frequently when they were as young as seven. Mary Bell was hired out by the year to take care of three children starting when she was seven. John Mullanphy noted that he had living with him a four-year-old mulatto girl, whom he willed to the Sisters of Charity in the event of his death. George Morton sold to his daughter Ellen "a certain Mulatto girl a slave about fourteen years of age named Sally, being the child of a certain Negro woman named Ann." The only state that put any conditions on sales that separated mothers and children was Georgia, which in 1854 passed a law about the settlement of the legacies of slaveowners who died intestate. It provided that children under five should not be sold away from their mothers "unless such divisions cannot in any wise be [e]ffected without such separation." The many newspaper advertisements, like one in the September 1835 *St. Louis Republican* that looked to buy "young slaves (two girls and one boy) each from 10 to 15 years of age," testified to the thriving market in children.[4]

Slave girls often wound up in the houses of aspiring white middle-class families. In 1819, William Lane wrote his wife about a mutual friend who had made the mistake of marrying a poor man and should, he thought, be pitied. "One hardship at present is the want of a girl: She [their friend] does most of the washing, in preference to paying $1. Per dozen.—when I last saw her, she endeavoured to hide her hands, but I distinctly saw that the skin was rub'd off her wrists & fingers." Probably the most significant difference among white wives was the presence or absence of a "girl." With some household help granting them free time, white wives could become the focus of family life, instilling sensitivity in their children and directing family attention toward religion and emotion. They were able to impart to their children the sense of attachment and accountability that was the earmark of middle-class membership and the qualification for success in the world of growing opportunities. Without a "girl," the workload was usually too much to do anything but raise children to help shoulder some of the burden.[5]

A "girl" was an all-purpose tool in family life. For wives without them, the work was never-ending, and many wished that they had not moved out west.[6] The word "girl" applied to any working female who did not yet have children. She might be a hired white or free black, but she was more likely to be a slave. If she was white and American, her employers might fret about her pretensions or the likelihood that she would leave. If she was white, she was also likely to place conditions upon her work and expect decent treatment. She might have come from Ireland, in which case she would have fewer options than would an American. But slaves were in most ways preferable. In the long run they cost less. Once the outlay of $350 to $400 was made, there was no weekly wage to worry about. An enslaved girl could be anywhere from nine or ten to her mid-teens. A typical ad for a "woman" requested slaves from "10 to 15 years of age." It added, "Subjects from the country would be preferred." (Slaves from St. Louis were harder to control. They were too worldly-wise and too likely to have family connections nearby. They also probably had some education.) Sometimes they were younger than nine.[7]

Wherever slavery existed it stigmatized manual labor of all kinds, but particularly heavy household work, which the "girl" was likely to do. In 1830 a priest wrote, regretfully, that the white brothers would not do the cooking or washing, take care of the cattle, or do the other household duties "in the land where there are negroes. For no one wants to be a subject, to do the lowest jobs in the house and sometimes even, this spirit of republican pride infects those who by their profession and their vocation ought to love dependence, submission, and humility." He missed half the point in assuming that this was an entirely racial prejudice, for of course it was also about gender.[8]

In one guise or another a "girl" solved labor problems in a wide range of white families, rural and urban, middle class and aspiring.

Because she had no gender in her work life, a "girl" was able to be put to almost any kind of work. She provided freedom for other girls to be young, nurtured, and educated. Without her, household work overwhelmed white women and made them turn to their daughters for aid. Without her, middle-class husbands noticed that their wives were exhausted and miserable. A "girl," especially if she was black, required no financial or emotional maintenance, no empathy. She was drawn in disappearing ink.[9]

White Relatedness: Letters Home, 1820–1845

The thriving market in black (and to a much lesser degree white and Indian) girls made possible the mass training of white girls to be ladies. The first generations of St. Louis girls to be sent to boarding schools in the early nineteenth century learned to be members of the city's new, growing elite. Girls' letters suggest that the boarding school experience identified them as privileged not only by the kinds of knowledge they acquired and the kinds of activities in which they became proficient but also by emotional characteristics: enhanced dependency and a highly developed attention to relationships. For these girls, an anxious focus on separation shaped their understanding of being female, endowing one of the supposedly natural female priorities with special force. The new emphasis on dependent intimacy, enhanced in some by the experience of boarding school through separation from home as well as passionate friendships at school, burdened many nineteenth-century elite women with special sensitivity to and anxiety about separation.[10]

Through the first four decades of the nineteenth century in and around St. Louis, the precise intellectual content of privileged girls' education was in dispute, but most still shared the assumptions of the previous century: that girls were to learn to be pleasing company and to ornament genteel domestic life. As William Lane deliberated over a name for a new daughter, he wrote that he wanted a "decent Christian-like appellative, which will sound well either in prose or poetry, and which a plain, blunt, western-man, (to whom I hope to marry her some 20 years hence,) will think becoming." Girls needed to be acquainted with a body of refined literature, to acquire attractive handwriting, and to speak and write with some grace in both French and English. Unlike elite southerners, who believed their girls and boys should have a relatively equivalent education, educators in Missouri generally favored an education for girls that emphasized literature over science and correct behavior over great intellectual exertion.[11]

A significant but implicit lesson girls learned, which derived from their experience of being away from home and parents, was heightened concern for the maintenance of relationships. Raised in a mobile culture in which separations were omnipresent, girls understood the stark necessity of relationships as well as their fragility.

Relatedness, which Carol Gilligan has posited as fundamental to the female psychological and moral maturation process, is a quality that can be accentuated or diminished by place and circumstance. Since the late eighteenth century, middle-class society valued relatedness in women and saw it as a moral imperative, not just a natural characteristic. Among late-eighteenth-century gentry, in both Great Britain and America, the intensity of the experience of relationship, empathy, and feeling for others came to mark refinement and sensibility. Exhibiting these feelings was one sign of membership in the elite. Similarly, independence, the foundation of manliness, was contingent upon the ownership of property; thus it too was class-specific in the eighteenth century. Both sexes can and do experience both relatedness and independence, but strong variations exist in the way the need for relationship figures in the imagination, and these variations are at least partly socially produced. For middle- and upper-class girls in the early nineteenth century, when the need for and care of relationships were their highest priorities, the experience of separation on going away to boarding school was not a secondary experience incident to the acquisition of education as it was for boys. It was in itself an object lesson in the value and cultivation of relationships.[12]

By leaving home for educational institutions where girls learned that correct behavior and tending to relationships were more impor-

tant than any intellectual achievements they might attain, girls naturally nurtured a preoccupation with and anxiety about relatedness
that came to be identified with middle-class attributes like the much
celebrated tender heart, melting disposition, sweetness, and dependence on the presence and approval of others. Parents also explicitly
tutored daughters in the appropriate degrees of relatedness to sustain among different kinds of intimates.

Elite Franco- and Anglo-American girls' letters reveal mild involvement with or curiosity about their studies. Sara Lane, in a letter
to her father, wrote that she would "tri to appli my salf to my book."
The nearly ubiquitous apology for a letter's appearance and excuse
for its brevity or poor writing are the one exception to girls' disinterest in their education. Their anxieties about their intellectual abilities
coalesced in wishing to carry out their epistolary relationships and
responsibilities elegantly. Letter writing was widely known to be
woman's work in the nineteenth century, and girls learned early to
deprecate their correspondence.[13]

Absence and its attendant insecurities may have accelerated a
tendency in girls to criticize their own performances. They persistently refer to their inadequacies as writers and as partners in relationships. The apologies helped relieve anxiety while demonstrating
the desire to please and a humble willingness to accept blame for
failures. They also show how difficult it was to acquire and wield the
rhetoric of elite women.[14]

Adult correspondents trained girls to see their letters as social
performances, the appearance and correctness of which would influence others' opinions of them. Wealthy girls' performance would include the ability to display facility in both English and French. Julia
de Mun wrote painstakingly that she had not written her father for a
long time but that she hoped her "letter . . . will please you better
than any one that you have received from me because it is in English
and I assure you that no person did correct it." Penmanship was also
an essential part of the performance in letters. Bryan Mullanphy
wrote a young niece: "It looks very pretty in a little girl to write a neat
& clean hand." He recounted the story of a young girl living in a
small village in France who wrote asking a favor of a wealthy man.

"That person was so delighted with the neatness of her letters, that he sent for the young woman and granted her request. In addition to this, he presented her with a handsome portion and gave her away in marriage to a distinguished officer in the army." In other words, a girl's future fortunes could depend significantly on how others responded to her.[15]

Girls blamed themselves with monotonous frequency for being faulty correspondents. Behind the excuses they tried to calibrate just the right amount of attention to pay to each relationship to secure it. At the heart of all these letters, exchanging news or simply greetings, was a desire to stay in touch with all those people who secured these girls in their world and constituted them as members of their family and their family's community. Over and over, the letters reflect their writers' desire for and effort to sustain relatedness. Jane mentioned hearing from her "dear mother," about her sister Anne's illness, about baby Meziere's learning to walk, about hoping her aunts would visit, about a schoolmate who would be visiting St. Louis, about writing to her sister Ellen, about sending a greeting to a different aunt, and about her intentions to write still another aunt.[16]

Girls' letters are usually deferential in tone and free from complaints, except to note correspondents from whom they have heard nothing. Sometimes they express openly the fear of being forgotten. Jules de Mun, in writing to his daughter Louise, after complaining that her sisters had not written, expressed the unthinkable: "I hope that you, dear child, will not forget me and that you will write me quite often." The possibility of being forgotten posed an existential threat, one that might terrify a girl alone, where the lifelines from home were so vital and scarce. Americans in St. Louis were people who had just arrived and had left people behind. Health along the river was often poor, and lives were often cut short. Exchanges of phrases of remembrance, so commonplace as to be invisible, exposed the underlying fragility of relationships frighteningly visible when a girl was sent from home.[17]

In their letters parents trained girls to nurture a circle of reciprocal relationships usually limited to people of their own class and color. Adults gave a wide variety of explicit and implicit instructions on which members of the household merited full relationships. Family news sometimes included greetings from and news about servants and slaves, but such news was sporadic and phrased to emphasize the nonreciprocity of the relationship. In a letter to his girls in school in Philadelphia, William Lane wrote a note introducing an acquaintance named Samuel Owens, whom he described as a "backwoods gentleman" they would "see at once where to place." He continued by saying that with all the "half-bred, & the vulgar" they should adopt a more carefully courteous attitude than with well-bred people or they might "fancy themselves to be overlooked, and are apt to be offended." It was important for his girls to recognize fine gradations of rank among people if for no other reason than to marry within or above their own. But as Americans and members of a democracy, they also needed to know how to pretend to overlook those gradations.[18]

The letters of privileged girls expressed the underlying, sometimes explicit, more often implicit concern of their education: to nourish the relationships on which they did and would continue to depend. Girls learned to stir up the embers of affection and remembrance and to prevent absence from meaning disappearance. While relatedness is an aspect of the human condition and particularly the female human condition, it was in the early nineteenth century an important aspect of an elite girl's education. Her special susceptibility to the demands of relationships as well as her mastery of their subtleties marked her as a member of a privileged class.

The other key aspect of class training for white girls was sexual restraint. Middle-class membership demanded modesty for girls. Middle-class young men and women found themselves surrounded by a wide-ranging and often silly collection of rules. The rules circumscribed middle-class social contact, but they could also be a source of hilarity as young men and women tried to sort out for themselves how far propriety required them to practice reproving silences and circumlocutions. These social strictures provoked men to challenge them and young women to find them ridiculous. But middle-class women usually found it safer to obey and mock them than to defy them altogether.[19]

Sometimes confusion and incomprehension resulted as young women tried to assume properly modest and virtuous airs without

knowing what they were defending. "A matter of fact man" described, in a newspaper article, his utter inability to understand the
conduct of a young woman whom he offered to accompany home
one evening. She did not speak to him but took his arm. He did not
know whether she wanted him to walk her home or not. She did not
say a word to him, nor did she the next time they met. During a third
meeting she talked to him for two hours, worrying that he was offended "but could not conceive why. She begged me to explain; but
gave me no chance." She asked him to call on her. Yet after he saw
her through her window one day, he called but was told she was not
at home. When they next saw each other, she criticized him for ne-
glecting her. For his part, the author criticized the young lady for acting in a way that she thought was both genteel and alluring but that
was merely confusing. Hers was the behavior of someone unsure
whether or not to do what she was told to do by a man she did not
know and could not yet assess. He searched for facts, but she had
been taught postures.[20]

A burdensome code of restraint combined with pretensions to
gentility could powerfully constrain girls' ability to identify and consult their own wishes. The notion of sentimental individualism for
girls who had been raised to subdue not only their own behavior but
also that of the males around them had a pronounced logical incon-
sistency. Young women knew that even more important than divining
their own desires was the need to protect themselves. One young
woman recorded her fear of the ease with which some misreported
or misunderstood indiscretion could destroy a woman socially.
Her strategy was to withhold sentimental information, to behave
prudently, to be vigilant. In her journal she remarked on "how very
careful ought ladies to be—The least word or look is remembered—
there is always someone to catch at any thing and when least thought
of it is remembered." Restraint, not candor, informed this woman's
behavior with young men.[21]

In trying to assure girls' modesty, American moralists cautioned
them against vanity in dress. Girls were to keep sight of the seriousness of choosing husbands on right principles, not on sexual attraction or money, and to make sure that they did not dress beyond their

means. Finally, one way or another, moralists usually wound up stressing that attention to externals inevitably distracted from attention to internal issues of morality.[22]

Although the French trained daughters to premarital chastity, they did so without trying to repress pleasure in self-adornment, flirtation, and emotional expressivity. The Catholic Church did not find coquettish behavior on the part of young women looking for husbands much of a sin. Moral writers did try to discourage flirtation, but the ethicist Jean Benedicti came close to sanctioning it, calling it "at the very most a venial sin." Marmontel described efforts to please in women as moral excellence.[23]

In St. Louis the French enjoyed the pleasures of dress, flirtation, and the stylized but relatively free play of feeling. Emilie de Mun wrote her cousin in 1842 that she had been "very much abused" in St. Louis, although she admitted "that [she] was wild." She went on to say that she had changed but shed doubt immediately on her claim by asking her cousin to tell her friend Mr. March "that she hopes often again to be able to drink eight glasses of champagne with him and try to walk a line on the rug without swaying from side to side."

Other parts of Emilie's letter recorded her feelings with all their contradictions and drama, one after another, as they came to her. "Sometimes, dear Louise, I get into sad moods, and I believe then that death would be welcome to me—I miss my mother very much, even more than I thought I should have done." Some of the letter was devoted to the special affection she had for Louise, to whom she felt she could say anything. She signed off, "Goodbye dearest one . . . and believe me ever your devoted & attached." The letter is remarkable for its effusive affection and unimpeded communication of a wide range of emotions. While decorum and sexual continence were essential to elite French girls, the St. Louis French had a spontaneous emotive ability less often expressed among Anglo-Americans. The French Americans trained their daughters in less repressive ways than Anglo-Americans. Nor did they destine their girls to arbitrate society's sexual morality.[24]

The deep moral and social value Anglo-American middle-class

parents gave to their daughters' chastity and training in the maintenance of relationships stands out even more dramatically when compared with the way slave society tried to strip both relationships and
sexual continence from black girls.

Relationships were the only positive context for middle-class
white girls. Conversely it was essential for the slaveholding world
to describe female slaves without relationships. It thus kept black
girls suspended in what was, for a woman, an amoral world. Louisa,
twelve, and Clara, thirteen, runaway slaves advertised in the *St.
Louis Enquirer*, were described in language designed to make criminals of them. The newspaper focused exclusively on their appearance. One was "small for her age," and the other was "middle size,
African face, heavy built." Clara had "toes somewhat turned inwards
and scattering," while Louisa had "slender feet for a negro." More
tellingly, Louisa had a "bad face and bad expression." In the absence
of any mention of family and with a few details, the girls became sin-
ister adults. Their owner, on the other hand, was described in terms
of her tender relationships and, just as compelling, her lack of them:
a "helpless widow" with "three little children." In a couple of eco-
nomical strokes, Henrietta Jacobs emerged as vulnerable, virtuous,
and in need of protection from these delinquents.[25]

The girls may have been sisters and were likely just separated
from their mother. The emotion-laden word "orphan" was never applied to slave children, whereas white children missing only fathers
qualified. Similarly, "poverty" was never used to describe the economic condition of slaves. By describing Clara and Louisa without
the connections that would have situated them in the moral world of
females, the editor deprived their behavior of emotional and ethical
logic. Thus they bore the implicit blame not only for their flight but
also, by the editor's comparison with their owner, for their absence of
family. They emerged from their description as unlovely and unlov-
able—loners by choice—miscreants with malicious countenances,
not motherless girls running from misery. A one-line item in the *St.
Louis Beacon* about a "coloured girl" of eleven years and two months
who "gave birth to a healthy female child" expressed, by omission,
the white community's view of this abused and exploited little girl.[26]

Family details would have transformed the stories of female slaves into tragedies about little girls raped and abused, not demonstrations of the unregulated passions and fecundity of African Americans. This disparity points to the inability of slaves—and free African Americans as well—to control the public moral and emotional meaning of their own experiences. Just as shattering, the social isolation of slave girls may have prevented them from holding on to their own understanding of these experiences. If the girls had been sold away from their mothers, as seems likely given their vulnerability, they might have had no one to affirm their version of who was responsible for what happened to them and what it meant. In addition to the traumas of rape and childbirth at young ages, the girls would assume the blame for their victimization. What had been confusing, painful, and deeply frightening experiences would never be recognized or treated as such.[27]

Robert Newson, a seventy-year-old Missouri grandfather, was in want of a "girl" and bought fourteen-year-old Celia. He raped her on the way back from purchasing her and continued to rape her over the next five years. By this time she was pregnant with their third child and sick. According to the testimony of Newson's daughter, Celia threatened to harm him if he continued to rape her while she felt sick, but he came to her cabin anyway. She hit him twice with a stick, killing him. She burned his body in the fireplace and later spread his ashes on the pathway. In court Celia's lawyer said she had the same right of self-defense as a free Missouri woman would have had and that Newson's purchase of a slave woman did not include the right to rape her. The judge instructed the jury, to the contrary, that Newson should have been able to come to her cabin for any reason and to have had intercourse with his girl slave when he wanted. The jury found against Celia, and pregnant and possibly still sick, she escaped from jail. She was returned. She was not executed until she had delivered Newson's third baby, a potential slave, but stillborn. Celia was hanged sometime in the winter of 1855–56.[28]

African slaves knew, without being told, what researchers now tell us about healing the damage of psychic trauma. They knew that for life to have meaning, it must be lived out in sustaining relationships

with others. When slavery threatened to overwhelm the value of being alive, they knew that "recovery [could] take place only within the
context of relationships; it [could] not occur in isolation." Some have
argued that the maternal role inhibited female slaves from running
away. It would be incorrect to say that children stood in the way of
mothers' realizing their "resistless love of liberty." Maternity indeed
sometimes healed some of the psychic damages of slavery. Mothers
and fathers could find in their children the motivation to cherish,
protect, and love, acts that inherently affirm the value of life. The
needs of children, however hard for parents to fulfill, provided goals
that taught patience, fortitude, and perseverance. Mothers were
more likely to strengthen these skills in the context of facilitating the
survival of another, not in solitary heroic feats. If daughters became
free, mothers often had a hand in it, either practically or emotionally,
or both. Liberty, among the most frequently invoked words in the
antebellum period, commonly meant for white women emotional
freedom of expression. For slave girls it meant something much
more tangible, the freedom to live with their families, especially their
mothers, unmolested.[29]

Bitter Lessons:
Incidents in the Lives of Slave Girls

Precisely the qualities that society fetishized in white girls were sys-
tematically denied to black girls: chastity, dependence, refined sensibility. White notions that dependence and hypersensitivity were
attractive parts of a young woman's character were foreign and indeed subversive to the experience and needs of slave girls. While
moralists, with unwholesome fervor, thrust on white girls the responsibility for national chastity, slaveowners routinely stripped it from
black girls. And whereas white girls learned to cultivate men who
would take care of them, black girls on plantations and in towns had
to learn to take care of themselves. The most thrilling dream for a
slave girl was freedom, not marriage. Slave mothers tried to raise independent daughters because most slave girls simply would not be

able to count on anyone else. Furthermore, the production of white girls suitably dependent upon their mothers, fathers, and husbands required bonded female labor.[30]

Because Missouri was just across the Mississippi River from Illinois, St. Louis slaves often sought their freedom. But proximity to the border worked both ways, and free blacks in Illinois were not particularly secure in their liberty. Slave catchers brought them back to Missouri long before the 1850 Fugitive Slave Law required their return. In addition, in southern Illinois, a proslavery region, legally free blacks were sometimes held as slaves. St. Louis had a thriving slave market, which sent large gangs of chained-together slaves down the Mississippi to be sold in the lower South. Slave girls dealt with the possibility of freedom, the reality of exploitation, and the shocks of separation.[31]

The parents of enslaved children in St. Louis and its environs craved freedom for their children despite its high emotional cost. Freedom could mean the severance of ties with one's family, a pain not unlike that of being sold away. If a mother wanted freedom for her child, she might have to face losing her forever, and the child had to be independent enough to leave. Paradoxically, finding the strength to be free often came from loving relationships. Sufficient love and care were required to render a girl or boy secure enough to dream of freedom and to imagine giving up that love and care.

Polly Wash's daughters, Nancy and Lucy, clearly grew up believing that freedom, no matter how it was obtained, was sufficiently valuable for them to stay alert for any possibility of achieving it. They also believed that after reaching the age of competence they should be strong enough to leave their mother if freedom required it. They further believed that leading a double emotional life—one genuine and one of faked subservience and simulated accord with white rule—was a necessary expedient for life in an unjust society. Both sisters married, but freedom, not romance, gave direction to their lives. Both were raised to be self-reliant, watchful, brave, and discreet. These were not typical middle-class girls' values, and they helped create forceful, careful women capable of acts of heroism.

Polly Wash's epic battle for freedom provides some links to her daughters' struggles. The theme of separation is omnipresent. Separation or just the fear of it caused pain deep enough to motivate enormous risk-taking and life-changing events. Polly, a slave born in Kentucky, was purchased at seven, and at fourteen went with her owner, Joseph Crockett, to Madison County, Illinois. She therefore lost her mother completely at fourteen, if the separation had not actually been final seven years before. Although living in the free state of Illinois had legally entitled Polly to her freedom, in 1821 Crockett sold her to a Major Berry who lived in St. Louis. She married one of Berry's slaves and had Lucy and Nancy. Berry died, and his wife, Fanny, inherited Polly, her husband, and her children. Fanny Berry subsequently married Judge Robert Wash, and when she died, Robert Wash sold Polly's husband downriver. During her years in St. Louis, Polly worked as a seamstress, laundress, and nurse.

Nancy escaped to Canada after the sale of her father (Polly's husband). At that point, Nancy's erstwhile owner sold Polly to a slave trader, Joseph Magehan, who took her downriver. Lucy remained with Polly's former owner. Polly managed to escape and walked to Chicago, but she returned to St. Louis when she began to fear for Lucy's safety on account of her escape. In 1839 Polly sued Magehan for her freedom and damages to pay for her time as a slave in the free territory of Illinois. Four years later she won her liberty but only a single dollar in damages in the St. Louis circuit court, payment for four years of illegal servitude in a free state. (Ironically, she sued successfully on the same grounds that failed to support Dred Scott's suit in the heated climate of the late 1850s.) In 1844 she sued for Lucy's freedom on the basis that a child's condition follows its mother's. She and Lucy won.[32]

Lucy Delaney, Polly's daughter and the principal narrator of this drama, recorded in her memoir Polly's elation over the escape of Nancy. She recorded how her mother put on a show of irritation and displeasure for her owners. Yet slave mothers who prepared their children for freedom had to reckon with the possibility of a separation as permanent as those caused by sales. They also had to consider that those left behind might be used as hostages in blackmailing the runaways. All slaves had to balance the value of freedom against the possibility of lifelong separations from beloved family members. Children early learned the paradox that freedom became more thinkable when slave life was most unbearable, probably at moments of extreme suffering over the loss of parents or children. Otherwise the commitment of African American mothers and daughters to each other could make the choice to escape nearly as agonizing as being sold.[33]

Mattie Jackson's story of childhood in St. Louis demonstrates how close slavery and freedom could be in a border state. Mattie and her parents tried to realize their dreams of freedom, but partial separation, complete separation, and fear of separation shaped their lives. In slavery the Jacksons were a divided family. Mattie's father walked twenty miles every Sunday from his owner's place in St. Charles, north of St. Louis, to see her and her mother in the village of Bremen. Mattie and her mother were then forced to endure the sale of her father, taking him farther from them. Eventually Jackson, discouraged by his inability to see his family even once a week, escaped to Chicago, where he wrote his wife and children letters that never arrived.

Two years after his escape Mattie's mother, Mattie, and her sister ran away, preferring the greater risk of trying to flee together to the anguish of running separately. They reached Illinois in two days, but they were caught and taken back to St. Louis before they could reach Chicago.[34]

As the lives of Polly Wash and Mattie Jackson make clear, abrupt, wrenching separations with attendant feelings of abandonment, despondency, and unfulfilled dependency characterized numerous slave childhoods. But these narratives also show that separations did not necessarily cripple and that the example of strong parents, particularly strong mothers, made children capable of bearing heavy burdens of responsibility, sorrow, and loneliness.[35]

If white girls learned relatedness, black girls learned to labor independently. At twelve Lucy Delaney was given the job of taking care of an infant and soon was ordered to do the laundry. Laundry was probably the most common job performed by black women, slave and free, in St. Louis and elsewhere. Of the twenty-nine free black women listed in the city register for 1838, seventeen de-

clared washerwoman their trade. Laundry was so extremely time-
consuming and laborious that it was the chore that Catharine
Beecher singled out for housewives to pay someone else to do if they
had any discretionary cash whatsoever. William Lane's sister specified that she would pay for her own laundry when she came to visit
"to prevent any thing unpleasant." One wash required fifty gallons of
water, which weighed around four hundred pounds. In St. Louis a
laundress was likely to get the water from the Mississippi. She often
had to provide her own soap; that meant boiling animal fats, ashes,
and lye together. Riverboats sold ashes to women at the wharves.
The laundress sorted the clothes, soaked them overnight, then
scrubbed and wrung them out. At that point, she covered them with
water and boiled them on a stove or over an open fire, stirring with a
wash stick. Not only was it backbreaking, but also in St. Louis it was
mysterious to the uninitiated. Lucy Delaney recalled: "After soaking
and boiling the clothes in . . . the earthy depths [of the Mississippi],
for a couple of days, in a vain attempt to get them clean, and rinsing
them through several waters, I found the clothes were getting darker
and darker, until they approximated," she added with dry humor,
"my own color." Eventually Lucy learned from other slave women
the secrets of river rinsing, but not without being whipped first for
stained laundry.[36]

If white mothers and fathers looked to marriage as the great goal
of their daughters' lives, coping with separation was the best and
worst of slave life. Emotional strength and independence were the
variables that predicted how slave girls and women would react to a
sudden sale or to an opportunity for freedom. When slaves formulated their own moral code with freedom and human connection at
its center, they condemned the majority of Americans who participated in or passively condoned slavery, placing the protection of
property, particularly property in people, at the heart of white freedom. No paternalistic compromise could reach slaves who were so
profoundly, morally estranged from the dominant society.[37]

Many records attest to mothers' wishing for their daughters' freedom, but none exists to demonstrate a slave mother's wish to see her
daughters marry. In Missouri slave marriage was forbidden by law

though this did not stop many slaves from marrying. But slave mothers knew that marriage would have no legal support. Slave women's experience of being exploited not only for their labor but also for their sexuality and their reproductive capacities underlay broader claims for ownership of their bodies. To them it made little sense to cede rights to their bodies to husbands after claiming them back from slaveowners. Hence the apparent exclusion of marriage from their hopes for their daughters may have represented an early radical critique of marriage as duplicating aspects of slavery for women.[38]

Thus freedom, including the freedom to control their bodies and to sustain their maternal and social obligations, shaped the moral views of black women. It was freedom to form and carry out the duties and enjoy the pleasures of relationships. It derived not simply from the biological facts of motherhood but also from African traditions of extended maternal and infant intimacy and the solidarity of women's societies. The sudden, traumatic separations of slavery threw into relief the strength-giving and healing potential of ties between parents and children, particularly mothers and daughters. Paradoxically, the stronger these ties, the greater the ability of slaves to bear the consequences of freedom.[39]

15

ST. LOUIS MARRIAGES:

CROSS-CULTURAL PERSPECTIVES

ON SEX, LAW, AND FEELING

Oh, it is sweet to hear the sigh
That trembles on the lip of beauty!
To wipe the dew that wets the eye
Of her who pines 'tween love and duty!
—"Woman," *St. Louis Enquirer*,
October 27, 1819

The American Revolution confirmed a belief in voluntarism, the right of all to choose freely and to pursue happiness. The increasing insistence on the moral correctness of sentiment meant that feeling was to be respected.[1]

Puritans had also advocated love in marriage, but the nineteenth-century idea of love differed in essential ways. Puritan men were to be attracted to their wives, and women were to believe they could willingly serve their husbands, but for both sexes earthly happiness was serendipitous; the goal was to serve and glorify God through well-ordered family life, not emotional satisfaction. Virginians too had looked for affection in marriage, but obligation and the subordination of wives were components of domestic arrangements that outweighed and often displaced dreams of happiness. In nineteenth-century ideology, woman's love had displaced both divine love and women's subordination at the core of domestic experience. Her exercise of sentimental individualism—her free choice of her husband—was the foundation of the loving home.

Women were indeed free to choose whom to love, but new ideas about womanly love as unrelenting and redemptive, giving significance to and rewarding life's struggles, made it duty as well as freedom. Numerous St. Louis newspapers published poems and stories confirming the expectation of both men and women that the affection and instruction of wives and mothers purveyed the existential meaning of family life.

Fundamental to this ideal view was the tenderhearted and vulnerable woman, loving, long-suffering, giving meaning to a weary man's daily struggles by her patient sweetness. The corollary of this view was that women experienced love more deeply and fully than men and hence suffered more when it went awry. Intensity of dependent love could also be dangerous. The heroine who died, or was about to die, of a broken heart was a commonplace in fiction of the period, and she appeared in numerous St. Louis newspaper stories.[2]

Woman's love was to be a potent force for national good. Her loving and quiet heroism "brings down the conqueror, calms the stormy soul, and forces the blood-thirsty monarch of the wild to kneel and worship." Woman was all-powerful unless she actually tried to rule. If she tried to use power, "[t]hen comes a returning darkness, deeper than has yet been upon the earth." National purposes depended on the elevation of the female character. This belief was part of the larger providential history of the United States, which women wrote as well as read. History began with the birth of Jesus, moved briskly to the English Civil War, and lingered over the United States, which was leading the world into a new reign of Christendom. Such histories saw the Reformation as only partially completed and looked to the United States to lead the conversion of the rest of the world.[3]

Woman's transcendent self, not her material or carnal one, was crucial to this endeavor. She could be an angel by serving "the godly part of her nature." But if she misguidedly chose to compete on the material plane with man, she was foolish. Furthermore, if she chose

to please her senses, she became a prostitute. Worse, female impurity endangered the mental and physical health of American men. St.
Louis newspapers looked to rural wives as the touchstone of practi-
cality and rational republican virtue. According to the author of
"What a Farmer Wants," the farmer looking for a bride desires "a stable mind," industriousness, steadiness, and someone to soothe his
cares. With this in hand he will then enjoy "bliss unknown / To those
the world calls greatest / Known only to the good alone." In this fantasy of the rewards of simplicity, the farmer's wife was to be part of
his bliss, although it is less clear if she was to experience it herself.
The poem exudes nostalgia for an arcadian—or idealized republican—past, when wealth and idleness did not attract the good yeo-
man, and his wife made him her only object of concern.[4]

At the same time, the urban middle class was intent on differentiating itself both from the sexual looseness that it believed characterized the poor and from rusticity. Middle-class people mocked the
rude and uneducated for pretending to a culture that they could not
possess. In published stories rustic people mime their betters, imperfectly reproduce polite discourse, and generally make fools of
themselves. This dialogue parallels newspaper squibs devoted to the
presumed pretensions and ignorance of slaves. Malapropisms and
ridiculous conclusions characterize both groups. St. Louis, fifteen
years after statehood, had a self-conscious middle class, defending
itself against imitators and interlopers. The young city celebrated
agrarian virtue in nostalgic verse but skewered the ignorance and social pretensions of farmers in satiric prose.[5]

The increasing authority given to refined feeling in domestic life
defined and was limited to the middle class. Moral authorities specifically exempted the "lower orders," as well as rural folk, from being
capable of empathy, hence of deserving it themselves. Coming from
poverty into "service" was a rude shock, one that the poor made with
difficulty. *The Young Lady's Own Book* told women that servants
could not be expected to have good values on their own and that it
was up to mistresses to set examples they could follow. In a world in
which the possession of sympathy and empathy defined the sensibility of members of the middle class, the lack of these powers was a

moral deficiency and represented a threat to the master's security as well. Even moralist Abigail Mott, who argued for empathy with black children, agreed that the poor were prone to habits of "idleness and dissipation." Empathetic wives would ensure that they would understand and sympathize with their husbands' interests. Understanding would obviate the presumed but now infrequently articulated need for obedience.[6]

The moral vision of marriage as female submission and of women as industrious helpmeets still activated traditional women, particularly rural women. In a world where husbands still exercised the ultimate authority at home and female self-sacrifice was the ultimate virtue and foundation of the republic, it was still exceptional for women to believe that their emotional lives would be a central concern of their marriages. The goal of traditional marriage had been, and still was for the majority of families, an economic partnership, which could be tested by its productivity. This moral vision entailed a view of life that was founded on thrift, industry, regular habits, and limited horizons.[7]

Refashioning assorted ideas of emotional satisfaction, obedience, and work, evangelical women spliced together a third ideal view of marriage as submission to God and the realization of a meaningful life by executing His desires. They rejected conventional earthly pleasure and sentimental individualism, substituting in their stead joy in executing the divine will and "liberty" in expressing it. The freedom they aspired to was a flowing, unrestrained emotional state, not something they expected from marriage. In submitting to their husbands, they looked for liberation from the individual self in union with God. Mary Sibley, evangelical St. Louis educator, often mentioned the experience of freedom in the context of prayer—e.g., "Had some freedom in prayer." Evangelicals also spoke of their experience of freedom from the slavery or bondage of sin or a concern with worldliness and self. The emotional goal was the relief felt in throwing off restraints in accord with God's will.[8]

These ideas about love, virtue, the safety of the republic, the imperatives of sentimental individualism, and emotional spontaneity and its dangers all took shape in a context of ethnic diversity in which the cultural traditions of various groups mingled or collided with stereotypes and fears about one another's cultures. The French seem to have been the most emotionally expressive and to have incorporated sentimental individualism most thoroughly. The Anglo-Americans seem both to have yearned for emotional freedom and greatly to have feared it. They routinely projected this freedom onto African Americans, who, paradoxically, had to bear the burden of hiding most feelings and shaping those they displayed.

From the sixteenth through the eighteenth centuries the French elite female world of feeling and sentiment had preeminence over the Renaissance male values of domination and patriarchy. Key to the increased importance given to sentiment and tenderness was the reevaluation of marriage as representing a highly evolved and enviable form of equal and shared love. French women moralists of the Enlightenment, like the Comtesse de Genlis, admired Rousseau, whose *Émile* and *La Nouvelle Héloïse* confirmed sex in virtuous and tender relationships as one of life's great pleasures. As the reputation of marriage changed and improved, so too did the reputation of women and their values.[9]

The French saw woman's sexual role not as innocent novice or partner in a holy and blessed relationship but as redeemer and sensible regulator of passion. Unlike Americans who would not openly write of a woman's sexual agency or domain, French moralists thought women should manage the sexuality in a marriage. Marmontel wrote a story set in a harem in which the pleasures of a love chosen rather than a love imposed so intrigue the bored Soliman II that he proposes marriage to the European Roxalana, forsaking "his slaves from Asia." Roxalana announces that she will share his throne with him, and if he will not do that, to please send her home, "where all pretty women are sovereigns, and much more absolute than I should be here, for they reign over hearts." As Soliman conducts Roxalana to the mosque to marry, he asks himself, "Is it possible that a little turned-up nose should overthrow the laws of an empire?" The answer is obviously yes, that a woman's right to refuse sexual access to herself gave Western women power denied in the "Orient."[10]

American moralists found heterosexual life more problematic.

Abigail Mott exhorted "females" to "maintain their proper dignity." If they would "discountenance that familiarity which gives confidence to the other sex . . . it would contribute very much to the improvement of society." She looked to a repressive female propriety to reform men and institute a single standard of chastity for all. Lydia Maria Child, in telling mothers not to let their daughters learn about sex from anyone but them, cautioned, "[V]ery often their young minds are polluted with filthy anecdotes of vice and vulgarity. . . . A girl who receives her first ideas of these subjects from the shameless stories and indecent jokes of vulgar associates, has in fact prostituted her mind by familiarity with vice. A diseased curiosity is excited."[11]

Both American authors wrote of the pleasure of domestic relations in terms like "holy and blessed," making marriage's earthly pleasures sacred. Child cautioned mothers not to criticize the marriage relation or to urge their daughters to "enjoy themselves while they're single." While warning mothers not to reveal the dark side of marriage, Child insisted on the respectability and pleasure of remaining single for women. Anglo-American moral writers presented sexual relations in this period in America as dangerous and a potential source of conflict between the sexes. Women's goals in marriage were a sacred union in which they would improve themselves, their children, and their husbands morally. Sexual and emotional contentment was not necessarily to be expected. Furthermore, women were expected not to forgive or try to reform sexually impure men. Their tools were to be withdrawal, disapproval, and, in the extreme cases of sexual purity activists, exposure and public shame.[12]

Anglo-Americans, African Americans: Emotion and Sexuality

The legal condition of slaves in Missouri fell into doubt twice between 1800 and 1820. First, when the United States took over the territory, enslaved blacks anticipated liberation, hoping that the freedom granted people in the Northwest Territory would apply to those living in the Louisiana Territory as well. Then, in 1820, was when it was unclear whether Missouri would enter the Union as a free or a slave state. The battle ranged over economic and moral grounds, embracing the emotional and sexual role of black women.

Since many of the lawyers who were proslavery were bachelors, as Thomas Hart Benton was at the time, critics accused them of wanting slavery to provide for their sexual desires. As an article in the *Missouri Gazette* said, "Is the right to engage in the discussion of slavery and give an . . . opinion upon it, really confined and secured to none but an old sinful, obdurate bachelor, a father of negroes, and a murderer?" Most of Missouri wanted unrestricted slavery in the state, but many worried about making available illicit sexual opportunities to passionate men who were precisely those creating a corrupt and self-interested public political and economic sphere. White men carrying on sexual relations with black women evoked not images of rape but of mutual, sordid passion, making possible other vile crimes. Thus a slave, Pauline, imprisoned, beat, and starved her mistress and children because "the husband of the woman had instigated his slave, who was also his paramour, in the commission of this horrid outrage."[13]

According to nineteenth-century white thought, Africans were a sinfully passionate people to start with. And then slavery evoked passions of all kinds, not only in slaves but also in their owners. The famously expressive style of blacks, particularly on display in interracial congregations, put pressure on white women to exercise extreme caution in the ways they showed emotion and pleasure, particularly pleasure in the opposite sex. White women, the guardians of and experts on feeling, had much to lose by being identified with the unrestrained passions of African Americans. Overlapping emotional styles between white women and blacks might cause observers to see white women as irrational at best, unchaste at worst.

The context in which white women demonstrated their ideas about sexuality and their "passionlessness," the ambient ideology about unrestrained black passion, and the belief in black emotionality developed apace as whites and blacks came together in congregations in the Great Awakenings. In the early nineteenth century white women who were struggling for national moral leadership would have had reason to restrain their expressive behavior, including, but not limited to, sexual behavior to distinguish themselves from African Americans.[14]

Since the earliest days of slavery whites had described blacks as lascivious and sexually incontinent, and white men had justified the rape of black women on this ground. As we have seen, legislation in Virginia was designed to ensure white men sexual access to black and white women and to deny white women to black men. These early laws were foundational to beliefs that southern white women were "pure" while black women were not, stereotypes the press constantly kept alive. But the biracial experience at the church and camp meetings threw white and black women together in passion-evoking pastimes offering uncomfortable comparisons and parallels.[15]

The well-documented emotional expressivity of evangelical blacks included their religious dances, deeply felt singing, shouts, trances, ecstatic behavior, and generally intense level of emotional involvement. By the nineteenth century notable emotionalism was increasingly ascribed to black practitioners and had come to be seen as both frightening and inferior. In 1831 the St. Louis press called for regulating black worship. The repose "of the whole neighborhood is effectually destroyed by the unusual length of time to which their meetings extend, and the yellings which invariably attend them."[16]

In integrated congregations, white women too experienced excesses. Local chroniclers had to portray both white and black women forgivingly or criticize both. A series of local stories portrayed ecstatic trances and the jerks, convulsive movements that overtook worshipers, as abnormal behavior that was usually the province of black and white women. For white women interested in respectability, this blurring of racial lines must have been worrisome. One vignette played on the theme of the danger of mocking God's medium for transmitting His message. A young white girl imitating the jerks for the amusement of her friends, proved unable to stop, and, as in a fairy tale, jerked until she collapsed exhausted. Another anecdote demonstrates the strange routineness of the movements in the lives of white women believers. A group of four white women tied up their hair carefully and proceeded to jerk rhythmically and even decorously back and forth until the dinner horn sounded, at which point "they all quieted down, and went back to the table and ate as healthy as anyone." Yet a third story presents female vulnerability. A white mother and daughter both have the jerks, to the entertainment of young men, who allow dogs to attack the jerking girl and tear off her clothes.[17]

In a final anecdote, a black woman has the most inexplicable experience of all. A slave, identified only by her owner, is known for often getting the jerks at meetings. After one episode she remains unconscious and seemingly dead for a day or two. The series of accounts displays a bemused respect for the inexplicable but divinely inspired behavior of pious women. Black and white women are equal before God and equally susceptible to uncontrollable emotional responses to His presence. To male observers this confirmed both positive and negative stereotypes of women. To white women concerned with respectability, however, this behavior could suggest a troubling identity with black women.[18]

Some black preachers contributed in a different way to the merging of white women's culture with African American culture. The Reverend Hosea Easton, of the Hartford, Connecticut, African Methodist Episcopal Zion Church, published in 1837 his *Treatise on the Intellectual Character, and Civil and Political Condition of the Colored People in the United States*, in which he assigned womanly, gentle qualities to African Americans who would not reveal their true genius until the aggressive, destructive white race did them justice. Blacks would, through patience and gentleness, thus redeem whites (or the "Angry Saxons," as Anna Julia Cooper later wrote) and in the process reject their own arrogance, brutality, and greed. Other African American intellectuals, like the Reverend James W. C. Pennington and Henry Highland Garnet, sometimes upheld Easton's claims for a kinder, gentler black "race" because of its presumed female qualities of meek endurance in the face of terrible oppression.[19]

Mary Sibley, the evangelical Presbyterian who helped found Sunday schools for rural whites, blacks, and Germans, reacted ambivalently to the expression of emotion. Her anxieties seem indicative of the ways the merging of black and white women in religious experience may have encouraged some white women to exert special control over themselves. Of all her students, she remarked only upon the black children's emotive intensity. Noting the growth of African

American membership, she wrote, "The simple prayer of some of these poor people at the closing of school is really affecting." Sibley, who frequently castigated herself in her journal for her own lack of emotion ("so cold, so unfeeling"), believed display of sincere emotions to be a mark of authentic religious experience.

Over time, as many Puritans had done, Sibley came to use sexual metaphors of ecstasy as the best language for understanding religious rapture. She found an acceptable place in respectable religion for passion, as had the Puritans. But she remained wary of passionate language. Sibley wrote that she had been moved by the Song of Solomon but worried that it was in the Bible because of the corruption of men. She came to understand, however, that "no extravagance of language can express what the soul feels in view of the beauty and excellency of Him."[20]

Like sensuality, deep feeling for Christianity was admirable, yet it too was dangerous. Sibley saw "[e]vil passions and depraved hearts" everywhere. Passion in the service of anything other than God, particularly for evangelicals, but especially for most Protestant women, was the road to sin. An article in a St. Louis paper noted that a person who did not master passion, "no matter whatever else he is master of, is a slave." Passion collapsed the distance between master and slave, between white women and the stereotype of African American women. Evangelicals could respond to sudden emotion only with caution and suppression of feeling. When Mary Sibley's husband, George, joined her church after years of her pleading with him, she was overjoyed but studiously contained her reaction: "I retired to my room to give vent to my feelings."[21]

The Legal Framework for Love

Legal measures framed these varying ideas and attitudes toward sexuality, feeling, and marriage. Among the French, property arrangements in marriage were far more favorable to women than was true within American customs. In 1792 the French had passed laws giving women the right to marry and divorce under the same rules as men and establishing a family court that gave wives nearly equal rights with their husbands in supervision of the children. Women also had been guaranteed equality of inheritance with their brothers and other male heirs. Married French women in Louisiana, unlike married English and American women, had long been able to hold property and undertake contracts without prenuptial agreements.[22]

Anglo-American law responded to the new freedom to choose with protections for women vulnerable to seduction and falsehood. Community sanctions forcing men to marry pregnant women had been weakening since the colonial period, and women could rely less and less on their neighbors to protect them. Consequently they were exercising more self-control. Postrevolutionary courts made it possible for women to sue men who had promised to marry them and had reneged. However, it was dangerous to go to court over breach of promise because it could ruin a young woman's reputation. Rachel Jenckes reported to her sister in St. Louis about their congressman, who, engaged to one young woman in his district in Illinois, had "gone crazy in love" with another in Washington, D.C., and become engaged to her as well. The most motivated to recapture the congressman was the jilted fiancée's mother, who twice managed to pressure him into renewing his agreement to marry her daughter. Twice he escaped. "Ellen apparently bears it very well laughs and talks and tries to be gayer than ever—Mrs. Jones [Ellen's mother] is raging—says her Family is disgraced for ever and abuses every body that was at all intimate with [him]."[23]

A prevalent threat in a society committed to romantic free choice and mobility was bigamy. Ann Lane wrote her father that an old friend of her mother's was married, "[a]nd some say very badly. I heard some people say that her husband has a wife and children in the Lower country and that he only came away to escape from his creditors."[24]

At the time of Missouri statehood (1821) the question arose of how easy divorce should be. The informal method—a wife (usually) decamped, and her husband advertised that he was not responsible for her debts—persisted. Formal territorial procedure had husbands and wives petition for divorces from the legislature, and this continued into early statehood. But divorce by legislative decree was cumbersome and favored those with the money and connections to find lawyers and pay for the process. After 1830 Missouri legislators moved to liberalize divorce law, bringing it more in line with the northeastern (and French) notion that marriage was a civil contract that could be terminated. In January 1835 the legislature made divorce obtainable in circuit and chancery courts as well as in the legislature itself, and it broadened grounds for divorce beyond impotence, bigamy, adultery, and desertion to include conviction for a felony, two years of habitual drunkenness, and a definition of cruelty that included the psychological as well as physical, "when a partner shall be guilty of such cruel and barbarous treatment as to endanger the life of the other, or shall offer such indignities to the person of the other, as shall render his or her condition intolerable."[25]

Although many Missourians used the liberalized access to divorce, most marriages ended informally in a de facto divorce. The requirement that divorcing couples had to find one party at fault and the other guiltless very often meant the creation of unrealistic scenarios or the couples' collaboration on a story. It also meant that the party found guilty would not be allowed to remarry for five years. Whatever the drawbacks of divorce in the early republic, women suffering abuse and unable to move away found divorce a great relief. Some were willing to brave community shock to escape dreadful unhappiness.[26]

Following closely on the liberalization of divorce laws, antidivorce sentiment became louder and more potent. Winning the legal ground for divorce happened at the same time as losing the moral ground. Once the women's movement emerged in 1848, women found it far easier to mobilize protective sentiments toward them as dependents than to achieve consensus on their rights as individuals.[27]

In theory the laws concerning marriage, breach of promise, and divorce applied to free blacks as well as whites. However, the lawlessness of slavery was an ever-present danger. Free blacks were never completely secure from reenslavement or from loss of their property, and slave marriages, of course, had no legal recognition. Free blacks married to slaves lived with the constant threat of disruption to their families.

16

ST. LOUIS MARRIAGES:

VIEWS FROM THE INSIDE

Postrevolutionary marriage for whites, especially those of the incipient middle class, provided the only valid framework for virtuous women. Obedience and chastity combined with the absence of economic and political power all contributed to women's habitual lack of assertion that seemed to demand protection and to define purity.

Choosing a Spouse

In Missouri in the early nineteenth century young women by and large married. It is probably not surprising that Protestants snatched their daughters from the hands of the nuns as soon as the girls expressed an interest in convent life. But some Catholics were eager to do so as well. The Chouteaus forbade Emilie Chouteau from entering. Young Irishwomen were more likely to take vows than French because they were poorer.[1]

In practice, relatively few young women freely exercised sentimental individualism in selecting mates. Their choices were hedged about by the circumstances of transience—their own and others'—by isolation if they were rural, by economic necessities, by their dependent condition, and by doubts about their own judgment. While the urban middle class and evangelicals tried to marry among their own, western agricultural life around St. Louis threw together men and women of different nationalities and classes. Mobility and diversity militated against predictable coupling.

Courtship in the St. Louis hinterland tended to be short even though it was commonly accepted that courtship was more agreeable than marriage. This corresponded to masculine domination of a social scene that in a more bourgeois setting became more complex and favored the social skills of women. A story about a man's marrying a thirteen-year-old is suggestive of the haste and making do in some marriages. He waited for his breakfast the day after the wedding and entered the cabin to find her playing with dolls on the floor. The emphasis on haste underscores the limited choices young rural women had and the rush men felt to be married. Susan Vanarsdale, who taught in rural Missouri in the early 1840s for two years, accumulated more than ten marriage proposals, many from older widowers whom she barely knew.[2] In the backwoods, niceties could not prevail.[3]

Men spoke of marriage as "changing their condition," suggesting the transforming power of marriage. But for women, the changes went even deeper and included their bodies and health. Marriage also had a profound impact on their moral autonomy by situating their husbands between them and the world of practical politics. Rural women tended to regard marriage as a sacrifice, not an opportunity. Women who were in charge of naming the wedding day usually postponed it while their prospective grooms wished it earlier. The choice of a husband was a graver decision than the choice of a wife. For men, marriage confirmed their assumption of adulthood. Women were almost entirely dependent upon their spouses as they left the security and comfort of their homes; often men constituted their wives' link to the world, their economic foundation, and their emotional support. Marriage almost inevitably meant many children, which meant many brushes with death.[4]

Men who were concerned with the future did not marry until they were financially ready. Ambitious American men saw attaining

independence as the key rite of manhood, one that marriage confirmed but did not initiate. Young men who achieved professional
equilibrium in a new fast-growing city like St. Louis were often on
their own. Establishing independence in the West underscored the
individualism of the achievement, a competency far from home, often without help.[5]

Though men did not think of themselves as marrying *for* money,
money was never too far from their thinking about marriage. In 1807
Will Carr referred to finding a wife as searching for household help.
He wrote his brother that he had to mend his own shirts, but he
hoped the situation would soon be changed. Within a few months he
had met someone who might do his sewing for him although she
would disappoint friends who wished for him a rich heiress. Ann Elliott was not rich. Nevertheless, Carr presented his marriage as
something that would help ensure that he would achieve personal
worth. For him worth was someone with money. He observed that
he was turning into a "miser . . . for I discover that the sight of a Dollar is much more pleasing to me than it was formerly—and I have
not now such an itching to get it out of my pocket almost as soon as I
get it in—I can keep it one whole week." His remarks painted hopes
for accumulation of cash over a traditional matrimonial landscape of
industry and thrift.[6]

Will Carr's work simultaneously illuminated and overshadowed
his plans and feelings about his wedding. The judiciary calendar
dominated Carr's life and calmed or rechanneled any nervousness he
might have experienced. This marriage, he wrote, was to be "entirely
subservient to my conveniences." Ann Elliott had given up the right
to name the wedding date. Carr was one of those new American men
more alone with money than ever before in history. Money was usually fungible with almost anything. When it was not, he felt he had
reached the limits of his ability to express himself. He wrote his
brother that the Frenchwomen in Louisiana "are undoubtedly the
greatest sluts in the world. . . . I would not marry a French girl if she
[were] worth a million."[7]

In marrying men like Carr, women had to accommodate to the
reality of their driving economic individualism. Some women de-

scribed their proper pursuit as seeking a "superior" man, usually
meaning someone older, more experienced, and more educated. As
Mary Sibley put it, "I never wish to see that society in which the no-
bler sex can not be looked up to as superior in knowledge, as they are
in strength and energy of character. It would destroy half the delight
of our associations if we were not permitted to feel that we have a
protector in man whom we can regard as superior." Sibley's attribu-
tion of women's delight in male company to the latter's superiority,
probably typical of many women in St. Louis, suggests how women
contributed to male dominance. A happy hierarchy with men at the
top provided both comfort and camouflage to women who, like Sibley, were undermining the ideology of patriarchy while playing by
the rules.[8]

Given the complexities surrounding the choice of a spouse, most
women in the early decades of the nineteenth century did not embrace sentimental individualism wholeheartedly but often asked for
help in choosing their life partners. Men, too, sometimes solicited
advice.

Harriet Ewing wrote her sister Mary Lane in 1826 for advice on
her engagement. She announced that both her "duty and affection"
urged her to tell Mary of her intention to marry Mr. Farrington,
"with the consent and approbation of all my friends here. . . . Should
it be so unfortunate that this connection would not meet your approbation I have said it must stop—though they say they do not believe
me to be in earnest, but I am, for such is the strength of my love and
affection for you, I could not be happy to go against it. . . . I must
know before *matters* can proceed any further." Her willingness to
break the engagement, pending her sister's opinion, makes it clear
that her wishes in this matter were of less importance to her than the
considered opinions of others close to her. Her hesitancy suggested
not only that she doubted her own judgment in a transient and
volatile world but also that she did not consider emotional individualism her undisputed natural right. She thought the decision to
marry complex, one that might be beyond her wisdom and experience.[9]

A young man, writing to Mrs. Linn, the wife of Missouri's Senator

Lewis Linn, asked for her advice on a woman who intrigued him. He wanted her to write him "freely and frankly on the subject," because the young woman's "personal appearance, her education, habits, age, parentage, every thing is calculated to make her very interesting to me not a day passes but I think of her." Mrs. Linn's evaluation of her and the information she could provide locating this young woman socially in a new and growing town would carry real weight.[10]

Believing, as Quakers did, that the religious community had an important part in the selection of the members' husbands and wives, evangelicals offered advice freely about marriage. Religious women who counseled unsettled men sometimes chose for themselves the life work of redemption along with a husband. Their apparent strength and moral certainty could attract and reassure men uncertain of their way in the turbulent world.[11]

The wife as redeemer became a common nineteenth-century trope. The moral superiority of women was an antebellum given, providing familiar roles for courting couples. In the 1840s Dabney Carr, Will Carr's son, had been forbidden to visit any "ladies" in the wake of running up debts and flunking out of school. Breaking the rules, he visited a certain Mary, who forgave him "under the condition that [he] would sign a temperance pledge." The happy afterglow of this moral barter, following so closely upon Carr's humiliation, persuaded him to marry Mary. Her discipline sanctioned and possibly heightened his desire. Mary's sternness and forgiveness and Carr's willingness to submit to her correction illuminate the darkly tangled imaginative pathways of nineteenth-century middle-class love.[12]

In contrast with Anglo-American concerns, sentimental individualism at its most undiluted seemed to characterize members of the French elite. Their ideal of marriage was the union of two people who loved each other and would make each other happy. Jules de Mun's mother wrote him that she hoped that his lack of a fortune would not keep him from seeking in marriage the young woman whom he loved. The revolutions in France and in Haiti had wiped out the de Mun assets. Fortunately for Jules, the father of fifteen-year-old Isabelle Gratiot respected the wishes of his daughter and permitted her to marry the poor but well-connected de Mun.

The individualism of the two spouses was tempered by the fact that they united two large and important families whose continuing prominence depended upon a significant degree of corporate cooperation. Isabelle Gratiot and Jules de Mun selected each other from among a small pool of well-to-do French in St. Louis, just as Virginia gentry chose one another from among the local elite. The sentimental choices of members of both groups consequently were limited by the economic and social differences dividing them from the rest of society. French law and tradition gave Isabelle control over the property her family bestowed on her at the time of her marriage. She was therefore less dependent on her husband than an American wife would be. This seems to have steadied her confidence and, perhaps, her affection over time.[13]

The German settlers who poured into Missouri in the 1830s and later (125,000 in the 1830s, 375,000 in the 1840s, and 1 million in the 1850s) brought with them a class system compatible with but considerably more rigid than that of the United States. Middle-class German women were acutely aware of class differences among themselves and witnessed with pain marriages facilitated by New World needs that breached the old status order. Henriette (Jette) Bruns, the daughter of a mayor and wife of a doctor who had arrived in Missouri in 1836, had to stand by while her brother, Franz, married her "girl," Trude. Jette wrote home that she believed that Trude would take care of the house well after a year and a half of Jette's supervision. But she wanted "to confess to you that the changed relationship is still somewhat strange to me and," she wrote prophetically, "that she has probably gotten a very critical relative."[14]

German brides usually brought at least linens and bedclothes, but Trude brought no dowry with her, working, like most poor Germans, for her family, not herself. Elite Germans, like Americans, believed that poor people had less sensitivity than wealthy people. Jette grudgingly allowed that Trude expressed more feeling than her employer had anticipated.[15]

Jette's feelings of superiority toward Trude never diminished, although American circumstances forced Jette to live in apparent equality with her sister-in-law. An indication of the limits of the welcome Jette gave Trude was that she continued to use the formal *Sie* with her instead of the friendly, intimate *du*. Defending herself to her family back home, she wrote, "You cannot put yourselves in our position. One can be quite well inclined toward a person without the 'Du.'" Bourgeois Germans arranged ways to maintain class distinctions in the face of American democracy, but the old system could not be transported intact.[16]

Love and Obedience: Disciplining Desire

Reconstructing married life, its moral problems and solutions, is hard given the limited direct evidence from the two central players. Exchanges and diaries do exist, however, and church records and local histories provide fragments of stories that permit making reasoned inferences. The following exchanges illustrate some of the ways wives thought of the uneasy relationship between obedience and affection. Obedience provided moral shelter from most conflicts and was likely to sustain the affection of husbands, although frequent recourse to it was likely to stifle the spontaneous affection of wives.[17]

Marriage in and around St. Louis often started out in a subordination very similar to that women experienced with their fathers. Women usually married very young. Twenty-eight-year-old Daniel Morgan Boone, Daniel and Rebecca's son, married fourteen-year-old Sara Lewis. In Callaway County a farmer married the thirteen-year-old daughter of a preacher. These age discrepancies ensured a husband's much lengthier acquaintance with the world, which could not help reminding a wife of her forfeited ability to decide many matters for herself. Most of the wives quoted referred to their husbands as "mister" throughout their marriages. The exchanges between these couples were often caring and concerned but formal and polite. The teasing intimacy of the late nineteenth century was absent from these letters. However, usually with the advent (and departure) of children, and often through shared religious beliefs, middle-class wives were likely to wield considerable moral and emotional weight within their households.[18]

Jules de Mun (1782–1843) was thirty when he married sixteen-year-old Isabelle Gratiot. He had a title; she was a pretty colonial girl who spelled poorly. He was sophisticated, well educated, widely traveled, and a refugee from two revolutions. He often referred to her as "his friend" in the style of Rousseau, but equally often as his "child."[19]

Their disagreements over letter writing display the moral paradox that demanding affection represents. De Mun wrote his Isabelle: "We have already missed two mails from St. Louis, I am all the more angry because I hoped they would bring me letters from you. Since I have been here I have received only one small letter. Perhaps, dear child, you wanted to make them more desirable by making them scarcer, but, good Isabelle, if I received some every day, I do not think I would ever receive enough. . . . I am irritated, dear child, to repeat the same thing so often, but, dear friend, you force me to it by your bit of negligence."[20]

Whatever the dynamics of individual marriages were in creating an imbalance in letter writing, Isabelle de Mun's reply (which no longer exists) to a similar plea from her brother-in-law sheds light on one reason women did not write more often. She told Auguste de Mun that she thought her letters must bore him. He protested, of course. Nevertheless, to wives and mothers at home, where it often seemed as if nothing were happening, a letter detailing the ways in which nothing happened could appear dull to read and a chore to write. Its affection-bearing function may not have seemed particularly urgent to tired housewives. Wives might also avoid writing because letters were usually shared with family and friends, and women feared performing badly. Anna Adams expressed the self-consciousness that was nearly universal among wives. She begged her brother William Lane not to show her letter to anyone because "I have not written a letter for years no comments on the bad spelling bad diction and bad writing, A."[21]

Letter writing was regarded as a female function, and women were the designated family correspondents, yet they often fell down on this particular job in the eyes of their husbands. Some passively resisted the pressure on them to produce affection on demand, and they could not have failed to see the similarity between their situations and those of their children at school. In any case, husbands perceived it as a failure to love. Lane wrote, for example, "[Y]ou must write every fortnight during our separation; if you do not, the comfortless conclusion that I am forgotten,—aye, & forgotten too by her, whose reminiscence I value most here below, will be inevitable." A husband's demands for affection were never far removed from the issue of a wife's obedience.[22]

In the background of wives' accommodations to obedience was the reality that some husbands enforced their desires with violence. Susannah Boone was Daniel and Rebecca Boone's high-spirited daughter, who at fourteen had a reputation for sexual freedom. The story has it that her father warned her husband-to-be, Will Hays, but he married her anyway. Others questioned the picture of her as sexually outspoken. While Susannah's sexual reputation is disputed, it is clear that her husband drank and habitually whipped his wife. Relatives remembered with bitterness that he would caution her to cover up warmly so as not to get cold but the real reason was to keep her "bloody stripes" from showing to her father. Mother of ten children, she died at forty just after the family had moved to Missouri.[23]

Nineteenth-century marital obedience required self-mastery and the ability to subordinate one's feelings without causing a fuss. Jette Bruns criticized her sister-in-law for "always believ[ing] herself to be ill." In fact, Trude was right; she died of tuberculosis not long after her marriage. But good German women were supposed to suppress or control unpleasant feelings in the interests of marital serenity. Jette thought Trude rude and "moody."[24]

The kind of restraint that some American middle-class women, especially but not exclusively evangelicals, experienced could and did slow or block the flow of human sympathy and empathy even when it was supposed to run freely. Reserve and restraint, essential in disguising the discomforts of obedience, could blind some women to the pleasures of human contact. William Lane thought his wife so uncommunicative and difficult that he felt a need to write to their daughters explaining her silence and brooding behavior to them. At first, he wrote, he "really thought her vastly indifferent" to him after some years of marriage, but a dangerous illness he contracted convinced him otherwise. As for them, he assured them he knew, and "high heaven can atest it,—she loves you, notwithstanding her man-

ner, now & then, better than she loves her own life." In regard to the
cause of her difficulty in communicating her true feelings, he wrote
that it was the result of "neglected education & badly formed
habits."[25]

An anonymous contributor to the St. Louis Enquirer wrote "The
Evils of Reserve in Marriage," in which she described the tragedy of
both her and her husband's inability to communicate. She related
several instances of marital silence and misunderstanding and years
of misery that turned her from a cheerful person into a melancholic.
"The little pleasure my husband found at home induced him to seek
it abroad." Like other members of the growing middle class, her husband worked in the center of the city, and they lived at the edge of
St. Louis. This meant a considerable walk home for her husband, so
she spent long, lonely days at home, often weeping. In his final illness she was unable to break through her own or his reserve, so others attended him in death. "That sensibility which might have given
birth to the purest and exquisite pleasures, was from the want of
candour and explicitness changed into an instrument of torture."
American and English moralists praised reserve, particularly in
women, as a means of masking the unpleasant emotions generated
by habitual obedience as well as expressing disapproval of unpleas-
antly familiar behavior. It could, however, chill even the "blessed" relationship moralists recommended marriage to be.[26]

Mary Sibley worked out questions of obedience by seeing them
through her desire to submit to God. For instance, before his conversion, George Sibley was ill disposed toward prayer meetings. Although Mary knew that their house was the most spacious and hence
logical for such meetings, she could not invite her fellow evangelicals
into her home. "The Lord," she believed, "will change his heart in
His own good time." Her evangelical faith helped her to accept passively the authority of her husband. At war within her were the social
demands on good women for caring, soothing, obedience, and empathy with the concerns of their families and the radical demands of
evangelical faith to risk her earthly relations by pushing them to
Christ. The vocabulary of Christianity and the republican rhetoric
criticizing interest intersected and reinforced the abhorrence she felt
for self-generated and self-serving action. But selflessness and sub-

mission to God's will could be interpreted to support either action or inaction. Sibley's social training to defer to authority dampened evangelical Christianity's authorization to challenge it.[27]

She remained an obedient wife to Major Sibley as well as a tense and conflicted but submissive daughter to her parents. Her ambivalent resolution of this struggle led her to a restrained feminism in which she upheld the public silence and the private subordination of women while claiming moral authority through Jesus. When Harriet Livermore, the Pilgrim Stranger, an itinerant woman who had preached all over, from Jerusalem to Washington, D.C., arrived in St. Charles, Sibley noted her own agreement with St. Paul's doctrine that women were not to speak publicly in churches. Respectability and dependence required obedience for their maintenance. Sibley balanced the demands of action and inaction by submitting to those on whom she was dependent and challenging those she did not fear or need like the poor, Germans, and slaves.[28]

For devout but nonevangelical women, silence and resignation to the status quo was a clearer moral path and a less stressful emotional one than criticizing the beliefs of husbands, relations, and friends.[29]

Obedience included curbing one's temper. This was a wife's job in all circumstances, and husbands who aspired to mutuality in marriage assumed responsibility for their tempers as well. Over the years Mary Lane and her husband exchanged poignant apologies for their difficult tempers after storms in their marriage. Both aspired to self-improvement, but she offered obedience and painted him as a good spouse and herself as incorrigible. They never found a comfortable equilibrium. Mary spent more and more time at the home of her family, where submission was not frequently required. William Lane eventually admitted marital failure and became the second territorial governor of New Mexico. They effectively created a no-fault separation for themselves.[30]

Marriage: Free Blacks and Slaves

Free black wives were likely to participate in their marriages more equally than elite white women. The submissive reserve that white wives cultivated fitted awkwardly into their challenging lives; goodness and indeed psychological survival in a racist world required resistance, not acquiescence, to white ideology. Rebellion might be overt or hidden in the heart, but it hung over most aspects of black life.

In 1835 a free black needed to post bond from one hundred to one thousand dollars to receive permission to remain in Missouri on condition of good behavior. For a border state, Missouri had very few free blacks, and after this law they melted away, leaving only 2,618 in 1850, compared with Maryland's 74,723. By then slaves and free blacks constituted only 5.21 percent of St. Louis's residents. The passing riverboats provided work for many and escape for others. Residents ran barbershops, hotels, boardinghouses, eating and drinking establishments, and a bank, and also provided a variety of services, including nursing, needlework, carting, laundry, and prostitution.[31]

The "colored aristocracy" was a small elite within this free black society. It consisted mainly of descendants of mixed unions between French or Spanish and Africans, many of whose ancestors had been freed during Spanish rule. Glimpses of marriage among free blacks suggest that women wished to be economic partners, if not equals, in their marriages and relationships. In St. Louis under the French, free black women had the same rights as white women and could own property, dispose of it, and participate in legally recognized marriages. Free black women desired to be financially independent in a world in which everything, including their children and their freedom, might be taken away from them. After 1835 the law not only required permits for free blacks to remain in Missouri or a white person to vouch for them but also that the county courts hire out or, in effect, enslave free black children from seven to twenty-one years old. Free parents with enough money could protect their children from that fate. In free black marriages, wives worked as hard as their husbands to secure their livelihoods, but they also often took precautions to be sure that their financial security remained in their hands alone. This represented a realistic assessment, not of their husbands' untrustworthiness but of the countless ways white society had to interfere in African American marriages and business dealings. This economic individualism flew in the face of the gender conventions of white America.[32]

In the white middle class, husbands frequently expressed affection and control and underlined the dependence of their wives with purchased goods. Among free blacks, the language of consumption did not necessarily have the implication of control or emphasize wives' dependence. Gifts and necessities did not circulate only from husbands to wives and hence did not substitute for a flow of emotion specifically from male to female. Also, since husbands were not the only ones able to make these purchases, they did not obscure wives' economic contributions to the marriage, whether paid or unpaid, as they could in white marriages.

Some free black women had money for luxuries. Rebecca Reynolds had a guitar, Pelagie Rutgers a piano, and Pelagie Foreman a carriage. Among the wealthiest free blacks were Pelagie Rutgers and her husband, Louis Rutgers. She had been a slave but had bought her freedom. Over time, and after the death of her husband, she managed to accumulate considerable real estate, probably overvalued by free black chronicler Cyprian Clamorgan at five hundred thousand dollars. Rutgers's husband, who had been arrested and imprisoned, had lost nearly all his property, but hers remained intact.[33]

There were several female-centered families among the free black elite, but more widespread was a pattern of extended families living together. Pelagie Rutgers, for example, presided over a household including her twenty-year-old daughter, an eighty-nine-year-old white woman, a Frenchman who worked as a gardener, and a white friend from Louisiana. Pelagie Nash headed a household that included her three children and a sixty-nine-year-old mulatto woman. Marie Aubuchon's house contained six free people of color, including her. Samuel Mordechai's household sheltered his wife, their three daughters, and three mulatto women, one from Kentucky and two from Pennsylvania. Robert Wilkinson's home held his wife and three children and three unrelated black barbers from Virginia.[34]

The notable number of female-centered households reflected the reluctance of free black widows to remarry. Instead they frequently lived in expanded households of various combinations of children, grandchildren, longtime friends, lovers, and boarders. This pattern reproduced widespread West African customs, in which mixtures of

relatives and friends often extending beyond a single residence constituted families. Family life among free blacks in St. Louis reflects
values of broad inclusiveness and mutual aid. If a West African
woman became a widow, she still lived in a group, and if she remarried, her new husband joined the extended family along with his
kin. Similar behavior showed up in St. Louis. Five years after Marie
Aubuchon's husband, Francis Aubuchon, died, she appeared in the
census sharing her home with Alexander Pellerin and his nieces and
nephew, Elise, Josephine, and Sylvester. Wives as well as husbands
had a say in how extended family groups were composed.[35]

Although many free black women seem to have had more autonomy than did white women, it would be wrong to romanticize their
independence. For Lucy Sessan, Fanny Valiant, Harriet Henry,
or any of the fourteen others identified as washerwomen in the
St. Louis Directory for 1838–39, autonomy did not imply a comfortable life. It meant that free black women, married or not, were
still responsible for making their way in the world. For the great
majority of free black women, work strategies always accompanied
marriage in plotting a life course. Nancy Lyons, for example, came
to St. Louis from Illinois with her husband and left soon after, for
a year, to travel as a nurse with a wealthy white family in France.
As a widow she ran a boardinghouse in St. Louis. Even for African American women with educations, household service jobs
remained about the only work available until after the Civil War,
when there was a demand for teachers. All free blacks who could afford it, men and women, owned property, real estate being the most
common and safest investment in a city where property values were
growing.[36]

Free blacks could not imagine marriage in the same terms that
whites did. This is not to say that marriage did not embody their
hopes for enduring love, sympathetic companionship, and children,
but it could not be expected to provide a safe haven where the
husband-protector reigned supreme. The necessity for most free
black women to bring income to the family made it unlikely that
wives' obedience to husbands would be a central feature of their
marriage. Some antebellum free black husbands and wives advocated

adopting a white middle-class model of marital respectability, but African custom, the fallout from slavery, and the poverty endemic to most free black life militated against it.[37]

Clamorgan claimed that the antislavery agitation in Missouri before the Civil War was entirely due to the work of the wealthy free black men of St. Louis who believed that with the abolition of slavery, their status would rise to equal that of white men. He overlooked women's important contribution. Antislavery work included education, and free black women were active in that field. Blacks in St. Louis set up schools wherever they could. Elizabeth Keckley had a school for seamstresses, but it evidently taught a great deal more than sewing. This was true of other schools that purported to teach crafts, as well as the five schools in the basements of five black churches in the city. Despite laws against the education of slaves and the exclusion of free blacks from white educational institutions, many St. Louis blacks found ways to become educated.[38]

Churches were centers for covert black resistance. Women, more likely to be church members than men were, played a leading role. Slaves and a very few free blacks met in John Meachum's Baptist church. The popular Methodist church of Richard Anderson, a slave freed when he was two years old by the territorial governor Frederick Bates, had a congregation of a thousand, about half of whom were free. The African Methodist Episcopal Church had its own building after 1830. It was part of the Methodists' black separatist movement, which began with the election of Richard Allen as the black minister of his own church in Philadelphia in 1816. By 1830 the AME organization had more than ten thousand members, most of them in the Middle Atlantic states and western Ohio. Black St. Louis Methodists knew about abolitionist work but could not share such information publicly. In 1831 Allen inaugurated annual conventions where African Americans would come together to debate issues crucial to their well-being, like abolition, education, job discrimination, and emigration. It is clear that among the St. Louis free elite there was considerable interstate communication. One St. Louis free black couple, for example, sent their two girls to a Quaker-run school in Philadelphia.[39]

Abolitionist activity in slave states was punished so quickly and so dramatically it could not take place in public. Even in the North, black civil rights activity was dangerous. In Cincinnati in 1829 a black protest against the revitalized Ohio Black Codes of 1804, which dramatically restricted the rights of free blacks, resulted in an ultimatum by town officials that each black come up with five hundred dollars or leave town. While free blacks were trying to cope with this crisis, whites rioted and set fire to the black part of town. The 1829 publication of David Walker's incendiary *Appeal* to his fellow blacks to recognize and resist the evils of slavery, the appearance of William Lloyd Garrison's outraged abolitionist newspaper, the *Liberator*, and the rebellion of Nat Turner, all within two years, shook the South. The Antislavery Society, established in Philadelphia in 1833, distributed more than a hundred thousand pamphlets over the next year. In 1835 there were riots in many cities. In St. Louis, Mayor William Lane chaired a meeting to deal with the threat of rioting. He set up vigilance committees to control mob action. They were to report anyone engaged in preaching or publishing abolitionist ideas. Antiabolition sentiment in and around St. Louis grew very violent after the lynching in St. Louis of the free black steamboat steward Francis McIntosh, who stabbed a sheriff in fleeing from arrest. Elijah Lovejoy, the abolitionist publisher, attacked the lynchers repeatedly in heated language and for his safety removed from St. Louis to Alton, Illinois. He continued to publish his views and was murdered soon after.[40]

Self-purchase was safer than abolitionist activity. A number of free black women had bought their own freedom. Indeed women brought many of the freedom suits in St. Louis, for even more was at stake for them than for men. For women, freedom would also free subsequent children as well as provide protection against sexual violation. Thus women's freedom not only was an investment in the freedom of others but also provided them with sexual moral autonomy and bodily security.

St. Louis was the site of more liberations than any other part of Missouri. Part of the reason was that urban slavery was not particularly profitable, and selling slaves their liberty could be good business. A few masters freed their slaves willingly, especially in the 1850s. Some even charged only nominal prices. Pelagie Rutgers paid only three dollars. Elizabeth Keckley, on the other hand, paid twelve hundred dollars for herself. Another reason for the high proportion of liberations was that information and education circulated in the city as they could not on isolated farms in the countryside. People learned routes to freedom, and opportunities for earning money were relatively plentiful.[41]

Slaves

Marriages for slaves, even more than for free blacks, rested on moral ideas different from those animating white women. Slaves, married or single, desperately desired autonomy, the very thing that white wives were to sacrifice in order to share in the influence purported to accrue to pure women. While few slave women could achieve autonomy, neither their marriages nor the circumstances of their lives could permit the kind of dependence that produced the sentimental style marking middle-class white homes. The absence of legal protection in slave marriage, the prohibition on the accumulation of property, the automatic enslavement of children of slave mothers all meant that the structures and relationships that gave moral definitions to American white women's lives would make slave women moral outcasts. Instead the circumstances in which slaveowners forced them to establish married life ensured that the humiliating appellations Anglo-Saxon men thought up to describe women who were neither virgins nor married would apply to them. If they were, by definition, outside the pale of middle-class purity, they also never partook of the compromised dignity of legal dependence that characterized white women.

A young slave woman was under various pressures when she passed puberty. Her owners wanted her to marry so she would start to have children, thereby increasing their wealth. The consequences of a young woman's delaying a marriage too long meant she would be sold or forced into a marriage of her owners' choosing. Owners, in varying degrees, insisted on having control over her choice of husband. Owners usually permitted only strong and physically mature slaves to marry, thus guaranteeing strong children. If a slave had to visit another plantation to court a girl, he usually needed a pass, another obstacle to unimpeded courtship. Young men had the prerogative to initiate courtships, while mothers tried to persuade their daughters to put off courtship as long as possible. They succeeded so well that slave women generally began childbearing an average of three to four years after they were physically ready—at nineteen or twenty—but two years before white women. In larger plantations there were parties, dances, quilting bees, and other get-togethers where young people could meet. By and large, premarital sex was neither uncommon nor a cause of disapproval. Men and women were expected to choose someone who pleased them, but a woman's goal was not solely pleasure. Young unmarried women were expected to be sexually attractive not only for the pleasure their beauty could give others but also as living symbols of the promise of future generations. Sometimes young women married the fathers of their first children; sometimes they waited and formed lasting relationships with other men. In spite of coercion and pressures, great numbers of slave women married, although they often married off the plantation even when they might have chosen otherwise. One reason for this choice was the West African tradition of strict exogamy. Another may have been the need for some psychological distance or independence from loved ones or a young man's desire to experience a broader world. A third reason may have been resistance to marry according to the convenience and preferences of an owner.[42]

In the late eighteenth century most slaves did not marry in religious services. This would have implicated their owners in morally binding pledges that the couple remain together for life. In the nineteenth century, however, particularly after churches had split into northern and southern factions, southern ministers married slaves without vows or regard to their future to prove that the church could make religion comfortable for slaveowners and slaves as well. In one service the minister told the couple that they would be man and wife until "death or distance" did them part.[43]

Marriage could not define slave women as it did white women; the institution's moral and emotional claims had to give way legally to the claims of slavery. Marriages could be interrupted or terminated from one moment to the next. One slave in St. Louis remembered that a Mr. Cleveland always separated husband and wife at sales. Coping with the moral and emotional consequences of this random domestic terror shaped expectations of what kind of transformation marriage might bring. Wives could not promise obedience to their husbands when they were already involved in a struggle over the obedience their owners demanded. Whether they were externally compliant or resistant, the issue was always present. Neither the hierarchical marriage with husband as patriarch nor the companionate marriage, in which husband and wife sought to understand and to complete each other, really could apply, the former because slave men could not become patriarchs, the latter because sentimental individualism required leisure, comfort, and peace of mind to imagine and explore each other's desires and preferences. Both versions gathered imaginative force from the assumption that lifelong fidelity, at least on the part of women, would accompany marriage. The expectation of women's fidelity within marriage, and the high price women paid for disobeying this shibboleth, were essential to the idea that white wives' bodies belonged in the custody of their husbands. Few white women would have subscribed to the moral idea that they should have control over their own bodies. But for African American women who had experienced slavery, it would have been an obvious desire.[44]

Under slavery lifelong fidelity was a hope, but in practice it was rarely attainable, while rape and serial monogamy because of separations were not unlikely. The West African model, emphasizing a married couple as part of a larger community, divided by gender allegiances and centering on the production and protection of children, was more apt. This ideal too was hard to realize in Missouri, where slaveholdings tended to be small and the slave market increasingly active. Whereas marriage did not and could not achieve the sentimental and moral importance and potential in the eyes of slave women as it did in the eyes of free women, freedom was an ideal that never dimmed. Slavery put questions about autonomy at the core of every slave's life. Thus slave women, married or not, had to confront the existential responsibility for themselves far more directly than did married white women, who might submerge this question in their daily efforts to be obedient to their husbands.[45]

For slaves in Missouri, marriage was essentially a private commitment producing emotional and psychological changes, not legal ones. Catholic slaveowners were supposed to respect slave marriages and not separate spouses. This had been among the protections guaranteed in French law covering slaves, the Code Noir. But it was a largely unenforced commitment.[46]

Non-Catholics had a moral obligation to respect slave marriages only if their individual consciences required it, and very few did. Of seventeen notices advertising the sale of black women between 1819 and 1822, only two mention a husband in the sale, and only one specifies that couples should be kept together. The first advertisement presents five Negroes for sale, a man and wife, a girl, sixteen, and a little boy and girl, two and four. It was not specified that any of the group be sold together.[47]

Marriages were broken up on the way to Missouri as well as in Missouri. William Brown was married in Virginia, and when his owner decided to move to Missouri, Brown's wife's owner offered to buy him. "William is old, and his family are here; his work won't amount to much now," the prospective buyer argued. But Brown's owner said in three years he would get the $220 asking price out of the slave and would not sell.

Slaves were themselves objects of consumption for wealthy whites. Legally they could not buy or own anything, including themselves, and most were largely kept out of the labor market, meaning that consumer behavior penetrated their economic and emotional lives only minimally. Emotional and sexual interaction was not, as it was in the white middle class, often translated into the languages of purchases, money, and gifts. Thus it was not often, on the one hand, vitiated by material substitutions or, on the other, enhanced by the heightened individualism that money and the market provided.

Dred and Harriet Robinson Scott's history and lawsuit show the ways that marriage, freedom, and the possibility of separation could affect slaves. There is strong evidence to suggest that Scott's wife was the moving force behind the lawsuit and that it was part of the Scotts' long-term fight to remain an unviolated family. Scott is famous for being denied freedom despite having lived for considerable periods of time in the free Northwest Territory. There Scott, a mature man who worked for one Dr. Emerson, was married to young Harriet Robinson by her owner, Major Taliaferro, the commanding officer of the military installation. It would have been strange for Taliaferro as an officer to officiate at a wedding he did not consider to be between free people. He later said in a newspaper interview that he gave Harriet her freedom. And Dred Scott, by virtue of residence in the Northwest Territory, should have been free. But the Scotts followed Dr. Emerson out of the free territory to the South and sued for their freedom only when he died, years later, in 1846. Why not before? The answer seems to be that as long as they were with Dr. Emerson, they could stay together safely as a fairly autonomous family: husband, wife, and two growing daughters. At Emerson's death, however, they inevitably would be sold off separately. Harriet, then about twenty-eight, was still very valuable, and the girls would have been just the right age to be sold south. Dred was sick and in his late forties, old for a male slave and, in terms of the market, of little value. Sale from St. Louis was always sale to the South, and the Scotts, who had seen Louisiana up close in 1838 and had young daughters, fought as hard as they could against a fate they knew firsthand would be worse than death.[48]

They found both allies and information in the free black community of St. Louis. Harriet was a member in the Second African Baptist Church, which was led by the Reverend John Anderson, a former slave who had freed himself and his family. This connection probably helped her to the first of the lawyers who took Dred's case, Francis Murdoch, who had known Anderson when the latter had worked for the abolitionist Elijah Lovejoy. Murdoch had worked in Alton, Illinois, to investigate the vigilantes who had murdered Lovejoy. Freedom became a necessity for Harriet and Dred Scott when the terror of separation pressed on them. Murdoch opened the suit in 1846, when it seemed like a relatively strong case. He dropped out, however, and as time went on, the case became a political football. The Supreme Court eventually denied Scott his freedom in a split decision that outraged free-soilers and delighted slaveowners. The Scotts were emancipated, ironically, by Dr. Emerson's widow's new husband, Clifford Chaffee, an antislavery congressman from Massachusetts, in 1857.[49]

It may seem contradictory to include free black and slave marriages in a section about views of matrimony from the inside since the outside pressed relentlessly on these couples. Slavery and the poisonous insecurity it spread into the lives of free blacks as well as slaves affected their moral and emotional lives. Women's choices of husbands were limited by geographical immobility, West African strictures about exogamy, laws, and their owners' desires. On large plantations, which existed in Missouri only in the seven central-western counties constituting Little Dixie, sentimental individualism could guide some slave courtships. In these cases the pressures on young women were different from those on white women. Historians have described young slave women caught between their mothers' desire for slow courtships and prolonged freedom from the responsibility for children and their masters' desires for early "marriage" and rapid childbearing. The vulnerability of slave women to rape and the lack of legal protection to married slave couples combined to make premarital female chastity irrelevant or impracticable. Sexual autonomy must have felt far more important a goal than purity, which, in any case, was a label whites reserved only for white women.[50]

The fact that slaves legally owed obedience to their owners curtailed their aspirations to the pursuit of individual happiness. White wives shared with slaves to some degree a view of married life through the filter of obedience. For both it was supposed to provide a lens through which to view moral questions. But slaves largely rejected this perspective. They shared a critique of slavery that "was grounded in an analysis of the human condition as a moral quest for affiliation and self-assertion, an analysis that led to the conclusion that slavery was wrong because it unacceptably frustrated moral and affiliational behavior." White wives might see obedience to their husbands' views and commands founded justifiably in their own voluntary choice of spouse. No slave would have seen obedience as anything but an unfortunate necessity to be avoided if possible. Slave men and women shared this insistence, however often frustrated, on affiliational and moral autonomy. Slave wives did not imagine that marriage would or should disrupt this commitment. An enslaved wife's view from inside her marriage would not have been like that of a free white bride. She could not shift from her shoulders the burden of her full moral autonomy even if she wished to.[51]

17

ST. LOUIS MARRIAGES:

VIEWS FROM THE OUTSIDE

This chapter looks at some common experiences white St. Louis women would have had as wives, but not necessarily experiences that were directly related to their marriages. Women lived surrounded by violence. White men fought each other, attacked Native Americans, and brutalized African Americans. With this as a background and dependence on their husbands in the foreground, white women participated obliquely in politics, the economy, and more directly in the social world. Successful participation meant adhering to the forms of respectable behavior and not challenging prevailing political ideas, particularly about Indian policy. The extreme violence of antebellum male culture underlay white women's exclusion from the economic and political machinery of the early republic and encouraged many women to remain morally passive in evaluating the exploitation and brutalization of poor whites, blacks, and Indians. Obedience, submission, and the desire for family peace and harmony, not to mention the growing benefits of being middle class, assured that most elite women would exercise their moral mandate to sympathize and empathize only so far as to sustain and intensify immediate intraclass relationships, rarely reaching very far beyond.[1]

Western men permitted "respectable" women privileges of passage through and spectatorship of their activities, but never let them forget their marginal status. In part reflecting the violent world they created and presided over, western men managed to seem respectful of modestly behaved white women, yet somehow menacing in public at the same time.[2]

Violence, Native Americans, and Fear

As Americans moved into St. Louis, it became the eye of a hurricane of American violence against Native Americans. There were almost always Indians in the city, and their cultural expressions frequently frightened white Missourians. Jessie Benton, Thomas Hart Benton's daughter, remembered attending a tribal dance, a "horrible thing . . . [that] threw me into a panic." Evangelical religion in rural disputed areas was infused with fear and hatred of Indians, giving violence toward Native people a central place in Christian worship. One Baptist minister, James Lee, was "celebrated" because he "used to preach under the tree with his gun standing by his side, apprehending an attack from Indians." Indian warfare and the fear of it made Christian worship a martial endeavor requiring courage and vigilance. The border between whites and Native Americans was a frequently violent place, where American women's fears ran high. Susan Gratiot coined a phrase to describe the most exhausting and disruptive events: "equal to an Indian war."[3]

U.S. military initiatives were ongoing in the Southeast, the Ohio Valley, and the Great Lakes region. When Americans began pouring into the Louisiana Territory, the bloody relations that had accompanied Anglo-American settlement in the Ohio Valley moved inevitably westward. Those tribes that had been displaced were pushed into what we think of as the Midwest. Winnebagos, Sauks, Foxes, Miamis, Wyandots, Kickapoos, and others in the North were losing homelands. Native Americans under the Shawnee leaders Tecumseh and Tenskatawa put together a multitribal Indian resistance. Tecumseh perished in battle at Moraviantown, Canada, in 1813. At the same time, the Americans were pushing Indians on the southern front.

Under the leadership of Andrew Jackson, and with help from the Cherokees, the U.S. military intervened in the Creeks' civil war and came away with fourteen million acres of Creek land, the largest Indian cession ever. Despite the help the Cherokees had provided in subduing the Creeks, as president, Jackson determined to oust the Cherokees from their homelands. Some Cherokees, seeing the handwriting on the wall, began moving in the late 1820s to the Arkansas Territory, just south of Missouri. The rest were forcibly removed in 1838. Three years after its acquisition of Florida in 1821, the United States was using the military to force the Seminoles onto a reservation or to remove them to the West. This did not conclude till the last Seminole War in 1858. In 1827 the Winnebagos went to war with the settlers of Illinois over disputed land. The Black Hawk War erupted between the Sauks of Illinois and the Americans in 1832 in southern Wisconsin. Even in New England, where the military had long since done its job, the status of the small remaining Indian population was precarious and fiercely debated. In Massachusetts the 1820s and 1830s were decades of struggle for the political autonomy of the remnant Mashpee community, and complaints surfaced throughout these debates about the immodesty, intemperance, and poor working habits of Indians.[4]

It was almost impossible in the early years of the republic to open a newspaper in St. Louis without finding an article about Indians, usually in association with violence. If the stories were not of formal military confrontations, they were of conflicts among the Indians or between the Indians and settlers. The Missouri General Assembly petitioned Congress in 1821 to extinguish Indians' claims to Missouri land, to prevent further Indian migration into Missouri, and to remove eastern tribes already placed there by federal policy. The United States negotiated treaties between 1823 and 1832 to accomplish these goals and put Osage and other Missouri groups in Kansas, on land considered undesirable for white settlers. A particular problem area was Arkansas and southern Missouri, where Cherokees were moving onto land already occupied by the Osage Indians. This problem grew much worse after 1830 and the passage of the Indian

Removal Act, which forced the rest of the Cherokees, the Creeks, the Seminoles, the Chickasaws, and the Choctaws into Osage territory. To the west, hostilities flared up intermittently among the Osages, the Pawnees, the Comanches, and the Kiowas.[5]

Smallpox and cholera both struck the Osages in the late 1830s, further destabilizing their society. In 1833 the state government authorized five sheriffs in northwestern Missouri to recruit vigilantes to prevent Indians from hunting in the state. In 1836 settlers in northwestern Missouri, frightened by false rumors generated by some white liquor peddlers, feared Osage attacks and wanted to force them entirely out of Missouri. Under the direction of Governor Lilburn Boggs, local men formed a militia to search out Osage raiders. Finding only some mixed-blood women living near the old mission at Harmony, they seized them. Federal troops from Fort Leavenworth arrived, saved the women, and tried to disband the militia. The troops failed, and the militia went on to hunt down some starving Osage families foraging for food and forced them out of Missouri. Two years later the Osages, weak from illnesses, political disunity, and constant violence, had to abandon neighboring ancestral land in Oklahoma to make room for the Cherokees, whose Trail of Tears ended on formerly Osage land.[6]

Indians in Missouri were never subjected to wholesale slaughter, but they became increasingly unwelcome there. A group of Shawnee and Delaware farmers forced out of the East tried to live peacefully on the Missouri River near St. Louis. Several served as guides for militia companies, and William Clark praised them for the help they provided settlers. But as white settlement grew, Americans took their lands and forced them to move west, eventually to Oklahoma.[7]

By the 1830s Indians were no longer a regular presence but a special, worrisome occurrence in St. Louis. Indian-European war had always been a part of the North American landscape, a fact of life. But in the nineteenth century conflict was unceasing until the 1880s. Missouri hoped to mobilize women to a frame of mind appropriate to the "stalwart and rugged" atmosphere of constant border wars. The wide-ranging aggression characteristic of American Indian policy needed women's support, and to whip up enthusiasm for dispossession, newspapers published frightening tales and applauded female courage.[8]

The Missouri newspapers were consistently in favor of the removal of the "Civilized" tribes, distrusting all Indians and being contemptuous of "friends of aboriginies" who failed to understand their true, vengeful, and warlike nature. Typical was the outrage expressed at eastern sympathy with the defeated and imprisoned Sauk chief Black Hawk: "[T]his savage, copper-colored subject . . . shed the innocent blood of many of the enterprising inhabitants of our frontier."[9]

Anglo-Americans moving into the St. Louis area after 1800 were likely to have a family history of violence with Indians. Many Missourians came from settler families that had implemented or accelerated removal policy by taking lands where Indians still had claims. The grandfather of Lewis Linn, Missouri's enthusiastically proJackson senator (1833–1843), was a settler-scout in the Indian wars in the Ohio Valley. He and his wife both were killed in 1781. These wars, into which Linn's parents were born, lasted twenty years. Like Andrew Jackson's, Linn's early years were saturated with fear and violence.[10]

American women in and around St. Louis usually had little alternative but to support a violent military policy toward Indians. Their fathers, husbands, and sons were often directly involved. In October 1837 a regiment of white soldiers left St. Charles County for the Seminole War. Students of the female college of Columbia, Missouri, presented the soldiers "a beautiful silk flag."[11]

Missouri's senators made sure their constituents understood that they were beefing up military reinforcements with the arrival in the vicinity of uprooted eastern nations. In St. Louis during a period of massive immigration and settlement the differences in the way white men and women treated Native Americans do not seem to have been substantial. Anglo-American middle-class women's empathic emotional style inside the household seems to have translated into support for dispossession and removal coupled with the hope that it would not be unpleasant. Evangelicals often wished to convert Indians to Christianity and American culture. Women living on or near contested lands were fearful; a few were violent. Fear often resulted in male protection, which itself confirmed the reasonableness of the fear and increased the distance it placed between white women and Native people.[12]

A more noticeable difference in attitude lay not between the sexes but between the French and the Anglo-Americans. Under French and Spanish rule, relations with the surrounding Indians had been reasonably peaceful. In part this was because the French and Spanish settler populations were small. In addition, the Chouteaus, St. Louis's founding family, had made cultural and familial alliances particularly with the Osages who inhabited Missouri. The French had sent boys, often orphans, to live with Indians to learn their languages and become sufficiently bicultural to spy on them. The Chouteau boys grew up learning the language and customs of the Osages. Although the policy could backfire, creating Frenchmen who adopted an Indian way of life rather than loyal French informants, it established a tradition of bicultural life at least for some men. Also, French and Spanish traders not infrequently married Indian women.[13]

Frenchwomen, whose husbands mediated their relationships with Indians, were more fearful than their men. But as members of French fur-trading families, usually on good terms with Indians, Frenchwomen had less to fear than representatives of the perpetually warring United States. Adele Gratiot remembered, when she lived in the wilderness,

> four tall Indians, with guns in hand, coming up to the house. I was so taken by surprise that the bowl fell from my hands, to the great dismay of the children. I ran in to apprise the gentlemen. . . . They were friendly Winnebago chiefs, who came to tell us that, on account of the encroachments of the whites upon their territory, they could not restrain their young men, who were going to declare war.[14]

Both French and Anglo-American women's fear was an important part of the atmosphere through which men conducted relations with Indians and increased the cultural distance between the sexes. When

Jules de Mun went among the Kansas Indians in 1816, he wrote his wife not to have any fear for him. He went on to tell her about a Pawnee attack on his brother's party, in which three men were wounded and one died. But, he said, it was the victims' fault.[15]

American men tried to protect their women but also praised those who turned their aggression against Native Americans. Agnes Lindsay of St. Charles was celebrated for being brave and resolute and "had killed several indians during her life." Women in Daniel Boone's family were memorialized for molding bullets, nursing the wounded, loading rifles, and generally taking a hand in the skirmishing against Indians that accompanied early settlement. The missionary and western promoter Timothy Flint wrote scathingly of wives who feared to agree to their husbands' wishes to move west.[16]

By the late 1830s the Indians in Missouri generally appeared to have been rendered harmless. In 1838 Jette Bruns noted that Indians had been twice near her home. She remarked: "There is no thought of danger or attack. They obey as soon as they are told." The expectation of peace brought with it the expectation—or the hope—that the Indians were about to die out. The painter George Catlin, in St. Louis five times between 1830 and 1836, decided to create "an ethnographic record of a dying race." There were approximately forty novels published between 1824 and 1834 about the vanishing American Indian. A story in the St. Louis Beacon in 1832 announced that "they are . . . doomed, by an Infinite Wisdom, to give way gradually and retire further and further before the enterprize of intelligence and civilization. Such has ever been their fate hitherto . . . and such, in all probability, will continue to be so, so long as there remains on this continent a remnant of their unfortunate and devoted race." American women who recoiled from the brutality of violent dispossession nevertheless saw the demise of Indians as inevitable. Even the handful of women writers who dealt sympathetically with Indian life, like Catherine Sedgwick and Lydia Maria Child, supported removal.[17]

While the long Anglo dehumanization of Indians effectively ensured that most women (and men) of the middle class would probably not be tempted to extend their feelings of empathy and sympathy to Native people, a few opposed the dominant view. Some Missouri women worked to convert the Indians to Christianity. George and Mary Sibley promoted religious and moral transformation in the hope that the Osages would become less Osage; they supported removal but wanted it to be painless. Indeed, as a commissioned Indian agent in Fort Osage in 1808, George Sibley advocated fair treatment for the Osages, the Pawnees, the Kansas, and all other Indians still at large. He thought the Osages had a strong religious bent but doubted that they would ever become "civilized until [they adopted] the religion of Jesus Christ." He also believed they would have to move from the land they had traditionally inhabited.[18]

Mary Sibley joined her husband in 1815 at Fort Osage, where they spent their early married years. She worked to convert the Indians and, according to mission records, "purchase[d] a thirteen year old Osage girl and called her, Mary E. Sibley." Whatever Sibley's hopes and plans for her namesake, the politics of removal interfered. In 1824 the missionaries established a new mission at Neosho, farther west in Kansas. It attracted some Osages as federal pressure pushed them west.[19]

Anglo-American women inherited centuries of fear of Indians. Fear cancels out empathy. Nearly constant violence and the power of the myth that Indians were unfit for the modern world, hence already dying out, convinced most Anglo-American women that coerced dispossession was proper policy. Military and political leaders worked to mobilize women and their moral support for the American project of dispossession. In the name of religion, civilization, liberty, and patriotism most women followed their husbands into disputed borderlands and defended their cabins.

Gender and Greed

Boosterism in the western cities of the new nation grew out of the new American equation of patriotism with individual success. Economic individualism dominated the courtship patterns of striving western Anglo-Americans and continued to dictate the rhythms of their married lives. The difference between the early nineteenth century and what had gone before was a matter of degree for some and of kind for others, who were newly experimenting with market endeavors. While the Revolution encouraged both economic and sentimental individualism, there were few brakes on the former. Through stories, allegories, and the use of certain recurrent metaphors, St. Louis writers struggled with the moral issues that rapidly growing commerce created, such as economic inequality, cycles of boom and bust, regulating consumption, and finding wives' proper place in the scramble for wealth. St. Louis men struggled, sometimes violently, to make their fortunes against a backdrop of rising anxiety about women's consumption. Absent from public discourse but omnipresent were workingwomen.[20]

St. Louis men daily tested themselves, their acumen, virility, and stamina against others in achieving riches, particularly through land speculation. More money circulated in the early republic than ever before; more slaves were being sold and bought; more household goods were being purchased than produced. Like the national economy, St. Louis's economy expanded and contracted alarmingly in the antebellum period. The city and the rest of the West had experienced prosperity during and after the War of 1812. When St. Louis was handed over to the Americans, its earliest years were dominated by ferocious fighting over land between shifting coalitions of old French families and new American immigrants. Defending interests was a life-and-death struggle. Everyone knew that land values in the territory would climb precipitously with the American takeover, and this struggle, with a changing cast of opponents and supporters of the Spanish land claims, went on well after statehood in 1821.[21]

White women watched as their husbands accumulated or lost money, bought or sold land and slaves, competed with other men, fought duels, and were, or were not, elected to office. Men's business commitments shaped married life. William Lane's growing practice meant less and less time for his wife. In one letter he gushed, "When do we meet? Say the word?" Despite his enthusiasm, he warned her that he had little time to help her return to St. Louis: "It is vitally important to me not to be long absent from my business."[22]

Women were to provide their men a respite from these titanic struggles and to remind them that "riches and grandeur" would not produce the "contentment" that was all a person really needed or

should seek in life. "Goodness of heart" was the only worthy goal.
This would rein in the envy that might destabilize a society growing
more unequal. A virtuous husband worried about providing for others, not satisfying his ambitions, and gave as freely as he could. A disinterested wife purchased with caution and asked for little. Goodness
of heart signaled a family devoted to one another through sentiment.
And sentiment, in the words of one critic, was "a strategy for claiming cultural status independent of one's financial status."[23]

Moralists Abigail Mott and Lydia Maria Child reminded readers
of the republican goal of disinterestedness. They opposed the accumulation of excess wealth altogether. Both criticized men for trying
to acquire more than a "competency." The wholehearted pursuit of
wealth, Mott thought, created lopsided men, deficient in cultivation.
She emphasized frugality and economy in both earning and living.
Mott, unlike many moralists who focused solely on issues inside the
home, pointed out the moral cost of acquiring riches. If Americans
worked for a competence, not wealth, then the United States would
be "built, not on the quicksands of extended commerce; not on
bloodstained treasure of the east or west; but on the solid rock of
public and private virtue." She pointed to the suffering of many who
were instrumental to the riches of others and to the instability of an
economic system that encouraged speculation. For the most part,
however, moralists tried to deal with the results of inequality, not to
criticize its origins.[24]

Newspaper articles honoring domestic life explained that the only
thing that "reconcile[d] a man of trade" to the "toil of business . . .
the fastidiousness and impertinence of customers . . . many hours of
tedious confinement" was "the caresses of his family." He will "be-
hold the desire of his eyes and the children of his love, for whom he
resigns his ease; and in their welfare and smile, he will find his recompense." The author cautioned the rich to appreciate the life of
laboring men: "See his toil worn countenance assumes an air of
cheerfulness; his hardships are forgotten; fatigue vanishes; he eats . . .
his plain repast . . . and is satisfied." Innocence and purity marked
those who remained, because of gender or class, outside the economy. At home the wife, detached from worldliness, ruled in republican virtue over a loving husband and a faithless economy. Retreat

from the wider world to sweet domesticity signaled the triumph of sentiment over the corruption of the marketplace.

The other face of this idealization of wives and a reminder of the scorn awaiting those who grasped at luxury was a persistent long-term fear of women's supposed greed, susceptibility to temptation, and insatiable appetite for wealth. Given the peace and respite wives should be providing their market warriors, it was so much the worse, then, when the impure female element poisoned men's economic chances. The prerevolutionary critique of British politics and morals based in the language of luxury, vice, and femininity reappeared after the contraction of 1819 had begun to hurt St. Louis, particularly in editorials and articles about banking. Prostitutes and parasites, these feminized institutions were the cause of men's economic woes, not just the messengers of them. In times of economic crisis, western men believed these banks had seduced and abandoned them to destitution and ruin, revealing their true identity as servants of the interests of rich, powerful men in the East.[25]

The tradition of feminizing debt and the institutions involved in it derived from the association of dependency with women. Independence instead represented all that was debt-free, incorruptible, and masculine. Psychologically, credit-giving institutions seem to have been female because men saw their relationships with them as intimate, confiding, and built on men's sharing their deepest desires and dreams. To the extent that magical thinking—then and now—usually accompanies male-female relationships, so too it accompanies hopes of becoming rich.[26]

Along with these metaphorical links between women and economic insecurity, more direct ones joined women to men's economic woes. In sermons and the popular press, a wife's greed intruded in the marriage bed, marking her transformation into a prostitute. Selfish disregard for her husband's financial striving made a pretty woman ugly in the eyes of her worried spouse. In St. Louis, where more and more goods were available for cash, identity of spouses' financial interests, or rather the purification of the husband's self-interest through the wife's disinterestedness, had become necessary to social stability and hence marital love.

Consumption

The expanding array of goods and increasing demand for them meant that consumption played a significant part in the emotional and moral economy of early-nineteenth-century St. Louis. Moralists argued for frankness between husband and wife about money. They also emphasized restraint in hospitality and dress. Men's clothes, relatively drab and uniform, made it harder for males to declare their status through their clothing. Women's dress, on the other hand, represented both the status of the couple and the generosity of the husband. An emphasis on measured display was to show restraint and respectability and minimize differences of wealth in a culture generating a growing class of the newly rich. Domestic moderation helped create a harmonious nation.[27]

Husbands used goods as expressions of affection and approval and sometimes as representations of the family's status. Wives tried to keep their material wants to a minimum, wishing to draw little from the marital budget, thereby emphasizing their increasing dependence. Married women also equated husbandly love with presents and objects. On the one hand, this emerging language of commodities could express affection in new and pleasing ways. On the other hand, in a climate where husbands' careers dominated their marriages, it frequently substituted goods for emotional and sexual exchange. Also, since men were engaged in market activities far more regularly and reaped more financial rewards than did women, the flow of gifts went one way. This equation had the effect of making women's consumption seem gratuitous and unhitched it from their contributions to the household. One woman wrote of her husband: "I get all I want by asking for it. . . . I have all I wish and nothing to complain of." Her expression foregrounded his generosity and obliterated her work.[28]

Most wives in early St. Louis considered consumption a moral issue about which they were to be responsible both to their husbands and to an ideal of frugality. Many consumed with great care, demonstrating their good taste and enjoying new possessions. Consuming for the family, in this case the extended family, was a middle-class woman's duty as well as a tempered expression of her individuality. Saved from self-assertion and greed by family purposes, Sarah von Phul Mason was an astute consumer of the adornments of middle-class life but parsimonious in her own personal decoration, exemplifying the ideal virtues for her social position. She was not personally self-indulgent but was sophisticated in those purchases that confirmed families' respectability. She taught her careful consumption habits to her adolescent daughter years later.[29]

After two years of marriage Mason equated her happiness in marriage with her husband's giving her the things she wanted. She was sure that because her wishes were few and well thought out, he would agree to them. She told her sister-in-law: "I cannot recollect a single instance of his so much as contradicting me, my wishes have often been anticipated, and always gratified to the extent of his power, I feel as perfectly assured of a happy life . . . as a frail mortal ought to be."[30]

However, a wife who let her own desires be known too clearly was open to criticism. Wives might importune their husbands on behalf of other family members, but not for themselves. Dorcas Bent Carr, married to the extremely prosperous judge and widower William Carr, seems to have expressed a desire to buy something beautiful for her stepdaughter, and Judge Carr wrote her from Philadelphia that he was perfectly happy for her to "rig out your husbands daughter," but that he wanted her to dress well also. "It is neither my wish nor shall it ever be so if I can help it, that you should be so obscure as to be overlooked in a crowd. . . . I will not consent that either of you appear as a foil to the other—neither of you could do without at least two or three more changes than what you brought on & I hope you will get good ones." Like Sarah Mason, Dorcas Carr displayed frugality toward herself and a desire to give to those close to her. Her husband encouraged her desires to include herself in a transaction typical of affectionate marriages. Husbands became trustees of their wives' desires. The Carr women, by shining in society, would represent both Will Carr's prosperity and his generosity, while they would exercise their taste in a prudent display of ornamentation.[31]

Acquisition troubled Mary Sibley, and she expressed this in her choice of words. She became aware of her own wealth compared with the poverty of the women she visited to bring the Word of God. "The Lord has blessed me with many comforts and luxuries which she has not," she wrote after meeting with one poor woman. Sibley disapproved of material accumulation and did not buy clothing to adorn herself, but she did enjoy her "comforts." "Comfort" evolved as a kind of British code to distinguish virtuous bourgeois commodities from aristocratic "luxuries." Sibley's use of the word "comfort" domesticated the objects she owned. It renamed them as "sentimental possessions" beyond market crassness, rather than as purchases. But her use of "luxuries" implicated her in mean-spirited acquisition, which she and her husband so deplored.

Wives of well-to-do men in the early nineteenth century expressed an ambivalent identity as consumers. Consumption was a new language in which objects could stand in for husbands' physical and verbal expressions of fondness. Some wives interpreted the satisfaction of their wants as marital happiness, but wives' expressions of emotional satisfaction seem like muted translations, not resounding affirmations. Consumer goods, like physical attraction, stimulated desires that women were to throttle down. Purchasing for pleasure required husbands' implicit consent and encouragement. Thus wives' consumption for themselves was likely to be tentative. However, wives brought little ambivalence and considerable seriousness to purchases for the family. They carefully selected items that both constituted and expressed their social standing. Their unhesitating engagement in consuming for others did not threaten the fiction that wives were disinterested. Thrift and words like "comfort" helped dissociate purchases from their origins in the market. For widows, years of thrift and the sense of being guardians rather than proprietors of money and goods were hard-to-change outlooks. For evangelicals, religious belief might reinforce republican ideals of a competency, but their goal was not austerity. Sibley did not wish to divest herself of possessions, or to share them, but to remind herself that they were from God's goodness.[32]

Women's Market Participation

The fiction that women were disinterested and selfless because they were outside the market provided a "private" retreat in which men could purify themselves. But women of course were neither outside the market nor selfless, even if they did resist defining themselves fully through economic activity. Employed women often aimed at the republican goal of independence, or competency, which meant having some kind of skill to sell and avoiding factory work. They usually hoped to be useful, while men frequently dreamed of success and wealth. Wives who did not work for money had an oblique and often, but not always, critical relationship to the economy. Some openly disapproved of the opportunities for self-centered accumulation.

St. Louis in the 1830s congratulated itself on the fact that its economy, while volatile, did not force children and women into factory work. In fact, there was little manufacturing yet in St. Louis. Adolph Meier was to open a cotton factory in the early 1840s and advertise for seventeen- and eighteen-year-old "girls," but in the 1830s St. Louis could look at Great Britain and New England with satisfaction that conditions in Missouri were wholesome by comparison. However, while the papers ran stories on labor legislation in Great Britain to protect children from night work and to protect children under nine from working at all, Missourians, worried about the moral conditions of their environment, concentrated on factories as a symbol of heartless industrialization and wage slavery, not on whether children should work. Poor children in nineteenth-century Missouri, white and black, worked and worked hard. Yet compared with New England, Missouri insisted that it protected its women and children from the insatiable industrialization that was overtaking Europe and New England. This was part of the larger argument that slavery offered a kind of lifetime social security to slaves, unlike wage laborers, who were left to die on the streets when they were too old to work. Although there was little factory work for women, there were nevertheless plenty of women working.[33]

The first women to make a notable economic contribution to the growth of St. Louis were Native Americans, especially the Osages with whom the Chouteaus had initiated fur trade. The disappearance of game in the nineteenth century, warfare with the United States, and the policy of dispossession began to reduce the trade and women's labor in it. Women continued to do the agriculture essential to survival but had little more to do with the expanding American economy. Indeed across the United States in the nineteenth century Native men and women participated in prophetic movements that rejected European consumer objects as well as practices, seen to pollute Native American societies by diverting them from their traditional, sacred ways. Americans saw individual ownership of land and the satisfaction of individual desires as key to "civilizing" the Indians. But the Osages did not give up their ideals and practices like communal landownership despite the growing pressures on them to do so.[34]

White women in the Midwest were more likely to participate in the cash economy as consumers than as earners, but many did both. Rural women might market dairy products. A few women worked as teachers, midwives, dressmakers, corset makers, governesses, and milliners, and in the early 1840s a few girls worked in St. Louis's cotton factory. For the most part, black women served as maids, cooks, and laundresses. Both white and black ran boardinghouses and brothels. White women taught English, French, geography, history, science, voice, piano, guitar, sewing, fancy needlework, lace embroidery, and dancing. In 1821 the census for St. Louis listed 18 employed women; by 1840 the number was 141, of whom 54 were African Americans, although they constituted less than 10 percent of the population. Women working for wages were, for the most part, a uniquely vulnerable group, selling skills that usually had little market value. Female teachers were paid fairly well, although half as well as their male counterparts. In 1838 the St. Louis Board of Education paid Edward Leary $168.75 and David Armstrong $225 for teaching from April 25 to July 2, while it paid Sarah Hardy $93.75 and Mary Salisbury $125 for the same period.[35]

Susan Vanarsdale, a teacher from Illinois in Audrain County, Missouri, evinced little economic ambition but a powerful desire to "do some good." She wrote, "If I may only be enabled to be of service to others . . . 'tis all I ask." Emily Austin, a milliner, worked hard her whole life, moving every three or four years into and later out of Missouri, sometimes in poverty so great it meant giving up her children to foster care. Her most republican of ambitions was for "independence." She wrote that she had "ever looked at avarice as my worst foe. . . . To emulate the example of the good Samaritan effectually, one must be in possession of an independence."[36]

Utility, production, and ambition organized and gave meaning to these women's lives. Austin explicitly rejected accumulation, and Vanarsdale never even mentioned economic considerations. If men were more alone with money in this period than ever before in history, it was only one of several concerns for these women and apparently of equal weight with helping out their families and making some kind of contribution to their society.

Women in the middle class were eager not to lose whatever independence they had achieved. Sarah von Phul Mason visited the Bradleys, who had recently lost all their money. Nevertheless, she remarked, "They keep up appearances very well." Mrs. Bradley had eleven children, all still living at home, and had taken in student boarders. Their rent allowed the couple to seem to keep their large house, although the Bank of the United States actually owned it. General Bradley's daughters did the housework. The Bradleys had maintained their standard of living and avoided wage labor.[37]

Mary Sibley, financially comfortable with her husband, was highly critical of accumulation and saw hope for an improved United States only in conversion to Christ. She found in evangelicalism both a critique of the widespread ethos of material gain and political advancement and a path to the disinterestedness that had once characterized good citizens, but increasingly applied only to women.[38]

Despite married women's contributions to the family economy, whether in cash or labor, when the Missouri legislature considered an act granting married women property, proponents argued for it in terms of protecting women from men's unwise participation in the market, not of any right women might have to their own "competency." In 1837 a severe panic afflicted the country. Missouri felt its full effects in 1842 and for the next few years. In response to the seizures of property for debts, Mississippi passed in 1839 the first statute guaranteeing married women security in their property. In 1845 the Missouri legislature considered such a statute, but by and large men rejected the notion that wives and husbands had two separate economic interests as French law presumed. One supporter even wrote that husbands assumed financial responsibility voluntarily for their wives. In return the wife "guards the home, and, by her presence and affection; gives it a value inestimable and a charm above price." Here the wife's contributions had no market value.[39]

By the Civil War seventeen states had passed similar legislation. These laws provided to all married women a general legislative protection that had previously been available only to the rich through their husbands and fathers. Although that was not its intent, the reform gave legal reality to the possibility of differing financial interests between husband and wife. Its defenders saw themselves as protectors of exploited wives. However, this legislation also spurred on feminist activity designed to recognize and sustain a vision of married women as economic agents. Ironically, French American women in St. Louis would have been getting back part of what they had sacrificed by becoming Americans through this legislation. French law had long permitted wives to hold property in their own names and to renounce their dower rights if they were smaller than a fair share of their husbands' estates would be.[40]

Public Life: Violence, Tolerance, and Reform

Just as women were engaged in the economy, so they were engaged in public life but not through the majority (Democratic) party in Missouri. Democrats, who favored cheap land, states' rights, and minimal government, practiced boisterous politics that could frighten and alienate women. They did not welcome or encourage women's support till mid-century. Whigs, on the other hand, who favored governmental encouragement of institutions and projects that contributed to the nation's economic growth, like canals, roads, and the United States Bank, courted women's participation. Women watched and participated at the far edges of Missouri party politics and through reform.[41]

The violence of early national party politics effectively ensured women's distance, as much as ideas of true womanhood did. Women watched and feared, or mourned, as political disputes turned violent, sometimes resulting in death or in the ruin of reputations. Intemperance, brawling, toxic gossip, and the unpredictable spark that could ignite deadly feuds designated "real" politics. St. Louis was particularly interested in the ferocious war between President Andrew Jackson and the Bank of the United States because Thomas Biddle was the brother of the bank's president, Nicholas Biddle, and Thomas was married to Ann Mullanphy, the daughter of the very wealthy Irishman and St. Louis benefactor John Mullanphy. The Democratic papers in St. Louis attacked the bank and its supporters, but the issue went beyond verbal violence. Thomas Biddle beat with a cane the Democratic candidate for Congress (and bank opponent), Spencer Pettis. Subsequently, in 1831, the two fought a duel on Bloody Island in the Mississippi. Because Biddle was nearsighted, the men fought with pistols at a distance of five feet; both died, and Ann Mullanphy Biddle, who had not even known her husband was planning to fight, was suddenly a widow.[42]

Other duels claimed other victims and left women mourning. Thomas Hart Benton killed young Charles Lucas. William McArthur, Lewis Linn's brother-in-law, killed Auguste de Mun in 1834. Judge Will Carr spit in the face of the publisher Joseph Charless and put a pistol to his chest. Charless retaliated by throwing stones at him. Dr. William Lane reassured his worried wife, Mary, that he would not engage in a duel. "I despise the practice and love you too well," he wrote in 1819. His political activities did bring him at least one challenge and the choice of weapons. He is reported to have responded that he and his opponent should sit together on a keg of powder to see who would be shot the farther toward heaven.[43]

While domestic middle-class culture was becoming more centered on emotions, physical bravery and the command of violence helped legitimize a man's claim to leadership in western communities. Some urban middle-class men of St. Louis began joining women in disapproval of duels, particularly after Benton's killing of young Charles Lucas and another notorious duel in the 1820s. The legislature started passing antidueling acts in 1822. Legislators made dueling the equivalent of murder and enjoined those running for politics to take a vow not to duel. Legislation in 1835 made even presence at a duel a misdemeanor punishable with a year in jail, and six months for anyone challenging or "posting" (publicizing) another's unwillingness to fight. Individually women could do little about dueling, but the spread of middle-class domesticity slowly undermined its acceptance in more settled communities.[44]

Women's views of the contested center of power, where men fought over economic and political issues, were both critical and distant. But even the periphery of politics—i.e., the social lives of men and women around the president and Congress—became dangerous with the advent of Andrew Jackson, whose behavior contravened a generation of assumptions about the direct relationship between national leadership and gentility.[45] Democratic, Jacksonian politics were not genteel nor did women's moral standards provide a reassuring background for its programs and plans.

Judge William C. Carr made a trip to Washington to attend the trial of his fellow judge James Peck of St. Louis, against whom an attorney, the wonderfully named Luke Lawless, had initiated a movement to impeach. The case arose out of a violent argument in Peck's courtroom between Lawless and Judge J. B. C. Lucas over the latter's right to give testimony as a friend of the court. Peck had Lawless jailed and fined for intemperate behavior, and Lawless responded with impeachment proceedings. Carr, a very old friend of Lucas's, observed to his wife that the opening speech against Peck was "the most violent and abusive effort I have ever heard."[46]

Moral risks in Andrew Jackson's Washington included socializing. Carr filled his wife in on a party he attended at the notorious Margaret Eaton's house a few nights earlier. He marveled to her: "a backwoods Missouri Judge (sometimes mistaken for a member of the Presbyterian Church) to attend one of Mrs. Eaton's parties!" Peggy Eaton, the pretty, lively wife of Jackson's close friend the secretary of war John Eaton, was a controversial figure in Washington. Mrs. Eaton, as bold and forthright in her way as Jackson in his, had worked in her family's boardinghouse, an occupation both vulgar and surrounded with temptation. She had an open and unreserved style that enemies read as sexual impurity. Jackson was convinced of her chastity and tried to force his cabinet members to see it that way, but they could not and would not try to control their wives, who refused to return Mrs. Eaton's calls or associate with her in public places.[47]

Mob violence, especially to support slavery, in addition to party violence and the violence that could be done to reputations, further limited the scope of political activities in which St. Louis women might engage. Elijah Lovejoy, nativist and abolitionist publisher in St. Louis, was a sometime guest at the Sibley house. But Lovejoy's uncompromising views on abolition began to make the Sibleys, who advocated colonization of freed slaves in Africa, uncomfortable. Many of Mary Sibley's close friends and associates remonstrated with Lovejoy over what they thought was his intemperate attack on the lynchers of Francis McIntosh and on slavery altogether. Her husband canceled his subscription to Lovejoy's newspaper, just prior to Lovejoy's murder at the hands of a mob.[48]

How did some women enter politics in largely Democratic Missouri? Mary Sibley's experience provides some answers. Sibley was a passionate supporter of Henry Clay, Whig senator from Kentucky, and she embodied what one historian has called Whig womanhood. In addition to colonization, she was interested in temperance and joined the Female Benevolent Society. Her main interest was in promoting education, which she did by organizing her own school, and helping to see that the education beyond Sunday school of selected poor children was paid for. She also organized Sunday schools for Germans and slave children.[49]

The blend of Sibley's political and religious views demonstrates how evangelical religion imparted the confidence to participate. Before she could enter politics, Sibley had to redimension men to her size—the size of all God's creatures. Through religion, she lost both the paralyzing deference she was trained to feel for some men and her class contempt for others. Just after her conversion she heard two sermons from an old preacher: "[T]he Old man was a real follower of the Lord Jesus that notwithstanding he was illiterate and shabbily arrayed. My prejudices . . . were subdued and I could love him." On another occasion she confessed that when the itinerant minister began to preach, she was disposed to laugh at him for his "sad mistakes in grammar and the use of English words, but I checked myself with the reflection . . . [that] this poor ignorant man might be far more highly favored in the sight of our God than myself or any of our more learned brethren."[50]

Just as she was troubled by her prejudices toward the rough-hewn, so she was troubled by her feelings of respect and admiration for polished and powerful men like the Reverend Mr. Potts of St. Louis, who became the president of Marion College. She needed to bracket her excess of enthusiasm for a fellowman who, she worried, threatened to fix her attention on this world, not the next. She fought to suppress the excitement she felt from his good opinion of her. The democracy implicit in evangelical religion helped Sibley recast her dangerous feelings for Potts as Christian fellowship and nothing more.[51]

Sibley gained authority from the democratic (and empathic) possibilities of evangelical faith. But despite her abhorrence of censoriousness, she could not imagine the humanity of Catholics. Other St. Louis women, including some Presbyterians, however, found Catholics kinder and gentler than their fellow worshipers. A founder of the Presbyterian church in St. Louis, Susan Hempstead Gratiot wrote her brother in St. Louis that "the love that I have for so many dear friends that are Catholick give me more charity . . . than many . . . [but] I cannot condemn them in fact we have no right to condemn each other."[52]

More typical among Protestants, however, was Sarah Ward, the wife of an Episcopal minister, who conceded to a recent Catholic convert that she was "equally under the care of Divine providence as a good Catholic or as an Episcopalian." Nonetheless, she hastened to enter into controversy, saying, "[W]ithout wishing . . . to enter into any religious controversy . . . permit me to differ from you in opinion, that there is any similarity between the two Churches in question." She went on to enumerate the Episcopalian rejections of numerous points of Catholic doctrine, particularly any special devotion to the Virgin. The widespread authority of Protestantism could support both democracy and intolerance.[53]

When Protestant women embarked on reform activities, it was a tentative and stepwise process. The authority they found in religion was not to lead them to disturb the authority of their husbands, nor was it to challenge the authority of men engaging in politics or business. Protestant reformers displayed cringing submission to men publicly while insisting that reform politics was not really politics. In line with women of northern cities, however, they could assume moral authority over and on behalf of select subordinates: children, the poor, and slaves.

In 1824 an association led by Anglo-Americans and supported as well by Frenchwomen founded the Female Benevolent Society of St. Louis, hoping to "relieve distressed females and children" and to encourage industry among the poor . . . (particularly during the sickly season)." The constitution assured readers that the women were not about to abandon "that dearer scene of duty which lies at home" but only to "employ whatever time, energy and money they had left over." It noted that as individuals they could accomplish little but that together "the limits of our power for good or evil cannot be easily fixed." They affirmed that retiring from the world was one of the "most lovely traits in the female character, yet it must not be allowed to shrink from acknowledged duty, simply because that duty is to be performed in public." The managers were obliged to report cases of distress to the board of directors, which would decide on "the propriety of affording relief, except in cases of sickness or pressing necessity, when application to the first directress shall be sufficient." The directresses framed their mission in the language of true womanhood.[54]

In St. Louis, Catholics preceded Protestants into the familiar areas of benevolent work, establishing schools, orphanages, and hospitals to care for the sick and the destitute, who, in the turbulent economy of the early republic, were having trouble making their way. The nuns, unlike Protestant reformers, did the actual work of cooking, cleaning, tending the sick, teaching children, and caring for the orphans. They had no need to issue statements or draw up constitutions inasmuch as their mandate was long since established in Catholic tradition. For wealthy Catholic women, the nuns were their delegated emissaries of mercy, whom they supported with both money and friendship. St. Louis Catholic charities probably helped

motivate Protestant women in St. Louis to engage in reforms, and
the Protestant-organized movement gathered momentum from its
urge to compete with the well-organized and institutionally savvy
Catholics. It was a morally sanctioned way for socially prominent
Protestant women to establish themselves as the new aristocracy, displacing the Creoles, who left reform work to the nuns. It was also a
chance to offer help to needy Protestant children who might otherwise come under Catholic influence.[55]

The Catholics founded an orphanage for girls in 1827, and in
1834 the Sisters of Charity moved their Carondolet orphanage to St.
Louis. Catholics received money and a building for the first project
from John Mullanphy. He promised funding for twenty girls, including ten dollars for bedding, five dollars for upkeep, and a gift at
departure. More came from his daughter, Ann Biddle, and his son,
Bryan Mullanphy. The Sisters of the Sacred Heart ran the orphanage
along with their free school and their paying school. The bishop provided the Sisters of Charity with money for the second. Typically, a
male board of trustees controlled the funding for Catholic charities
while the sisters ran the internal operations.[56]

Sixteen Anglo-American women, Methodists, Presbyterians, and
Episcopalians, with financial support of women from French families, including the Chouteaus and the Bertholds, established in 1834
the St. Louis Association of Ladies for the Relief of Orphan Children, which called its creation the St. Louis Protestant Orphan Asylum. This was in part a response to the cholera epidemic of 1832,
which left many orphans and half orphans in its wake. Article 1 of the
bylaws was against sectarianism, stating that this was the united
effort of Protestant Christians on behalf of the destitute. Mary Sibley was listed as one of sixty-five life members, each paying five
dollars annually. There were 106 annual subscribers at a dollar each.
These women seem to have been from both elite and evangelical
backgrounds and were bound together by common moral and class
interests.[57]

The asylum volunteers distinguished, with abject rhetoric, their
humble work from men's "dignified cares of government, and all the
honors which talents can obtain in the various roads which lead their

sex to fame and eminence." The authority women were claiming appears colored with uneasy, submerged competition with their husbands.

The Protestant women, while protesting their humility, reached for more control than the nuns in defining, controlling, and having access to the orphans. Part of their mission was to draw an old but increasingly important line distinguishing real suffering from false or insufficient distress. They also positioned themselves to acquire and dispose of potential laborers.[58]

In establishing the genuineness of the orphan's need and his or her status as orphan, women were contributing to the creation of "fair" rules for participation in the growing economy. One of the middle-class tasks in a society characterized by economic inequality was to help establish the justness of the regulations through which people became haves or have-nots. The managers were concerned not to have capable but lazy people take advantage of their charity and unburden themselves of responsibility for their children. Disqualifying some poor as ineligible for charity, through their own fault, firmed up the moral ground under the feet of the well-off.[59]

Women setting up the asylum took over the capacity customarily exercised by overseers of the poor laws. The association members had first "preference" when it came to "placing the children in families." The association functioned as an employment agency for the young poor, placing the children out as workers in families needing labor. Before the asylum even had a building, an association member desired one of the five certified orphans to "spend the winter with her to assist in the care of a child." As the middle class grew, so did the demand for servants. (In Washington, D.C., at the same time, poor children were increasingly apprenticed as house servants.) The St. Louis Protestant women, more in line with northern than with southern asylums, defined an orphan as having either no parents or one indigent parent. In addition, they insisted on control over the orphans who came to them. Their bylaws stipulated: "No relation or friend shall interfere in the management of the children of the Asylum, nor visit them but in presence of the Matron or teacher nor at any time that such visits are disapproved by the Board." Reformers hoped that by substituting orderly habits and moral direction for the assumed chaos of destitution, they could train poor children to be productive members of the new republic. Obtaining children's obedience was key in this transformation, and this required their complete dependence upon the managers.[60]

The managers tried to avoid or at least to charge for being used as a temporary refuge for struggling parents. If they were to take on dependent poor, they wished the privileges that went with having dependents. They had a form for relatives to sign when relinquishing a child that stipulated that they would not

> interfere in the management in any respect whatever or to visit (Him or her) without their [the managers'] consent—and in consideration of their benevolence I do relinquish all right or claim to (his or her) services until the age of eighteen years. And I do engage neither to ask or receive any compensation for the same—or to induce (him or her) to leave the family where they may be placed by the Managers of this Institution.

Mr. Boswell, for example, placed three children with the asylum "in the expectation of death"—i.e., his own. When he recovered, he wanted his children back, but "the society declined until some arrangement was made personally with Mr. Boswell." Six months later the secretary noted that "John Boswell a boy belonging to the institution was decoyed away." Six months after that the three Boswell children went back to their father when he provided a promissory note for expenses the children had incurred. Relations of the three orphans paid seventy-two dollars for the boarding of those children. Poor parents were, by Protestant Americans' definition, unfit parents, from which flowed many consequences. Managers neither employed themselves nor expected to instill in the children the genteel attributes of empathy and refined sentiment. They worked to instill simple obedience.[61]

Despite frustrations and setbacks, the annual meetings were a time when the Protestant women reflected with satisfaction on what they had undertaken. A minister who came to their meeting in 1841 heard an "appropriate Hymn by the little Orphans" and "expressed the gratification he felt in meeting with the society, of the duty of Christians to comfort the Fatherless, and encouraged and excited the members to a faithful performance of their duty, picturing the delight of doing good, and of the glorious reward laid up in reserve for those who love and serve the Lord." These and other public acknowledgments of the association's virtue provided one of its members' rewards, as did the satisfaction of helping the helpless.[62]

The Catholic arrangements for orphans provided more indirect rewards to the women running things. The nuns' satisfactions came with living out their vocation, including living within a community of women. The labor of Catholic orphans was beneficial to, indeed went far toward, supporting the orphanage. But it did not benefit individuals. The orphan girls often became seamstresses, making school uniforms and men's shirts, which were sold. They also made artificial flowers for sale, the proceeds going for clothing for them and materials for sewing. Moreover, they did the orphanage housework. Although the nuns' care of orphan girls was no doubt without frills, and the orphan girls and charity students expressed jealousy of the privileged paying students at the school, nevertheless, Catholics shielded them against the potential for exploitation as live-in help. Domestic service has always been, after all, the least desirable work in the United States. The convent also offered poor girls an alternative to a life of housework and marriage. Regarding the collective life of community service more attractive than marriage and children, many Catholic orphan girls found their vocation as nuns, becoming teachers and workers with the sick, the elderly, and the handicapped. (By comparison, few men were attracted to the priesthood.)[63]

As in other southern communities, women limited their benevolence to the spread of religion and the care of the white poor. Increasingly, slavery proponents wished to distance themselves and their communities from any national charitable societies based in the North. They insisted on a greater and greater separation of religion from any form of social relief. Temperance and tract societies, spreading abstinence and the word of God, throve in St. Louis. Women's reform remained circumscribed.[64]

Sociability

Married women were to substitute compliance for moral autonomy
on issues outside the household and in disputed domestic issues. For
most wives this meant focusing inward on domestic moral values,
overdetermining personal, moral, and emotional life because it was
closer to hand and more malleable than public issues. Nevertheless,
women's personal behavior had both moral and public components.

Like marriage, sociability had acquired positive value in the eyes
of eighteenth-century thinkers as encouraging the development and
refinement of sentiment. Scottish moral philosophers, including
Hume, and others, like Montesquieu, praised sociability as the activity
through which people learned to be humane. Isolation was thought to
breed incivility and misanthropy. Advice manuals incorporated this attitude. "By cheerfulness and sympathy, the powers of conversation are
called forth to peculiar advantage, and the heart is opened to the impressions of tenderness and benevolence. Sentiments are developed,
which, obtaining approbation and currency from their real value,
amuse, instruct, and ennoble the mind." Marriage and sociability offered endless occasions to improve morally through mutual exchanges
of affection and confidence. These improvements would be personal
and would not touch the determining framework of society.[65]

Sociability might or might not promote the moral growth of the
individual, but it decidedly facilitated the exchange of goods and information that linked successful elites. Sociable behavior reinforced
ties, widened the circles of acquaintanceship, spread information,
and reconfirmed the status of the elite. As sentimental culture more
and more dominated middle-class life, distinctions between those
within and without crystallized in countless ways, including the use
of language, dress, ornamentation, and child rearing.[66]

Evangelicals gave sociability an overtly Christian purpose and instituted meetings for praying and mutual improvement as well as for
visiting the needy to offer religious advice, criticism, and occasionally
material aid. These moral purposes overlapped with the pleasures
and practices of the emerging middle class, which, through visiting—
or refusing to visit—reaffirmed its friendships, respectability, and
judgments on correct and incorrect behavior.[67]

Evangelicals particularly charged women with patrolling the social borders between the sexes to avoid improper encounters. Evangelicals used the formats of sociability to regulate aggression and
other undisciplined behavior. After her conversion, Mary Sibley gave
up visiting for worldly pleasure and began visiting to do God's work.
Once she visited a fellow church member with whom she "conversed
nearly all the night. . . . I had for some time thought it my duty to tell
her that she made herself liable to be spoken about by the enemies
of religion by her attentions to Mr. H. riding with him alone. . . . She
took my advice kindly and I felt satisfied that I had done my duty."
Expressing criticism and trying to persuade people of things they
might not want to hear were tricky but potentially satisfying aspects
of being a Christian. They were particularly tricky, and perhaps particularly satisfying, for women precisely because both required aggression, normally forbidden to them.[68]

Evangelical sociability took place among a group of strivers who
opened themselves to one another's criticism of their efforts to lead
godly lives. Their understanding of a holy community was the same
as early Puritans' understanding: that the sin of one harms the whole
community. Churches discussed contentious and questionable behavior among parishioners and delegated members to speak to one
another about these problems. If that failed, the church elders took
up the negotiations. In practice, women, who were responsible for
compliance in marriage and virtue bearing in the republic, were held
to more rigorous standards of orderly and nonaggressive behavior
than men were. White women were usually disciplined for aggression in one form or another, and black women for sexual offenses.
White men were almost always the investigators and always the
judges. If women were assigned to visit, men generally followed
up with another visit. Not surprisingly, white men were the least
frequently excluded from membership as a punishment. They also
joined churches in substantially smaller numbers than women. In the
one church that provided a count in 1838, white women outnumbered white men in the congregation by more than two to one, and
blacks represented slightly over 10 percent.[69]

Men confessed and remained in these churches despite sins like
"being overtaken in passion and prepar[ing] for combat," speaking

badly of other members, lack of attendance, "great impropriety," and not paying debts. Women criticizing or acting aggressively received surveillance, censure, and often exclusion.[70]

While congregations made the rules for religious gatherings and visits, starting in the 1820s a rush of etiquette books for middle-class readers regulated secular visiting. When Sarah Mason arrived in Lexington, after a ten-year absence, she made a round of "friendly calls" or visits to close friends not bound by any formal rules. These could occur at almost any time and without special attention to dress. But when her husband joined her, the couple executed a more formal "round of visiting." The proliferation of rules ensured that making calls was something only educated people knew how to do properly, and their forms required participants to have—at a minimum—a "girl." The Masons' ceremonial visits effectively stated who were friends and who were not. Such visits could be made by leaving calling cards as well as actually seeing the friends. Servants patrolled visitors, admitted some but not all, depending upon the desires of the visited. Visitors needed to stay no more than fifteen minutes and did not relinquish their hats or shawls to the servants, to indicate that they had come on a ceremonial, not a friendly, visit.[71]

Sociability for the wives of doctors, politicians, and others working with the public had obvious economic advantages. William Lane, as mayor and doctor, wished his wife to make ceremonial calls, whereas Mary was barely interested in the friendly kind. When Mary was back at her parents' in 1821, William scolded her for not returning the calls "that you have received at your Father's." William said he was mortified. "It is unjust to your visitors, and injurious to yourself. When here [in St. Louis] I could rarely get you abroad." To refuse to return a visit was to reject a relationship or to express moral and social disapproval. William Lane wondered if it was the problem of "fixing up" that kept Mary from visiting and told her that it was bad to "mope always at home." The outgoing doctor and politician put his authority as a husband behind urging Mary to do her wifely duty, to pay attention to her appearance, and to solidify their social position.[72]

For the bold and well connected the rewards of sociability could be dramatic. Senator Lewis Linn customarily wrote to his wife that the honors of his world were of little meaning, and that her world of domestic comfort and religion was where happiness truly abided. Still, Mrs. Linn knew President Andrew Jackson, Vice President John C. Calhoun, Supreme Court Justice Roger Taney, and other elevated Democrats, and they often sent her greetings through Mr. Linn. She knew her husband's allies and foes and treated them with judiciously applied cordiality and caution. As a widow Elizabeth Linn used the years of sociability that she had put in to get her friend the Reverend William Henry Milburn made chaplain of the House of Representatives. Through careful sociability in person and epistle, she managed to secure a political plum for a friend while enjoying true woman status.[73]

Secular sociability also served a regulatory function. It informally rewarded female mildness and checked aggression. Sarah von Phul Mason, renewing old friendships in Lexington, observed that a newlywed of her acquaintance had "altogether laid aside her satirical manner, which was the only fault I ever laid to her." Mason was pleased to pass on an announcement of moral improvement.[74]

Sociability provided women with a public form of critique, although it is richly ironic that the acceptable expression of aggression for well-bred women was silence. Elizabeth Linn's brother wrote her that her friends were angry at Senator Thomas Benton, who had prevented Mrs. Linn's son from getting a government appointment. To express her outrage, a friend of Mrs. Linn's received three visits from the Bentons before she returned their calls. She drove her carriage to the door, intending to leave only her card, but "the [Benton] ladies came out, which compelled [her] to make a personal call for a moment . . . which they had reason to think she wished to avoid." The mute response, the ultimate act of reserve, was the weapon the middle class entrusted to women. In this way, Mrs. Linn's friends tried to inform the Bentons of their moral disapproval, but the Bentons hijacked the intended snub and wrung an unwilling visit out of their enemies.[75]

18

MOTHERS AND MORALS

In the wake of the American Revolution and its victory over monarchy and patriarchal authority, women acquired, at least in theory, moral authority over the home and family. Moral writers quoted Montesquieu, who observed: "The safety of the State depends on the virtue of the women." Since the workplace and, increasingly, politics were the sites of self-interested conflict, women were left to exemplify and teach republican virtue in the ideally private, peaceful, disinterested atmosphere of the home. The purity of private life, particularly the exquisite goodness of mothers, was to redeem and cleanse the filthy stables of public life. The rolling revivals of the Second Great Awakening progressively aroused a far wider public to moral issues than did the rapidly fading memories of revolutionary republicanism. Women participated in revivals in considerably greater numbers than men, finding in obedience to God a motive and a model for the demands for obedience at home. Through the revivals, republican virtues elided with Christian self-sacrifice, obedience, empathy, and the repression of aggression. Women's presumed penchant for piety made them natural carriers of these virtues. Moralists now praised motherly love, only recently rescued from the stigma of fondness, as the purest expression of virtue and the necessary accompaniment to the education of a child worthy to play a part in the new United States.[1]

Women's moral influence on family governance had to support the burden of the nation's mission. The white family's redeeming moral value acquired an extra shimmer of reflected purity from the widespread representation of its supposed negative, the slave family. Slaves could not protect an intimate domestic space that was withdrawn from the economic world since the inhabitants were marketable items themselves. Nor could slave fathers hold or exercise patriarchal authority, absorb the properties of their wives, exercise their civic rights for them, or have the legal right to discipline them. By keeping African Americans enslaved, white Americans in St. Louis and the surrounding countryside had intimate views and often relationships with people who could not establish the conditions considered necessary for sustaining virtuous republican life. To sustain woman's virtue, to shelter the hearth, and to have the time and energy for raising good children, the labor of the less virtuous was required.

To exist, the moral system of the emerging middle class, with its demands for chastity and disinterestedness from females and economic success from males, had to rest on top of a contrasting set of ideas about the moral potential of poor whites and slaves. In practice, white mothers in private homes often practiced one moral system to train their children and another to discipline poor orphans, servants, and slaves under their control. Empathy, sympathy, and mutuality were to shape mother-child relations; authority determined mothers' relations with the poor and enslaved.

For the new nation to maintain its purity it needed citizens who, in the absence of many institutions or other restraints, could pursue virtuous lives. Self-control and decorous behavior were primary among the qualities children needed to learn to join the growing middle class. Because every impression was of great impact on a tiny child, mothers had to adjust their own comportment to show only tranquillity and love. "Gentleness, patience and love are almost everything in education. . . . If he look up in the midst of his play, a smile should always be ready for him, that he may feel protected and happy in the atmosphere of love." Mothers' love was to exemplify self-control within heroic self-suppression, not only restraining mothers' desires but measuring and controlling their emotions so as to display only mildness, care, and pleasure in their children's progress. Such behavior would lead not only to a child's salvation, the ultimate goal of a mother's instruction, but also to the mother's salvation. Failure could haunt her to her death.[2]

The stress on empathy and sympathy with one's children in the early nineteenth century derived of course from the sentimental and genteel culture of the previous century. Following on most evangelicals' rejection of Calvinism's emphasis on damnation and original sin, mothers were to focus on their oneness with their children as a way to understand and control their behavior. Mothers made the love and dependence they and their children shared central to their didactic purposes. Linked with correct precepts, love and dependence would instill voluntary, reliable compliance. "Coercion may, in childhood, produce prompt obedience, but if it destroys affection, what hope can we reasonably entertain, that when such children get from under parental authority, they will retain a respect for what they have been compelled to adopt . . . ?" The empathy and reciprocity that should characterize parent-child relations would save children from the abundant opportunities for sin in the growing United States.[3]

Mothers were to raise children to defer gratification, save money, suppress impulses and sensuality, exhibit refined and gentle behavior, and both exert and defer to what they believed was legitimate authority. Mothers typically approved behavior exhibiting these qualities while they punished exhibitions of roughness, self-assertion, impulsiveness, excessive bodily freedom, and sensuality, all signs of coarseness in adults. Withdrawal and the withholding of affection were the tools of discipline in private, as withholding a visit was a tool of public discipline. As in refusing to visit, middle-class women often did not have to expand on their displeasure, disapproval, or criticism; a glance or a word might suffice.[4]

In helping their children repress untoward urges, Anglo-American mothers appear to have been more zealous and more thorough than their French counterparts in excising sensuality and

instilling an anxious conscience. Breast-feeding is a case in point. Arnaud Berquin's *The Children's Friend* commences with the tale of
Fanchette, a five-year-old girl whose mother has just given birth to a
brother. Fanchette wants to give her crying brother something good
to eat. Her father explains that he has no teeth, and her mother adds,
"God has put milk in my breast to nourish your little brother."
Fanchette wants to know if she also took milk from her mother. Her
father explains that her mother took "infinite pains to get her to suck
a few drops of milk." For two long years she required the same care,
troubling her exhausted mother's rest. Over and over her mother
would run to Fanchette's cradle and present the tiny girl with her
breast. While this story deals directly with allaying sibling rivalry and
with encouraging maternal tenderness in a little girl, it also demonstrates the casual and comfortable way this French writer talked
about nursing.[5]

In the French community in St. Louis the same ease appears to
have prevailed. Jules de Mun wrote his young wife in 1815 to find
out if their daughter Isabelle was weaned. "I cannot tell you how eager I am to see her again, and when she no longer has to be nursed,
to put her to sleep in my lap, as I think mademoiselle will not refuse
me that." He also observed that he hoped his wife would not neglect
taking purgatives as a health precaution when she was weaning. A
year or so later, while traveling among the Kansas Indians, de Mun
wrote about a favorite image he had of their (by now) two children:
"I love to picture my pretty Julie on your lap toying with the breast
and watching you with her pretty little smile: at your side the big Isabelle caressing her little sister and the mother admiring them both."
De Mun's obvious comfort in writing about his wife's body and its intimate functions is in striking contrast with the silence of American
men on such topics.[6]

American moralists did not mention body parts and spent little
time on nursing, a change from the franker discussions of earlier
times. Nor is there evidence in St. Louis of Anglo-American husbands writing so uninhibitedly to their wives. Husbands expressed
affection, but little physicality. English moralists whose works were
sold in the United States wrote that mothers should be willing to

"sacrifice a little amusement, a little company, or a little repose, for the sake of nursing their infants." The American evangelical Lydia Maria Child's only reference to nursing was that children had died of convulsions when nursing from a mother "under the influence of violent passion or emotion; and who can tell what *moral* evil may be traced to the states of mind indulged by a mother, while tending the precious little being, who receives everything from her?" Child's characteristic preoccupation with the inner spirit and motivations reminded the reader that only constant moral vigilance could keep a mother from harming or even killing her child with her unsubdued passions and thoughts. The observation would be unlikely to induce maternal pleasure in breast-feeding.[7]

In terms of discipline, French parents scolded and tried to mold their children, but it seems to have been done on top of a strong, confident base of physical and emotional affection and cautiously, not to inflate the stature of the failing. As Jules de Mun wrote his wife, "Do not reprove . . . except with the greatest sweetness and above all, never lose your calmness; and . . . [Julie] will learn to obey and will love you even more, and if you are obliged to punish her, she will see that it is not from capriciousness or anger, but only that the little fault makes you do it."[8]

The more anxious American style was likely to make the love dependent on the molding. Excessive praise was dangerous. Mrs. Child wrote that one should praise a parsimonious child for generosity "even more than you would think safe under any other circumstances." Americans were as likely as not to use irony and offer conditional love to their relatives. Senator Lewis Linn wrote one of his daughters that "Father is very anxious to do well for his children and to see them good, virtuous, religious and happy, so that his gray hairs may not be brought with sorrow to the grave by their wicked conduct. This I hope you will never forget, when you want to [do] as anything sinful or bad."[9]

Self-sacrificing mothering whose goal was the installation of the mother's conscience had, as its reward, the creation of dependent children who reflected the good mother back to her. In vibrant reciprocity, mothers and children loved and needed each other. The mothers' sacrifices were well recompensed in dependence and love.

As one writer put the bargain, bluntly, "She will be loved in proportion as she makes those around her happy,—as she studies their tastes, and sympathizes in their feelings."[10]

Because the mother's moral and disciplinary bond with the child depended on mutuality, she needed her children's love and approval almost as much as they hers. As middle-class fathers worked longer hours away from the household, a mother was often isolated with the children, and her lifeline to self-worth and pleasure was through the affection and, to a lesser extent, the good behavior of her children. This mutual dependence, masked by the ideology celebrating the purity of mother's love and exacerbated by the physical, and often the emotional, distance between spouses, could make mothers emotional hostages to their growing children. They needed their children to need them for their own sense of well-being. The widespread mothers' depressions that are evident over the frequent deaths of children suggest that this suffering—always agonizing—became even more acute in the nineteenth century.[11]

The moral and emotional links between mothers and children were also particularly intense in the antebellum period because physical health was believed to be, at least partly, a moral issue. Although it was unclear what precisely caused or prevented disease, nineteenth-century moralists joined the purity of a mother's care with her child's health, both spiritual and physical. In the eighteenth century vice made girls ugly. In nineteenth-century literature it could make them sick.

The relationships middle-class mothers created with their children were intense and concerned. This of course had been true of Puritan mother-child relations, but it was now more widespread. Furthermore, middle-class mothers had less company and fewer productive occupations than before. Moreover, the sentimental lives of all family members had achieved heightened importance in the postrevolutionary world. Individual desire had acquired new validity. For middle-class women desire was circumscribed to mean the desire to enjoy certain emotional states, such as feeling beloved, righteous, content. These feelings often depended upon the behavior of their children.

Gilligan's relatedness bloomed for the first time across an emerging middle class in the early republic. Many women saw themselves largely in terms of the quality of their relations with their children and husbands, finding moral direction in the maintenance and health of those relationships. As wives and mothers were increasingly cut off from the moral questions and intrusions of economic and village life, their moral compasses responded to smaller, more personal dilemmas. Self-worth and self-definition depended more and more on the quality of a few relationships.[12]

While moralists recommended empathic mothering for the middle class, they specified authoritarian treatment of the potentially lazy and drunken poor who sometimes became the responsibility of respectable mothers. Middle-class family virtues, these moralists argued, might save the poor from sloth and a dissolute life if absorbed early enough. The emphasis on this rescue operation, however, was not on developing a mother's empathy with needy children but on the shared goal of the middle class: that poor children work hard and eschew liquor.[13]

Despite the moralists' advice, most white middle-class mothers in St. Louis worked hard *not* to be alone with their children. They do not appear to have been worried about interference with their systems of moral management but wanted to curtail their own loneliness and give their children opportunities to learn, get out of St. Louis, and become attached to their wider families. Neither French nor Anglo-American families hesitated to combine families and remnants of families for reasons of company, health, and economy. The Gratiots, especially the sisters, enveloped Susan Hempstead Gratiot with visits when she was frequently without her husband, Henry, and alone with her children in Illinois or Wisconsin. Being alone for Susan was a great trial, as it was for all women in rural areas. She had no wish to raise her children in isolation and worked hard to import congenial company.[14]

Cece de Mun Depestre wrote her sister-in-law Isabelle de Mun about the visit of Isabelle's elder daughter when Isabelle had just had her second daughter. She described how she and her cousin Claire had become the best of friends and played mother and child with each other. She assured Isabelle that the little girl was never sad and urged Isabelle to bring her new infant and come spend two months with her since her husband had to be away for three months. She also reported how much she appreciated the presence of the child of a cousin of Isabelle's and wished Isabelle to tell the girl's mother how grateful she was for the "mark of confidence" and to assure her that she thought of the little visitor as her own child. The exchange of children seems to have been not only desired but also symbolic of trust and respect between mothers.[15]

Moralists expected mothers to have somewhat more influence with their daughters than their sons. Nowhere was the establishment of an empathic tie between mother and daughter more important than in a daughter's marriage. Moralists thought daughters, rightly raised, would consult their mothers on choosing a husband. They usually ascribed girls' desires to marry wealthy men to bad maternal values; giddy and foolish mothers made giddy and foolish daughters. A daughter's "poisoned" relationship with her husband should be the lifelong burden on her mother's conscience. "When such a mother lies upon her deathbed, will she feel no melancholy regret for a daughter's *past*, and no dreadful anticipation of her *future* indiscretions?"[16]

Some mothers were ambitious for their daughters beyond marriage. Many saw education or a combination of education and religion as the route to a better life. Sally McConnell Spencer had four daughters. She and her husband had a herd of thirty cows and milked them for dairy products, which she sold for cash with which she made sure all her daughters got an education. All of them subsequently taught school. Ensuring an education was about the only way mothers could give their daughters the possibility of avoiding the dangers, tedium, and backbreaking, unremitting labor of married rural life in the West.[17]

Mothers were likely to bring the family's attention to religion. Mrs. Wells Marvin, a Baptist, was married to a New England man without religion. She instilled devotion in her children. One, who became a missionary to China, remembered years later sitting on her lap while she wept and sang "Alas! Did my Savior bleed." Another son remembered that his conversion at eighteen had little to do with any minister and much to do with the influence of his mother. Despite Mrs. Marvin's success, and while mothers were expected to have great influence with their daughters, their confidence in their ability to guide their sons was low. Young boys on the verge of manhood worried their mothers and other female relatives. Ann Ewing wrote her son William one of many injunctions to think about his future: "Tell William my heart is sore when I think of him for I know he is too lazy to work on the farm and what is to become of him I know not." She also expressed to her daughter her worry that William would have no future: "He want[s] ambition . . . poor boy he will have to come home and go to the plough and the hoe."[18]

Parents marshaled not only their own moral pressure but also that of sisters and aunts. Jane Mullanphy Chambers wrote her brother Bryan that she "was surprised to find some expressions, in your letter to my Father . . . denoting some dissatisfaction and impatience at remaining any longer at Stonyhurst." She went on to say that she certainly hoped he was going to become "an excellent scholar . . . uniting the mild, affable, unassuming character of the polished gentleman, and that you will . . . make amends for the many, very many anxious days and nights his [father's] love and fears for you have occasioned him." All she wanted, she said, was for him to be "a comfort and an honour" to his father and the whole family. She concluded with some thoughts on the future importance of cleaning his teeth properly.[19]

Beyond a certain age, mothers' influence over their sons gave way to their fathers', which contributed to maternal anxiety. Despite his mother's warning, Daniel and Rebecca Boone's son Israel got up off his sickbed and volunteered for an Indian fight that was at hand. He was killed in the action. The militant ethos of westward-moving men usually overrode mothers' worries for the safety of their children—at least that of their sons. Concerns over manliness would not permit much empathy between fathers and sons about suffering, fear, and loss. Fathers did not usually expect girls to exhibit fearlessness, so they could shelter for a time under whatever protection their mothers could offer.[20]

The anxious, ambitious white family, huddled in concern around its children, was alive to the opportunities and the pitfalls of its new world. There were fortunes to be made and lost, careers to succeed or fail, land to settle, buy, squat on, or lose, institutions to be imagined, armies to be led, debts to incur, whiskey to drink, duels to be fought, marriages to be made. Everything on this earth and in the next depended upon one's choices, and making the right choices depended on how children were reared. In early-nineteenth-century thought one drink could lead to a lifetime of debauchery, one evening in the company of "low" people to sin, syphilis, and death. All this communicated a kind of millennial fervor to relations between parents and children, especially the sons exposed to these pitfalls. The level of emotion between mothers and sons could be particularly intense; women had no other weapons but feeling and rhetoric, and they were ignorant of many of the experiences about which they preached. By displaying their fears and uneasiness to sons and brothers, women were hoping to mobilize the mutuality they had worked to establish over the years. This was women's "influence," the designated moral mortar of the United States.[21]

African American Mothers

If middle-class white culture exaggerated and isolated the vital ties between mothers and children, market practices, legal realities, racist usages, and the construction of slave motherhood tried to deny the same emotional connections for black families. By insisting that African Americans' feelings were not strong, by separating families through sale, and by forcing slaves to bury their grief at the sales of relatives, friends, and themselves, white society was attempting to bring African American motherhood into accord with the needs of the consumer market in people.[22]

Missouri, a western end point for many slaveowners as well as home to a thriving market, was often a place where slave families ended up. St. Louis, the central western market for the upper South, was the place slaves were sent from the surrounding territories to be sold downriver. More than two dozen slave traders had agents in St.

Louis. In the numerous slave pens or jails, traders, like "Colonel"
John White, imprisoned, fed, dressed up, and tried to improve the
appearance of the slaves they were about to sell. Frequent auctions
and, on January 1, the annual hiring out of slaves whose owners
rented them took place in front of the Old Courthouse, across the
square from the slave pen. On another corner was the whipping
post.[23]

The conditions under which most slave mothers raised their children were unspeakably anxiety-provoking. Unlike middle-class white
mothers, slave mothers were unable to isolate their children from
outside influences and had little time to give the combination of love,
surveillance, and careful control that was assumed to produce purposeful, self-controlled, and socially discriminating white Americans.
Slaves and their owners agreed that infants needed to be breast-fed,
but for field hands this might mean having to leave a baby nearby in
a field while working. Women working in the house usually could
keep their children near, but getting work out of slaves rivaled and
usually won out in importance over aspects of mothering other
than providing food. Mothers could never forget the threat of sale.
George Morton sold to his daughter for one dollar the fourteen-year-
old "Mulatto" girl Sally, "being the child of a certain Negro woman
named Ann." Morton's daughter could have the girl, but if she sold
her, she had to sell her out of state or the terms of the sale would be
invalid. Morton's conditions would have moved Sally farther from
her mother if she had been sold again.[24]

Early impressions, counted so important to white children, im-
printed themselves on slave children unfiltered, straight out of the
brutal system under which they lived. Sometimes children suffered
physical trauma; sometimes they saw their parents or siblings suffering. Separations from mothers and other family members often came
without preparation. Anxiety, rage, and despair reached dangerous
levels in many mothers because of the conditions under which they
were forced to have and to rear children. Even slave mothers who
lived in fairly stable circumstances sometimes could not resist the
pressures they were under from distorting their maternal practices.
Fil Hancock of Missouri grew up owned by the same woman who

had owned his grandmother and mother. He remembered that his master was not allowed to touch him and his family because they belonged to his "Old Missus." It was his mother who whipped them most. "My own mammy whipped us good and proper—she used a razor strap, and sure poured it on us." He added later, "I can see now I needed more'n I got." Hancock's mother may have seen whipping as a kind of prophylaxis, whereby her sternness would ward off her children's future misbehavior and hence any worse punishments that her owners might provide. She may have believed she was protecting, guiding, and morally strengthening her children by beating them regularly. Whatever moral message she was trying to send, sadly, she also seems to have communicated to her son a suggestion of his own moral unworthiness, which he kept as part of her legacy.[25]

Most slave mothers went to extraordinary lengths to achieve freedom for their children. Jenny, a "free woman of color," sued Ephriam Musick in 1825 for her freedom and that of her daughter, asserting that she had been wrongfully held in slavery. From 1805 through 1834, three Scypion women, Catiche and Celeste and Marie their mother, all sued for freedom.[26]

William Wells Brown described the enormous sacrifices of his mother. Elizabeth had him and six other children, each by a different father, in Lexington, Kentucky. Their owner took them all to Missouri, north of St. Louis, where William grew up on a farm with about forty slaves. When he was a young man, he and his mother and siblings all were sold to different people in St. Louis. Brown, working on a riverboat, often thought of escaping but did not because of his mother and sister. He remembered his mother's stories of taking him as an infant on her back to the field where she worked. She also spoke of enduring many whippings in order to nurse him. When his sister was sold south, he resolved to escape with his mother. Slave catchers intercepted their attempt. Elizabeth told her son he should try to get his freedom, that she would not last long in the South; he last saw her chained to another woman on a steamboat. The principles of Brown's mother's behavior, as he understood them, were to protect and aid him and her other children to freedom, if possible. Living up to her own standards of mothering in slavery condemned her to lawbreaking and grievous physical and emotional suffering. Bearing up under a lifetime of stigma and torture enhanced her moral authority in the eyes of her son. Brown's lifelong abolitionist and reform work carried on the redemptive tradition initiated by his mother.[27]

The moral and emotional key to the power of Brown's story, like that of so many nineteenth-century autobiographies and inspirational tales, hinges on his mother's love, suffering, and prayers for him. Brown's mother was a far cry from Lydia Child's chaste, mild, dispassionate, cheerful disciplinarian. But his tale became an abolitionist classic because a mother's loving sacrifice was the nineteenth century's primary symbol of goodness and pathos. The imagined family of the postrevolutionary middle class—a loving, pious mother and her children—constituted a sacred tableau in the new republic. Appeals to political rights or to economic rights, even a republican competency, remained appeals in the profane areas of partisanship and self-interest. The most evocative token of disinterestedness was a mother's love.[28]

Mothering, Illness, and Loss

As the promise of a mother's love had so much riding on it in the early nineteenth century, so the potential heartbreak of a lost mother's love was the greater. Easily terminated by illness, death, and geography, the mother-child bond was not only the most important human tie but also one that was severed frequently enough to make it especially precious. While a mother's love became increasingly identified as a sacred love, maternal love replaced original sin as the origin of the core of virtue in the American citizenry, because of both its disinterestedness and its fragility.[29]

When in 1854 Harriet Beecher Stowe published *Uncle Tom's Cabin*, featuring a seemingly endless chain of separation of both black and white mothers and children, it hit an American nerve sensitized by anxiety over a shortage of the comfort of maternal love. This brought many northern white readers to empathize with African

American characters deprived of the secure enjoyment of the delights of domestic coziness that Stowe drew so artfully. The language
of sentiment, including words like "comfort" to describe home fur-
nishings, nostalgically evoked the love, or lost love, of mothers. Sentimental domesticity vehemently rejected anything sexually "impure"
since that signaled women's deviation from the national project of
selfless love. Instead domestic rhetoric, as many critics have pointed
out, not only idealized and sweetened mother love but, by eschewing
Puritan and Anglican stoicism, also made the possibility of its loss a
constant presence in middle-class antebellum society.[30]

The deteriorating health of women in the nineteenth century
meant that motherhood would be even more perilous physically than
it had been in the eighteenth. Furthermore, the isolation and intensity of the mutual dependence of mothers and children seem to have
aggravated the pains and griefs of motherhood and even childbirth
itself. One scholar has linked mothers' fear of death with an actual
increase in the experience of pain in the early republic. "The more a
person feels her existence threatened by the source of pain, the more
pain she is likely to feel." This, combined with the growing individu-
ation of family life, the stress on the identity of mother and child,
and the ideological focus on families as the site of private, domestic
happiness, put new and considerable pressures on women while re-
moving traditional activities, props, and community buffers between
mothers and their children.[31]

Everyone, particularly children and the elderly, was susceptible to
a variety of diseases for which there were no cures and for which
medical help was often worse than the disease itself. As Germans observed disapprovingly, Americans used calomel very widely. Tuberculosis was widespread. And pregnancy exacerbated tuberculosis.
Pneumonia, bronchitis, and influenza attacked forcefully. Then epidemics of cholera, dysentery, yellow fever, diphtheria, and measles
carried many off in waves. The Mississippi Valley was more unwholesome than more northerly parts of the United States. Mosquitoes,
breeding rapidly, carried malaria, and bacteria-loaded water bore
various intestinal maladies. August, September, and October seem to
have been particularly sickly months for malaria and other insect-

and water-related diseases, while the pulmonary infections tended to cluster in January and February. One historian has estimated that 20 to 33 percent of all children died in these years.[32]

Urban life in the nineteenth century was more hazardous to health than rural life because of overcrowding, poor water, and the presence of sewage. St. Louis was slow to take steps that would inhibit the spread of disease. It established a board of health in 1822, but it did little. Cholera—rapid, cureless, and potentially fatal—traveled to the United States from Europe in 1832, hitting St. Louis that summer. There was little coordinated response. A second, devastating epidemic in 1849, however, produced many urban improvements. The reason for the differing reactions seems to be that in the absence of scientific information about the cause and transmission of the disease, many thought it had to do with the supposedly bad habits, intemperance, and generally undeserving character of the black and white poor. Thus spending citizens' money on useless improvements seemed beside the point. The second time, cholera hit St. Louis worse than any other American urban center and did not spare the prosperous.[33]

Thus, for a variety of social, medical, and demographic reasons, early-nineteenth-century motherhood regularly confronted women with the meaning of their lives and life in general. Fathers faced the loss of their children as well, but they were not responsible for their daily care, sitting up at nights, watching—with no adequate remedies—the range of human maladies, from colds and stomachaches to the agonies of death.[34]

The birthrate for white native-born women dropped over the course of the nineteenth century. They went from having 7.04 births in 1800 to 5.42 births in 1850. The reasons are not entirely clear, although declining health among American women may have contributed. However, the birthrate in the South did not decline for white or black women, and it is unclear how prosperous southern women were contesting unlimited childbearing. Maternal and infant mortality was higher in the antebellum South than in the North. The hinterland of Missouri can be considered southern in this context because of its climate and agricultural economy, while St. Louis tended to follow a more northern pattern. Pioneering families were prolific, and late-nineteenth-century historians attributed the high numbers to the "heroic" patriarchs, presenting a formula for virility that counted all the children a man had fathered divided by his number of wives: "One hardy and hearty pioneer had no less than 29 sons and daughters by 2 wives." Rural wives usually had as many children as they were physically able to have. At the same time, women often wished to stop having so many children for both their own and their children's sakes.[35]

Starting in urban areas doctors were increasingly replacing midwives in attending laboring women. Statistics are not firm, but historians think that women had a better survival rate with midwives than with doctors. Regardless, doctors began outnumbering midwives. Dr. William Carr Lane, for example, had a growing practice and many women patients. In the hinterland, midwives still predominated. There is evidence that the introduction of forceps and their enthusiastic overuse increased risks from infection and tearing. Some doctors in the late eighteenth and early nineteenth centuries also administered laudanum, prescribed for false labor but sometimes administered to women in real labor, thereby temporarily—and sometimes with danger to the mother and child—stopping contractions. A third intervention possible during the early republic was the administering of ergot, a drug that powerfully stimulated uterine contractions. Finally doctors were sometimes inclined to bleed their patients, a dangerous and unnecessary procedure. Midwives were less likely to take these four steps and were also likely to have considerable experience with the things that could go wrong and with repositioning the baby if necessary.[36]

Doctors, unlike midwives, linked elite status with increased suffering and danger in childbirth. According to a growing medical consensus, women of lesser status could be expected to deliver their babies with less fuss and difficulty. As the century wore on, only elite women were offered anesthetics as they became available.[37]

Motherhood signaled entry into the world of health care for women. No matter how young the mother, her status initiated her partnership in discussions of health. Charles Gratiot, father of the seventeen-year-old Isabelle Gratiot de Mun, wrote her in 1814 detailing her mother's lameness and her need to wear flannel all the time for her pain. A mother or father might have shared this information with an unmarried daughter. But Gratiot also wrote of the measles infecting a whole group of schoolgirls, including his own Adele, who got ill. This kind of news he probably shared with his seventeen-year-old daughter because she herself was now a mother. The responsibility for the day-to-day health of the family was usually the most taxing of a mother's obligations.[38]

Women near delivery tried to be with mothers, sisters, or trusted relatives for childbirth and recovery. Husbands were sometimes there, but by no means always. The family ties among women were usually the strongest and most comforting in times of childbirth. Sarah Mason, whose mother had died, had her sister Maria with her for the birth of her first child. Isabelle de Mun gave birth to her daughter Isabelle with her mother nearby in her sister's compound in Gratiot's Grove, Illinois, while her husband was away. Mary Lane went to her mother's for the birth of her daughter Sarah and for most of her subsequent births.[39]

Early-nineteenth-century childbirth involved myriad difficulties, both physical and logistical. Mrs. Ramsey suffered both kinds. Indians attacked her house in Warren County, near St. Louis County. They tomahawked three of her six children in the yard and shot Mrs. Ramsey, who was pregnant. When Harriet Ewing, Mary Lane's and Rachel Jenckes's sister, was about to be confined, she had a severe pain in her head, despite or because of preventive dental work. "[W]hile we were at Terre Haute she had a tooth drawn and a hole made in the cheek bone so as to let the matter come down in her mouth instead of the nostril." The danger posed by the infection was great and because of Harriet's already weak condition contributed to her death soon after.[40]

Mothers of dead children had to mourn while continuing to sympathize and empathize with the survivors. To give way to paralyzing grief and loss was thought to enact a rebellion against God. Lydia Maria Child advised mothers not to share with their daughters the darker sides of marriage, including sadness. Some women were able to manage their despair, but others found it impaired them emotionally and hence kept them from their moral obligations. Mary Lane, having lost many children, sent her two daughters away to school in Philadelphia, in part because she could not educate them at home but also because her depression was preventing her from being a good mother.[41]

Elizabeth Linn's sister-in-law wrote about desiring death herself, another common response to the pain of losing a child: "Too well I know, from my own bitter experience, how utterly unavailing are all the consolations of friendship. . . . I thought I never could have survived the dreadful blow, which deprived me of him, whom I can never cease to mourn, until I too shall be numbered with the dead. . . . He was so entwined around every fibre of my heart, that I shall carry this aching void to my grave." She went on to say that although the death remained a mystery to her, she at least knew that God knew why it had happened. Religious consolation did not necessarily offer an explanation, but faith offered the belief that an explanation at least existed.[42]

Jette Bruns, trained to the same standards of refined sentiment and its precise articulation, wished to die when three of her children died in close succession. After her own illness and deepest depression had passed, she wrote home with excruciating details of her children's misery and uncomprehending suffering. She focused on their sweetness, innocence, and vital connection to her.

> With all of them the last words and the dying glance was "Mother!" And so it is not surprising that I wished I could have gone with them. . . . Now all wishes, all striving have been quieted! I even no longer wish to go back to you, to germany! . . . I had been provided with the last sacrament. . . . It really hit me too hard that I also had to lose little Rudolph. . . . I myself sewed his shroud. . . . Oh how lovely he was, how dear.[43]

These maternal reactions to the deaths of children reflect darkly the more and more common experience of merging between empathetic mother and child. Middle-class mothers' love for their young was constructed as so strong and so binding that mothers felt the deaths of children as their own partial deaths. Puritan moralists had exhorted mothers that their duty to their children was to crush signs of the original sin into which they had been born. Nineteenth-century moralists, however, had constructed a maternal embrace that left middle-class mothers with almost no defenses against the loss of their children.[44]

Women, as they always had, thought about birth while considering the possibility of death. This often produced careful preparations, including examining one's spiritual state and making bequests. Sarah Mason wrote her sister-in-law Rosalie and brother Henry a farewell letter just before she was to deliver a child. She delivered, safely, a daughter, named for her sister, Maria. In anticipating her own death, she had solicited her sister-in-law to take care of the child, should it survive its mother, and predicted that this new, closer relation to Sarah's husband would only increase her respect for Mr. Mason. Sarah, in thinking about relinquishing her life, wrote, "I am blessed at this moment with such a feeling of resignation that I trust I may be enabled to say if called, 'Yea Lord thy servant is ready.'" Sarah felt equanimity at the prospect of giving up her life if need be. But motherhood replaced peace with anxiety about the responsibilities and obligations of child rearing. Mason's relatively serene 1820 letter about her own state of resignation prefaced the central drama of most married women's lives: how they learned to cope with sickness, dying, and death in the years when they had young children. Mason's sense of her identity and moral value shifted dramatically after she had had a child, replacing her calm resignation to the possibility of her own loss with persistent anxiety about the loss of a child.[45]

Sarah von Phul Mason's father had died in Philadelphia of yellow fever. She lost her sister, confidante, and midwife, the watercolorist Anna Maria, to disease in 1823. She had also lost her mother, to whom she and her siblings were extremely attached, not long before that. Anna Maria wrote on her late mother's birthday that recollection of her "still plays around my heart and often beguiles me of tears which sooth my aching bosom." Their mother had lived, according to Sarah's and Anna Maria's brother George "an afflicted saint, and she died a triumphant Christian—The last words she uttered in this world were in prayers for her children—Hallowed, forever, as the memory of that mother whose example in life and in death was their precious inheritance." Sarah's mother had set a high standard for self-sacrifice, sympathy, and piety. Her example and her loss predisposed Sarah to find motherhood initially overwhelming.[46]

Catholics often circulated religious articles to strengthen the prayers of the ill and their caretakers. Isabelle de Mun's sister-in-law, hearing that her niece was sick, sent Isabelle a silver medal with the image of the Virgin Mary on it; Cece de Mun Depestre's priest had blessed it along with four copper ones for other children. She urged Isabelle to employ the medals and read a little book that she was sending along with it. "How do we know if God will not grant our prayers joined with those of the holy virgin, who has promised particular protection to those who will wear the medal and invoke her with confidence." Remembering that St. Louis was not a community entirely made up of Catholics, she added a postscript begging her sister-in-law to be discreet and not speak of the miracles the medal could facilitate to people "to whom they would be useless, and who . . . would joke about them." Jette Bruns gave a medal to her ailing sister-in-law Trude, who was very pleased. "She shouted with joy, she told everybody and showed it to everybody who came."[47]

Statistics about slave pregnancy and childbirth are not very reliable, but the number of live slave births was much lower than among white women. One historian has posited that more than 50 percent of slave babies died before reaching one year, a rate more than twice that of white infants. Poor health from overwork, poor nutrition, inadequate clothing, anxiety, and depression weakened slave women, making repeated pregnancy and childbirth even greater health hazards than they were for white women. Fertility rates in the years between 1830 and 1860 declined for slave women, reflecting the increased work demands caused by cotton production, increased family disruption through sales to the deep South, and generally declining health nationwide.[48]

Slaves usually could not choose the conditions under which they would bear children. Dorcas Carr gave her slave Rachel to her nephew to hire out. A year later her niece wrote her that Rachel had died. Rachel had lost a child about ten days before her death and had been extremely ill ever since. If Rachel was afraid of giving birth, it is not recorded. If she'd wished she'd had a mother or a sister present, it made no difference; the mother of her owners attended her. In the discussion of her and her baby's death, no one mentioned the father of Rachel's child, any surviving children, or anyone who might care for human reasons. Their concerns were with the economic liabilities of Rachel's employment circumstances. By refusing attention to human ties among black people, slaveowners constructed the negative version of relatedness, an emotionally anesthetized people with whom whites needed to feel no empathy.[49]

RACE, MORALITY, AND MOURNING

The obituary was probably the most widespread genre for describing middle-class women's virtues in the antebellum period. It was the only legitimate format in which women could appear in the newspapers. Its formulaic tableaux of women featuring their courage and uncomplaining suffering fitted, with small adjustments, most shapes and sizes of white respectability. Women's strong and correct attachments accompany and often overshadow most other traits. The death of a sixteen-year-old produced a picture of a "humble and obedient" daughter, a "kind and affectionate" sister whose interment therefore gathered "a large number of respectable citizens." Nineteen-year-old Catherine Senter, a Methodist who had enjoyed "true and vital religion," had been of the "most respectable obedience to both parents."[1]

Friends and relatives wrote informal obituaries for one another conforming closely to newspaper notices. George Sibley's grandmother Elizabeth Hopkins wrote him that his mother, who had died when he was very small, "was one of the best of mothers—to all who knew her she was agreeable—Elegant in her form—beautiful in her countenance—amiable in her disposition, accomplished in her manners, and engaging in all her deportment. She sustained a variety of trials and supported with a dignity which few women possess. And what adds a lustre to her character, she was (we doubt not) a true Christian—soon after you was [sic] born she made a public profession of religion, and dedicated your brother and you, to God by Baptism." Sibley's grandmother hoped he would benefit from his mother's "many prayers."[2]

The authors of two elaborate obituaries of two well-known women excused themselves for giving voice and publicity to their own suffering with the defense that feelings must be allowed to express themselves although silence, indicative of resignation to God's will, would be a better moral choice. The women's elite status presumably justified a relatively prolonged demand on public attention. Sarah G. Stother, wife of a wealthy attorney and head of the Female Benevolent Society, had "amiable qualities" that included "fervent yet humble piety," and her colleagues had a "duty to [their] feelings" to record their "deep regret for the loss [they had] sustained." In the case of Harriet K. Clark, second wife of the explorer and superintendent of Indians for Missouri, "were it not for the uncontrollable feelings of sorrow and sympathy" for her relatives, the writer would stop. But the author was forced to continue: Mrs. Clark was a "mild, equable and conciliatory wife," a "gentle, affectionate, indulgent" mother, a tender and devoted sister, and "mild and generous to the poor . . . and indefatigable in the number and delicacy of her attentions to the sick and distressed."[3] In these and other obituaries virtuous women could legitimately claim moral value: for years of love, care, grief, and empathetic suffering. These were their sources of moral authority and reasons for action.

The death of a mother was of particular import because she was laden with sentimental power. A vignette from the American Tract Society, an interdenominational association devoted to disseminating Christian writings, entitled "The Mother's Last Prayer," narrated the conversion in 1807 of George Vining, a lifelong scoffer at evangelical religion. He finally converted, remembering his mother's death when he was a small boy. "Just before she breathed her last," he confided, "she took me in her arms and blessed me and gave me up to God." His minister recorded Vining's work to convert his children and

grandchildren, praying, "Give me poverty—chain me in the dun-
geon—bind me to the martyr's stake, but deny me not *the prayers of
a godly mother.*" Moralists and doctors were writing by mid-century
that for those who survived into old age, pain and misery were the
result of sin, not any inevitable physical decay. Thus the mother who
could remember her children in death possessed mighty virtue and
was to be ignored at peril. Harriet Beecher Stowe used this well-
worn evocation in narrating the life of Simon Legree, who was
cursed for disregarding his dying mother's prayers for him.[4]

Women presided over death practically and spiritually. Until the
Civil War they were responsible for washing and preparing corpses
for burial. They also created jewelry and ornaments with the hair of
the dead. The education of middle-class girls often included lessons
in drawing mourning pictures. These pictures featured mourners,
willow trees that signified grief, urns that signified the spirit of the
dead person, and evergreens connoting life everlasting.[5]

Women wielded their greatest authority among intimates at
home. Their everyday struggles to obey their husbands were an aspect of their larger struggles to find meaning in renunciation and suffering: their own or that of those for whom they cared. The death of
beloved intimates, often following long periods of exhausting care-
taking, raised in its most baffling form the question of why God allowed suffering and loss. It was woman's ability to field this question,
in action and in words that gave her moral authority.[6]

Key to women's informal moral power was their ability to mani-
fest and interpret emotions that sustained a belief in personal sacrifice and God's wisdom. The spread of evangelical religion infused
Protestant sects with heightened emotionalism, and that in turn
made way for increased attention to feelings as moral markers in the
progression toward perfected Christianity. Mary Sibley's journal is a
case in point. She began writing to narrate her conversion and continued to provide a didactic glimpse of the ups and downs of her
feelings as a reborn Christian. Her conversion increased the significance and authority she gave her own feelings; for the first time she
found them worthy of recording. For Sibley, like Puritans before her,
a good guide to failure as a Christian was the absence of feeling,

marked by coldness and dullness. She many times reported her own coldness or that of another that reminded her of her own. "My sins weigh heavily upon me I try to repent, but can not feel that brokenness of heart which I ought." Trying to experience the right feelings was part of Sibley's emotional and moral discipline.[7]

Sibley's conversion came because of the death of Eliza Lindsay, and her description of the events is a remarkable demonstration of the persuasive power of women's expressive and interpretive agility. The deathbed had been a scene that excited Puritans' intense curiosity, but it was not usually the site of their conversions. New England Puritans increasingly saw conversion as the result of a process that was in part rational—derived from the conscientious study of Scripture—and guided by a minister. The First Great Awakening placed more emphasis on the emotional aspect of faith and conversion. Congregations were now demanding that ministers excite their emotions and help them bring their realizations of weakness and sinfulness to Christ for solace and support. In the vast camp meetings of the Second Great Awakening, which extended greatly the tendencies of the First, the emotional conviction of damnation and the release in experiencing the presence of God were available to anyone, whether or not he or she was already prepared, knew the presiding minister, or was literate. Mrs. Lindsay had monitored Mary Sibley's readiness for conversion, and in her dying days she and Sibley shared their concerned affection, grief, fear, and awe. This heady experience of release, love, and self-authorization led the repressed and self-critical Sibley to declare herself before her congregation.[8]

Mary Sibley described her relations with Eliza Lindsay as "those of sinner and saint. . . . She was the saint watching over me with the tender care of a Mother, praying unceasingly for me, taking every opportunity that offered to lead me gently into the way of life, never out of patience at my frowardness [perversity] and open ingratitude to my Maker." When Sibley visited her during her last days, Lindsay said, "O! I am so glad to see you! You are my own dear child, I have wrestled in prayer for you and glory be to my Saviour. He will rescue you from the pit of destruction." The dying woman insisted on her maternal relation to Sibley and proudly took credit for her struggle for Sibley's soul against the demons of worldliness and sin. For Sibley, a wife at fifteen and at thirty-five still afraid of her own mother, Mrs. Lindsay's motherly concern was powerfully soothing. Sibley wrote, "I never saw so much patience, mildness, uncomplaining endurance of pain—so much thankfulness for the most trifling attention conferred, such a continual attention to the feelings and comforts of others exhibited by anyone." Lindsay's disinterest, sensibility, and empathy for others distinguish the perfected Christian and the perfect American mother.

Lindsay's major concern on dying was the religious state of her acquaintances. She used her disinterested empathy for God's purposes, inquiring about attendance at church meetings. She wanted Sibley to tell her who had shown up. She wished particularly to know about Sibley's feelings. "If you feel any changes in your feelings while attending this meeting, you must just write a little note and tell me about it." Sibley added, "I felt her sickness had already softened my heart and that I thought I could pray much more in faith than formerly." Lindsay and Sibley were looking together for a particular, recognizable, emotional change, for a broken heart. The existence of a calibrated emotional scale on which a sinner could judge herself recalls the Puritan morphology of conversion. The emotional cycle was predictable and therefore something the sinner could imagine. Having imagined it, of course she would be more likely to experience it. Lindsay, the Christian priestess, helped Sibley identify the correct feelings of grief, helplessness, and acceptance of her dependence on God required for conversion. Her strong, unwavering maternal concern made it safe for the self-doubting Sibley to experience and give Christian value to her own sorrow and weakness.[9]

By the time Mrs. Lindsay died, Sibley had demonstrated her readiness to succeed her friend in authority. Lindsay wondered why God did not simply allow her to die since she was in such misery. Sibley told her that "perhaps her work was not done here; you are not, I hope, unwilling to stay if it is God's will." At first Lindsay seemed willing to contravene the Lord, saying, "I would rather go," but then she reconsidered the question and affirmed, "Oh yes His Holy will be done." Again, just before she died, Lindsay asked why she could not "be absent from the body and present with the Lord, do see if you can't find out the cause, I know his loving kindness is so great." The priestess turned to her acolyte to sustain her faith in a moment when she could neither understand why she was being allowed to suffer nor question God's mercy. Sibley, a willing assistant teacher, wondered if perhaps she was there to "show us how his children ought to die, that your example may do us good." Instead Mrs. Lindsay blamed her friends and husband for being unwilling to give her up. Once she had instructed her husband and others to relinquish her, the group sang two hymns, and Eliza Lindsay died.[10]

Three ministers conducted Lindsay's funeral, but she and Sibley had conducted her death. Both were public events, one large and formal, overseen by men, the other smaller, a free form improvised by the two women. Mrs. Lindsay's journey to death proceeded as a mother-daughter dialogue punctuated with familiar hymns and prayers and witnessed by mourning intimates. Implicit in Sibley's version was Lindsay's passing on of her mantle of disinterested Christianity. A saint ascended, and a sinner was saved. A mother was lost, and a mother was born.[11]

Mary Sibley wrote up this event and sent it to Lindsay's mother, who undoubtedly shared it with others. It appears twice in Sibley's journal; no doubt Sibley also shared it. Lindsay's death demonstrated both the absolute virtue of patience and resignation in the face of suffering as well as obedience to the will of God and optimism about His inexplicable dark side. It also portrayed a communal Christianity, whose meanings and solace emerged through feelings shared and explained in an egalitarian setting infused with motherly love. Through the gentle guidance of the two women principals, the friends and family of Eliza Lindsay arrived together at reaffirmed faith and consolation through their collective loss. And Mary Sibley was saved to continue God's work.

There is a richness of detail, affection, and clarity in these braided stories that contrasts dramatically with Sibley's brief and worried account of her husband's conversion. Sibley's confidence in setting the tone of the vigil and her willingness to attempt to interpret Lindsay's Christian duties are striking in comparison with her abruptly foreshortened response to what should have been positive feelings aroused by George's conversion. One historian has noted that when women wrote about the deaths of their husbands, they used unusual detail. "These writers are excited . . . to notice themselves, to have been noticed, and to be free from any coercion, regardless of how genuinely fond they may well have been of their husbands." Sibley was able to write about Lindsay because her friend's uncoercive, motherly concern brought Sibley alive to herself and allowed her to explore her own feelings. The demands of wifely obedience and women's concerns about the suppression of self blocked her spontaneity and affection in writing about her husband. But the gratitude she freely experienced for Lindsay's nourishing affection and the excitement she felt to be a participant at the heart of a morally important event permitted her to recover it with specificity and intensity of detail.[12]

Religion continued to embolden Mary Sibley to initiate and coordinate gatherings and to interpret the meanings of other people's behavior and feelings. Her husband's conversion gave her a new affection for him. That fondness probably sustained her ability to bring her interpretative abilities to a new, more confident dialogue with him.

The mortal struggles of their intimates emboldened women to examine their feelings as indicators of important truths. Anna Maria von Phul, describing a slight improvement in her sick sister's condition, queried rhetorically, "What were the emotions I then felt?" She answered herself: "Gratitude to God that she was spared: and that patience and resignation where [sic] the predominant traits of her exalted mind." Her emotional experience: humility, grateful thanks to the Lord, and awe at her sister's noble character made a commendable offering to her sister-in-law. Von Phul was joining in a moral, not a material, hierarchy. Just as material objects sometimes substituted for emotions, so emotions sometimes became objects in middle-class life. In addition to confirming one's sensibility and status, they could be shared and considered.[13]

The moral, persuasive power ceded to white women derived from a perception of their close acquaintance with renunciation and their willingness to subordinate their own desires to attend to weakness, grief, illness, and death. Slave women's experience was nothing if not steeped in renunciation, weakness, grief, illness, and death. That should have made them uniquely powerful bearers of moral influence in the United States, but of course the opposite was true, at least in white society. White insensibility toward the sacrifices of blacks altogether as well as their obsession with female chastity disqualified black women from participating in the symbolic power of white women.[14]

Enslaved African women do not seem to have lent enslaved African men moral authority or even symbolic authority. The social and legal isolation of individuals under slavery meant that men and women did not form morally intradependent units of man and wife. Moral power resided in individuals struggling for freedom, like Elizabeth Keckley and William Wells Brown. White American men glorified their women's self-sacrifice to purify but not to change a rapacious economic system. By contrast, men and women who fought against slavery and for black rights acquired real moral power in the antebellum black community. Every woman in Missouri who sued for freedom, purchased herself, or escaped joined a collective of freedom fighters and leaders of the black community.

Black women had celebrated special rites of mourning in West Africa, and in America they usually washed and shrouded the dead. African American men and women both sat up all night with the dead in wakes that could go on for many hours, even days. Then each individual took his or her leave of the dead. In a menacing world, these leave-takings and the celebratory rites gave meaning to the contributions of the deceased and encouraged the living. Funeral traditions that had crossed the Atlantic from Africa included dances, processions, and merriment to accompany the dead on his or her way. The notion that death represented a homecoming and should be celebrated was an idea Virginia whites shared with and adapted from African beliefs at the time of the First Great Awakening. Notions like heaven as home and the reassurance that the living would meet the dead in the hereafter became commonplace in the late eighteenth and early nineteenth centuries. Nineteenth-century white women certainly drew sustenance from the idea of heaven as a far better home than earth for their beloved dead. Ideas of reunion with family and joy and triumph in death were foundational in the consolation literature white women and ministers elaborated in the nineteenth century. Black culture contributed to white thinking about the hereafter, but this contribution was not acknowledged.[15]

Some slaveowners permitted blacks to organize the elaborate funerals their traditions required. (A procession for a well-celebrated funeral ranged from three to seven hundred people.) Others put dead slaves in coffins, buried them, and the matter ended there. Free blacks quickly established burial societies that proliferated throughout free black communities. These were predominantly all-male societies although some women also formed their own groups. That these societies were among the first African American community organizations suggests how important slaves and free blacks considered the proper rites in sending the dead to the next world. Because most nineteenth-century white communities would not permit blacks to be buried in white cemeteries, African American funeral societies had to set up their own.[16]

Black men and women suffered uniquely not only from the early, sometimes brutal, often needless deaths of family, friends, and acquaintances but also from the frequent inability to celebrate the proper rites. The accelerating diaspora of nineteenth-century slavery meant that family and friends were often distant and frequently ignorant of the deaths of loved ones. The white community consumed black deaths as horrific entertaining anecdotes. This assortment of mentions comes from only one paper during one year (1845) in St. Louis. A black barber shot the "colored girl, Elizabeth Ballard" and then killed himself. Under the title "Free Negroes at Work" was a story about an enslaved man and woman helped by a free Negro to run away but shot trying to escape. A slave tried to cut the throat of his wife and was found hanged. Four blacks at a camp meeting were to be executed for allegedly beating a white man to death in a dispute over some cake. A black girl named Sophy was hanged for killing her master's son. Two black men and a white man were charged with raping a "young white female." The white man was sentenced to forty-two years; the black men were to be hanged. One story detailed a white mistress's torture and murder of a slave woman. A story titled "Paper Hangings" about the execution of a black father and son named Paper constituted humor. The white community interpreted these deaths as examples of the violent and chaotic life of blacks. Black men and women tried to find moral meaning through lovingly celebrated funerals and by trying to end slavery.[17]

White women's power in the nineteenth century was symbolic and derived from a collective history of their suffering, self-sacrifice, caring, and presumably exalted emotions. Black women's power, expressed through desperate independence and service in their communities, resulted from accomplishments and endurance. White women's power depended absolutely on a perception of their chastity. Black women's power existed in spite of persistent attacks on their sexual integrity. The two groups were entwined in each other's lives and moral ideas. To continue elaborating their moral system built on empathy and sympathy, white women depended on the labor of black and poor white women. White women often searched for emotional "liberty," but it frequently escaped them. White women's moral history is of considerable self-sacrifice and courage in tending the people for whom they were responsible combined with the nearsightedness that accompanied their deprivation of full ethical adulthood and their often unthinking exploitation of those who provided their lives with comfort and time. Black women's history is of endurance rising frequently to heroism. Paradoxically, despite slavery, they may have experienced more emotional liberty than white women. They survived in a society that thrust them into adulthood and into what Elizabeth Cady Stanton called "the solitude of the self" while they were still children. At the same time, that society denied not just the validity but even the existence of their hard-won moral vision.

EPILOGUE

The early republic depended on its white women to be very good. The terms of their conduct had been laid out over the previous two hundred years and required of them chastity, selflessness, modesty, frugality, and self-regulation. Prisoners of purity and sworn to obey their husbands, women, in exchange, were to have respect, a free hand at home, and such material rewards, including household service, as the burgeoning economy and their husbands' imaginations could provide. After more than one hundred years of African slavery had distorted the colonies' moral perceptions, white Americans in the new nation were agreed that only white women could provide a symbol of purity and virtue to which white American men could dedicate their labors. Rigid standards for white women accompanied low moral expectations of women who were not white, expectations that permitted the latter to be sexually and economically exploited. The development of complementary moral systems meant that the labor of different groups of women would have different meanings and strikingly different rewards. It further meant that different moral and emotional styles would mark members of different groups, making them easy to identify and ascribe status to. These varied ethical evaluations of women according to race, as well as ethnicity and class, also meant that white women should be the good shepherds of those with lesser moral potential.

Without an official public voice in shaping the nation's policies but assured that their influence would persuade men to behave justly, white women were to elaborate a moral and emotional interior world where empathy reigned supreme. Within the white home, mothers trained their daughters in sentimental expression while black or poor white girls with their rougher manners did the housework. Women refined a system of moral and emotional communication based on empathy and delicacy for the middle class that ensured its exclusivity. Its participants faced inward. Outside the family, white Americans employed other, harsher styles to achieve their temporal goals, justified by the evidently flawed moral values of the poor, the black, and Native Americans.

In splitting off the morality of white women from that of other Americans and in positing female sexual purity as the basis of virtue, early Americans made it very difficult for them and their descendants to arrive at a mature and realistic moral code flexible enough to deal with a broad range of complex problems. Displacing serious public questions onto the body and carriage, as the Puritans would say, of women is only one of the unfortunate legacies of the nineteenth century. Just as egregious in distorting public policy and justifying gross social and economic inequities has been pitting the mythical chastity of white women against the equally mythic salaciousness of black women. Thinking in false dichotomies about sexuality has encouraged prurience, not sexual maturity. Fetishizing chastity has alienated many women from their own sexuality, no less certainly than it has distorted sexuality for many white men and kept them from integrating sexuality into their view of women of their own color and class. It has also been one of the most enduring hindrances to women's equality. And it has forced on women an unhealthy concern for appearances in place of the chance to participate freely in the political debate around them. Making women's moral credibility equivalent to their chastity has circumscribed women's imaginations as well as their activities and suggests that self-renunciation and fatalism are higher responsibilities than challenging abuses of authority.

Separate moral codes for prosperous whites and all others has permitted the dominant group not to give weight to the critiques of those who have profited less or not at all from the economic and political system. Ascribing inferior morals to the poor masks the effects of inequality and calls individual character into question when the real issue is injustice.

NOTES

PROLOGUE

1. This is derived primarily from Charles Taylor's magisterial *The Sources of the Self: The Making of Modern Identity* (Cambridge, Mass., 1989).
2. See Carolyn Merchant, *The Death of Nature: Women, Ecology and the Scientific Revolution* (San Francisco, 1980) and *Ecological Revolutions: Nature, Gender, and Science in New England* (Chapel Hill, N.C., 1989).
3. See Amanda Porterfield, *Female Piety in Puritan New England: The Emergence of Religious Humanism* (New York, 1992), especially the Introduction, for a discussion of the elevation of family life. Joseph Hall, quoted in Taylor, *Sources*, 223.
4. See, for example, Laurence Hauptman, "The Pequot War and Its Legacy," in Laurence Hauptman and James D. Wherry, *The Pequots in Southern New England: The Rise and Fall of an American Indian Nation* (Norman, Okla., 1990), 69–80.

   Jill Lepore, *The Name of War: King Philip's War and the Origins of American Identity* (New York, 1997), 71–96, discusses this defense and denial as a conscious choice. It seems to me that for many it was probably an unconscious response to desires Puritans had trouble admitting to themselves. Carol Karlsen, *The Devil in the Shape of a Woman: Witchcraft in Colonial New England* (New York, 1997), and Ann Kibbey, *The Interpretation of Material Shapes in Puritanism* (New York, 1986), both document this process and how it affected women.

1. CHILDREN AND ADOLESCENTS

1. Karlsen, *Devil in the Shape of a Woman*, 160–81; Angeline Goreau, *The Whole Duty of a Woman: Female Writers in Seventeenth-Century England* (New York,

1985), 1–20, 75–159. For a view of the shifting definitions of gender in a broader context in this period, see Kathleen M. Brown, *Good Wives, Nasty Wenches, and Anxious Patriarchs: Gender, Race, and Power in Colonial Virginia* (Chapel Hill, N.C., 1996), 13–41. Anthony Fletcher, *Gender, Sex, and Subordination in England, 1500–1800* (New Haven, 1995).

2. Cotton Mather, *Ornaments for the Daughters of Zion* (Boston, 1691), 82, 4; Robert Pope, *The Half-Way Covenant: Church Membership in Puritan New England* (Princeton, 1969), 213; Mary Maples Dunn, "Saints and Sisters: Congregational and Quaker Women in the Early Colonial Period," *American Quarterly*, vol. 30 (1978), 594; Elizabeth Reis, *Damned Women: Sinners and Witches in Puritan New England* (Ithaca, N.Y., 1997), 41–54, 121–54.

3. John Calvin, *The Institutes of the Christian Religion* (Basel, 1536), trans. Henry Beveridge (New York, 1962), 267; Cotton Mather, *A Family Well-Ordered* (Boston, 1699), 10–12. See Peter Gregg Slater, *Children in the New England Mind in Death and Life* (Hamden, Conn., 1977), 18–41; Joseph Illick, "Child-Rearing in Seventeenth-Century England and America," in *The History of Childhood*, ed. Lloyd deMause (New York, 1974), 303–50; John Walzer, "A Period of Ambivalence: Eighteenth Century American Childhood," in *Childhood*, 351–82; ibid., 358, 365; David Leverenz, *The Language of Puritan Feeling: An Exploration in Literature, Psychology and Social History* (New Brunswick, N.J., 1980), 1–10, 74–78. Emory Elliott, *Power and the Pulpit in Puritan New England* (Princeton, N.J., 1975), and Sanford Fleming, *Children and Puritanism* (New Haven, 1933), have stressed the controls, fears, and resulting anxieties that Puritans instilled in their young. See also Vivian Fox and Martin Quitt, *Loving, Parenting and Dying: The Family Cycle in England and America, Past and Present* (New York, 1980).

4. Ross Beales, Jr., "In Search for the Historical Child: Miniature Adulthood and Youth in Colonial New England," *American Quarterly*, vol. 27 (1975), 379–98, believes that there was a recognized stage known as youth in Puritan culture. Others agree: Roger Thompson, "Adolescent Culture in Colonial Massachusetts," *Journal of Family History*, vol. 9 (1984), 151–54, and John Frye, "Class, Generation, and Social Change: A Case in Salem, Massachusetts, 1636–1656," *Journal of Popular Culture*, vol. 11 (1977), 744–51.

See John Phillips, *Eve: The History of an Idea* (New York, 1984), chs. 5 and 6, for a discussion of the Reformation interpretation of the Fall as Eve's doing; Karlsen, *Devil*, 173–79, for a discussion of Eve as the partially submerged Puritan view of woman as evil; Cotton Mather, *Memorials of Early Piety Occurring in the Holy Life and Joyful Death of Mrs. Jerusha Oliver* (Boston, 1711), 4. Lyle Koehler, *A Search for Power: The "Weaker Sex" in Seventeenth Century New England* (Urbana, Ill., 1980), 29, notes that embryological lore implicated the female fetus in dreary and uncomfortable pregnancies, while the male was supposed to exit more quickly and was thought to receive his soul earlier in the womb. Anne Bradstreet, *The Works of Anne Bradstreet in Prose and Verse*, ed. John Harvard Ellis (Charlestown, Mass., 1867), 151.

5. Nathaniel B. Shurtleff, *Records of the Governor and the Company of the Massachusetts Bay in New England*, 2 (Boston, 1853), 6–7, 26, 203; Jennifer E. Monaghan, "Literary Instruction and Gender in Colonial New England," *Am. Quarterly*, vol. 40 (1988), 30–31; Robert St. George, " 'Heated' Speech and Literacy in Seventeenth-Century New England," in *Seventeenth-Century New England*, eds. David D. Hall and David Grayson Allen (Charlottesville, Va., 1984); Edmund Morgan, *The Puritan Family* (New York, 1944), 10.

6. Perry Miller, *The American Puritans* (Garden City, N.Y., 1956), 324; Elizabeth Joceline, *The Mother's Legacie to Her Unborne Childe* (London, 1624), 1. C. Mather, *Ornaments*, 82, 4; Richard Allestree, *The Ladies Calling* (Oxford, U.K., 1673), 9; Samuel Sewall, "The Letter-Book of Samuel Sewall," *Collections*, Massachusetts Historical Society, vol. 1, Ser. 6 (Boston, 1866), 19. C. Mather, *Memorials*, 4–7.

7. Patricia Caldwell, *The Puritan Conversion Narrative: The Beginnings of American Expression* (New York, 1983); First Parish Church (Dorchester, Mass.) Records, Massachusetts Historical Society, 93; John Eliot, "The Rev. John Eliot's Records of the Church of Roxbury," *New England Historical and Genealogical Register*, vol. 33 (Boston, 1881), 289. The age of sixteen had significance in criminal law by demarcating the age at which a person might be executed for specific crimes, such as arson, denial of the infallibility of Scripture, and cursing or smiting parents. Other crimes, such as sodomy and lying, required the maximum punishment for those fourteen and over. See Edwin Powers, *Crime and Punishment in Early Massachusetts, 1620–1692: A Documentary History* (Boston, 1966), 442–43, and James Axtell, *The School upon a Hill* (New Haven, 1974), 40.

    Charles F. Adams, *Antinomians in the Colony of Massachusetts Bay, 1636–1638* (Boston, 1894), 155; John Cotton, *Singing of Psalms, a Gospel Ordinance* (London, 1647), 43; Jane Kamensky, *Governing the Tongue: The Politics of Speech in Early New England* (New York, 1997), 72–73; see 71–98 for her discussion of women's speech, and for a fuller discussion of Hutchinson, see ch. 4. See also Michael Ditmore, "A Prophetess in Her Own Country: An Exegesis of Anne Hutchinson's 'Immediate Revelation,' " *William and Mary Quarterly*, 3d Ser., vol. 57 (2000), 349–92.

8. Hugh Peter, *A Dying Father's Last Legacy to his Daughter* (Boston, 1717), 26; Sewall, "Letter-Book," *Collections*, Ma.H.S., vol. 5, Ser. 5, March 1687; "Middlesex," Middlesex County Courthouse, Folio 152, January 1692; Adam Winthrop, ed., The Winthrop Papers (Boston, 1929–), vol. 4, 378; Ann Maria Plane, *Colonial Intimacies: Indian Marriage in Early New England* (Ithaca, N.Y., 2000), 101–2; Lawrence Hammond, Diary, March 1688; Ma.H.S.

9. Winthrop, ed., *Papers*, vol. 4, p. 378; Plane, *Colonial Intimacies*, 116, 96–128, on Indian servitude. See Gloria Main, *Peoples of a Spacious Land: Families and Cultures in Colonial New England* (Cambridge, Mass., 2001), 131–38, on comparative English and Indian practices.

10. For these and other examples, Peter Thacher Diaries, May 23, 1679; June 24, 1679; September 29, 1679; December 26, 1679; April 16 and 19, 1680; Ma.H.S. George F. Dow, ed., *Records and Files of the Quarterly Courts of Essex County, Massachusetts*, vol. 3 (Salem, Mass., 1911), 22; "Suffolk," Suffolk County Court-house, vol. 24, p. 147; "Testimony of Sarah Eaton," April 9, 1672, Ma.H.S.; Elizabeth D. Hanscom, *The Heart of the Puritan* (New York, 1917), 41; "Middlesex," Middlesex County Courthouse, Folio 157. See Cornelia Hughes Dayton, *Women Before the Bar: Gender, Law, and Society in Connecticut, 1639–1789* (Chapel Hill, N.C., 1995), 70–71, for a discussion of the remarkable accessibility of the New Haven legal system to women.

11. James Axtell, "The Scholastic Philosophy in the Wilderness," *William and Mary Quarterly*, 3d Ser., vol. 29 (1972), 354; John Josselyn, *An Account of Two Voyages to New England* (Boston, 1865), 99. Eli Faber, "Puritan Criminals: The Economic, Social and Intellectual Background to Crime in Seventeenth-Century Massachusetts," *Perspectives in American History*, vol. 9 (1977–78), 83–144, 94–95, observes that Puritans thought Indian family life disordered. Salisbury, *Manitou*, 137; Axtell, "Scholastic Philosophy," 355. See also Main, *Spacious Land*, 64, on the sexual freedom of children. William S. Simmons, "Cultural Bias in the New England Puritans' Perception of Indians," *William and Mary Quarterly*, 3d Ser., vol. 38 (1981), 58. Ann Kibbey's work (*Interpretation*) is based on the inversion of these ideas. See also James P. Ronda, " 'We Are Well as We Are': An Indian Critique of Seventeenth Century Christian Missions," *William and Mary Quarterly*, 3d Ser., vol. 34 (1977), 71, 75, 79; Yasuhide Kawashima, *Puritan Justice and the Indian: White Man's Law in Massachusetts, 1630–1763* (New Haven, 1986); Lepore, *Name of War*; Winthrop Jordan, *White over Black: American Attitudes Toward the Negro, 1550–1812* (New York, 1968), 68–69. Winthrop, ed., *Papers*, vol. 3, 435. John Winthrop to William Bradford, 1637: William Bradford, *Bradford's History of Plymouth Plantation* (Boston, 1901). See Hauptman and Wherry, *Pequots*, especially Hauptman, "Pequot War," 69–80, 76.

12. Lepore, *Name of War*, 28–29, 116; "Suffolk," Suffolk County Courthouse, vol. 17, 138; Thacher, Diary, May 14, 1679; ibid., August 18, 1679. Alden Vaughan, *New England Frontier, Puritans and Indians, 1620–1675* (New York, 1979), argues that the Puritans before King Philip's War treated the Indians with considerable fairness but that the war eroded their egalitarian attitude. Francis Jennings is the most vociferous among those who accuse the Puritans of bad behavior and bad faith from the beginning: *The Invasion of America: Indians, Colonialism, and the Cant of Conquest* (New York, 1975).

13. Beales, "Search," 384–85, demonstrates that in Dorchester between 1640 and 1730, 8.9 percent of the communicants converted in their teens. Of the three conversions that took place in under seventeen-year-olds, all were girls. The majority, 52.9 percent, converted in their twenties. See also Mary Ramsbottom, "Religious Society and the Family in Charlestown, Ma., 1630–1740," Ph.D. dissertation, Yale, 1987. See also Betty Sewall's conversion: Samuel Sewall, "Diary of Samuel Sewall," *Collections*, Ma.H.S., vol. 5, Ser. 5 (1882), 345, 348, 359.

14. Laurel Thatcher Ulrich, "Vertuous Women Found: New England Ministerial Literature, 1668–1735," in *Puritan New England*, ed. Alden T. Vaughan and Francis J. Bremer (New York, 1977), 220, argues: "In a very real sense there is no such thing as *female piety* in early New England . . . [T]he same Christ-like bearing was required of both male and female." Charles Cohen, *God's Caress: The Psychology of Puritan Religious Experience* (New York, 1986), 222–23, agrees, as does Caldwell, *Puritan Conversion*, 9–15. Amanda Porterfield challenges this view in *Female Piety in Puritan New England: The Emergence of Religious Humanism* (New York: 1992). See C. Mather, Diary, Cotton Mather Papers, November 7, 1697, Ma.H.S.; C. Mather, *Memorials*, 10, 13.

15. Thomas Cobbett, *A Fruitfull and Usefull Discourse Touching the Honour Due from Children to Parents, and the Duty of Parents Towards their Children* (London, 1656), 7; Thomas Hutchinson, *A Collection of Original Papers Relative to the History of the Colony of Massachusetts-Bay* (Boston, 1769), 174; Shurtleff, *Records*, 14; John Cotton, *Milk for Babes* (London, 1646), inscription by Mary Patrick on flyleaf. John Demos, "Infancy and Childhood in the Plymouth Colony," in *The American Family in Social History Perspective*, ed. Michael Gordon (New York, 1973); John Demos, *A Little Commonwealth: Family Life in Plymouth Colony* (New York, 1970), 100–104, 134–39; Demos, "Notes on the Life of Plymouth Colony," *William and Mary Quarterly*, 3d Ser., vol. 19 (1965), 264–66; Philip Greven, *Protestant Temperament* (New York, 1977), 27–28, 37.

16. Peter, *Legacy*, 21; Allestree, *Calling*, 43–44; Bradstreet, *Works*, 124; Joceline, *Legacie*, 38.

17. Much of my evidence comes from the unpublished Suffolk Court Files: Original Depositions and Other Materials from the Proceedings of the Quarterly Courts of Suffolk Co. Mass. Boston, 1650–1700, and the unpublished Middlesex County Court Files: Original Depositions and Other Materials from the Proceedings of the Quarterly Courts of Middlesex Co. Mass., East Cambridge, 1649–1700. I have also used the published George F. Dow, ed., *Records and Files of the Quarterly Courts of Essex County, Mass.*, 1–5 (Salem, 1911), and John Noble and Joseph F. Cronin, eds., *Records of the Court of Assistants of the Colony of Massachusetts Bay 1630–1692*, 1–3 (Boston, 1901–1928). My heavy reliance on court evidence is out of necessity and entails certain problems. There is little or no other evidence about the large numbers of Massachusetts women who had no clergymen to memorialize them and were neither poets nor heretics. The glimpses one catches of the poor of three hundred years ago are therefore distorted by either their extreme misfortunes or their unusual defiance. On the other hand, the glimpses we have of extremely "good" women are comparably distorted by what appears to be their unusual submissiveness as well as their proximity to powerful males. In the absence of an abundance of women's voices recording their own experiences, court records are the best extant source of material about them. They must, however, be read in light of the fact that women in court were usually in an adversarial situation.

18. See John Demos, *Entertaining Satan, Witchcraft, and the Culture of Early New*

England (New York, 1982), 157–65, 97–111, for his lucid explanation of the psychic conflicts many adolescent girls experienced. Cotton Mather, "Memorable Providences," in *Original Narratives of Early American History* (New York, 1914), 267, 270, 276. See C. Mather, Diary, Cotton Mather Papers, 1695, Ma.H.S. See Karlsen, *Devil*, 222–51, for a rich discussion of possession and its sociology. See also Reis, *Damned*, 123, on the envy and guilt of the possessed.

19. Peter, *Legacy*, 27. See Kamensky, *Governing the Tongue*, 73–98, who points out that when Anne Hutchinson arrived, she merely represented the dissenter tradition of women's lay prophesying. See Phyllis Mack, *Visionary Women: Ecstatic Prophecy in Seventeenth-Century England* (Berkeley, Calif., 1992), especially 1–124, on these women in their English context. St. George, "Heated," 275–322, 310–11; Mary Beth Norton, "Gender and Defamation in Seventeenth-Century Maryland," *William and Mary Quarterly*, 3d Ser., vol. 44 (1987), 4–39, finds a high female participation in slander in the Chesapeake. Saint George, "Heated," 314; Brown, *Good Wives*, 99–100, maintains that women used gossip as a powerful and informal political tool. See Kamensky, *Governing the Tongue*, 19–22, 190. It is disheartening that men still believe that women talk and interrupt more than men when study after study shows the reverse to be true. Deborah Tannen, *You Just Don't Understand: Women and Men in Conversation* (New York, 1990), 188–89. Ulrich, "Vertuous Women," 218, argues that godly women were supposed to converse. C. Mather, *Memorials*, 16–17.

20. Bradstreet, *Works*, xv, 4–7; Winthrop, *Papers*, vol. 3, 214–15; C. Mather, *Memorials*, 5.

21. Allestree, *Calling*, 7.

22. Paul L. Ford, ed., *New England Primer* (New York, 1897, reprint 1962), not paginated. [Thomas Shepard], "A breefe answer . . ." 1642?, Photostats, Ma.H.S. Shurtleff, *Records*, vol. 2, 21.

23. *The Psalms, Hymns and Spiritual Songs of the Old and New Testament Faithfully Translated into English Meeter. For the Use, Edification and Comfort of the Saints in Publick and Private, Especially in New England* (London, 1680), ch. 19, verse 1. Karlsen's *Devil* is the best exploration of the contrasting ideologies about women; another fascinating treatment is Porterfield's *Female Piety*. David Flaherty, "Law and Morals in Early America," *Perspectives in American History*, vol. 5 (1971), 244, asserts that for Puritans sin and crime were one and the same and that the state's cease-fire on morals prosecution represented its acknowledgment of its failure to control community sexual behavior. He remarks too that the result was many fewer prosecutions against men. John Murrin, "Magistrates, Sinners, and a Precious Liberty," 188, in *Saints and Revolutionaries*, ed. David Hall et al. (New York, 1984), 196, also argues that sin and crime were identical to Puritans, noting that by the end of the seventeenth century the community had changed. Dayton, *Women Before the Bar*, 60, says that men were beginning to use lawyers to defend themselves against fornication charges, and lawyers were rejecting the testimony of accusing women because of their poverty and alleged lewdness. C. Mather, *Ornaments*, 11. Cotton Mather, *Mag-*

nalia Christi Americana: or, the Ecclesiastical History of New England from Its First Planting in the Year 1620 unto the Year of Our Lord 1698 in Seven Books (New York, 1967), 213. Leverenz, *Language*, 155. Hutchinson, *Collection*, xx. Suffolk County Courthouse, vol. 44, 23; vol. 11, 137.

24. Barbara S. Lindemann, "To Ravish and Carnally Know: Rape in Eighteenth-Century Massachusetts," *Signs*, vol. 10 (1984), 63–82.

25. John Winthrop, *The History of New England from 1630 to 1649*, 1 (Boston, 1853), 54, 41; Shurtleff, *Records*, vol. 2, p. 12; "Fairfield Case" [1656?], Boston Public Library. Much of the discussion is in Latin to prevent the nonelite and women from reading it. See also Else L. Hambleton, " 'Playing the Rogue': Rape and Issues of Consent in Seventeenth-Century Massachusetts," in *Sex Without Consent: Rape and Sexual Coercion in America*, ed. Merril D. Smith (New York, 2001).

26. Powers, *Crime*, 266.

27. "Middlesex," Middlesex County Courthouse, vol. 1, 119; Koehler, *Search*, 96, notes that servants, while only 10 percent of the population, were a third of the rape victims. See also Sharon Block, "Lines of Color, Sex, and Service: Comparative Sexual Coercion in Early America," in *Sex, Love and Race: Crossing Boundaries in North American History*, ed. Martha Hodes (New York, 1999), 142–63. "Testimony of Ruth Parsons," September? 1654, Photostats (these are photocopies of selected trials heard before the General Court and filed in the Suffolk Courthouse), Ma.H.S.; "Suffolk," Suffolk County Courthouse, vol. 8, 32–33.

28. N.E.H. Hull, *Female Felons* (Urbana, Ill., 1987), 57. "Suffolk," Suffolk County Courthouse, vol. 18, October 12, 1676; Robert C. Twombley and Robert H. Moore, "Black Puritan: The Negro in Seventeenth-Century Massachusetts," in *Puritan New England*, 191; Dayton, *Women Before the Bar*, 249.

29. "Suffolk," Suffolk County Courthouse, vol. 12, 101. I use the word "leniency" in the context of a society that was not, on principle, opposed to the death penalty although its use was diminishing. Lindemann, "To Ravish," 79, 81.

2. MASSACHUSETTS: CULTURAL PERSPECTIVES ON SEX, LAW, AND FEELING

1. See John D'Emilio and Estelle B. Freedman, *Intimate Matters: A History of Sexuality in America* (New York, 1988), 4–5; Morgan, *Family*, 62–64, and "The Puritans and Sex," *New England Quarterly*, vol. 15 (1942), 591–607; Koehler, *Search*, 71, argues that Puritans thought sex a "base and contemptible thing," but that is only one part of the story. Kathleen Verduin, " 'Our Cursed Natures': Sexuality and the Puritan Conscience," *New England Quarterly*, vol. 56 (1983), 200–237. Leverenz's *Language* finds Puritans ambivalent. They routinely condemned female sexuality but displayed "a healthy acknowledgment of sexuality among the faithful" (6). See also Reis, *Damned*, 105–7, and Karlsen, *Devil*, 168–69, 194–96, 217–18. See Thomas A. Foster, "Deficient Husbands: Man-

hood, Sexual Incapacity, and Male Marital Sexuality in Seventeenth Century New England," *William and Mary Quarterly*, 3d Ser., vol. 41 (1999), 723–44, and Main, *Spacious Land*, 64–70, on Puritan ideas of a husband's sexual responsibilities.

John Allin, *The Benefit of a Well-Ordered Conversation* (Boston, 1682), 37. Verduin, " 'Our Cursed Natures,' " 200; Porterfield, *Female Piety*, 27–29.

See Cornelia Hughes Dayton, "Was There a Calvinist Type of Patriarchy?: New Haven Colony Reconsidered in the Early Modern Context," in *The Many Legalities of Early America*, ed. Christopher Tomlin and Bruce Mann (Chapel Hill, N.C., 2001), 349, on the evenhandedness with which the New Haven colony under Theophilus Eaton prosecuted male and female fornicators. After Eaton's death the double standard began replacing gender fairness; Norton, "White Women's Experience," 608; Mary Beth Norton, *Founding Mothers and Fathers: Gendered Power and the Forming of American Society* (New York, 1996), 8–17. Murrin, "Magistrates, Sinners," 196; Morgan, "Puritans and Sex," 595–96; Henry Bamford Parkes, "Morals and Law Enforcement in Colonial New England," *New England Quarterly*, vol. 5 (1932), 431; Daniel Scott Smith and Michael S. Hindus, "Premarital Pregnancy in America, 1640–1971: An Overview and Interpretation," *Journal of Interdisciplinary History*, vol. 4 (1975), 549–50; Koehler, *Search*, 193; Powers, *Crime*, 368–69; Hull, *Female Felons*, 52–53.

2. "Middlesex," Middlesex County Courthouse, Folio 31, 1662. "Suffolk," Suffolk County Courthouse, 44, October 5, 1699, 23; Lindemann, "To Ravish," 66; see Dayton, *Women Before the Bar*, 232, on acquaintance rape and the difficulties of prosecuting in Connecticut in this period when English evidentiary standards, including heavy scrutiny of the woman's reputation, were being applied. Massachusetts, unlike Connecticut, also employed the lesser charge of attempted rape. Laurel Thatcher Ulrich, *Good Wives: Image and Reality in the Lives of Women in Northern New England, 1650–1750* (New York, 1982), 78–105, introduces a perplexing question, arguing that "many New Englanders" had not internalized guilt. Thus external controls had to substitute for conscience. Murrin, "Magistrates, Sinners," 196, disagrees, as do I. The difference may be that my evidence is largely urban while Ulrich's is rural.

Main, *Spacious Land*, 138, remarks on the greater supervision afforded wealthier girls. See Murrin, "Magistrates, Sinners," 164, 196, for the pressure the accused were under to confess and the 90 percent conviction rate achieved in Puritan Massachusetts. See Kamensky, *Governing the Tongue*, 134, for the importance Puritans gave to unsaying slander and libel and how penitence was a particularly comfortable position for women. The authorities were likely to call for their repentance through silence, while men often unsaid in public their offending sentences. Reis, *Damned*, 121–63, discusses women's susceptibility to seeing themselves as inwardly corrupt and available to the devil rather than as just people who sometimes sinned.

3. I do not believe confessing was simply about self-defense, however. Reis, *Damned*, 121, 124.
4. Murrin, "Magistrates, Sinners," 204–5.
5. In the colony of New Haven—i.e., before 1666—fornication was rare, most people confessed, and men and women were punished equally (Dayton, *Women Before the Bar*, 175–78). The same remained true for some years after New Haven had become part of Connecticut except that whipping became rare and was used almost exclusively to humiliate black offenders. Karlsen, *Devil*, 154–161; Leverenz, *Language*, 148; C. Mather, Diary, 1702, Cotton Mather Papers, Ma.H.S.; Hanscom, *Heart*, 66–68, 70–71; Page Smith, *Daughters of the Promised Land* (Boston, 1970), 50; Verduin, " 'Our Cursed Natures,' " 231, 235. "Confession of Elizabeth Healy," Photostats, July 26, 1667, Ma.H.S. See also Jane Stoddard in "Suffolk," Suffolk County Courthouse, vol. 34, 51. "Middlesex," Middlesex County Courthouse, Folio 167, 1698, 166–67. First Parish Church (Dorchester, Mass.) Records, 1692, Ma.H.S. See also Abigail Merrifield, ibid., March 1679, May 1679, April 1683. See also Mary Modesly, in "Suffolk," Suffolk County Courthouse, vol. 44, 35.
6. Thompson, "Adolescent Culture," 141–54. See also Frye, "Class, Generation, and Social Change."
7. For example, see Captain Patrick and Elizabeth Surgis in "Middlesex," Middlesex County Courthouse, Folio 131, December 31, 1689. See also ibid., Folio 52; "Pulsifer," vol. 4, 63. Winthrop, ed., *Papers*, vol. 4, 17; see Block, "Lines of Color."
8. Thompson, "Adolescent Culture," 146, includes Holmes, it seems incorrectly, in his youth culture. She had testified about the books explaining sex, and he speculated about a rebellious group of girls reading such books together. Much of his evidence is from Langhorn's attacks on her, which makes it suspect.
9. "Middlesex," Middlesex County Courthouse, Folio 143, April 1691; Sewall, "Diary," May 17, 1686, *Collections*, Ma.H.S., vol. 5, Ser. 5. For how Connecticut handled this problem, see Dayton, *Women Before the Bar*, 202–5.
10. "Middlesex," Middlesex County Courthouse, Folio 78, 1677; "Pulsifer," vol. 3, 196, 232, 255. George Lee Haskins, *Law and Authority in Early Massachusetts* (New York, 1960), 153; "Middlesex," Middlesex County Courthouse, Folio 78, 1677. Savin had emmenagogic properties, and the dried leaves were used to obtain abortions (*OED*). On early abortion techniques, see Linda Gordon, *Woman's Body, Woman's Right* (New York, 1977), 35–39.
11. "Middlesex," Middlesex County Courthouse, Folio 112, April 1685.
12. Second Church (Boston, Mass.) Records, April 4, 1697, Ma.H.S.
13. Ibid., 29; Hull, *Female Felons*, 57, suggests one thousand for the number of blacks in 1700, which agrees with the estimate of Lorenzo Greene, *The Negro in Colonial New England* (Port Washington, N.Y., 1966), 11; Hull, *Female Felons*, 57, 102; Faber, "Puritan Criminals," 100. Richard Slotkin, "Narratives of Negro Crime in New England, 1675–1800," *Am. Quarterly*, vol. 25, (1973), 3–31, says that black men were represented as sexually rapacious from the moment they

appear in the records. Daniel Cohen, "Social Injustice, Sexual Violence, Spiritual Transcendence: Constructions of Interracial Rape in Early American Crime Literature, 1787–1817," *William and Mary Quarterly*, 3d Ser., vol. 56 (1999), 481–526, 482; ibid., 29; Hull, *Female Felons*, 102; Faber, "Puritan Criminals," 100.

14. Ira Berlin, *Many Thousands Gone: The First Two Centuries of Slavery in North America* (Cambridge, Mass., 1998), 47–63; Jordan, *White over Black*, 67, 32–43; David Eltis, *The Rise of African Slavery in the Americas* (New York, 2000), 127; Samuel Sewall, *The Selling of Joseph: A Memorial*, ed. Sidney Kaplan (Amherst, Mass., 1969), 10.

15. Sidney Kaplan (Sewall, *Selling*, 31) calculated, using Lawrence Towner's figures ("Fondness for Freedom: Servant Protest in Puritan Society," *William and Mary Quarterly*, 3d Ser., vol. 19 [1962], 210–19), that protest behavior on the part of blacks constituted 7 percent of servant "crime" from 1629 to 1659, 29 percent from 1660 to 1689, and 48 percent from 1690 to 1719.

16. Winthrop, *History*, vol. 2, 31. Second Church (Boston, Mass.) Records, November 13, 1698, Ma.H.S.; Bernard Rosenthal, "Puritan Conscience and New England Slavery," *New England Quarterly*, vol. 46 (1973), 62–81, 67, quotes Ezra Stiles lamenting in his journal that there were " 'perhaps 26, and not above 30 professors out of Twelve hundred Negroes in Town.' " Of these, seven were members of his own church. Cotton Mather, *Rules for the Society Negroes* (1693 reprint, New York, 1888), not paginated.

17. "Jonathan Farnum's Testimony," 1670?, Ma.H.S.; "Middlesex," Middlesex County Courthouse, January 1692. In some instances the folio numbers are missing; in those places dates have been used instead. "Suffolk," Suffolk County Courthouse, vol. 9, 113, 114; Sewall, *Selling*, 51; ibid., 11.

18. For slave breeding on Noddles Island, see Josselyn, *An Account*, 26. Before the miscegenation law of 1705, I found no successful prosecutions of white men by pregnant black women. "Middlesex," Middlesex County Courthouse, Folio 123, April 19, 1686; Miscellaneous Manuscripts, April 15, 1669, Ma.H.S.; "Middlesex," Middlesex County Courthouse, Folio 42, May 8, 1669. The miscegenation law of 1705 imposed "fixed penalties . . . on both races. Fornication was no longer left to judicial decision: Negro offenders were banished and the white consort, male or female, assumed responsibility for the offspring" (Twombly and Moore, "Black Puritan," 196).

19. Norton, "White Women's Experience," 612. See, for example, the case in Northampton of the midwifery books or the illicit love affair of Martha Root and Elisha Hawley in Patricia Tracy, *Jonathan Edwards, Pastor* (New York, 1979), 160–61, 164–65, for her account of Edwards's failure to force the town of Northampton to support him in reviving the understanding that sexual misconduct was more than a private affair. David Flaherty, "Law and Morals," 244; Murrin, "Magistrates, Sinners," 188, 206. See Dayton, *Women Before the Bar*, 60–61, for the shift from Puritan to English legal practices in this period in Connecticut, protecting men from prosecution for sexual offenses.

20. Mary Maples Dunn, "Saints and Sisters: Congregational and Quaker Women in the Early Colonial Period," *Am. Quarterly*, vol. 30 (1978), 594. See Kenneth Silverman, *The Life and Times of Cotton Mather* (New York, 1984), 139; David Levin, *Cotton Mather: The Young Life of the Lord's Remembrances* (Cambridge, Mass., 1978), 104–5; Robert Middlekauf, *The Mathers: Three Generations of Puritan Intellectuals* (New York, 1971), 213–30. This is of course the starting point for Ann Douglas, *The Feminization of American Culture* (New York, 1977). Pope, *Half-Way Covenant*, 213. Dunn, "Saints and Sisters," 582–601; according to her statistics, Massachusetts women began outnumbering men in church admission in the decades 1640–1649: 55 percent; 1650–1659: 61 percent; 1660–1669: 64 percent; 1670–1679: 71 percent; 1680–1689: 66 percent; 1690–1699: 68 percent; 1700–1709: 65 percent; 1710–1719: 60 percent; 1720–1729: 67 percent (590). Michael Zuckerman, *Peaceable Kingdoms* (New York, 1970), 12–13.

3. PURITAN MARRIAGES: VIEWS FROM THE INSIDE

1. Robinson, *Works*, ed. Ashton, 237. See also Rev. John Cotton, *A Meet Help* (Boston, 1699), 16; C. Mather, *Ornaments*, 32, 87; John Dunton, "John Dunton's Letters from New England," *Prince Society*, vol. 4 (Boston, 1867), 101–2; Alice Morse Earle, *Colonial Dames and Goodwives* (Boston, 1895), 50. On marriage as a model for society-wide order, see Plane, *Colonial Intimacies*, 6; see also Norton, *Founding Mothers*, 94–95.

2. Greene, *The Negro*, 192–93; Note 17, "Massachusetts: Cultural Perspectives . . . ," "Middlesex," Middlesex County Courthouse, Folio 85, 1691; "Testimony of Hagar Blackmore," April 15, 1669, Ma.H.S.

3. Peter C. Hoffer and N.E.H. Hull, *Murdering Mothers: Infanticide in England and New England, 1558–1803* (New York, 1981), 80; Hull, *Female Felons*, 51, 58.

4. Plane, *Colonial Intimacies*, 63–66. See Tom Hatley, *The Dividing Paths: Cherokees and South Carolinians Through the Revolutionary Era* (New York, 1995), for a similar view of the Cherokees and English.

5. Plane, *Colonial Intimacies*, 6, 20–26, 68. For a view including Virginia Indians, see Karen Ordahl Kupperman, *Indians and English: Facing Off in Early America* (Ithaca, N.Y., 2000), 144–49. See also Main, *Spacious Land*, 63–64.

6. Plane, *Colonial Intimacies*, 69–70, 37–38, 65.

7. Thomas Gataker, *Marriage Duties Briefly Couched Together* (London, 1620), 8–9; John Wing, *The Crowne Conjugall or the Spouse Royall Discovered* (Middleburgh, Netherlands, 1620), 21, 31. Marylynn Salmon, *Women and the Law of Property in Early America* (Chapel Hill, N.C., 1986), 6–8; Ulrich, *Good Wives*, 107, has written that the notion of a "meet help" to Reformation Protestants "combined a radical theology with a conservative social system, simultaneously releasing and constraining two powerful sources of female power. . . . In early New England [sexuality and spirituality] were uneasily linked in the consort's

role." In her discussion of marriage (108–25) she emphasizes (and in this she agrees with Edmund Morgan; Edmund Leites, *The Puritan Conscience and Modern Sexuality* [New Haven, 1986], 75–104; and James Johnston, "The Covenant Idea and the Puritan View of Marriage," *Journal of the History of Ideas*, vol. 32 [1971], 107–18) love, mutuality, and equality over subjection and constraint. Koehler, *Search*, 160, argues for a considerably more dour view of Puritan marriage for women. Fox and Quitt, *Loving*, 30–31, have incorporated both positions in a view that seems more balanced. Karlsen's balance in *Devil* between implicit and explicit thinking about women places her in the middle as well, although implicit thought is dangerous because it is semiconscious. Crane, *Ebb Tide*, 165–73, argues that women were disadvantaged economically and legally in southern New England but initially may have evaded many of these disabilities as long as they comported themselves deferentially. Mary Beth Norton, " 'Either Married or to Bee Married': Women's Legal Inequality in Early America," in *Inequality in Early America*, ed. Carla Pestana and Sharon Salinger (Hanover, N.H., 1999), 41, maintains nevertheless that seventeenth-century Anglo-American wives were "subordinated to husbands, [and] their independent identities were literally erased from society's consciousness. The consequences of that erasure for all women were momentous." In *Founding Mothers*, 67–69, Norton also argues, however, that Puritan men and women frequently affirmed their marital choices with consensual premarital sex.

My evidence supports the middle view. Many Puritan marriages were warm and loving despite their patriarchal, authoritarian framework. Sometimes wives sidestepped some of the ill effects of their subjection. However, the institution of marriage, as it evolved in Massachusetts, did both legally structure women's subordination and ideologically elevate dependence, subservience, and doubt to female virtues. This significantly eroded the spiritual equality that Puritanism offered women and created economic realities in addition to psychological and emotional patterns that outlived the theology that justified them.

8. Peter, *Legacy*, 38.
9. John Cotton, *Practical Commentary, or an Exposition with Observations, Reasons and the Uses upon the First Epistle General of John* (London, 1656), 131. Edmund Leites, among others, says that Puritan writers thought husbands and wives equal in desiring sexual pleasure. He quotes Richard Baxter, who wrote that husbands and wives were to love each other, saying, "[T]he first Duty of Husbands is to Love their Wives (and Wives their Husbands) with a true intire Conjugal Love" (*Puritan Conscience*, 85). Main, *Spacious Land*, 67, similarly argues that Puritans assumed strong desire in women once their husbands sexually awakened them. See also Wing, *Crowne*, 99, 100; Robinson, *Works*, 240; Seaborn Cotton, "Commonplace Book of Reverend Seaborn Cotton" (Ms. A1454), R. Stanton Avery Special Collections Department, New England Historic Genealogical Society.
10. Peter, *Legacy*, 34.
11. See Roger Williams, *The Complete Writings of Roger Williams* (New York, 1963), for the example of his daughter. Letter to John Winthrop, December 10,

1649: Winthrop, ed., *Papers*, vol. 3, 214–15. Winthrop, ed., *Papers*, vol. 5, 23. Philip Greven, Jr., "Family Structure in Seventeenth-Century Andover, Massachusetts," in *American Family*, 83–84, shows that first marriages occurred at a later age in Andover, Massachusetts, than historians suspected, at twenty-six for men ("men" here means first son, each later son marrying about two years after) and about twenty-three for women. He writes that "marriages throughout the seventeenth century and the early part of the eighteenth century were rarely fortuitous; parental authority and concern, family interests, and economic considerations played into the decisions determining when particular men and women could and would marry for the first time" (82). See related arguments: Ulrich, *Good Wives*, 119–22; Smith and Hindus, "Premarital Pregnancy," 537–70; Fox and Quitt, *Loving*, 22. Main, *Spacious Land*, 80–81, refines Greven to show that women married at about 20.5 until 1675 and between 22 and 23 thereafter. "Middlesex," Middlesex County Courthouse, "Pulsifer," vol. 1, 71, 85, 101.

12. Sewall, "Diary," January 4, 1699, *Collections*, Ma.H.S., vol. 5, Ser. 5; Sewall, "Letter-Book," vol. 1, 213.

13. Wing, *Crowne*, 13; Whately, *Bride-Bush*, 5; Gataker, *Marriage Duties*, 38–40. Winthrop, ed. *Papers*, vol. 6, 283; Shurtleff, *Records*, vol. 1, 211.

14. David Cressey, *Coming Over: Migration and Communication Between England and New England in the Seventeenth Century* (New York, 1987), takes issue with the ascription of a religious motive to many of the English who came to New England in the 1630s and thereafter (74–106). His argument may be more relevant to some women than men. The Puritan insistence on wifely obedience was as important to wives as the demands of their religion—in some cases more. Cressey's book does not, unfortunately, address questions about gender.

15. See, for example, Bradstreet, *Works*, xv; Roger Thompson, *Women in Stuart England and America* (London, 1974), 103. Winthrop, ed., *Papers*, vol. 3, 87. The court encouraged togetherness as well. See Dow, ed., *Essex*, vol. 1, 166. "Middlesex," Middlesex County Court, "Pulsifer," vol. 1, 22. Dow, ed., *Essex*, vol. 1, 152, 173.

16. Virginia DeJohn Anderson, *New England's Generation: The Great Migration and the Formation of Society and Culture in the Seventeenth Century* (New York, 1991), 15, 18, 21; Young, *Chronicles*, 530; Winthrop, ed., *Papers*, vol. 2, 68; Young, *Chronicles*, 432. C. Mather, *Magnalia*, 309.

17. Earle, *Colonial Dames*, 18; C. Mather, *Magnalia*, 309.

18. Winthrop, ed., *Papers*, vol. 3, 279, 232–33. Elizabeth Poole, August 24, 1644. (Photostats of original in the Jeffries Family Papers, Ma.H.S.) See also Mrs. Saltonstall's return: Saltonstall Family, *The Saltonstall Papers, 1607–1858*, ed. Robert E. Moody (Boston, 1972), vol. 1, 128. Dorothy Crane just refused. See Winthrop, ed., *Papers*, vol. 4, 105.

19. Sewall, "Letter-Book," 138n.

20. Peter, *Legacy*, 34; Whately, *Bride-Bush*, 37–39; Wing, *Crowne*, 54–56, 120; Gataker, *Marriage Duties*, 10, 11.

21. Winthrop, *History*, vol. 2, 281. Two hundred years later Alexis de Tocqueville

echoed Winthrop's opinion. He wrote: "I never observed that the women of America consider conjugal authority as an unfortunate usurpation of their rights, or that they thought themselves degraded by submitting to it. It appeared to me, on the contrary, that they attach a sort of pride to the voluntary surrender of their own will and make it their boast to bend themselves to the yoke, not to shake it off" (*Democracy in America*) (New York, 1945), vol. 2, 223–24). See Ulrich, *Good Wives*, 106–25, on the improving images of Eve, and Norton, *Founding Mothers*, 56–62, 77–83, on marital subjection and its relation to theories of government. See also Peter, *Legacy*, 34; Robinson, *Works*, 240; Benjamin Wadsworth, *The Well-Ordered Family* (Boston, 1712), 38, 47. C. Mather, *Ornaments*, 89.

22. Whately, *Bride-Bush*, 40, 41, 44; C. Mather, *Ornaments*, 89. Paradoxically, as Robert St. George, "Heated," 314, has pointed out, women were assigned the role of regulating social morality. See Leites, *Puritan Conscience*, 90–91. Nevertheless, Puritan men were extremely ambivalent about the potential for aggression inherent in this activity. So while some men praised their critical wives, many others—indeed sometimes the very same men (e.g., C. Mather, *Ornaments*, 54)—enjoined them to be still. See also Larzer Ziff, *Puritanism in America* (New York, 1973), 115, 119, and Allin, *Conversation*, 1. See Kamensky, *Governing the Tongue*, 71–98, for the waves of anxieties that motivated Puritans' periodic efforts to control women's (and every subordinate's) proper use of language in New England.

23. Powers, *Crime*, 407, finds that the second most frequent crime that the Court of Assistants heard between 1630 and 1640 was "villifying the authorities," which was usually punished with whipping or a fine. "Suffolk," vol. 27, 107, October 8, 1684; Dow, ed., *Essex*, 182–83, December 1649; "Middlesex," Middlesex County Courthouse, "Pulsifer," vol. 1, 196. Kamensky, *Governing the Tongue*, 38–40, 127–49. See Norton, *Founding Mothers*, 234–37.

24. "Suffolk," Suffolk County Courthouse, vol. 19, 139.

25. John Winthrop, quoted in Miller's *American Puritans*, 92; Wadsworth, *Well-Ordered Family*, 25, 39; C. Mather, *Ornaments*, 98.

26. Bradford, *Bradford's History*, 232; Winthrop, ed., *Papers*, vol. 3, April 29, 1640.

27. Norton, *Founding Mothers*, 78; "Middlesex," Middlesex County Courthouse, 168; "Pulsifer," vol. 1, 166; Dow, ed., *Essex*, vol. 1, 25, January 30, 1641; *A Report on the Record Commissioners Containing the Roxbury Land and Church Records*, 6 (Boston, 1881), 85; First Parish Church (Dorchester, Mass.) Records, June 20, July 3, July 17, 1682, Ma.H.S.; Noble, *Records*, 108, July 29, 1641. Hull, *Female Felons*, 59. "Middlesex," Middlesex County Courthouse, May 7, 1669. The court fined Roger Draper forty shillings for beating his wife. Morgan (*Puritan Family*, 40–41) says that the courts enforced the provision against marital violence on numerous occasions. In the only example of wife beating he cites, the man's fine was lessened because his wife was shown to have been provoking him. It seems more likely that it was prosecuted infrequently and underreported. Ulrich suggests that women may have underreported such violence

for a number of reasons, including their fear of the legal system and their knowledge that submission was better protection at home than a court reprimand could be (*Good Wives*, 188–89, 80); Noble, *Records*, vol. 2, 60, 74; "Middlesex," Middlesex County Courthouse, Folio 42.

28. C. Dallett Hemphill, "Women in Court: Sex-Role Differentiation in Salem, Massachusetts, 1636–1683," *William and Mary Quarterly*, 3d Ser., vol. 39 (1982), 164–75; Hull, *Female Felons*, 101–2. See Crane's *Ebb Tide* for the deterioration of women's economic and legal conditions. Ulrich, *Good Wives*, first laid out this change in expectations of women's behavior.

29. See, for example, C. Mather, *Ornaments*, 95; Allestree, *Calling*, 28. "Suffolk," Suffolk County Courthouse, vol. 4, 41, June 1694. See Main, *Spacious Land*, 68–69, for men's particular worries about women's fidelity, and Norton, *Founding Mothers*, 392–39.

30. See, for example, Robinson, *Works*, 242; Michael Wigglesworth, *The Diary of Michael Wigglesworth, 1653–1657*, ed. Edmund S. Morgan (New York, 1946), 88; Thomas Shepard, *God's Plot: The Paradoxes of Puritan Piety, Being the Autobiography and Journal of Thomas Shepard*, ed. Michael McGiffert (Amherst, Mass., 1972), 55. Whately, *Bride-Bush*, 43–44; Ian MacLean, *The Renaissance Notion of Woman: A Study in the Fortunes of Scholasticism and Medical Science in European Intellectual Life* (Cambridge, UK, 1980), explains that woman's presumably cooler and moister humors, to which Whately refers, were the reason she was capable of bearing children, as well as the reason she was physically and emotionally inferior to men. Women were not thought to be as warm and dry as men because some of their heat was reserved to help their babies grow. The coldness and moisture were associated with lack of judgment, courage, stamina, and stability as well as untrustworthiness and passivity (45). On the Anglican custom of "churching," see Keith Thomas, *Religion and the Decline of Magic* (New York, 1971), 59–60. See also Main, *Spacious Land*, 100–101.

31. Winthrop, ed., *Papers*, vol. 2, April 29, 1640; First Parish Church (Dorchester, Mass.) Records, 26–27. Main (*Spacious Land*, 96) makes the same point.

32. Winthrop, *History*, vol. 1, 324–46, 393; vol. 2, 17.

33. C. Mather, *Ornaments*, 89–91; Whately, *Bride-Bush*, 7, 43; Leites, *Puritan Conscience*, 9, 91. Winthrop, ed., *Papers*, vol. 1, 366, 107; vol. 2, 3; vol. 1, 355.

34. Bradstreet, *Works*, 39. Her desire for heat calls up the Renaissance conceit of woman's colder, moister humors with all the womanly weaknesses that inhere therein (MacLean, *Renaissance*, 45). Norton, *Founding Mothers*, 76, has called the marriages of the Bradstreets and the Winthrops achieving the "asymmetrical ideal."

35. Cotton Mather, *Cares About the Nursery* (Boston, 1702), 81; Philip Greven, Jr., "Youth, Maturity, and Religious Conversion: A Note of the Ages of Converts in Andover, Massachusetts, 1711–1749," *Essex Institute of Historic Collections*, vol. 108 (1972), 129–30, placed most female conversions in the twenty-five- to thirty-four-year-old bracket. Women tended to marry between twenty-one and twenty-two (Kenneth Lockridge, "The Population of Dedham, Massachusetts,

1636–1736," *Economic History Review*, vol. 29 [1966], 330; Philip Greven, Jr., *Four Generations: Population, Land, and Family in Colonial Andover, Massachusetts* [Ithaca, 1970], 31–34). Wing, *Marriage Duties*, 9, 24–25; Winthrop, ed., *Papers*, vol. 3, 41.

36. Increase Mather, "Autobiography," American Antiquarian Society Proceedings, 121, pt. 51 (1961), 292–94; Winthrop, ed., *Papers*, vol. 4, 235, May 2, 1640.

37. Caldwell, *Puritan Conversion*, 119–25.

38. Ibid., 124; see Sacvan Berkovitch, *The American Jeremiad* (Madison, Wis., 1978), 3–17, for the double message, at once optimistic and pessimistic, within the jeremiad. I think women's experience would have inclined them to take more seriously the literal message that dwells on failure. See Kibbey, *Interpretation*, for a rich discussion of providential thinking. See also Kibbey, "Mutations of the Supernatural: Witchcraft, Remarkable Providence and the Power of Puritan Men," *Am. Quarterly*, vol. 34 (1982), 125–48.

39. "Middlesex," Middlesex County Courthouse, "Pulsifer," vol. 1, 1654, 1656. Winthrop, ed., *Papers*, vol. 1, 345; *Roxbury Land*, vol. 6, 212; Winthrop, *History*, vol. 2, 114; John Marshall, "Diary," vol. 1, May 1697, September 1697, 1701, Ma.H.S. Sewall, "Diary," vol. 5, 52, 163.

40. "Jonathan Farnum's Testimony," 1670?; Sewall, "Diary," vol. 5, 47.

41. William Adams, "Memoir of the Rev. William Adams," 4th Ser., vol. 1 (1852), *Collections*, Ma.H.S., 17–18; Young, *Chronicles* ("John Cotton's Letter to Puritan Ministers in England"), December 3, 1634. See Karlsen, *Devil*, 240, on discontent and witchcraft.

42. "Middlesex," Middlesex County Courthouse, Folio 114, October 1685; Emile Oberholzer, *Delinquent Saints* (New York, 1955), 170–71; George H. Moore, *Final Notes on Witchcraft in Massachusetts* (New York, 1885), 89.

4. MARRIAGES: VIEWS FROM THE OUTSIDE

1. Robinson, *Works*, 240.

2. John Cotton, *Singing*, 42; Pattie Cowell, "Puritan Women Poets in America," in *Puritan Poets and Poetics in Seventeenth Century American Poetry in Theory and Practice*, ed. Peter White (University Park, 1985), 24.

3. Over the centuries historians adopted Winthrop's attitude toward Anne Hutchinson. Exceptions begin with Jack Schwartz and Ann Withington, "The Political Trial of Anne Hutchinson," *New England Quarterly*, vol. 50 (1977), 225–40; Porterfield, *Female Piety*, 52, 81–82, 95–99, 106–7; and Kamensky, *Governing the Tongue*, 71–81. David D. Hall, *The Antinomian Controversy, 1636–1638: A Documentary History* (Middletown, Conn., 1968), 370, 383; Winthrop, *History*, vol. 2, 216. Husbands as well as wives came in for strong social pressure to conform to the ideals for their respective sexes. One can only feel touched by the courage it took Hutchinson to remain loyal to his notorious wife. After their exile Hutchinson told the remorseless Winthrop that "he was more nearly tied to his wife than to the church: he thought her to be a dear saint

and servant of God" (Winthrop, *History*, vol. 2, 396, 372). Ibid., 216, 276; Adams, *Antinomianism*, 328–29; Stephen Foster, "New England and the Challenge of Heresy, 1630–1660: The Puritan Crisis in Transatlantic Perspective" *William and Mary Quarterly*, 3d Ser., vol. 38 (1981), 624–660. See also Keayne, "The Apologia," ed. Bailyn, *Colonial Society of Massachusetts Publishers*, vol. 42 (1964), 278n, for the expulsion of Sarah Dudley.

4. Mack, *Visionary Women*, 57–58; on the Civil War experience, see ibid., 87–124; Margaret Hope Bacon, *Mothers of Feminism: The Story of Quaker Women in America* (New York, 1986), 25–26.

5. Winthrop, *History*, vol. 2, 29; see Lillian Handlin, "Dissent in a Small Community," *New England Quarterly*, vol. 58 (1985), 193–220, for a detailed account of Anne Yale Eaton Hopkins's descent into "irrationality." See also Kamensky, *Governing the Tongue*, 97, for the way the Hutchinson episode influenced the interpretation of Eaton's speech.

6. Bradstreet, *Works*, 101.

7. Porterfield, "Women's Attraction to Puritanism," 203, argues that this excessive deference was ironic.

8. C. Mather, *Memorials*, 13, 16; Michael McGiffert, ed., "Thomas Shepard's Memoir of Himself," in *God's Plot*; Young, *Chronicles*, 526; Ulrich, "Vertuous Women," 215–31, finds tension between Puritans' belief in the spiritual equality of men and women and the social inequality of the sexes but also that the emphasis Puritans placed on everyone's equality before God assured to women a valued place in society at least through the early eighteenth century. Crane, *Ebb Tide*, 31, asserts that "Despite Protestant assertions of female spiritual equality, a stronger commitment to hierarchy and patriarchy within the family probably overcame any egalitarian tendencies." See E. Jennifer Monaghan, "Literacy," 37, on the gift of literacy.

9. Porterfield, "Women's Attraction," 202–5, calls them moderates compared, for example, with Anne Hutchinson, who succeeded only in frightening Puritan men.

10. For examples, see C. Mather, *Magnalia*, 503, 522. Bradstreet, *Works*, xiv. Charles Hambrick-Stowe, *The Practice of Piety: Puritan Devotional Disciplines in Seventeenth-Century New England* (Chapel Hill, N.C., 1982), 140–41. See Ulrich, "Vertuous Women," 217–18; Leites, *Puritan Conscience*, 90. Saint George, "Heated," argues that men expected moral criticism from women and saw it as their moral function.

11. Whately, *Bride-Bush*, 24. Ulrich, *Good Wives*, 35–50, was the first historian to draw attention to the wives' role as deputy husbands; J. Cotton, *Meet*, 20–21; C. Mather, *Ornaments*, 93; Middlekauf, *Mathers*, 95. See Crane, *Ebb Tide*, 102–4; Laurel Thatcher Ulrich, "A Friendly Neighbor," *Feminist Studies*, vol. 7 (1980), 398; and Winifred Rothenberg, "The Market and Massachusetts Farmers, 1750–1855," *Journal of Economic History*, vol. 41 (1981), 283–314.

In Ulrich's view (see *Good Wives*), the clergy supported wives' as deputy husbands, and that ideology permitted more flexibility than the actual circumstances. Daniel Usner, *Indians, Settlers, & Slaves in a Frontier Exchange Economy: The Lower Mississippi Valley Before 1783* (Chapel Hill, N.C., 1992), places this theme in frontier conditions. He says that racial and gender ideologies bent before the demands of a constant labor shortage and lack of specialization so that almost anyone might end up doing just about anything.

12. See, for example, Mrs. Nathaniel Eaton's difficulties in Winthrop, *History*, vol. 1, 373. John Dane, "Sum poems . . .," Ma.H.S., manuscript, 1682.

13. Henry Dunster Petition, 1650?, Photostats, Ma.H.S. *Roxbury Land*, vol. 6, 83.

14. J. Cotton, *Practical Commentary*, 125; see Main, *Spacious Land*, 98, on beer for the neighbors and midwife at a birth. Winthrop, *History*, vol. 1, 390. Winthrop's failure led Increase Mather to inveigh against toast drinking in 1687 (Increase Mather, *Testimony Against Prophane Customs*, ed. William Peden [Amherst, Mass., 1953], 19); Allestree, *Calling*, 13. Cotton Mather, for example, does not mention drinking in *Ornaments for the Daughters of Zion.*

15. Second Church (Boston, Mass.) Records, Ma.H.S., vol. 1½, 45–47; ibid., vol. 1, November 2, 1692; First Parish Church (Dorchester, Mass.) Records, 96.

16. Oberholzer, *Delinquent Saints*, 152. Drunkenness was the most common crime for men and the eighth most frequent crime for women. "Middlesex," Middlesex County Courthouse, "Pulsifer," vol. 1, 301; James P. Ronda, "Generations of Faith: The Christian Indians of Martha's Vineyard," *William and Mary Quarterly*, 3d Ser., vol. 38 (1981), 369–94, 387; "Suffolk," Suffolk County Courthouse, vol. 40, 147; First Parish Church (Dorchester, Mass.) Records, April 4, 1684, 92.

17. Thomas Rogers Forbes, *The Midwife and the Witch* (New Haven, 1966), 126–27; Richard Sadler, "*Procul Ite*," 1640–1650, Ma.H.S. original from Library at Wales. See Norton, *Founding Mothers*, 203–6, 224–25, on the power of midwives.

18. See John Murrin's contention "To ask for a jury signalled a lack of contrition" ("Magistrates, Sinners," 164, 188); See Mary Beth Norton, " 'The Ablest Midwife That Wee Knowe in the Land': Mistress Alice Tilly and the Women of Boston and Dorchester, 1649–1650," *William and Mary Quarterly*, 3d Ser., vol. 55 (1998), 105–29, for a full rendering of the case.

19. Richard Wertz and Dorothy Wertz, *Lying-In: A History of Childbirth in America* (New York, 1979), 8; see Brown, *Good Wives*, 97–98; 102–3, on similar tensions among Virginia midwives. John Cotton, *John Cotton on the Churches of New England*, ed. Larzer Ziff (Cambridge, Mass., 1968), 238–39. See Norton, *Founding Mothers*, 222–39, for a discussion of what she calls the "women's childbirth community."

20. Adams, *Antinomianism*, 187; Hall, ed., *Antinomian Controversy*, 280–81; Anne Jacobsen Schutte, "Such Monstrous Births; A Neglected Aspect of the Antinomian Controversy," *Renaissance Quarterly*, vol. 38 (1985), 85–106, has identified Mary Dyer's infant as "anencephalic with spina bifida" (90).

21. Schutte, "Monstrous Births," points out that John Cotton helped Dyer conceal

the miscarriage. Shurtleff, *Records*, vol. 1, 224, 329; "Jane Hawkin's Petition," May 2, 1646, Photostats, Ma.H.S. See the chapter on mothers in St. Louis for the reluctance of some doctors to administer anesthetic to laboring women when it became available.

22. Plane, *Colonial Intimacies*, 96; Thacher, Diary, May 23, June 24, September 29, December 26, 1679, and April 16 and 19, 1680, Ma.H.S. "Suffolk," Suffolk County Courthouse, vol. 24, 147.

23. George Elliott Howard, *A History of Matrimonial Institutions* (Chicago, 1904), 166. By way of comparison, William Whately, *Bride-Bush*, 4, wrote that if a husband and wife committed adultery "through infirmity" and were contrite and wished to reform, the spouse should take his or her partner back "for the love of the married couple should be very fervent and abundant, and therefore able to passe by great, yea the greatest wrongs." See Dayton, *Women Before the Bar*, 117, 119–21, on the early years in New Haven when it was likely to grant divorces to prevent adultery, not to punish it severely.

24. Plane, *Colonial Intimacies*, 36–37, 1–4, 77. Hull, *Female Felons*, 30–31, 111; Shurtleff, *Records*, vol. 1, 243.

25. On adultery, Main, *Spacious Land*, 64–65, argues that the degree of criminality varied with the status of the partner, which would encompass race as well. Winthrop, *History*, vol. 2, 190. Ma.H.S., Photostats ("1645?" written on document; this probably should read 1643 or 1644, the year in which Mary Latham was executed). Winthrop, *History*, vol. 2, 190–91, 281; Noble, *Records*, 139.

26. Second Church (Boston, Mass.) Records, March 23, 1696; see also March 23, 1696, for the example of Hannah Bishop.

27. Dow, ed., *Essex*, n.d.

28. Koehler, *Search*, 149, maintains on the basis of two non-Puritan observers that adultery was widespread, but there is no supporting evidence. Powers, *Crime*, 407, 408. Powers found adultery ninth in frequency before the same Court of Assistants between 1673 and 1683. Hull, *Female Felons*, 31, found thirty-eight indictments for adultery between 1673 and 1774; thirty of them were women.

29. Nancy Cott, "Divorce and the Changing Status of Women in 18th Century Massachusetts," *William and Mary Quarterly*, 3d Ser., vol. 33 (1976), 586–614; K. Kelly Weisberg, "Under Greet Temptations Heer: Women and Divorce in Puritan Massachusetts," *Feminist Studies*, vol. 2 (1975), 2 3, 5; Oberholzer, *Delinquent Saints*, 112. Norton, *Founding Mothers*, 90–91, states that only in Connecticut could a woman obtain a divorce for desertion, but cases in Massachusetts indicate that it was possible there too.

30. "Suffolk," Suffolk County Courthouse, vol. 5, 115, September 9, 1664; Noble, *Records*, vol. 2, 138, March 5, 1644. Mary Bachiler, October 14, 1656, Photostats, Ma.H.S.; according to Koehler, *Search*, 150, the court had already refused her permission to marry when it discovered her adulterous affair with a married man.

31. Anna Lane Petition, 1658?, Photostats, Ma.H.S.; Dow, ed., *Essex*, vol. 3, 110, November 1663. See Foster, "Deficient Husbands," on this topic and his argument that seventeenth-century Puritans already evaluated men according to notions of sexual identity and did not simply note individual sexual behavior.

32. "Suffolk," Suffolk County Courthouse, vol. 19, 129.

33. Noble, *Records*, vol. 1, 30.

34. Winthrop, ed., *Papers*, vol. 5, 21. "Suffolk," Suffolk County Courthouse, vol. 9, 113.

35. Lepore, *Name of War*, 16. On the stereotypes of women as Beautiful Souls and men as Just Warriors, see Jean Bethke Elshtain, *Women and War* (New York, 1985), 3–13.

36. Taylor, *Sources*, 214, 218, 232; Michael Walzer, *The Revolution of the Saints: A Study of the Origins of Radical Politics* (Cambridge, Mass., 1965), 290. On the emotional patterns that accompanied the Puritan view of the godly vs. the ungodly, see Peter Lake, " 'A Charitable Christian Hatred': The Godly and Their Enemies in the 1630s," in *The Culture of English Puritanism, 1560–1700*, ed. Christopher Durston and Jacqueline Eales (New York, 1996).

37. Howard S. Russell, *Indian New England Before the Mayflower* (Hanover, N.H., 1980), 27; Indian population estimates are just that. See also Jennings, *Invasion of America*, 28–31. Salisbury, *Manitou*, 101, 9; Plane, *Colonial Intimacies*, 9. For Plymouth's hostile relations with the Indians, see Salisbury, *Manitou*, 110–66. For a fascinating discussion of the English style of appropriating Indian land, see Patricia Seed, *Ceremonies of Possession in Europe's Conquest of the New World, 1492–1640* (New York, 1995).

38. For King Philip's War, see Lepore, *Name of War*. See also Russell Bourne, *The Red King's Rebellion* (New York, 1990); Ulrich, *Good Wives*, 166–71, 215–36. For Rowlandson's narrative, see Alden Vaughan and Edward W. Clark, eds., *Puritans Among the Indians: Accounts of Captivity and Redemption, 1676–1724* (Cambridge, Mass., 1981). Ulrich has noted that early New Englanders praised and permitted women like Hannah Duston in her active assault on the Indians, but that later ideals for women promoted gentler virtues. Still, aggressive behavior specifically toward Indians may have varied less, perhaps, by historical period than by the proximity of Europeans to Indians. In the nineteenth century, writers celebrated western women, otherwise expected to adhere to the standards for True Womanhood, who turned violent against the Indians (see chapter 5, part III). Hauptman, "The Pequot War," 76. See also Lepore, *Name of War*, 116, 118.

39. John Demos, *Entertaining Satan*, 210. See also Lake, "Charitable Christian," 165–73, for a schematic description of Puritan projections onto the ungodly. See Mary Rowlandson, "The Soveraignty & Goodness of God, Together, with the Faithfulness of his Promises Displayed," for the repetitive, almost mechanical, invective she applies to her captors in Vaughan and Clark, eds., *Puritans*.

5. MOTHERS

1. C. Mather, *Ornaments*, 99. "Middlesex," Middlesex County Courthouse, 1654, 1656, vol. 1, 71, 85; "Pulsifer," vol. 1, 101. C. Mather, *Magnalia*, 517. Wertz and Wertz, *Lying-In*, 20–21; Main, *Spacious Land*, 104; Demos's estimates for Plymouth are higher: *Commonwealth*, 66, 131. See also David Flaherty, *Privacy in Colonial New England* (Charlottesville, Va., 1972); Kenneth Lockridge, "Population of Dedham," *Economic History Review*, vol. 19 (1966), 318–44; Daniel Blake Smith, "The Study of the Family in Early America: Trends, Problems, and Prospects," *William and Mary Quarterly*, 3d Ser., vol. 39 (1982), 3–28; Robert V. Wells, "Quaker Marriage Patterns in a Colonial Perspective," *William and Mary Quarterly*, 3d Ser., vol. 29 (1972), 415–42.

2. C. Mather, *Hour of Travail and Trouble*, quoted in Wertz and Wertz, *Lying-In*, 21; C. Mather, *Light in Darkness, Funeral Sermon for Mrs. Rebeckah Burnel* (Boston, 1724), 16. C. Mather, *Memorials*, 28.

3. Joseph Tomson, "The Journal of Joseph Tomson of Billerica," June 1667 manuscript, AM929, by permission of the Houghton Library, Harvard University, September 22 and 31, 1670; 1672.

4. Wigglesworth, *Diary*, 112–13. See also Thomas Shepard's ordeal: Shepard, *God's Plot*, 125. See Porterfield, "Women's Attraction," 200, for a discussion of the authority wives derived from their husbands' dependency.

5. Bradstreet, *Works*, 149–50; Laurel Thatcher Ulrich's wonderful *A Midwife's Tale: The Life of Martha Ballard, Based on Her Diary, 1785–1812* (New York, 1990) is based on a late-eighteenth-century diary with terse entries about Ballard's patients and life, but it is anything but forthcoming on the details of reproduction.

6. "Fond" in the seventeenth and early eighteenth centuries contained the idea of foolishness and excess within it (*OED*). Shepard, *God's Plot*, 36. See Porterfield, *Female Piety*, for discussion of Shepard's particular psychological orientation because of the loss of his mother.

7. Leverenz, *Language*, 5, 72–74, 92, 145, 157. Ulrich, *Good Wives*, 153–55, describes the division of labor in Puritan families between affectionate mothering and authoritarian fathering. Koehler, *Search*, 51, dismisses motherhood in a few paragraphs, missing the point that in mothering lay the opportunity for considerable creativity and moral leadership. Main, *Spacious Land*, 116, asks not whether Puritans loved their children, as they obviously did, but how they treated them.

8. C. Mather, *Ornaments*, 104; John Walzer, "A Period of Ambivalence," 365, writes that eighteenth-century "infants were probably almost all breast-fed," but he hesitates before the question of whether their own mothers fed them or not. Mather's insistence suggests at least that it was an issue. Allestree, *Calling*, 43–44. Illick, "Child-Rearing," 308, claims that most Englishwomen who could afford it gave their children to wet nurses. Male moralists unanimously condemned this; Leverenz, *Language*, 74. Demos, *Commonwealth*, 136, says that

mothers nursed their babies till they were about two and gave birth again when the children reached about three; he suggests that breast-feeding served a contraceptive function of which mothers were aware. Ulrich, *Good Wives*, 139, agrees that mothers were aware of the contraceptive potential of lactation.

9. C. Mather, *Family*, 37; C. Mather, *Ornaments*, 107. See also Illick, "Child-Rearing," 328, and Whately, *Bride-Bush*, 8.

10. *New England Primer*: "A wise son makes a glad father, but a foolish son is the heaviness of his Mother." C. Mather, *Help for Distressed Parents* (Boston, 1695), 8; *Cares*, 42; *Ornaments*, 107; *Family*, 37.

11. See, for example, the case of Martha Boyden, "Middlesex," Middlesex County Courthouse, Folio 113, 1685, July 7; "Pulsifer," vol. 1, 118.

12. Jernegan, *Laboring*, 119; Noble, *Records*, vol. 2, 5; Main, *Spacious Land*, 147. Norton, *Founding Mothers*, 118–19, inclines to think that Puritan parents treated their own children more kindly than their other dependents.

13. For the psychological mechanics of separation from the point of view of children, see John Bowlby, *Separation, Anxiety and Anger* (New York, 1973).

14. See Greven, *Protestant Temperament*, part 1, for a discussion of evangelical parenting and its emotional effects. Greven notes that mothers were extremely important partners in the reproduction of the evangelical temperament (22–24) but does not explore the ways in which gender shaped the process.

15. C. Mather, *Help for Distressed*, 8. For a discussion of moral communitarianism see chapter 1; for child-rearing methods in New England, see Morgan, *Family*, 65–86; Demos, *Commonwealth*, 131–44; Main, *Spacious Land*, 117–55; Illick, "Child-Rearing." In a general way, my interpretation is consistent with observations of Ulrich's in "Vertuous Women," 214–31. See also her *Good Wives*, 146–63: "Personal piety became a form of nurture" (148).

16. C. Mather, "Autobiography," American Antiquarian Society, *Proceedings*, vol. 71, pt. 2 (1961), 278; C. Mather, *Parentator*, 3–4; Middlekauf, *Mathers*, 82.

17. Michael Wigglesworth, "The Day of Doom," reprinted in Miller, *American Puritans*, 291; Shepard, *God's Plot*, 36.

18. See, for example, C. Mather, *Parentator*, 24; Frances Borland Diary, owned by Edinburgh University Library, Scotland, Ma.H.S. manuscript quoted in Ulrich, "Vertuous Women," 217; Dane, "Sum poems . . .," 1682, Ma.H.S. (I am using Vaughan and Clarke's version in *Puritans*, 33–75). See also Neal Salisbury's excellent new edition, *The Sovereignty and Goodness of God by Mary Rowlandson* (New York, 1997); Carroll Smith-Rosenberg, "Subject Female: Authorizing American Identity," *American Literary History*, vol. 5 (1993), 485. Vaughan and Clarke, *Puritans*, 36, 37, 39, 46, 49, 55.

19. Ibid., 56, 57.

20. Ibid., 75, 74.

21. Wing, *Crowne*, 126–27.

22. Elizabeth Saltonstall to her daughter, May 26, 1684, Thomas Prince Papers, Ma.H.S. See also Lucy Downing and her two daughters, Winthrop, ed., *Papers*, vol. 4, 307, about January 20, 1641.

23. "Middlesex," Middlesex County Courthouse, vol. 4, p. 22, Folios 81, 91, 9. Ibid., Folio 105, 1681.

24. Wigglesworth, Diary, 118. See also John Holman, Petition, Ma.H.S., Photostats, May 1656. For Thomas Shepard's unhappiness under his stepmother's regime, see Shepard, God's Plot, 38. See Dayton, Women Before the Bar, 139–40, for a Connecticut woman whose husband poisoned her relationship with her stepchildren.

25. Hoffer and Hull, Murdering, 54, 81.

26. Cotton Mather Papers, summer 1693, Ma.H.S. See Plane, Colonial Intimacies, 96–98, for an abandoned case of Indian infanticide. See Daniel Williams, Pillars of Salt: An Anthology of Early American Criminal Narratives (Madison, Wis., 1993), 86–87, for Mather's version of the white convict's confession.

27. Williams, Pillars, 71.

28. Cotton Mather, A Sorrowful Spectacle (Boston, 1715). See also Daniel Cohen, Pillars of Salt, Monuments of Grace, New England Crime Literature and the Origins of American Popular Culture, 1674–1860 (New York, 1993).

29. John Marshall Diary, July 1702, Ma.H.S.; Reverend John T. Rogers, Death: The Certain Wages of Sin (Boston, 1701), 131; Williams, Pillars, 95–109.

30. "Suffolk," Suffolk County Courthouse, vol. 41, 74. See Dayton, Women Before the Bar, 65, for the mid-eighteenth-century shift in Connecticut from prosecuting men and women equally to singling out poor women to bear the burden of increasing infanticide prosecutions.

31. "Suffolk," Suffolk County Courthouse, vol. 29, 82–85.

32. Winthrop, History, vol. 1, 335; Noble, Records, vol. 2, 78.

33. Hoffer and Hull, Murdering, 44–45.

6. AGING AND DEATH

1. Thomas Lechford, Plain Dealing or News from New England (New York, 1969), 2. John Cotton, Way of the Churches, 39, quoted in Darrett B. Rutman, Winthrop's Boston: A Portrait of a Puritan Town (New York, 1965), 218; Henry Dunster's Notebook, 1631, Ma.H.S.; Rutman, Winthrop's Boston, 218; Ulrich, Good Wives, 7–9. See also Thomas R. Cole, The Journey of Life: A Cultural History of Aging in America (New York, 1992), 40–53, for a discussion of the moral maturation expected of men and women.

2. C. Mather, Ornaments, 114. Karlsen, Devil, discovered that women likely to inherit property, who were usually but not always widows, were a group particularly vulnerable to witchcraft accusations. See Alexander Keyssar, "Widowhood in Eighteenth Century Massachusetts," in Loving, 425–45, for a discussion of the economic and familial situation of widows in the early eighteenth century.

3. C. Mather, Diary, February 22, 1699, Cotton Mather Papers, Ma.H.S. Sewall, "Diary," vol. 5, ser. 5, 345.

4. Winthrop, Journal, 471. C. Mather, Virture in Its Verdue (Boston, 1725), 27. See Cheryl Walker, "In the Margin: The Image of Women in Early Puritan Po-

etry," in *Puritan Poets*, for a discussion of how Puritan men denied the public significance of women's contributions to the survival of the early New England colonies.

5. Dunn, "Saints and Sisters," 594.

6. On romantic love, see E. Anthony Rotundo, *American Manhood: Transformations in Masculinity from the Revolution to the Modern Era* (New York, 1993), 154.

7. VIRGINIA GIRLS

1. On population, see John K. Nelson, *A Blessed Company*, 259. See also Helen Rountree, *Pocohantas's People: The Powhatan Indians of Virginia Through Four Centuries* (Norman, Okla.). On Williamsburg, see J. A. Osborne, *Williamsburg in Colonial Times* (Richmond, Va., 1935); Dumas Malone, *Jefferson the Virginian* (Boston, 1948), 62–65. On court days, see Rhys Isaac, *The Transformation of Virginia, 1740–1790* (Chapel Hill, N.C., 1982), 88–94; Charles Sydnor, *American Revolutionaries in the Making: Political Practices in Washington's Virginia* (New York, 1952), 77–80. On the *Virginia Gazette*, see Charles E. Clark, *The Public Prints: The Newspaper in Anglo-American Culture, 1665–1740* (New York, 1994), 220–53.

2. For Puritan exceptionalism, see Jack P. Greene, "Independence and Dependence: The Psychology of the Colonial Relationship on the Eve of the American Revolution," in *Imperatives, Behaviors and Identities: Essays in Early American Cultural History* (Charlottesville, Va., 1992), 174–80, 175; Kenneth Lockridge, *On the Sources of Patriarchal Rage* (New York, 1992), 92, 98; Greene, "Independence"; Isaac, *Transformation*, 135–36, 239; Brown, *Good Wives*, 319–24; David Hackett Fischer, *Albion's Seed: Four British Folkways in America* (New York, 1989), 252–56. See, for example, *Virginia Gazette*, January 21, 1772. See Bernard Bailyn, *The Ideological Origins of the American Revolution* (Cambridge, Mass., 1967); J. G. A. Pocock, *The Machiavellian Moment: Florentine Political Thought and the Atlantic Republican Tradition* (Princeton, N.J., 1975); and Gordon Wood, *The Creation of the American Republic, 1776–1787* (Chapel Hill, N.C., 1969), for discussions of this rhetoric. My thinking has been influenced by the work of Carroll Smith-Rosenberg, particularly in "Domesticating 'Virtue': Coquettes and Revolutionaries in Young America," in *Literature and the Body*, ed. Elaine Scarry (Baltimore, 1988); Toby L. Ditz, "Shipwrecked; or, Masculinity Imperiled: Mercantile Representations of Failure and the Gendered Self in Eighteenth-Century Philadelphia," *Journal of American History*, vol. 81 (1994), 51–80; Lockridge, *Patriarchal Rage*; Richard D. Brown, *Knowledge Is Power: The Diffusion of Information in Early America, 1700–1865* (New York, 1989); G. J. Barker-Benfield, *The Culture of Sensibility: Sex and Society in Eighteenth-Century Britain* (Chicago, 1992); David Kuchta, "The Making of the Self-Made Man: Class Clothing, and English Masculinity, 1688–1832," in *The Sex of Things*, Victoria de Grazia, ed. (Berkeley, Calif., 1996).

3. See Clark, *Public Prints*, 164, 220–53.

4. For an excellent discussion of colonial ambivalence about gentility, see Richard Bushman, *The Refinement of America* (New York, 1992); see chapter 3 for the Virginia planters' ascription of luxury and debt to corrupt femininity.

5. Beverly Fleet, "Virginia Colonial Abstracts," vol. 8, 27, New-York Historical Society. On the general subject, see Julia Cherry Spruill, *Women's Life and Work in the Southern Colonies* (New York, 1972), 185–231, and Brown, *Good Wives*, 295–98. See also Bertram Wyatt-Brown, *Southern Honor: Ethics and Behavior in the Old South* (New York, 1782); Daniel Blake Smith, *Inside the Great House: Planter Family Life in Eighteenth-Century Chesapeake Society* (Ithaca, N.Y., 1980); Joan R. Gundersen, *To Be Useful to the World* (New York, 1996), 77–93; Francis Mason, *John Norton & Sons, Merchants of London and Virginia* (Richmond, Va., 1937), 174–75, 138–39.

6. Spruill, *Women's Life*, 185–231; Mary Benson, *Women in Eighteenth-Century America* (Port Washington, N.Y., 1935, 1962), 1–75.

7. Alice Morse Earl, *Childlife in Colonial Days* (New York, 1899), 65. Landon Carter, *The Diary of Landon Carter of Sabine Hall, 1752–1778* (Charlottesville, Va., 1987) vol. 1, 521, 525; Fischer, *Albion's*, 346.

8. Spruill, *Women's Life*, 188–89; Smith, *Great House*, 61–68; Edmund S. Morgan, *Virginians at Home* (Colonial Williamsburg, Va., 1952), 17. Fleet, "Abstracts," vol. 14, 15; vol. 17, 15, 33, 58; vol. 7, 39. York County Court Records, February 1768, July 15, 1751; Monaghan, "Literary Instruction"; Fischer, *Albion's*, 346–47.

9. York County Court Records, June 1780; 1770. See, for example, the thirty-year contract for Frances Brooke with Edward Hudson: Fleet, "Abstracts," vol. 8, 39.

10. For a few instances, see Fleet, "Abstracts," vol. 5, 105; Colonel James Gordon, "Journal of Colonel James Gordon, of Lancaster County, Virginia," *William and Mary Quarterly*, 1st Ser., vol. 11 (1902), 98–112; Bishop William Meade, *Old Churches, Ministers and Families of Virginia* (Philadelphia, 1857); Osborne, *Williamsburg*; Edgar Pennington, "Thomas Bray's Associates and Their Work Among the Negroes," American Antiquarian Society, *Proceedings*, no. 48; Edgar W. Knight, *A Documentary History of Education in the South Before 1860* (Chapel Hill, N.C., 1949), 159; Thad Tate, *The Negro in Eighteenth-Century Williamsburg* (Colonial Williamsburg, 1965), 139–43; Luther P. Jackson, "Negro Religious Development in Virginia," *Journal of Negro History*, vol. 16 (1931), 170–80; (Marquis) François-Jean de Chastellux, *Travels in North America in the Year 1780–1781 and 1782* (Chapel Hill, N.C., 1963), 443. Fischer, *Albion's*, 346.

11. Mechal Sobel, *The World They Made Together* (Princeton, N.J., 1987), 86; Morgan, *Virginians*, 18, Anne Blair to Mrs. Mary Braxton, August 21, 1769, Blair, Bannister, Braxton, Whiting, Horner Papers, Swem Library, College of William and Mary; Carter, *Diary*, vol. 1, 194.

12. See particularly T. H. Breen, *Tobacco Culture: The Mentality of the Great Tidewater Planters on the Eve of the Revolution* (Princeton, N.J., 1985), for an ex-

cellent description of planter mentality. Edmund Morgan has written persuasively on the English settlers' dislike of labor in *American Slavery, American Freedom* (New York, 1975), 44–130. See also T. H. Breen, "Looking Out for Number One: Conflicting Cultural Values in Early Seventeenth-Century Virginia," *South Atlantic Quarterly*, vol. 78 (1979), 324–60. Sobel, *World*, 44–63.

13. Thomas Jefferson, *To the Girls and Boys*, ed. Edward Boykin (New York, 1964), 26–27; Sarah N. Randolph, *The Domestic Life of Thomas Jefferson* (Cambridge, 1939), for Jefferson's leisure pursuits. John Harrower, *The Journal of John Harrower* (Williamsburg, Va., 1963), 76; Harrower tutored at the plantation of Colonel William Dangerfield from 1774 to 1778. *The Ladies Library*, published and probably compiled by Sir Richard Steele in 1714, was one of the most popular books of advice for girls in colonial Virginia, vol. 2, 4; Benson, *Women*, 12, 22.

14. Mary Norton Stanard, *Colonial Virginia: Its People and Customs* (Philadelphia, 1917), 7.

15. See Deborah Gray White, *Ar'n't a I Woman* (New York, 1985), and Jacqueline Jones, *Labor of Love, Labor of Sorrow* (New York, 1985), 11–43, for discussions of female slave work; Carter, *Diary*, vol. 1, 194; Catherine Clinton, *The Plantation Mistress: Woman's World in the Old South* (New York, 1982), 49; Wilma King, *Stolen Childhood: Slave Youth in Nineteenth-Century America* (Bloomington, Ind., 1995), 22; Philip D. Morgan, *Slave Counterpoint: Black Culture in the Eighteenth-Century Chesapeake and Lowcountry* (Chapel Hill, N.C., 1999), 546.

16. Lucinda Lee Orr, *Journal of a Young Lady of Virginia* (Baltimore, 1871), 72.

17. Rev. James Fordyce, *Sermons to Young Women*, 14th ed. (London, 1814), 3. Benson, *Women*, 12. Fordyce was influenced by Francis Hutcheson, David Hume, Adam Smith, and other Scottish moral philosophers who found human virtues to be nourished in sociability and commerce. In this view, women were civilizing agents, teaching men manners. See Rosemarie Zagarri, "Morals, Manners, and the Republican Mother," *Am. Quarterly*, vol. 44 (June 1992), 192–215; Michael Ignatieff, *The Needs of Strangers* (New York, 1985), 83–103; Fawn Brodie, *Thomas Jefferson, an Intimate History* (New York, 1974), 220; Carter, *Diary*, vol. 2, 727.

18. Fordyce, *Sermons*, 77–78; François Fénelon, Archbishop of Cambray, *Instructions for the Education of Daughters*, trans. and rev. George Hickes, D.D. (Glasgow, 1750); Allestree, *Calling*.

19. Fordyce, *Sermons*, 78, 141.

20. Mason, *Norton*, 137. Fordyce, *Sermons*, 3; Ebenezer Hazard, "The Journal of Ebenezer Hazard in Virginia 1777," *Virginia Magazine of History and Biography*, 62 (1954), 400–23, 414.

21. Thomas Anburey, *Travels Through the Interior Parts of America* (Boston, 1923); Carter, *Diary*, vol. 1, 444. For textile making in West Africa, see Helen Bradley Foster, *"New Raiments of Self": African American Clothing in the Antebellum South* (New York, 1997), 75–133; Carter, *Diary*, vol. 1, 362, 383, 444, 493; vol. 2, 1040, 1141.

22. Carter, *Diary*, vol. 2, 1040. For a similar story from nineteenth-century Georgia, see Jean Friedman, *The Enclosed Garden: Women and Community in the Evangelical South, 1830–1900* (Chapel Hill, N.C., 1985), 80.

23. For a detailed discussion of slave clothing and a comparison between the relatively greater adequacy of clothing in the Chesapeake as opposed to the Lowcountry, see Morgan, *Slave Counterpoint*, 128–33; Foster, "*New Raiments*," 165. *Virginia Gazette*, October 18, 1770; ibid., October 27, 1752; ibid., December 22, 1768.

24. Foster, "*New Raiments*," 43, 71; Anne Elizabeth Yentsch, *A Chesapeake Family and Their Slaves: A Study in Historical Archaeology* (New York, 1994), 193. Personal information, Timbuktu, Mali, 1980.

25. Taylor, *Sources*, 230–32; Roger Smith, "Self-Reflection and the Self," in *Rewriting the Self: Histories from the Renaissance to the Present*, ed. Roy Porter (New York, 1997), 52, wrote of Montaigne that he "did not expect women or rather the ordinary person to possess the same reflective means to knowledge. Rather, he observed, 'the true advantage of ladies lies in their beauty; and the beauty is . . . peculiarly their property.' Thus, when he claimed the self as his own starting point, he denied the same quality of self to others." Montaigne may have denied the quality of self to women, but they experienced it anyway. It was nevertheless an experience in which girls had to abandon a reliable and ongoing communion with their interiors to make sure, over and over, that their exterior presentations were satisfactory.

26. Barker-Benfield, *Sensibility*, provides superb background on this culture; Cathy Davidson, *The Revolution and the Word: The Rise of the Novel in America* (New York, 1986), 38–54, explains how the novel subverted hierarchy through its unmediated relationship with each reader. See also Nancy Armstrong, *Desire and Domestic Fiction* (New York, 1987); for a fascinating discussion of the pleasures and tones of this world, see David Shields, *Civil Tongues & Polite Letters in British America* (Chapel Hill, N.C., 1997).

27. On the relationship among women, consumer culture, and sensibility, see Barker-Benfield, *Sensibility*, 154–214; see also Jan Lewis, *The Pursuit of Happiness: Family and Values in Jefferson's America* (New York, 1983), on the changing personal values in Virginia.

28. For a discussion of the birth of English individualism, see Alan MacFarlane, *The Origins of English Individualism: The Family, Property and Social Transition* (Oxford, U.K., 1978). For a brilliant discussion of the construction of the "naturally" economically motivated man, see Joyce Appleby, *Liberalism and Republicanism in the Historical Imagination* (Cambridge, Mass., 1992). Fordyce, *Sermons*, 125. Lady Sarah Pennington, in Hester Chapone, *The Lady's Pocket Library* (Philadelphia, 1792), 157.

29. Chapone, *Pocket*, 214; *The Matrimonial Preceptor* (London, 1765), 4. See, for example, Oliver Goldsmith, *The Vicar of Wakefield* (1766, London, 1985), 15; Robert Bolling, *Robert Bolling Woos Anne Miller: Love and Courtship in Colonial Virginia*, ed. J. A. Leo LeMay (1760, Charlottesville, Va., 1990), 5.

30. This was true everywhere the novel made its first appearance. Davidson, *Revo-*

lution, 40–45. Jefferson approved of *Pamela* but by 1818 had changed his mind and complained of the "Bloated imaginations, sickly judgment and disgust toward the real business of life" that he believed fiction engendered. Richard Beale Davis, *A Colonial Southern Bookshelf* (Athens, Ga., 1979), 123. On the history of the novel, see Michael McKeon, *The Origins of the English Novel* (New York, 1987); Josephine Donovan, "Women and the Rise of the Novel: A Feminist-Marxist Theory," *Signs*, vol. 16 (1991), 441–62; Margaret Anne Doody, *The True Story of the Novel* (New Brunswick, N.J., 1997). Davis, *Bookshelf*, 122–23. "The Library of Edmund Berkeley, Esq.," *William and Mary Quarterly*, 1st Ser., vol. 2 (1894), 250–52; Morgan, *Virginians*, 76.

31. Shields, *Civil Tongues*, especially 99–140. For women's contributions to this pleasant pastime, see Zagarri, "Morals, Manners," 201–05.

32. Orr, *Journal*, 26.

33. Steven Stowe, *Intimacy and Power in the Old South: Ritual in the Lives of the Planters* (Baltimore, 1987), 50–121, has written persuasively about the relationships among behavior, imagination, and reading in discussing courtship in the antebellum South. Eliza Ambler to Mildred Smith (Dudley), 1780, Ambler Papers, Colonial Williamsburg, on deposit at the Foundation's John D. Rockefeller Library.

34. Orr, *Journal*, 8–9.

35. Ibid., 10–11, 48–49. See Alexander Pope, *Pope* (New York, 1985), 68–76.

36. Orr, *Journal*, 8, 9, 10, 11, 24, 35, 37, 48.

37. Mildred Smith to Eliza Ambler, 1786, Ambler Papers, Colonial Williamsburg.

38. Mildred Smith to Eliza Ambler, 1785, Ambler Papers, Colonial Williamsburg. Eliza to Mildred, 1785, Ambler Papers, Colonial Williamsburg.

39. See Carol Gilligan, *In a Different Voice* (Cambridge, Mass., 1982). See also Gilligan, "Moral Orientation and Moral Development," in *Women and Moral Theory*, ed. Eve Kittay and Diana Meyers (Savage, Md., 1987).

40. Since nearly all gentry girls married, it is easy to say they were thinking about choosing husbands. See Shields, *Civil Tongues*, 103, for the connection between women's cultivation of sensible and polite discourse and attracting men.

41. *Ladies Library*, vol. 2, 2–4; Allestree, *Calling*, 14, 17.

42. See, for example, the Page household in Chastellux, *Travels in North America*, vol. 2, 383. See also the very obedient Martha Jefferson Randolph: Randolph, *Jefferson*, 44, 46, 114–15.

    For a detailed discussion of how boys were encouraged to be aggressive, see Wyatt-Brown, *Southern Honor*, 138–45; Fithian, *Journal*, 66, 80, 85, 88, 89; and Janet Lindman, "Acting the Manly Christian: White Evangelical Masculinity in Revolutionary Virginia," *William and Mary Quarterly*, 3d Ser., vol. 57 (2000), 393–416, 395.

43. Morgan, *Virginians*, 19.

8. THREE PERSPECTIVES ON GENDER AND SEXUALITY: ANGLO-AMERICAN, AFRICAN AMERICAN, AND NATIVE AMERICAN

1. Fordyce, *Sermons*, 27.
2. Richard Randolph to Frances Randolph Tucker, June 25, 1787, Tucker-Coleman, Swem Library, College of William and Mary. See, for example, Bolling, *Robert Bolling Woos*, 57. Smith, *Great House*, 69–76, argues that polarizing sexual difference gave women problems adjusting to marriage.
3. Morgan, *Virginians*, 18–19; *Gazette*, September 14, 1775; Baylor Hill, "Revolutionary Diary," in Fleet, "Abstracts," vol. 33, 66–73; Elizabeth Murray, *One Hundred Years Ago: The Life and Times of the Rev. Walter Dulany Addison, 1769–1848* (Philadelphia, 1895), 8–9; Orr, *Journal*, 29; Fithian, *Journal*, 45.
4. Bolling, *Robert Bolling Woos*, 5, 55.
5. Eliza Jacqueline Ambler to Mildred Smith, 1785, Ambler Papers, Colonial Williamsburg.
6. Brodie, *Thomas Jefferson*, 390.
7. Carter, *Diary*, vol. 1, 194, 215, 320–21, 345; vol. 2, 654, 713, 773; vol. 2, 814–15; vol. 1, 161, 183, 492; vol. 2, 830.
8. Hindus and Smith, "Premarital Pregnancy," 537–70; Ambler Papers. Revolutionary rates of premarital pregnancy were 30 percent and had dropped to 10 percent by 1850.
9. Fithian, *Journal*, 176.
10. See Sobel, *World*, 147–49, for an excellent discussion of the prevalence of miscegenation; Jordan, *White over Black*, 177–78. See Joshua Rothman, "James Callendar and Social Knowledge of Interracial Sex in Antebellum Virginia," in *Sally Hemings & Thomas Jefferson: History, Memory, and Civil Culture*, ed. Jan Lewis and Peter Onuf (Charlottesville, Va., 1999), 87–113.
11. William W. Hening, *The Statutes at Large: A Collection of the Laws of Virginia from the First Session of the Legislature in the Year 1619* (New York, 1823), vol. 3, 86–87; York County Court Records. See Morgan's *American Slavery* for the classic discussion of the relationship between the freedom of Virginia's planter elite and the slavery of Africans.
12. Hening, *Statutes*, vol. 2, 115, 167–68; vol. 4, 213. York County Court Records, July 1769, the case of Martha Brookes; case of Mary Burns, August 2, 1748; case of Sarah Rhodes, September 22, 1747; case of Catherine Harris. York County Court Records, September 22, 1747, May 16, 1748, October 6, 1749, August 2, 1748, June 18, 1750, July 1752, September 3, 1752, December 3, 1752, July 4, 1759, June 20, 1760, May 1764, May 1765, July 1769.
13. C. G. Chamberlayne, *The Vestry Book and Register of St. Peter's Parish, New Kent and James City Counties, Virginia, 1784–1786* (Richmond, Va., 1937), 277, 312; ibid., 312; C. G. Chamberlayne, *The Vestry Book of Stratton Major Parish, 1729–1783* (Richmond, Va., 1931), 215. Lucille Griffith, *The Virginia House of Burgesses, 1750–1774* (Northport, Ala., 1963), 259; Hening, *Statutes*, vol. 7, 374–77.

14. Hening, *Statutes*, vol. 3, 86–87, 452–54; vol. 6, 360; vol. 7, 374–77. Chamber-layne, *Vestry Book of Stratton Major*, 94.

15. Allan Kulikoff, "The Origins of Afro-American Society in Tidewater Maryland and Virginia, 1700–1790," *William and Mary Quarterly*, 3d Ser., vol. 35 (1978), 226–35, 230; Donald M. Sweig, "The Importation of Slaves to the Potomac River, 1732–1772," *William and Mary Quarterly*, 3d Ser., vol. 42 (1985), 502–24, 514; Douglas Chambers, "The Transatlantic Slave Trade to Virginia in a Comparative Historical Perspective, 1698–1778," in *Afro-Virginia History and Culture*, ed. John Saillant (New York, 1999), 15.

16. Kulikoff, "Origins," 231; Philip Curtin, *The Atlantic Slave Trade* (Madison, Wis., 1969), 156. The low estimate is Curtin's; the higher, Douglas Chambers, "My Own Nation: Igbo Exiles in the Diaspora in Slavery and Abolition," in *Routes to Slavery*, ed. David Eltis and David Richardson (London, 1997) from *Slavery and Abolition*, 18 (April 1997), 747–97. Thomas Hodgkin, *Nigerian Perspectives* (London, 1975), 194–95; Philip O. Nsube, *Ohaffia: A Matrilineal Ibo People* (London, 1974), 3; Curtin, *Trade*, 156; Allan Austin, *African Muslims in Ante-bellum America: A Sourcebook* (New York, 1984), 29–30; Donald D. Wax, "Black Immigrants: The Slave Trade in Colonial Maryland," *Maryland Historical Magazine*, vol. 73 (1978), 32–45, 35–36.

17. Olaudah Equiano, *The Interesting Narrative of the Life of Olaudah Equiano, or Gustavus Vassa, the African* (London, 1789). I have preferred to use eighteenth-century narratives by Africans when at all possible but have used accounts from the period by Europeans as well. I have also used contemporary anthropologists' work to look for continuity but have tried to avoid "upstreaming." Thomas Winterbottom, *An Account of the Native Africans in the Neighborhood of Sierra Leone* (London, 1803), 240; Mungo Park, *Travels in the Interior Districts of Africa* (London, 1799), 264; Arna Bontemps, ed., *Great Slave Narratives* (Boston, 1969), 6; Kamene Okonjo, "The Dual-Sex Political System in Operation: Igbo Women and Community Politics in Midwestern Nigeria," in *Women in Africa: Studies in Social and Economic Change*, ed, Nancy J. Hafkin and Edna G. Bay (Stanford, Calif., 1976), 50.

18. Herbert S. Klein and Stanley L. Engerman, "Fertility Differentials Between Slaves in the United States and the British West Indies: A Note on Lactation Practices and Their Possible Implications," *William and Mary Quarterly*, 3d Ser., vol. 35 (1978), 357–74, 358, 368–69; Joan Gundersen, "The Double Bonds of Race and Sex: Black and White Women in a Colonial Virginia Parish," *Journal of Southern History*, vol. 52 (1986), 351–72, 361; White, *Ar'n't I*, 104–6; Joyce Ladner, "Racism and Tradition: Black Womanhood in Historical Perspective," in *The Black Woman Cross-Culturally*, ed. Filomina Chioma Steady (Rochester, Vt., 1981), 269–88, 274–79; Philip Curtin, *Africa Remembered* (Madison, Wis., 1968), 66–77.

19. Curtin, *Trade*, 156; E. Osei-Koli, "The Family and Social Change in Africa," *Forskningsrapport*, no. 8 (Göthenburg, Germany), 9.

20. John Pinkerton, *A General Collection of the Best and Most Interesting Voyages*

and Travels in All Parts of the World, 16 (London, 1808), 234–38. For an account of an Angolan queen who came to power in 1624 and manipulated gender roles to maintain her legitimacy, see John K. Thornton, "Legitimacy and Political Power: Queen Njinga, 1624–1663," *Journal of African History*, vol. 32 (1991), 25–40.

21. Curtin, *Trade*, 156. Harry A. Galley, Jr., *A History of the Gambia* (London, 1964), 17. Austin, *Muslims*, 35, 124. See Boubacar Barry, *Senegambia and the Atlantic Slave Trade* (New York, 1998), on the religious wars and the slave trade.

22. Austin, *Muslims*, 29–30. Curtin, *Africa Remembered*, 49; Douglas Grant, *The Fortunate Slave* (London, 1968), 12–13.

23. Equiano, *Interesting*, 38. See for example, William Bosman, "A New and Accurate Description of the Coast of Guinea, Divided into the Gold, the Slave, and the Ivory Coast," in *General Collection*, 365; Austin, *Muslims*, 87; Equiano, *Interesting*, 38; Bontemps, *Slave Narratives*, 39. Equiano compared the modesty of these women with the treatment they and other African women received at white hands, recording that "clerks and other whites" with whom he worked when cargoes of slaves arrived to be sold made it "almost a constant practise to commit violent depredations on the chastity of the female slaves." He went on to say that his masters' employees routinely violated slave women on the voyage to America. Bontemps, *Slave Narratives*, 73; George F. Brooks, Jr., "The Signares of St. Louis and Goree," in *Women in Africa*, 35; Park, *Travels*, 264; Bosman, "A Description," vol. 16, 479; Grant, *Fortunate Slave*, 18; Asma El Dareer, *Woman, Why Do You Weep?: Circumcision and Its Consequences* (London, 1982), 1–5, 72–73, 79.

24. The Reverend Thomas Bacon, *Two Sermons Preached to a Congregation of Black Slaves* (London, 1749), 33, 57. See Nelson, *Blessed*, 259–72, on African American converts to Anglicanism in Virginia in this period.

25. *Virginia Gazette*, October 27, 1752, January 27, 1774, May 16, 1766, October 22, 1772.

26. See Brown, *Good Wives*, 42–74, for initial contacts between the Powhatans and the English; see also Morgan, *American Slavery*, 44–130, for an overview of Anglo-Indian relations. Material on the Powhatans comes from Rountree, *Pocahontas's People*, 15–127. Robert Beverley was an unusual observer of Indians who was not simply interested in making invidious comparisons with his own culture (*The History and Present State of Virginia*, ed. Louis B. Wright [Chapel Hill, N.C., 1947]).

27. Rountree, *Pocahontas's People*, 15–77; Isaac, *Transformation*, 11–17.

28. For another reading of this material, see Robert S. Tilton, *Pocahontas: the Evolution of an American Narrative* (New York, 1994), 16–23.

29. Rountree, *Pocahontas's People*, 5–6; William Byrd, *The Writings of Colonel William Byrd*, ed. John Bassett (New York, 1901), 8, 9, 56, 75, 98–99, 102.

30. Ann Maury, *Memoirs of a Huguenot Family* (Baltimore, 1967), 349–51. See Philip Morgan, "Interracial Sex in the Chesapeake and the British Atlantic World, 1700–1820," in *Sally Hemings*, 52–84. Morgan profiles a number of

cases of mulatto children of white planters and notes the increasingly hostile attitude toward interracial sex as the eighteenth century progressed.

31. Rountree, *Pocahontas's People*, 38–39; see Chastellux, *Travels*, 422; see also Tilton, *Pocahontas*, for a somewhat different version of these tales. For Bolling's writing, see J. A. Leo LeMay, "Southern Colonial Grotesque: Robert Bolling's 'Neathe,'" *Mississippi Quarterly*, vol. 35 (1982), 97–126, and Bolling, *Robert Bolling Woos*. For an excellent discussion of the Native Americans in this region, see Richard White, *The Middle Ground* (New York, 1991), 186–314. For Dunmore's War, see Hatley, *Dividing*, 186; Eric Hinderaker, *Elusive Empires: Constructing Colonialism in the Ohio Valley, 1673–1800* (New York, 1997), 190–95; Elizabeth Perkins, *Border Life: Experience and Memory in the Revolutionary Ohio Valley* (Chapel Hill, N.C., 1998), 13–14; Bil Gilbert, *God Gave Us This Country: Tekamthi and the First American Civil War* (New York, 1989), 66–70; Anthony F. C. Wallace, *Jefferson and the Indians: The Tragic Fate of the First Americans* (Cambridge, 1999), 9.

32. *Virginia Gazette*, 1775; quoted in Benson, *Women*, 37.

33. See Cynthia Kierner, *Southern Women in Revolution, 1776–1800: Personal and Political Narratives* (Columbia, S.C., 1998), 154.

34. *Virginia Gazette*, September 21, 1776. In early-eighteenth-century English hostilities with the French, narratives ascribed Indian violence to the French. During the Revolution, the British were the culprits. After the war the Indians' innate savagery was the target. See Kathryn Zabelle Derounian-Stodola and James Arthur Levernier, *The Indian Captivity Narrative, 1550–1900* (New York, 1993), 17–38.

35. For a discussion of the British offer of freedom to slaves and its effects on the Revolution, see Sylvia Frey, *Water from the Rock: Black Resistance in a Revolutionary Age* (Princeton, N.J., 1991), 55, 63, 66–67. *Virginia Gazette*, September 21, 1776; Kierner, *Beyond the Household*, 76.

9. MATRIMONY: INSIDE VIEWS

1. Catherine Clinton, *The Plantation Mistress* (New York, 1982), 60, argues that the young age of marriage for women was proof that planters considered women reproductive units, not people with individual destinies to fulfill. On inexperience and its consequences, see Ann Randolph to St. George Tucker, September 23, 1788, Tucker-Coleman Papers, Swem Library, College of William and Mary. Although Virginia girls were marrying young, they were waiting longer than they had in the seventeenth and early eighteenth centuries, as young men took longer to establish themselves. Lorena Walsh, "The Experience and Status of Women in the Chesapeake, 1750–1775," in *The Web of Southern Social Relations*, ed. Walter J. Fraser, Jr., R. Frank Saunders, Jr., and Jon. L. Wakelyn (Athens, Ga., 1985), 1–18. Hening, *Statutes*, vol. 3, 151; vol. 6, 81–88. *Virginia Gazette*, August 27, 1756; March 15, 1768.

2. On planters' reactions to their debts, see Breen, *Tobacco Culture*; on Whig rhet-

oric of debt, slavery, and corruption, see Bernard Bailyn, *The Origins of American Politics* (New York, 1967); on women and Scottish moral thought, see Zagarri, "Morals, Manners," 192–215.

3. *Virginia Gazette*, January 30, 1750, February, 1773, August 4, 1774, December 8, 1768; Fordyce, *Sermons*, 175; John Page to St. George Tucker, May 3, 1789, Tucker-Coleman Papers, Swem Library, College of William and Mary. See also Nathaniel Tucker to St. George Tucker, November 21, 1772; *Virginia Gazette*, March 7, 1771.

4. Mildred Smith to Eliza Ambler, 1780, York, Ambler Papers, Colonial Williamsburg.

5. On the wide prerogatives of southern white men to discipline the "family" as opposed to the greater reach of the law in the Northeast, see Peter Bardoglio, *Reconstructing the Household, Families, Sex and the Law in the Nineteenth-Century South* (Chapel Hill, N.C., 1995), part I. See also Fischer, *Albion's*, 279–80, 410–18; Wyatt-Brown, *Southern Honor*, 117–25. Thomas D. Morris, *Southern Slavery and the Law, 1619–1860* (Chapel Hill, N.C., 1996), 161–62, is suggestive of the way slaveholding changed the power distribution from that of a nonslaveholding society. Charles Sydnor identified the wide powers and influence of gentry men in *American Revolutionaries in the Making*, 60–73. See Frank L. Dewey, "Thomas Jefferson and a Williamsburg Scandal," *Virginia Magazine of History and Biography*, 39 (1982), 212–13, for a statement of a woman's virtuous choice of husband designed for courtroom consumption.

6. See Fordyce, *Sermons*, 18. For a discussion of eighteenth-century limits on the female sexual imagination in literature, see Carolyn D. Williams, " 'Another Self in the Case': Gender, Marriage and the Individual in Augustan Literature," in *Rewriting the Self*, 97–118. Lady Sarah Pennington, "An Unfortunate Mother's Advice to Her Absent Daughters" in *The Lady's Pocket Library* (Philadelphia, 1792), 174–75; "Our Modern Courtship," *Virginia Gazette*, February 22, 1770, reprinted in Osborne, *Williamsburg*, 59–60; *Virginia Gazette*, October 3, 1751.

7. Pennington, "Mother's Advice," 174–75; Marion Tinling, ed., *The Correspondence of the Three William Byrds of Westover, Virginia, 1684–1776* (Charlottesville, Va., 1977), 771; Carter, *Diary*, vol. 2, 939, for examples.

8. For negotiations, see Stanard, *Colonial Virginia*, 172. *Virginia Gazette*, April 1774, March 7, 1771, October 13, 1738, January 10, 1737, March 7, 1771.

9. *Ladies Library*, 40, 61; *Preceptor*, 8, 98, 254–55.

10. Carter, *Diary*, vol. 1, 249; *The Prose Works of William Byrd of Westover: Narratives of a Colonial Virginian*, ed. Louis B. Wright (Cambridge, 1966), 343; Chastellux, *Travels*, 408; Pennington, "Mother's Advice," 175–76.

11. Hester Chapone, "Mrs. Chapone's letter on the Government of her Temper" in *The Lady's Pocket Library* (Philadelphia, 1792), 187.

12. Fithian, *Diary*, 9; he witnessed a conversation in which the existence of women's souls was questioned.

13. See Isaac, *Transformation*, 61, 121, on gentry dominance. See Anita Rutman

and Darrett Rutman, *A Place in Time: Middlesex County, Virginia, 1650–1750* (New York, 1985), 124–25; a seventeenth-century Puritan might spend four to six hours in church on Sunday. Ibid., 125. Luther P. Jackson, "Negro Religious Development in Virginia," *Journal of Negro History*, vol. 16 (1931); Meade, *Old Churches*; William Stevens Perry, *Papers Relating to the History of the Church in Virginia, 1650–1776* (Hartford, Conn., 1870); Robert B. Semple, *A History of the Rise and Progress of the Baptists in Virginia* (Richmond, Va., 1810). See Isaac, *Transformation*, on the theatricality of worship and its cohesive social function through ritual. See Fischer, *Albion's*, 332–40, on the piety of great planters. See Nelson, *Blessed*, for the most extensive and sympathetic study of Virginia Anglicanism in this period. Reverend Samuel Davies, "The One Thing Needful," *Sermons on Important Subjects* (New York, 1802). See Lindman, "Manly Christian," for a discussion of a style of masculinity competing with planter assumptions of dominance. On doubt about women's souls, see Fithian, *Journal*, 9.

14. Kenneth Lockridge, *The Diary and Life of William Byrd II of Virginia, 1674–1744* (Chapel Hill, N.C., 1987), 53; Fordyce, *Sermons*, 88; Allestree, *Calling*, 6; Fénelon, *Instructions*, 125, 127; Fordyce, *Sermons*, vol. 1, 210–11, 230–33; vol. 2, 27.

15. *Ladies Library*, vol. 3, p. 232; Fordyce, *Sermons*, vol. 1, 124. *Virginia Gazette*, September 20, 1770; Stanard, *Colonial Virginia*, 350.

16. See Fithian, *Journal*, 82, on Mrs. Frances Tasker Carter and Mary Ann Maury's first sister-in-law in Maury, *Huguenot Family*, 323–25; Charles Andrews, *Memoir of Mrs. Ann R. Page* (New York, 1844), 15–18.

17. See Sobel's *World They Made*, especially chapters 14–17, for a discussion of the mutual effects of the Great Awakening on both races. See, for example, Thomas Lowry's opposition to his daughter's marrying a Baptist minister: Fleet, "Abstracts," vol. 28, 86. See Jon Butler, *Awash in a Sea of Faith: Christianizing the American People* (Cambridge, Mass., 1990), 142–63. For the antebellum *dernier cri* and one of the most complete discussions of this link, see Louisa McCord's review of *Uncle Tom's Cabin* in *Louisa McCord: Social and Political Writings*, ed. Richard Lounsbury (Charlottesville, Va., 1995).

18. Orr, *Journal*, 28; Morgan, *Virginians*, 47.

19. "By a Lady," *Virginia Gazette*, February 11, 1773. Barker-Benfield, *Sensibility*; Zagarri, "Morals, Manners"; on friendship, see Jay Fliegelman, *Prodigals and Pilgrims: The American Revolution Against Patriarchal Authority, 1750–1800* (New York, 1982), 41, 127.

20. See, for example, Ann Blair to Mary Braxton, August 21, 1769, Blair, Bannister, Whitney, Horner Papers, Swem Library, College of William and Mary. Fordyce, *Sermons*, vol. 1, 125, 126; *Ladies Library*, 68.

21. Fordyce, *Sermons*, vol. 1, 130, 126.

22. Morgan, *Counterpoint*, 530–40.

23. *Virginia Gazette*, July 1769, September 1768, April 1, 1775; Latham A. Windley, *Runaway Slave Advertisements: A Documentary History from the 1730s to 1790* (London, 1983), 222.

10. MARRIAGES: MORAL AND FINANCIAL ECONOMIES

1. See Jan Lewis, "Motherhood and the Construction of the Male Citizen in the U.S., 1750–1850," in *Constructions of the Self*, ed. George Levine (New Brunswick, N.J., 1992); Ruth Bloch, "The Gendered Meanings," *The Empire of the Mother: American Writing About Domesticity, 1830–1860*, ed. Mary Ryan (New York, 1985); Smith-Rosenberg, "Domesticating Virtue." These were staples of the genteel culture whose American roots we saw in early-eighteenth-century Massachusetts. For the English origins of sensibility, see Barker-Benfield, *Sensibility*.

2. *Preceptor*, 52. On commerce and effeminacy, see Amy Dru Stanley, "Homelife and the Morality of the Market," in *The Market Revolution in America: Social, Political, and Religious Expressions, 1800–1880*, ed. Melvyn Stokes and Stephen Conway (Charlottesville, Va., 1996), 84. *Preceptor*, 52; J. H. Hall, "Ancient Epitaphs and Inscriptions in York and James City Counties, Va.," *Proceedings*, Virginia Historical Society, Richmond, Va., 1892; for examples, see 69. Mason, *Norton*, 188. Carter, *Diary*, vol. 2, 805; vol. 1, 314–16; vol. 2, 950.

3. Thomas Jefferson, June 14, 1787, *Papers*, ed. Julian P. Boyd (Princeton, 1950–). For examples in the Byrd family, see Byrd, *The Great American Gentleman William Byrd of Westover, Virginia, His Secret Diary for the Years 1709–1712*, ed. Louis B. Wright and Marion Tinling (New York, 1963), 27, 29; Tinling, ed., *Three Byrds*, 623, 624–25, 653–54, 631–32, 635–36, 700–701, 707–8.

4. Stanard, *Colonial Virginia*, 349; *Virginia Gazette*, June 27, 1777, February 17, 1774, October 31, 1771.

5. Maury, *Huguenot Family*, 323–25; for this and a variety of similar conflicts, see Carter, *Diary*, vol. 1, 553, 314–15, 359, 462; vol. 2, 1027; vol. 1, 371; vol. 2, 742, 939, 942, 943, 990, 993, 994, 996–97, 998.

6. Frances Tucker to St. George Tucker, November 1787, Tucker-Coleman Papers, Swem Library, College of William and Mary.

7. Byrd, *Secret Diary*, 23, 25, 46, 48, 52, 53, 58, 78, 80, 88, 89, 91, 92, 103, 109, 120, 121, 124, 140, 147, 160, 172, 203, 215, 218, 221–22, 229, 231, 244.

8. On midwives and their fees, see *Virginia Gazette*, August 28, 1752, December 16, 1773, December 12, 1771. Chamberlayne, *St. Peter's Parish*, 281, 286; Louis Morton, *Robert Carter of Nomini Hall* (Williamsburg, Va., 1941), 116. On innkeeping, see Spruill, *Women's Life*, 291; York County Records, September 19, 1748, November 19, 1759, August 21, 1786. Chamberlayne, *Stratton Major Parish*, 195; Chamberlayne, *St. Peter's Parish*, 281, 282, 286, 287, 289, 306. On the cost of living, see Billy G. Smith, *The "Lower Sort": Philadelphia's Laboring People, 1750–1800* (Ithaca, N.Y., 1990), 109.

9. John Pendleton Kennedy, ed., *Journals of the House of Burgesses, 1770–1772* (Richmond, Va. 1906), 61; Fleet, "Abstracts," vol. 33, 18. For a discussion of the wartime and postwar dialectic and women, see Margaret Higonnet and Patrice Higonnet, "The Double Helix," in *Behind the Lines: Gender and the Two World Wars*, ed. Margaret Randolph Higonnet, Jane Jenson, Sonya Michel, and Margaret Collins Weitz (New Haven, 1987), 31–47.

10. Robert Gamble, "Orderly Book of Captain Robert Gamble," *Proceedings* of the
Virginia Historical Society, vol. 11 (1892), 253, 263. Robert Gross has argued
that the republican male hated luxury and complained that his wife was buying
expensive items which he had "to go out into the market to pay for—in effect,
blaming women for the economic revolution of the day, the rapid expansion of
commercial exchange, rather than assuming the responsibility for the ways in
which men made capitalistic society." Linda Kerber, Nancy Cott, Robert Gross,
Lynn Hunt, Caroll Smith-Rosenberg, and Christine Stansell, "Beyond Roles,
Beyond Spheres: Thinking Aloud About Gender; the Early Republic," *William
and Mary Quarterly*, 3d Ser., vol. 46 (1989), 576. See also Jean Boydston, *Home
and Work: Housework, Wages and the Ideology of Labor in the Early Republic*
(New York, 1990), for a complex discussion of the relations among men, women,
and the early cash market.

11. Edmund Pendleton, *The Letters and Papers of Edmund Pendleton, 1734–1803*,
ed. David Mays (Charlottesville, Va., 1967), 46; Pennington, "Mother's Advice,"
188; *Virginia Gazette*, December 8, 1768. H. R. McIlwaine, *Journals of the
House of Burgesses of Virginia, 1761–1765* (Richmond, Va., 1909), 7; *Virginia
Gazette*, November 30, 1759.

12. See, for example, Randolph, *Thomas Jefferson*, 42–43. Morgan, *Virginians*, 47;
Pendleton, *Letters*, vol. 2, 127. *Virginia Gazette*, Mrs. Sarah Thornton, June 27,
1777; Mrs. Lucy Dandridge, March 9, 1775; Mrs. Sarah Pitt, November 12,
1772; Mrs. Frances Horrocks, December 16, 1773; Stanard, *Colonial Virginia*,
349. On marriage, see anon. to Frances Tucker, March 24, 1783, Tucker-
Coleman Papers, Swem Library, College of William and Mary.

13. Fischer, *Albion's*, 286–97, details reasons for high levels of strife among Virginia
couples. Spruill, *Women's Life*, 184, also found more marital unhappiness than
in New England; Smith, *Great House*, 75–76, attributed it to girls' relative isolation from boys growing up.

14. Frank L. Dewey, "A Williamsburg Scandal," 47–48. See Norma Basch, *Framing
American Divorce, from the Revolutionary Generation to the Victorians* (Berkeley, Calif., 2000), 19–53, for a discussion of divorce in the revolutionary era.

15. *Virginia Gazette*, June 5, 1778.

16. Ibid., February 9, 1769, November 13, 1766, April 8, 1775, February 4, 1775,
January 21, 1775, September 11, 1779, September 18, 1779, February 22, 1752,
October 10, 1777, December 5, 1751. Fleet, "Abstracts," vol. 29, 64–65. *Vir-
ginia Gazette*, July 6, 1772, June 10, 1773, July 6, 1769, September 30, 1773,
December 2, 1773. Fleet, "Abstracts," vol. 29, 58, May 10, 1705. *Virginia
Gazette*, June 19, 1778, November 12, 1767, April 27, 1769, July 27, 1769, Feb-
ruary 22, 1752, December 5, 1751, April 27, 1769, April 18, 1755.

17. *Virginia Gazette*, January 17, 1768.

18. Ibid., February 6, 1772, February 17, 1774. Fleet, "Abstracts," vol. 28, 64–65,
1805.

19. Dr. Coltart to St. George Tucker, June 22, 1775; St. George Tucker to Dr.
Coltart, June 22, 1775; Elisabeth Coltart to St. George Tucker, October 15,

1779; St. George Tucker to Capt. Hunter, October 20, 1779, Tucker-Coleman Papers, Swem Library, College of William and Mary. See Wyatt-Brown, *Southern Honor*, 197, and Fischer, *Albion's*, 295–96, on wife beating.
20. Fleet, "Abstracts," vol. R 16, 82–91.
21. Lindman, "Manly Christian," 395.

11. FOND MOTHERS

1. Carter, *Diary*, vol. 2, 713; Jan Lewis and Kenneth Lockridge, " 'Sally Has Been Sick': Pregnancy and Family Limitation Among the Virginia Gentry Women, 1780–1830," *Journal of Social History*, vol. 22 (1988), 5; Roger Thompson, *Women in Stuart England and America* (London, 1974), 11; Sally McMillen, *Motherhood in the Old South: Pregnancy, Childbirth, and Infant Rearing* (Baton Rouge, La., 1990), 81, 94; Stevenson, *Black and White*, 248–49; Louis Morton, ed., "The Daybook of Robert Wormley Carter of Sabine Hall, 1766," *Virginia Magazine of History and Biography*, vol. 68 (1960), (July 15, 1766). Carter, *Diary*, vol. 2, 511–12, 514–16, 520; *Ladies Library*, 98.
2. Fithian, *Journal*, 67. See Richard Randolph to Frances Randolph Tucker on the latter's exhaustion, June 15, 1787, Tucker-Coleman Papers, Swem Library, College of William and Mary.
3. Morgan, *Slave Counterpoint*, 79–82; White, *Ar'n't I*, 106–7. See part 2, chapter 2. Todd L. Savitt, *Medicine and Slavery* (Urbana, Ill., 1978), 115; quoted in Gerald Mullin, *Flight and Rebellion* (New York, 1972), 55.
4. Helen Catterall, *Judicial Cases Concerning American Slavery and the Negro* (New York, 1968), vol. 1, 75. Berlin, *Thousands Gone*, 129. There is disagreement about this. White, *Ar'n't I*, 99–101, argues that the workload for pregnant slaves was significantly less and the food better; Marie Jenkins Schwartz mentions the incentives offered for bearing children (*Born in Bondage: Growing Up Enslaved in the Antebellum South* [Cambridge, Mass., 2000], 191). On this, see Jacqueline Jones, *Labor of Love, Labor of Sorrow: Black Women, Work and the Family from Slavery to the Present* (New York, 1985), 350–51; Schwartz, *Bondage*, 44–46; White, *Ar'n't I*, 152–53; Brenda Stevenson, "Gender Convention, Ideals and Identity Among Antebellum Virginia Slave Women," in *More Than Chattel: Black Women and Slavery in the Americas*, ed. David Gaspar and Darlene Clark Hine (Bloomington, Ind., 1996), 171–72.
5. McIlwaine, *Journals*, March 17, 1767, 83. Kennedy, *Journals*, vol. 1773–1776, 181; Roland Lewis, "Slave Families at Easly Chesapeake Ironworks," *Virginia Magazine of History and Biography*, vol. 86 (1978), 176–77. For a handful of other instances, see Morgan, *Slave Counterpoint*, 540. The prevailing mid-century prices for slaves reflected owners' present-mindedness, not the economic value of reproduction: A female would go for forty-five to seventy pounds, while males sold for seventy to eighty. See Louis Morton, *Robert Carter of Nomini Hall* (Virginia, 1941), 102. Ira Berlin quotes a Virginia planter saying, "Nothing is more to the advantage of my son," as he bought two fifteen-year-old

girls, "than young breeding negroes" (*Thousands Gone*), 127. There were seven listed as pregnant of 173 female runaways between the mid-eighteenth century and the Revolution: Windley, *Runaway Slave Advertisements*, vol. 1 for Virginia and North Carolina. I got a somewhat higher proportion counting directly from the *Virginia Gazette*, or approximately 15 percent.

6. Carter, *Diary*, vol. 1, 371–72, 554; vol. 2, 1036. Savitt, *Medicine*, 117. Stevenson, *Black and White*, 249, deals with Loudoun County, Virginia, in the antebellum period. For a broader view, see McMillen, *Motherhood in the Old South*, 94; she speculates convincingly that the presence of doctors, as opposed to mid-wives, at the labor of wealthier women was a health hazard in the pre–Civil War period. Certainly Landon Carter's procedures were terrifying.

7. Jacqueline Jones, "Race, Sex, and Self-Evident Truths: The Status of Slave Women During the Era of the American Revolution," in *Women in the Age of the American Revolution*, ed. Ronald Hoffman and Peter J. Albert (Charlottesville, Va., 1988), for her appraisal of the revolutionary nature of black women's efforts to hold the family together in the face of slavery and racism. Carter, *Diary*, vol. 1, 326, 424, 426, 496.

8. Mary (Dandridge) Spotswood Campbell's letter to John Spotswood, undated (Spotswood Family Papers, Virginia Historical Society, Mss., Isp687b10). See also Carter, *Diary*, vol. 1, 362; vol. 2, 865, and Morton, *Robert Carter*, 113.

9. *Virginia Gazette*, December 1, 1752. The value of the bourgeois style of life is highly disputed. See Stephanie Coontz, *The Social Origins of Private Life* (New York, 1988), 28–33, who argues with Lawrence Stone on the inevitability and preferability of affective individualism. See Berlin, *Many Thousands*, 17–28, 95–108, for the distinction; Illick, "Child-Rearing"; Philippe Aries, *Centuries of Childhood: Social History of Family Life* (New York, 1962); Fox and Quitt, eds., *Loving*; Randolph Trumbach, *The Rise of the Egalitarian Family* (New York, 1983), 1–11, 198; Linda Pollock, *Forgotten Children: Parent-Child Relations from 1500 to 1900* (New York, 1983), especially 1–67, 262–71. Pollock, who does not think parental love and attachment changed much over time makes the case for an exceptionally child-friendly Chesapeake in this period. See also Smith, *Great House*, 17–54; Coontz, *Private Life*, 34. See Barry Levy, *Quakers and the American Family* (New York, 1988), for a discussion of the earliest affective American families, and Greven, *Protestant Temperament*, for three styles of colonial child rearing.

10. See Fliegelman, *Prodigals*, 12–13, as well as Bushman, *Refinement*, 44–46, and Armstrong, *Desire*. See also Benson, *Women*, 62, for a discussion of what women were reading, and Davidson, *The Revolution and the Word*, for her discussion of the importance of fiction in the new republic.

11. See Armstrong, *Desire*; Ruth Perry, "Colonizing the Breast: Sexuality and Maternity in Eighteenth-Century England," *Journal of the History of Sexuality*, vol. 2 (1991); Ruth Bloch, "American Feminine Ideals in Transition: The Rise of the Moral Mother," *Feminist Studies*, vol. 6 (1978), 101–26. See Ellen Ross and Alice Adams, "Review Essays," *Signs*, vol. 20 (Winter 1995), 397–427, for discussions of differing points of view on recent literature on mothers and mothering.

My own view is that the historical experience of mothering must have helped fashion a characteristically female point of view on certain questions of morals and relationships. However, the conditions under which women mothered varied dramatically according to class and race. Lockridge, *Diary and Life of William Byrd II*, 158. See also Smith, *Great House*, 105–6.

12. Barker-Benfield, *Sensibility*, 141–48; Julie Ellison, *Cato's Tears and the Making of Anglo-American Emotion* (Chicago, 1999), 12–15.

13. For example, in *Richard II*, Act V, Scene iii, line 95, the virtuous Duke of York angrily calls his wife "fond" for defending their criminal son (William Shakespeare, *The Complete Plays and Poems of William Shakespeare* [Boston, 1942], 627). The bulk of the *OED's* citations unambiguously demonstrating foolishness and credulity to be an aspect of the meaning of "fond" are in the seventeenth and eighteenth centuries. See Lewis, "Motherhood," for inherent contradictions or limitations in the emerging liberal construction of manhood. See Barker-Benfield, *Sensibility*, 146, for the positive contribution of sensibility to trade. Kenneth Lockridge, *On the Sources of Patriarchal Rage* (New York, 1992), 43–44, argues that with the spread of enlightenment ideas it became increasingly unfashionable to accuse women of irrationality. It also became, according to Ellison, *Cato's Tears*, and Barker-Benfield, *Sensibility*, advantageous to join rather than fight the tide of sensibility. For Catherine Clinton's contention that one effect of slavery was to intensify patriarchy, see *Plantation Mistress*, 6–7. See also Mary Beth Norton, "The Evolution of White Women's Experience in Early America," *American Historical Review*, vol. 89 (1984), 593–619, for female moral authority in New England.

14. See Gilligan, *In a Different Voice*; Nel Noddings, *Caring: A Feminine Approach to Ethics & Moral Education* (Berkeley, Calif., 1984), especially 7–26. See Carol Gilligan, "Moral Orientation and Moral Development," 19–36; see also Annette Baier, "Hume, the Woman's Moral Theorist?" in *Women and Moral Theory*, ed. Kittay and Myers, 46.

15. Bloch, "Moral Mother," 120; see Nancy Chodorow, *The Reproduction of Mothering* (Berkeley, Calif., 1978), for the mechanisms by which relatedness is reproduced mother to daughter in societies in which mothers care for young children. See Smith, *Great House*, 42–55, on Chesapeake parenting. Children to the age of six or seven were primarily in their mother's company and under her control. Spruill, *Women's Life*, 43–63, emphasizes the exclusivity of mothers' involvement in the care of young children. See Smith, *Great House*, 250–51, on mortality; Fischer, *Albion's*, 251–52, 311, also on mortality.

16. Gilligan, "Moral Orientation," 2–21; see also Owen Flanagan and Kathryn Jackson, "Justice, Care, and Gender," 37–52, in *Feminism and Political Theory*, ed. Cass Sunstein (Chicago, 1990). Lockridge, *Patriarchal Rage*, 43–44, 80–81, 83–84, 88–89.

17. Cobbett, *Fruitfull and Usefull Discourse; Ladies Library*, 118; Allestree, *Calling*, 48. The comments in the two latter books are identical, so they were apparently lifted from Allestree. Cotton Mather, *Distressed Parents*; D. D. Raphael, *British Moralists, 1650–1800* (Indianapolis and Cambridge, U.K., 1991), 235.

18. Tinling, ed., *Correspondence of the Three William Byrds*, 457, 566. In many ways my reading of family changes agrees with Smith's *Great House* except that affectionate paternal behavior toward sons, I think, was not widespread in the first half of the century and that fathers came to express fondness in part through the example and challenges of their wives. Smith has two examples of early paternal affection. One is William Byrd II's encouraging his three-year-old daughter Evie not to eat the supper her mother wanted her to eat. Given that Byrd humiliated his wife at every chance possible, it seems likely that taking Evie's part had less affection in it for the child than malice toward the wife (Byrd, *Secret Diary*, 53, 105, 118, 225). Smith's other example is of Thomas Jones's pleasure in his nephew's noisiness and bullying behavior. It is consistent also with my interpretation to see fathers and uncles encouraging "manly" behavior in small boys. Smith, *Great House*, 51. "Letters of the Byrd Family," 120. Byrd, *Secret Diary*, 84, 113, 114, 117, 204, 187–91, 225, 181.

19. Tinling, ed., *Correspondence of the Three William Byrds*, 623–29, 653–54, 700–701.

20. Harrower, *Journal*, 103. Carter, *Diary*, vol. 1, 518. For a good discussion of changing medical practices in this period, see Ulrich, *Midwife's Tale*, 258–59. See also Savitt, *Medicine*, and Wyndham Blanton, *Medicine in Virginia in the Eighteenth Century* (Richmond, Va., 1931). Carter, *Diary*, vol. 2, 939, 942. Maury, *Huguenot Family*, 323–25.

21. Gundersen, "Double Bonds," 370; Windley, *Slave Advertisements*, vol. 1, 143–44, 194, 210, 197, 241, 276; "Memoir of Old Elizabeth, A Coloured Woman," in *Six Women's Slave Narratives*, ed. Henry Louis Gates (New York, 1988), 3–5. See Sylvia Frey, *Come Shouting to Zion: African American Protestantism in the American South and British Caribbean to 1830* (Chapel Hill, N.C., 1998); Morton, *Robert Carter*, 113.

22. Letter from Richard Randolph reprinted from *Poulson's Advertiser*, Georgetown, December 2, 1811, *St. Louis Free Press*, December 24, 1832. Smith, *Great House*, 103–4, argues for increased intimacy in this period. Intimacy and the ability to manipulate intimacy are not inconsistent.

23. Noddings, *Caring*, and Baier, "Hume," both write about a morality based on the resolution of conflict between and within individuals, a morality that may be contextual and contingent rather than abstract. Hume imagined people as social beings embedded in relations—voluntary and involuntary—rather than as people who see themselves as isolated individuals with rights who contract relationships only between equals. Richard Randolph to Frances Bland Randolph Tucker, June 25, 1787, Tucker-Coleman Papers, Swem Library, College of William and Mary.

12. THE LOGIC OF LUXURY

1. Byrd, *Prose*, 346.
2. *Ladies Library*, 217.

3. Allestree, *Calling*, 69; Steele lifted liberally from *Calling* in compiling *The Ladies Library*. Many passages, like this one, are identical; Allestree, *Ladies*, 75, 80.

4. *Virginia Gazette*, August 29, 1777, October 31, 1771, June 27, 1777, November 13, 1777, December 16, 1773, September 7, 1775.

5. Ibid., January 21, 1772.

6. Ibid., April 4, 1771; November 12, 1772; February 1767.

7. Byrd, *Writings*, undated, possibly 1720s or 1730s.

8. See Rutman and Rutman, *Place in Time*, 114–19, for mortality rates; Hening, *Statutes*, vol. 3, p. 335; Brown, *Good Wives*, 287–91, on declining influence of widows. Lois Green Carr, "Inheritance in the Colonial Chesapeake," in *Women in the Age of the American Revolution*, ed. Ronald Hoffman and Peter J. Albert (Charlottesville, Va., 1989), 186, 197; Smith, *Great House*, 240–41, argues that the withholding of administration of wills was to give women more time to focus on child rearing, but that does not fit with Carr's evidence.

9. Breen, "Looking Out for Number One," 342–60.

10. Bushman, *Refinement*, Chapters 1–6; Breen, *Tobacco Culture*, 36, 84–159.

11. York County Court Records, February 10, 1768, January 1769; June 15, 1747.

12. Ibid., November 1759, October 1766, July 1774. Hening, *Statutes*, vol. 5, 447; York County Court Records, February 10, 1768, January 1769, June 1774.

13. Despite the high mortality rate from childbearing, women tended to live longer than men if they made it through their childbearing years alive. Fox and Quitt, *Loving*, 401–02. York County Court Records, January 27, 1768, September 29, 1767, May 18, 1747; Chamberlayne, *Stratton Major Parish*, 101.

14. York County Court Records, November 16, 1767, February 10, 1768.

15. Mary (Dandridge) Spotswood Campbell to Lord Dunmore, n.d., Mary Campbell to her son, January 10, 1791?, John Spotswood Spotswood Family Papers, Virginia Historical Society, Mss. 1Sp687G15.

16. Mary (Dandridge) Spotswood Campbell to her son, Spotswood Family Papers, Virginia Historical Society, Mss. 1Sp687G11.

17. See Lockridge, *Patriarchal Rage*, particularly 69–89, for a discussion of Jefferson's rage at women and its origins in his father's death and widowed mother's control of his life and fortune. See also Dumas Malone, *Jefferson the Virginian* (Boston, 1948), 37–38. See Douglas Southall Freeman, *George Washington: A Biography* (New York, 1948), vol. 3, 280, 137B, 597, vol. 6, 159, on bad relations between mother and son. Spruill, *Women's Work*, 60. Karlsen's account in *Devil* of the repressed fears and resentments of women that underlay men's desires in New England a century before to keep property out of the hands of women has its parallel in the Chesapeake. The difference is that the fear and resentment of women were not implicit but explicit in Virginia culture.

18. Mullin, *Flight*, 118; Thad Tate, *The Negro in Eighteenth Century Williamsburg* (Williamsburg, Va., 1965), 46.

13. EARLY ST. LOUIS: AN INTRODUCTION

1. James Neal Primm, *Lion of the Valley, St. Louis, Mo.* (St. Louis, 1981), 85; John F. McDermott, "Culture and the Missouri Frontier," *Missouri Historical Review*, vol. 50 (1956), 356–58; R. L. Kirkpatrick, "Professional, Religious and Social Aspects of St. Louis Life, 1804–1816," *Missouri Historical Review*, vol. 44 (July 1950), 381; Louise Callan, R.S.C.J., *Philippine Duchesne, Frontier Missionary of the Sacred Heart, 1765–1852* (Westminster, Md., 1957), 391. See also Jay Gitlin, " 'Avec Bien du Regret': The Americanization of Creole St. Louis," *Gateway Heritage*, vol. 9 (1989), 2–11. For English mistrust of the French and particularly their sexual morality, see Reverend John Bennet, *Strictures on Female Education Chiefly as It Relates to the Culture of the Heart, in Four Essays* (Worcester, U.K., 1795), 44–45; Primm, *Lion*, 85. On the importance of looking at our own history of expansion comparatively see Jay Gitlin, "On the Boundaries of Empire: Connecting the West to Its Imperial Past," in *Under an Open Sky: Rethinking America's Western Past*," ed. William Cronon, George Miles, and Jay Gitlin (New York, 1992), 85–86. On similarities between French and southern elites, see Christie Anne Farnham, *The Education of the Southern Belle* (New York, 1994), 73, 32, 37, 59. See Jane Turner Censer, *North Carolina Planters and Their Children, 1800–1860* (Baton Rouge, La., 1984), 18–19, 40–41, 72 for a different view of elite culture. See Joan Cashin, *A Family Venture* (New York, 1991) on migration. See John Mack Farragher, *Sugar Creek* (New Haven, 1986), 49–50, for the origins of Missouri and Illinois pioneer families. Primm, *Lion*, 17, 61, 74, 80, 92; Charles van Ravenswaay, *St. Louis: An Informal History of the City and Its People, 1764–1865* (St. Louis, 1991), 110–14. See C. Dallett Hemphill, "Middle Class Rising in Revolutionary America: The Evidence from Manners," *Journal of Social History*, vol. 30 (1996), 317–44.

2. Carl J. Ekberg, *Colonial Ste. Genevieve: An Adventure on the Mississippi Frontier* (Tucson, 1996), 217–18; Sue Peabody, *"There Are No Slaves in France": The Political Culture of Race and Slavery in the Ancien Regime* (New York, 1996); see also William B. Cohen, *The French Encounter with Africans: White Response to Blacks, 1530–1880* (Bloomington, Ind., 1980), 62–70. For black population figures, see Lorenzo Greene, Gary Kremer, and Antonio F. Holland, *Missouri's Black Heritage*, rev. ed. (Columbia, Mo., 1993), 8–10, 17–22; Primm, *Lion*, 24–27.

3. Other families included the Saugrains, St. Vrains, de la Beaumes, Provencheres, and de Laurieres. Refugees from Haiti (Sainte Domingue) came to St. Louis, and another sizable influx of extremely wealthy French plantation owners from Guadeloupe settled there in the wake of the Revolution of 1848, which abolished slavery. Sister Mary Martina Stygar, "St. Louis Immigrants from 1820 to 1860," M.A. thesis, St. Louis University, 1937, 80–81. Alfred Hunt, *Haiti's Influence on Antebellum America: Slumbering Volcano in the Caribbean* (Baton Rouge, La., 1988), 37–39, 46–47. Harriet Jacobs, *Incidents in the Life of a Slave Girl* (Cambridge, Mass., 1987), 55, gives an account of a typical police

action against urban slaves and free blacks. Richard C. Wade, *The Urban Frontier* (Cambridge, Mass., 1959), 88–90; Lloyd Hunter, "Slavery in St. Louis, 1804–1860," *Missouri Historical Society Bulletin*, vol. 30 (1974), 233–65, 248, 253; Primm, *Lion*, 100.

4. Primm, *Lion*, 76–85; Callan, *Duchesne*, 599. See Winstanley Briggs, "Le Pays de Illinois," *William and Mary Quarterly*, 3d Ser., vol. 47 (1990), 30–56; Primm, *Lion*, 12–15. Charles Peterson, *Colonial St. Louis: Building a Creole Capital* (Tucson, 1993), 12–23. Briggs, "Illinois," 52. Primm, *Lion*, 87; C. E. Volney, *View of the Climate and Soil of the United States of America* (London, 1804), 384, quoted in Peterson, *Colonial St. Louis*, 6.

5. Ravenswaay, *St. Louis*, 195–201. For the honor code, see Joanne Freeman, *Affairs of Honor: National Politics in the New Republic* (New Haven, 2001). See also Joyce Appleby, *Inheriting the Revolution: The First Generation of Americans* (Cambridge, Mass., 2000), 40–45; Primm, *Lion*, 87.

6. See P. Ryan, *Empire of the Mother*; Mary P. Ryan, *The Cradle of the Middle Class: The Family in Oneida County, New York, 1790–1865* (New York, 1981); Coontz, *Private Life*, 116–60, on these changes. See also advice books like A. Mott, *Observations on the Importance of Female Eduction, and Maternal Instruction, with Their Beneficial Influence in Society* (New York, 1827) and Lydia Maria Child, *The Mother's Book* (Boston, 1831). Child mentions fathers rarely, and Mott points out how busy they are (*Observations*, 15–16). Ruth Bloch, "American Feminine Ideals in Transition," 101–26; Smith-Rosenberg, "Domesticating 'Virtue' "; Lewis, "Motherhood and the Construction of the Male Citizen"; Jan Lewis, "Mother's Love: The Construction of an Emotion in Nineteenth-Century America," in *Mothers and Motherhood: Readings in American History*, ed. Rima Apple and Janet Golden (Columbus, Ohio, 1997). See Shields, *Civil Tongues*, 320–21, 327–28.

7. For a catalog of the libraries of several French families, see John Francis McDermott, *Private Libraries in Creole St. Louis* (Baltimore, 1938); see also John McDermott, "The Library of John Hay of Cahokia and Belleville," *Missouri Historical Society Bulletin*, vol. 9 (1953), 185. The French moral texts I consulted include Arnaud Berquin, *L'Ami des enfants par Berquin* (Paris, 1845); this is a collection of a variety of the stories culled from the magazine; I could not find the magazine itself. Other prescriptive literature included: Comtesse de Genlis, *Nouveaux contes moraux et nouvelles historiques* (Paris, 1804); Jean François Marmontel, *Marmontel's Moral Tales*, trans. George Saintsbury (London, 1895); Mme Sophie Cottin, *Elizabeth, or Exiles of Siberia* (London, 1822); Jean-Jacques Rousseau, *La Nouvelle Héloïse*, trans. Judith McDowell (University Park, Pa., 1968); Jean-Jacques Rousseau, *Émile, or On Education*, trans. Allan Bloom (New York, 1979). For women's education in France, see Linda Kelly, *Women of the French Revolution* (London, 1987), 125–26; Harriet B. Applewhite and Darline G. Levy, eds., *Women and Politics in the Age of the Democratic Revolution* (Ann Arbor, Mich., 1993), especially Dominique Godineau, "Masculine and Feminine Political Practice During the French Revolution,

1793–Year III," 61–80, and Darline G. Levy and Harriet B. Applewhite,
"Women, Radicalization, and the Fall of the French Monarchy," 81–108. See
also Roderick Phillips, *Family Breakdown in Late Eighteenth-Century France:
Divorce in Rouen, 1792–1803* (Oxford, U.K., 1980), 14–15. Callan, *Duchesne*,
444, 487, 508, 560, 585, 683. On Lindenwood, see Mary Easton Sibley Journal,
Lindenwood College Collection, Missouri Historical Society.

8. Olwyn Hufton, *The Prospect Before Her* (New York, 1995), 458–62.

9. Berquin, *L'Ami*, 543–48.

10. On the French colonization style, see Seed, *Ceremonies of Possession*, 46, 55,
    58–59.

    This difference in emphasis is obvious in comparing Locke and Rousseau.
    In Émile's education, Rousseau directs his attention first and foremost to the af-
    fections, whose development and strategic manipulation, he believed, were the
    pathway to shaping the intellect and the will. Locke believed that appealing to a
    child's reason was the way to a noncoercive education. Rousseau scoffed at the
    circular notion that reason could be used to form and shape the reason. See
    Fliegelman, *Prodigals*, 30–31. For the other views, see Child, *Mother's Book*,
    130–31, 153–57; *The American Lady's Preceptor* (Baltimore, 1811), 32–34; Ben-
    net, *Strictures*, 41, 71, 74–75, 96; *Young Lady's*, 6, 57–58, 175–76, 179, 181, 187,
    202, 204, 277, 343; Mott, *Observations*, 41, 61, 72; *Mrs. Taylor and Jane Taylor:
    Correspondence Between a Mother and Her Daughter at School* (London,
    1817), 28, 69, 140; *St. Louis Beacon*, July 11, 1829; James K. Kenneally, *The
    History of American Catholic Women* (New York, 1990), 8. See, for example,
    Mott, *Observations*, 1; Child, *Mother's*, 17, 120–21.

11. See, for example, the records of St. Charles Borromeo Church from 1792 to 1846,
    vol. 1, Mo.H.S. for lists of baptism and marriages of blacks in the community.
    Bishop du Bourg had established a congregation for the slaves of French West In-
    dians in Baltimore before coming to St. Louis. William Barnaby Faherty, S.J., "The
    Personality and Influence of Louis William Valentine du Bourg, Bishop of
    Louisiana and the Floridas," in *Frenchmen and French Ways in the Mississippi
    Valley*, ed. J. F. McDermott (Urbana, Ill. 1959), 44; William Barnaby Faherty, S.J.,
    Dream by the River: Two Centuries of Saint Louis Catholicism, 1766–1980 (St.
    Louis, 1981), 4–5. Faherty claims that the French were less racist than the English.
    The Code Noir did offer some protection to slave families from separation. See
    Stafford Poole and Douglas Slawson, *Church and Slave in Perry County, Mo.,
    1818–1865* (Lewiston, N.Y., 1986); Cohen, *French Encounter*, 97, 85. See Berquin,
    L'Ami, 21–27, 29–53, 90–98, on fables, including blacks in the Caribbean;
    Rousseau, *Émile*; Hunt, *Haiti*, 4, 6, 21–22, 28–29; Sylvia Frey, *Water from the Rock*
    (Princeton, N.J., 1991), 230–32; Cohen, *French Encounter*, 101–7.

12. Thaddeus J. Posey, O.F.M., CAP, "Praying in the Shadows: The Oblate Sisters of
    Providence, a Look at Nineteenth Century Black Catholic Spirituality," in *This
    Far by Faith: Readings in African-American Women's Religious Biography*, ed.
    Judith Weisenfeld and Richard Newman (New York, 1996), 72–93.

13. Callan, *Duchesne*, 277; Callan, *The Society of the Sacred Heart in North Amer-
    ica* (New York, 1937), 80; Callan, *Duchesne*, 519. See Carol Coburn and Martha

Smith, *Spirited Lives: How Nuns Shaped Catholic Culture and American Life, 1836–1920* (Chapel Hill, N.C., 1999), on European houses for wayward, or sexually delinquent, girls.

14. Child, *Mother's Book*, title page, 117–19, 154–56; Mott, *Observations*, 7–8. For a view of the Jacksonian American as full of tricksters, see Karen Halttunen, *Confidence Men and Painted Women* (New Haven, 1992).

15. Berquin, *L'Ami*, 90–101, 110–19, 153–54, 507–20; Marmontel, *Tales*, 322; Genlis, vol. 2, 384–400. The entire plot of Mme Cottin's *Elizabeth* revolves around the effort of a brave young girl to restore her parents to their rightful country and throne.

16. Child, *Mother's Book*, 153–54.

17. See Basch, *Framing American Divorce*, for how this also supported the postrevolutionary enthusiasm for divorce. See Michael Grossberg, *Governing the Hearth, Law and Family in Nineteenth-Century America* (Chapel Hill, N.C., 1985), 24–27, for the emphasis on contractual relations in the early republic. See also Fliegelman, *Prodigals*, 125–55, and Gillian Brown, *Consent of the Governed* (Cambridge, Mass., 2000), for a discussion of the impact of Locke's ideas on colonial and postcolonial thinking.

18. See Gilligan, *In a Different Voice*. For a synopsis of the position, see "In a Different Voice: Women's Conceptions of Self and Morality," in *The Psychology of Women: Ongoing Debates*, ed. Mary Roth Walsh (New Haven, 1987), 278–320. Gilligan's original study was designed to correct the male bias in Lawrence Kohlberg, *Essays in Moral Development* (San Francisco, 1981). John Rawls's *A Theory of Justice* (Cambridge, Mass., 1971) most explicitly describes the ideal male liberal subject resulting from the kind of development Kohlberg describes. Philosophers, historians, and educators have argued over the virtues of relatedness among women. For a discussion among proponents and opponents of Gilligan's views, see Frances E. Olsen, *Feminist Legal Theory I: Foundations and Outlooks* (New York, 1995), 143–223.

19. Shirley Samuels, *The Culture of Race, Gender, and Sentimentality in Nineteenth-Century America* (New York, 1992), 17.

14. GIRLS AND FREEDOM

1. White, *Ar'n't I*, 107.

2. Melvin Dixon, "Singing Swords: The Literary Legacy of Slavery," in *The Slave's Narrative*, ed. Charles T. Davis and Henry Louis Gates, Jr. (New York, 1985), 314; White, *Ar'n't I*, 70–74.

3. For discussion of the precedence of consanguinity over conjugality, see Niara Sudarkasa, "Roots of the Black Family: Observations on the Frazier Herskovitz Debate," 77–87, and "African and African American Family Structure," 89–121, in *The Strength of Our Mothers: African and African American Women and Families, Essays and Speeches* (Trenton, N.J., 1996). See also Joyce Ladner, "Racism and Tradition: Black Womanhood in Historical Perspective," in *Black Woman Cross-Culturally*, 269–88.

4. Michael Tadman, *Speculators and Slaves, Masters, Traders and Slaves in the Old South* (Madison, Wis., 1989), 6–7, 12, 24; John Blassingame, ed., *Slave Testimony: Two Centuries of Letters, Speeches, Interviews and Autobiographies* (Baton Rouge, La., 1977), 286–87; Stevenson, *Black and White*, 183. William Wells Brown, "Narrative," in *Puttin' On Ole Massa*, ed. Gilbert Osofsky (New York, 1969), 95; James McGettigan, Jr., "Boone County Slaves: Sales, Estate Divisions and Families, 1820–1865," *Mo. Historical Review*, vol. 72 (1978), 176–196, 287–89; Philip Scarpino, "Slavery in Callaway County, 1845–1855, Part II," *Mo. Historical Review*, vol. 71 (1977), 270; Tadman, *Speculators*, quotes McGettigan saying that "the majority of Boone County slaveowners had little concern for the breakup of slave families" (138); Greene et al., *Heritage*, 35, 50. In this I disagree with R. Douglas Hurt, *Little Dixie*, 230–31, who argues that slaveowners and speculators rarely bought children under eight because they required parental supervision. The Will of John Mullanphy, 2, Mullanphy Papers, Mo.H.S. quoted in Morris, *Southern Slavery*, 83. See also *St. Louis Beacon*, October 20, 1831, advertising to buy a sixteen-year-old Negro girl; *Beacon* for April 1830 advertising to sell ten-, sixteen-, and nineteen-year-old Negro girls; see also an eighteen-year-old "Negro woman" (*Beacon*, July 4, 1829); a "Likely mulatto girl" (wanted in February 3 *Beacon*, February 6, 1830); "A Negro woman, 17 or 18 years of age" (*Beacon*, 1831); "a girl between 8 and 9 years old" (*St. Louis Enquirer*, December 1820); an eight-year-old girl, "capable of doing a number of things in a family" (*Enquirer*, September 23, 1820); "two likely young Negro Girls" (*Enquirer*, September 30, 1820); "for sale . . . a likely negro . . . girl, about fourteen years of age" (*Enquirer*, March 31, 1819); an advertisement wanting to buy a "likely Negro girl . . . from 15 to 20 years of age" (*Beacon*, September 16, 1830).

Norman R. Yetman, ed., *Voices from Slavery: 100 Authentic Slave Narratives* (Mineola, N.Y. [1970], 2000), 23; William Carr Lane, March 16, 1833, Carr-Lane Papers, Mo.H.S., George Morton bill of sale, June 31, 1837, Mullanphy Papers, Mo.H.S., April 26, 1824. David L. Browman, "Thornhill: The Governor Frederick Bates Estate," *Missouri Historical Society Bulletin*, vol. 30 (1974).

5. Will Carr to Charles Carr, August 25, 1809, Carr Papers, Mo.H.S. McGettigan, "Boone County Slaves," 274–75. For a discussion of the social aspects of this kind of work, see Tera Hunter, *"To 'Joy My Freedom": Southern Black Women's Lives and Labor After the Civil War* (Cambridge, Mass., 1997), 62–63. William Carr Lane to Mary Lane, April 17, 1819, Carr-Lane Papers, Mo.H.S. I was alerted to this subject some years ago when reading Ulrich's *Midwife's Tale*. She notes that Ballard's mood rose and fell according to whether or not she had help (222). Ann Ewing to Mary Lane, September 13, 1827, Carr-Lane Papers, Mo.H.S.

6. Anita Mallinckrodt, *From Knights to Pioneers: One German Family in Westphalia and Missouri* (Carbondale, Ill., 1994), 247. William Bryan and Robert Rose, *Pioneer Families of Missouri, with Numerous Sketches, Anecdotes, Adventures, etc. Relating to Early Days in Missouri* (St. Louis, 1876), 77–78.

7. Adolf Schroeder and Carla Schulz-Geisberg, eds., *Hold Dear, as Always, Jette: A German Immigrant Life in Letters* (Columbia, Mo., 1988), 130; see also Boydston, *Home and Work*, 78–80, on the "help problem." For a good discussion of the tensions among mistresses and their slaves and servants, see Barbara G. Carson, Ellen Kirven Donald, and Kym S. Rice, "Household Encounters: Servants, Slaves and Mistresses in Early Washington," in *The American Home: Material Culture, Domestic Space, and Family Life*, ed. Eleanor McD. Thompson (Winterthur, Del., 1998), 71–93. See also Faye Dudden, *Serving Women: Household Service in Nineteenth-Century America* (Middletown, Conn., 1983), 4–5. Dudden argues that there was a shift from the use of native-born white girls called help to Irish and other immigrants or "domestics." She specifically excludes slavery and the South from her study. Catherine E. Kelly, *In the New England Fashion: Reshaping Women's Lives in the Nineteenth Century* (Ithaca, N.Y., 1999), 35, talks of the value rural New England women gave to "help" because they understood so well the work they did. This did not seem to translate to St. Louis. Andrew Bowles to Ann Biddle, February 24, 1836, Mullanphy Papers, Mo.H.S., *St. Louis Republican*, December 11, 1835; Browman, "Thornhill," 95; *St. Louis Enquirer*, September 23, 1820.

8. T. B. Thorpe, "The Disgraced Scalp Lock, or Incidents on the Western Waters," in *Before Mark Twain: A Sampler of Old, Old Times on the Mississippi*, ed. John Francis McDermott (Carbondale, Ill., 1968), 238; John Mack Faragher, *Daniel Boone: The Life and Legend of an American Pioneer* (New York, 1992), 171; Poole and Slawson, *Church and Slave*, 156–57, 150–51.

9. Jean-Christophe Agnew, *Worlds Apart: The Market and the Theater in Anglo-American Thought, 1550–1750* (New York, 1986), 68.

10. Lawrence Cremin, *American Education: The National Experience, 1783–1876* (New York, 1980); for the southern experience in particular see Anne Firor Scott, *The Southern Lady from Pedestal to Politics, 1830–1930* (Charlottesville, Va., 1970); Christie Anne Farnham, *The Education of the Southern Belle: Higher Education and Student Socialization in the Antebellum South* (New York, 1994); Censer, *North Carolina Planters*, especially 41–59; Steven Stowe, "The Not So Cloistered Academy: Elite Women's Education and Family Feeling in the Old South," in *Web of Relations*, ed. Fraser, Saunders, and Wakelyn, 90–106. I agree with Farnham, who sees the experience of boarding school as crucial to creating membership in the southern elite. See also Kelly, *New England Fashion*, 77–84; Censer, *North Carolina Planters*, 18–19. Steven Stowe, "Not So Cloistered," 95, remarks on the importance to planters of receiving their daughters' epistolary testimonies of love, confirming the same point in a different way.

I am particularly indebted to John Demos's "Oedipus in America: Historical Perspectives on the Reception of Psychoanalysis in the United States" and "History and the Psychosocial: Reflections on 'Oedipus and America,' " in *Inventing the Psychological: Toward a Cultural History of Emotional Life in America*, ed. Joel Pfister and Nancy Schnog (New Haven, 1997). For two views of contemporary psychological development through adolescence, see Katherine Dalsimer, *Female Adolescence* (New Haven, 1986), and Marsha Levy-Warren, *The Adolescent Journey* (Northvale, N.J., 1996). See also Karin Martin, *Puberty, Sexuality and the Self: Girls and Boys at Adolescence* (New York, 1996), for the specific problems girls face at puberty compared with boys' relative ease on entering this phase of life. For a view of eighteenth- and nineteenth-century adolescence, see N. Ray Hiner, "Adolescence in Eighteenth-Century America," in *Loving*, 353–72, and T. Jackson Lears, *Fable of Abundance: A Cultural History of Advertising in America* (New York, 1994), 78, on Americans and "separation anxiety."

11. William Carr Lane to his daughters, May 21, 1836, Carr-Lane Papers, Mo.H.S.; *Young Lady's*, 32–33, 35, 37; Sibley, Journal, Lindenwood College Collection, Mo.H.S.; Farnham, *Belle*, 2–80; Scott, *Lady*, 6–9.

12. See *Fond Mothers*, Part II; Bushman, *Refinement*, 44–45, 56–58; Barker-Benfield, *Sensibility*, 27–28; Ellison, *Cato's Tears*, 1–22. For Gilligan, see "Moral Orientation"; see also Chapter I, note 61. For a discussion of Independence as an aspect of republican virtue, see John Murrin, "Can Liberals Be Patriots?: Natural Rights, Virtue, and Moral Sense in the America of George Mason and Thomas Jefferson," unpublished, January 1985. See also Pateman, *Sexual Contract*, 116–73, for the contrast between the construction of male independence and female dependence by the social contract philosophers. See Demos, "Oedipus in America," for a discussion of the basic building blocks of emotional life and how they can be reconfigured depending upon circumstances and exigencies.

13. See, for example, Marilyn Ferris Motz, *True Sisterhood: Michigan Women and Their Kin, 1820–1920* (Albany, N.Y., 1983), 5–6. Jane Chambers to her grandmother, Kaskaskia, Illinois, 1835, Eliza B. Chambers, Kaskaskia, November 1838, Mullanphy Papers, Mo.H.S.; Julia de Mun to her mother, September 3, 1832, De Mun Papers, Mo.H.S; the de Mun family papers are primarily in French, and some have translations attached; the translations here are mine. Anne Lane to Mary Lane, January 24, 1831; Mary Lane to Sarah, March 1830; Sarah Lane to William Lane, 1829, Carr-Lane Papers, Mo.H.S. Isabelle de Mun to her mother, August 7, 1832, De Mun Papers, Mo.H.S.

14. See Elizabeth Hampsten, *Read This Only to Yourself: The Private Writings of Midwestern Women, 1880–1910* (Bloomington, Ind., 1982), 48, 73.

15. Julia de Mun to Jules de Mun, January 27, 1832; Jules de Mun to Louise de Mun, October 16, 1831, De Mun Papers, Mo.H.S. See Stowe, "Not So Cloistered," for a discussion of letter writing as a means of communicating educational accomplishments and devotion to relationships simultaneously. Stowe argues that girls learned verbal skill also to fortify home ties. Brian Mullanphy to Margaret Chambers, December 4, 1830, Mullanphy Papers, Mo.H.S. See Bushman, *Refinement*, 90–95, for a discussion of the evolution of letter writing into an act of performance.

10. Julia de Mun to Jules de Mun, January 27, 1832, De Mun Papers, Mo.H.S. See,

for example, Ann Chambers to her grandmother, April 28, 1835; Eliza Chambers to her aunt, November 15, 1838, Mullanphy Papers, Mo.H.S.; Julia de Mun to Jules de Mun, January 27, 1832, De Mun Papers, Mo.H.S.; Ann Lane to Mary Lane, January 24, 1831, Carr-Lane Papers, Mo.H.S.; Isabelle de Mun to her mother, August 7, 1832, De Mun Papers, Mo.H.S.

17. See Hampsten, *Read This*, 73. Both Puritans in Massachusetts and Anglicans in the Chesapeake desired cheerfulness in women. Eliza Chambers, Kaskaskia, Illinois, November 28, 1838, Mullanphy Papers, Mo.H.S.; Julia de Mun to her mother, September 3, 1832, De Mun Papers, Mo.H.S.; Ann Lane, January 24, 1831, Carr-Lane Papers, Mo.H.S.; Ann Lane to Mary Lane, July 28, 1828, Carr-Lane Papers, Mo.H.S.; Jane Chambers to her grandmother, Kaskaskia, Illinois, April 15, 1835, Mullanphy Papers, Mo.H.S.; Jules de Mun to Louise, October 16, 1831, De Mun Papers, Mo.H.S.

18. William Carr Lane to Ann and Sarah Lane, March 26, 1836, Carr-Lane Papers, Mo.H.S. See C. Dallett Hemphill, *Bowing to Necessities: A History of Manners in America, 1620–1860* (New York, 1999), 142, 156–59, for a discussion of the tensions in the early national period as the middle class worked to distinguish itself. For examples, see Ann Lane to Mary Lane, July 19, 1828; William Lane to Sarah Lane, April 8, 1836, Carr-Lane Papers, Mo.H.S. Rachel Jenckes to Mary Lane, April 1822; Harriet Ewing to William and Mary Lane, June 21, 1824; Nancy Ewing to Mary Lane, October 7, 1822, Carr-Lane Papers, Mo.H.S.

19. "Pretty Good," *St. Louis Republican*, October 8, 1845; "False Delicacy," *St. Louis Beacon*, November 22, 1832. M. B. E. to Mary Lane, April 20, 1826; William Carr Lane to Ann Lane, February 26, 1836, Carr-Lane Papers, Mo.H.S. On cousin marriage, see Smith, *Great House*, 186–87. For a "western" woman, freer than her eastern sister, see "Western Women," *Missouri Argus*, October 28, 1836. For an analysis of how men in new urban centers solidified across class lines, see Timothy R. Mahoney, *Provincial Lives: Middle-Class Experience in the Antebellum Middle West* (New York, 1999), 62–112. Hemphill, *Bowing*, 129–59, stresses the similarities between changing behavior prescribed for male and female. See Jan Lewis, "Motherhood and the Construction of the Male Citizen in the United States," on how the ideal of republican virtue to be transmitted from wives to husbands failed.

20. "Matter of Fact," *St. Louis Beacon*, February 9, 1832. On repression, see also "A Kiss a l'Atlantique," *St. Louis Enquirer*, August 25, 1819. "The Infant Comparison," *St. Louis Free Press*, June 20, 1833.

21. Fragment of Journal, 1845, Potosi, Mullanphy Papers, Mo.H.S.

22. *Young Lady's*, 261–62; Child, *Mother's Book*, 122–28, 162–65.

23. Daumas, *La Tendresse*, 44 and n. 231. Benedicti's work was published first in 1584 and reprinted in the seventeenth century. See also Marmontel, *Moral Tales*, 170, 30–38.

24. Emilie to Louise de Mun, St. Louis, April 22, 1842, De Mun Papers, Mo.H.S.; see also Clara Berthold to Louise de Mun, September 22, 1836, De Mun Papers, Mo.H.S., emoting on her beloved brother's arrival. Clara Berthold was

the daughter of Pelagie Chouteau Berthold and Bartholomew Berthold (Ravenswaay, *St. Louis*, 99).

25. *St. Louis Enquirer*, December 20, 1823.

26. See Part II for why slaves were not proper objects of white charity; see also Barbara Bellows, *Benevolence Among Slaveholders: Assisting the Poor in Charleston, 1670–1860* (Baton Rouge, La., 1993), for a discussion of the proper dispensation of charity in Charleston, South Carolina. Walter Brownlow Posey, *The Baptist Church in the Lower Mississippi Valley, 1776–1845* (Lexington, Ky., 1957), 46.

27. Bryan and Rose, *Pioneer Families*, 71; *St. Louis Beacon*, May 24, 1832.

28. A. Leon Higginbotham, Jr., *Shades of Freedom: Racial Politics and Presumptions of the American Legal Process* (New York, 1996), 99–101.

29. White, *Ar'n't I*, 70–74; Eric Foner, *The Story of American Freedom* (New York, 1998), 29. Judith Lewis Herman, M.D., *Trauma and Recovery: The Aftermath of Violence, from Domestic Abuse to Political Terror* (New York, 1992), 133.

30. See, for example, Harriet Jacobs, *Incidents in the Life of a Slave Girl* (Cambridge, Mass., 1987), 201. "Reader, my story ends with freedom; not in the usual way, with marriage. My children and I are now free!"

31. Walter Johnson, *Soul by Soul: Life Inside the Antebellum Slave Market* (Cambridge, Mass., 1999), 45–49. For "Mr. Walker," see William Wells Brown, "A Narrative," 189; Katherine Corbett, ed., *In Her Place: A Guide to St. Louis Women's History* (St. Louis, 1999), 57–58.

32. For a good brief account of the Dred Scott decision, see Paul Finkelman, *Dred Scott. v. Sandford: A Brief History with Documents* (New York, 1997); see also Lea VanderVelde and Sandhya Subramanian, "Mrs. Dred Scott," *Yale Law Journal*, 106 (1997), 1033–1121. Morris, *Southern Slavery*, 21.

33. Jacobs's *Incidents* painfully illuminates the devastations of separations—from either sales or escapes—and the determination it required to face both eventualities. See Lucy A. Delaney, *"From the Darkness Cometh the Light," or, Struggles for Freedom* (St. Louis, 1891); an excellent short summary of this complex material is by Katherine Douglass, in Katherine Corbett, ed., *In Her Place: A Guide to St. Louis Women's History* (St. Louis, 1999), 56–58. See also the stories of William Wells Brown and Elizabeth Keckley: Brown, "Narrative," 203–4, 207, 209, 188; Keckley, *Behind the Scenes, or Thirty Years a Slave, and Four Years in the White House* (New York, 1868), 39, 44–45, 49–50.

34. William Andrews, ed., *Six Slave Narratives* (New York, 1988), 2–9.

35. See D. W. Winnicott, *Home Is Where We Start From: Essays by a Psychoanalyst* (London, New York, 1986), 63. So much was beyond parental control that failures to provide nurturing childhoods in slavery often had little or nothing to do with personal failures of slave parents and almost everything to do with the conditions in which they found themselves trying to raise children.

36. *The St. Louis Directory for 1838–1839* (St. Louis, 1838); George B. Mangold, *The Challenge of St. Louis* (New York, 1917), 55, 58. See Catharine Beecher, *A Treatise on Domestic Economy for the Use of Young Ladies at Home and at*

School (Boston, 1841); A. Adams to William Carr Lane, December 29, 1825, Carr-Lane Papers, Mo.H.S.; see Martha Saxton, "Woman Before the Vote," in *Not for Ourselves Alone: The Story of Elizabeth Cady Stanton and Susan B. Anthony*, ed. Ken Burns and Geoffrey C. Ward (New York, 1999), 52–57. See also Susan Strasser, *Never Done* (New York, 1982), 104–5; Jones, *Labor of Love*, 125–26; Dudden, *Serving Women*, 142–44, 223–25; Andrews, ed., *Six Slaves*, 2–9.

37. For the theory of paternalism, see Eugene Genovese, *Roll, Jordan, Roll: The World the Slaves Made* (New York, 1972), particularly 1–7; for a detailed discussion of slavery's relationship to the law, see Morris, *Southern Slavery*.

38. Greene et al., *Heritage*, 35. For abolitionists' varying interpretations of freedom, see Amy Dru Stanley, " 'The Right to Possess All the Faculties that God Has Given': Possessive Individualism, Slave Women and Abolitionist Thought," in *Moral Problems in American Life*, 123–43.

39. For the paradox that slaveowners were actually dependent upon the slaves, see Foner, *American Freedom*, 11; see also Peggy Davis, *Neglected Stories: The Constitution and Family Values* (New York, 1997), 38.

15. ST. LOUIS MARRIAGES: CROSS-CULTURAL PERSPECTIVES ON SEX, LAW, AND FEELING

1. See Ellen Rothman, *Hands and Hearts: A History of Courtship in America* (New York, 1984), 27, 37–38; see Norma Basch, *Divorce*, on how this also supported the postrevolutionary enthusiasm for divorce; see Grossberg, *Governing the Hearth*, 24–27, for the emphasis on contractual domestic relations in the early republic. See also Fliegelman, *Prodigals*, 123–55, and Brown, *Consent of the Governed*. See Crane, *Ebb Tide*, 225–41, for the view that Locke's more egalitarian writings on the family and women were easily dismissed in the revolutionary settlement that officially disenfranchised women.

2. See, for example, William Gilmore Simms, *Richard Hurdis: A Tale of Alabama* (New York, 1855), for not one but two heroines who die for love. Newspaper articles include "From the Sketch Book," "Woman," *St. Louis Enquirer*, December 22, 1819; *St. Louis Republican*, June 12, 1835; "The Broken Heart," *St. Louis Enquirer*, October 30, 1819; "The Broken Hearted," *St. Louis Beacon*, April 12, 1832; "Romance in Real Life," *St. Louis Republican*, September 4, 1835.

3. "Woman: A Rhapsody," *St. Louis Republican*, June 12, 1835, quoted in Crane, *Ebb Tide*, 225, from Fletcher, *Gender, Sex*, 400. See Nina Baym, *American Women Writers and the Work of History, 1790–1860* (New Brunswick, N.J., 1995), 4.

4. "What a Farmer Wants," *Missouri Argus*, June 5, 1835. See also Kelly, *New England Fashion*, for a fascinating discussion of the lives of provincial Massachusetts women coping with a society increasingly responsive to capitalism. "Intriguing and Madness; Influence of the Stage," *St. Louis Beacon*, December 16, 1830.

5. In *City of Women: Sex and Class in New York, 1790–1860* (New York, 1986), Christine Stansell argues that female factory workers had a much more open attitude toward nonmarital sex than did members of the middle class (125–27). "What the Farmer Wants"; "Matrimony—A White Gentleman Wishes to Marry a *colored lady . . .*," *St. Louis Republican*, July 12, 1845; "Courting Below," *Republican*, October 23, 1835; "Who Is a Beautiful Woman!," *St. Louis Beacon*, April 13, 1829; "dere mr edditur," *Beacon*, February 10, 1831; "Courting Below," *Missouri Argus*, October 3, 1835. See, for example, "Negro Logic," *Argus*, July 27, 1839. As Hemphill says, "So manners were essential in republican America. The only alternative was true equality" (*Bowing*, 159). She also points out that the profusion of manners was elaborated only for the wealthy into a complex code that defined who was out with ever more specificity (156–58).

6. Hemphill, *Bowing*, 119, asserts that middle-class etiquette in a sense prepared the way for the middle class or helped challenge the upper class early in the mid-eighteenth century and did not wait upon material circumstances to produce separate spheres for this to happen, an argument similar to one Nancy Armstrong and Leonard Tennenhouse make in "The Rise of the Domestic Woman," *The Ideology of Conduct: Essays in Literature and the History of Sexuality* (London, 1987), 22. But middle-class values that originated in the sensitive woman, not in the authority of her father, husband, minister, etc., could not be acted upon freely until men were out of the home, i.e., after the beginning of American industrialization. On the patriarchy prevalent in rural nineteenth-century families, see Daniel Walker Howe, "The Market Revolution and the Shaping of Identity in Whig-Jacksonian America," in *Market Revolution*, 268; Bennet, *Strictures*, 226, 227; *Young Lady's*, 220; Mott, *Observations*, 40.

7. Motz writes of rural Michigan, "Women expressed a strong sense of duty to marry any man who met certain standards of decency, was an adequate provider, was moral and religious, and could be expected to treat his wife kindly" (*True Sisterhood*, 15).

8. For the prevalence of discussions of liberty in the early republic, see Foner, *American Freedom*, 47–48. For evangelicals and freedom, see Andrews, ed., *Sisters of the Spirit: Three Black Women's Autobiographies of the Nineteenth Century* (Bloomington, Ind., 1986), 47; Mary Sibley, Journal, Lindenwood College Collection, Mo.H.S. See Catherine A. Brekus, *Strangers and Pilgrims: Female Preaching in America, 1740–1845* (Chapel Hill, N.C., 1998), 233–64, and Sibley, Journal, on evangelical criticism of commerce.

9. Mme. de Genlis. See particularly "Le Journaliste," *Contes Moreaux*, vol. 3, 1–50. Daumas, *La Tendresse*, chs. 1 and 2.

10. See, for example, Genlis, *Contes Moreaux*, vol. 2, 405–53. American novelists frequently used the trope of kindness to animals to demonstrate virtue as well as the French. Witness Mrs. Bird in Harriet Beecher Stowe's *Uncle Tom's Cabin*, who can become roused out of her placid benevolence only by cruelty to a kitten or by the drowning of George's dog by his wicked owner as metonymic for the evils of slavery. Marmontel, *Moral Tales*, 2, 16, 18.

11. Mott, *Observations*, 75–76; Child, *Mother's Book*, 151–52.

12. See Carroll Smith-Rosenberg, "The Beauty, the Beast and the Militant Woman: A Case Study in Sex Roles and Social Stress in Jacksonian America," in *Disorderly Conduct* (New York, 1985), 109–28; Child, *Mother's Book*, 165–66.

13. *St. Louis Republican*, January 24, 1845, "Fiendish Barbarity by a Slave." Blacks appear with extreme rarity in letters of the St. Louis French. Cohen, *French Encounter*, 64–65, observes that they were not very interested in them. See Carole Pateman, *The Sexual Contract* (Stanford, Calif., 1988), 117–19, for some of the many ways in which the division of family labor, enforced by social contract theory, has been made to look natural; Cohen, *French Encounter*, 117–19. On the distrust of bachelors and the prohibitions on their even addressing white women without an introduction, see M. H. Dunlop's fascinating *Sixty Miles from Contentment: Traveling in the Nineteenth-Century American Interior* (New York, 1995), 168–69. *Missouri Gazette*, May 10, 1820; see also April 19, 1829, signed "A Head of a Family," quoted in Anderson, "The Social and Economic Bases," 30; Perry McCandless, *History of Missouri*, vol. 2 (Columbia, Mo., 1987), 6–8; Maximillian Reichard, "Black and White on the Urban Frontier: The St. Louis Community in Transition, 1800–1830," in *Missouri Historical Society Bulletin* (October 1976–77, July 1977), 3–17, 16.

14. Nancy Cott, "Passionlessness: An Interpretation of Victorian Sexual Ideology, 1790–1850," in Nancy Cott and Elizabeth Pleck, *A Heritage of Her Own: Toward a New Social History of American Women* (New York, 1979); Daniel Scott Smith, "Family Limitation, Sexual Control, and Domestic Feminism in Victorian America," ibid., discusses sexuality and its repression for political, ideological, or family motives. Karen Lystra's *Searching the Heart: Women, Men, and Romantic Love in Nineteenth-Century America* (New York, 1989) speaks in favor of a vibrant married sexuality but discusses relatively sophisticated couples, most of whom lived in the later part of the century. D'Emilio and Freedman, *Intimate Matters*, 55, argue that the significance and experience of sexuality changed over the course of the nineteenth century, moving from one of reproductive importance and of only moderate emotional importance to one detached from fertility and with greatly heightened emotional significance.

15. See Jordan, *White over Black*, 32–35, 150–51, for one of the earliest explorations of a ubiquitous historical theme.

16. The Concord Baptist Records, vol. 1, Mo.H.S. Greene et al., *Heritage*, 35. Mr. and Mrs. Francis Emmett Williams, *Centenary Methodist Church of St. Louis: The First One Hundred Years, 1839–1939* (St. Louis, 1939), 2, 6, 7; Duncan, *A History of the Baptists in Missouri* (St. Louis, 1882), 86–87; Morgan, *Slave Counterpoint*, 645. See Sobel, *World They Made*, 178–213, for a detailed account of blacks and whites at revivals of the First Great Awakening. Frey and Wood, *Come Shouting to Zion*, 147–48; see also Michael A. Gomez, *Exchanging Our Country Marks* (Chapel Hill, N.C., 1998), 268–69; *St. Louis Republican*, September 20, 1831, quoted in Reichard, "Black and White on the Urban Frontier," July 1977, 16.

17. Bryan and Rose, *Pioneer Families*, 84–86.

18. Ibid.; see Morgan, *Slave Counterpoint*, 645, for the suggestion that such behavior originated in African traditions of possession and trance. See also Susan Juster, "Mystical Pregnancy and Holy Bleeding: Visionary Experience in Early Modern Britain and America," *William and Mary Quarterly*, 3d Ser., vol. 57 (2000), 249–88, on the changing forms of ecstatic behavior and the new medical paradigm making it harder for women to find transcendence and spiritual authority.

19. Mia Bay, *The White Image in the Black Mind: African American Ideas About White People, 1830–1925* (New York, 2000), 38, 44–55, 236 n. 70.

20. Sibley, Journal, Lindenwood College Collection, Mo.H.S. See Cynthia Lynn Lyerly, "Passion, Desire, Ecstasy: The Experiential Religion of Southern Methodist Women, 1770–1810," in *The Devil's Lane: Sex and Race in the Early South*, ed. Catherine Clinton and Michele Gillespie (New York, 1997), 168–86, for an interesting discussion of the difference between white and black women's experience of religion. See also Friedman, *Enclosed Garden*, and Cynthia Lyerly, *Methodism and the Southern Mind, 1780–1810* (New York, 1998).

21. Sibley, Journal, Lindenwood College Collection, Mo.H.S.; *Missouri Argus*, October 21, 1836; Sibley, Journal.

22. James F. Traer, *Marriage and the Family in Eighteenth-Century France* (Ithaca, N.Y., 1980), 138, 192; see also Corbett, *In Her Place*, 13–17, for the kinds of economic transactions in which French women, white and black, could participate under French law.

23. See Scott and Hindus, "Premarital Pregnancy," 200–211, for the rising illegitimacy rate accompanying the Revolution. Much literature in the postrevolutionary period dealt with the increased sexual and social vulnerability of women in a culture where men had more and more freedom and women were considered responsible for men's sexual behavior: Susannah Rowson's *Charlotte Temple* (1794), for example; Hannah Foster, *The Coquette* (1797); and Tabitha Tenney, *The Female Quixote* (1801). Rothman, *Hands*, 45. See Friedman, *Enclosed Garden*, 11, on the end of church discipline in the 1830s for sexual crime. See Rachel Jenckes to Mary Lane, April 1822, Carr-Lane Papers, Mo.H.S., and on George Ewing's illegitimate children.

24. Rachel Jenckes to Mary Lane, August 28, 1825, Carr-Lane Papers, Mo.H.S. See Grossberg, *Governing*, 34–44, for a description of the breach of promise suit's development in the new Republic. On seduction: "Dismissing a Lover," *St. Louis Republican*, February 2, 1845; "A Case of Seduction . . . ," *Republican*, June 21, 1845; "A rash case of what is called 'breech of promise' . . . ," *Republican*, May 9, 1845; "Seduction Case," *Republican*, September 5, 1845; "Abduction and Suicide," *St. Louis Beacon*, October 25, 1832. On coquetry: "To an Elderly Coquette," *St. Louis Enquirer*, September 1, 1819; "Oh! 'Tis Sweet to Think," *Enquirer*, April 7, 1819; "The Lady Who Swore by Her Eyes," *Enquirer*, March 31, 1819. See D'Emilio and Freedman, *Intimate*, for the origins

of antiseduction legislation in the Female Moral Reform Society, 144; see Smith-Rosenberg, "The Beauty, the Beast" on women's anger over the double standard. *St. Louis Enquirer*, September 1, 1819; *Enquirer*, June 2, 1819. Ann Lane to William Carr Lane, August 28, 1830, Carr-Lane Papers, Mo.H.S. See also Henrik Hartog, *Man and Wife in America: A History* (Cambridge, Mass., 2000), 87–91.

25. Before statehood Francois Labrosse announced he would not pay the bills of his wife, Celeste (*St. Louis Enquirer*, June 2, 1819). Sixteen years later Mildred Lewis left Samuel Lewis, and he disclaimed responsibility for her debts (*St. Louis Republican*, September 9, 1836). Also that year Ann Mackinnon Kinkaid left her husband, "P. Kinkaid" (*St. Louis Republican*, July 8, 1836, and *St. Louis Enquirer*, December 1, 1821). Mary Husky petitioned the state legislature for a divorce from John Husky (*St. Louis Enquirer*, June 24, 1820). George Breckenridge to his wife, January 6, 1833, George Breckenridge Papers, Mo.H.S., McCandless, *History of Missouri*, vol. 2, 89–90. According to the unpublished compilation made by Lois Stanley, George Wilson, and Mary Wilson ("Divorces and Separation in Missouri, 1808–1853" in the Mo.H.S.), there were thirty-nine separations and thirty-eight divorces between 1831 and 1839, but these figures do not correspond with those in the statute books, which suggest there were more.

26. Mallinckrodt, *Knights to Pioneers*, 192. See *Laws of the State of Missouri Passed at the First Session of the Sixth General Assembly Begun and Held at the City of Jefferson* (1830), 107–13; *Private Acts of the Third General Assembly of the State of Missouri at the Session Begun and Held at the Town of St. Charles* (*St. Louis Enquirer*, 1824), 44; *The Revised Statutes of the State of Missouri, 1835* (St. Louis, Argus), 129–38, 66–67, 225. See also Basch, *Divorce*, especially 19–67, and Hartog, *Man and Wife*, especially 167–192. William Carr Lane to Mary Lane, January 17, 1831, Carr-Lane Papers, Mo.H.S. See Hartog, *Man and Wife*, 87–92; Duncan, *History of the Baptists*, 214.

27. See Basch, *Divorce*, 67.

16. ST. LOUIS MARRIAGES: VIEWS FROM THE INSIDE

1. Hattie Anderson, "The Social and Economic Bases of the Rise of the Jackson Group in Missouri, 1815–1828," reprinted from the *Mo. Historical Review* (April 1938–April 1940), 30; Callan, *Sacred Heart*, 96–98.

2. Carla Waal and Barbara Korner, *Hardship and Hope: Missouri Women Writing About Their Lives, 1820–1920* (Columbia, Mo., 1997), 38. See Kelly, *New England Fashion*, 158–59, for courtship in provincial Massachusetts. Bryan and Rose, *Pioneer Families*, 175, 182, 213, 245, 302; Waal and Korner, *Hardship and Hope*, 28–47. This was 1847–49, but conditions in the Missouri hinterland did not change very much over forty years.

3. Hamsten, *Read This*, 73, 233.

4. Rothman, *Hands and Hearts*, 63; see Kelly, *New England Fashion*, 108–9, for a

contrasting interpretation. See also Nancy Cott, *The Bonds of Womanhood* (New Haven, 1977), 78–83. Crane, *Ebb Tide*, 223–41, argues that the ideals of the Revolution were for men only, as does Joan Hoff Wilson. For this debate, see also Mary Beth Norton, *Liberty's Daughters: The Revolutionary Experience of American Women, 1750–1800* (Boston, 1980); Linda Kerber, *Women of the Republic: Intellect and Ideology in Revolutionary America* (Chapel Hill, N.C., 1980); and Joan Hoff Wilson, "The Illusion of Change: Women and the American Revolution," in *The American Revolution: Explorations in the History of American Radicalism*, ed. Alfred E. Young (De Kalb, Ill., 1976), 348–415. Hartog, *Man and Wife*, 93–95. See Janet Farrell Brodie, *Contraception and Abortion in Nineteenth-Century America* (Ithaca, N.Y., 1994), 57–135, for a discussion of contraception information and possibilities.

5. Stuart Blumin, *The Emergence of the Middle Class: Social Experience in the American City, 1760–1900* (New York, 1989), 187–88; Appleby, *Inheriting*, 56–89.

6. Will Carr to Charles Carr, February 10, 1807, Carr Papers, Mo.H.S.

7. Quentin Anderson, *Making Americans: An Essay on Individualism and Money* (New York, 1992), 5–6. Will Carr to Charles Carr, June 21, 1804; Will Carr to his brother, October 28, 1807, Carr Papers, Mo.H.S. See Rotundo, *Manhood*, 96–103; Will Carr to his brother, July 3, 1807, Carr Papers, Mo.H.S.

8. Sibley, Journal, Lindenwood College Collection, Mo.H.S.; Bardaglio, *Reconstructing the Household*, 24, 27–28, 32–34.

9. Harriet Ewing to Mary Lane Ewing, August 28, 1826, Carr-Lane Papers, Mo.H.S.

10. A. Moulton to Mrs. Lewis Linn, December 26, 1840, Lewis F. Linn Papers, Mo.H.S.; Rotundo, *Manhood*, 102; Lears, *Fables of Abundance*, 53.

11. Ravenswaay, *St. Louis*, 153, 356, 369, 881; Corbett, *In Her Place*, 58.

12. Rotundo, *Manhood*, 107; Dabney Carr to Walter B. Carr, December 16, 1849, Carr Papers, Mo.H.S.

13. John Darby, *Personal Recollections of Many Prominent People Whom I Have Known* (St. Louis, 1880), 405–08; Mahoney, *Provincial Lives*, 17–18; Primm, *Lion*, 53–54; Ls. de Mun D. Orbigny to Jules de Mun, February 26, 1812, De Mun Papers, Mo.H.S.; Corbett, *In Her Place*, 6, 9.

14. Kathleen Neils Conzen, "Patterns of German-American History," in *Germans in America: Retrospect and Prospect*, ed. Randall Miller (Philadelphia, 1984), 15; Carol Piper Heming, "Schulhaus to Schoolhouse: The German School at Hermann, Mo., 1839–1855," *Mo. Historical Review*, vol. 18 (April 1988), 280–98; Richard J. Evans and W. R. Lee, eds. *The German Family: Essays on the Social History of the Family in Nineteenth- and Twentieth-Century Germany* (Totowa, N.J., 1981), 36–37, 53–55, 71–77; Schroeder and Schultz-Geisberg, *Hold Dear*, 46, 107, 134.

15. Linda Schelbitzki Pickle, *Contented Among Strangers: Rural German-Speaking Women and Their Families in the Nineteenth-Century Midwest* (Urbana, Ill., 1996), 47; Schroeder and Schutz-Geisberg, *Hold Dear*, 107, 144.

16. Schroeder and Schutz-Geisberg, *Hold Dear*, 120.

17. Norma Basch makes a similar point in *Framing American Divorce*, for example, 126–29, as does Karen Lystra in *Searching the Heart*.

18. Mary Sibley was fifteen and George Sibley in his thirties. George Sibley to his brother, August 20, 1815, Lindenwood College Collection, Mo.H.S. Isabelle Gratiot de Mun was sixteen and Jules de Mun was thirty (Bale, "A Packet of Old Letters," 159; Nettie H. Beauregard, "De Mun Family in America," in *Missouri Historical Collections*, vol. 5 [1927]). Tilman Agee married the thirteen-year-old daughter of a preacher in Callaway County (Bryan and Rose, *Pioneer Families*, 302). Couples on the Oregon Trail and in Texas were not particularly youthful (Julie Roy Jefferey, *Frontier Women: The Trans-Mississippi West, 1840–1880* [New York, 1971]). In the South they were. See Clinton, *Plantation Mistress*, 59; Wyatt-Brown, *Southern Honor*, 203–06; Faragher, *Daniel Boone*, 281, 350; Bryan and Rose, *Pioneer Families*, 302. Karen Lystra's evidence is largely from the postbellum era, and when it is not, the couples are remarkably liberal (*Searching the Heart*, 192–226).

19. Jules de Mun to Isabelle de Mun, February 15, 1815, De Mun Papers, Mo.H.S.; Beauregard, "De Mun Family."

20. See, for example, William Carr Lane to Mary Lane, April 17, 1819; William Carr Lane to Mary Lane, September 16, 1819, Carr-Lane Papers, Mo.H.S., 21. Jules de Mun to Isabelle de Mun, February 1, 1815; Isabelle de Mun to Jules de Mun, March 20, 1817(?); Jules de Mun to Isabelle de Mun, February 1, 1815; Isabelle de Mun to Jules de Mun, March 20, 1817(?), De Mun Papers, Mo.H.S.

21. August de Mun and Ls. de Mun d'Orbigny to Isabelle de Mun, August 12, 1813, De Mun Papers; A. Adams to William Carr Lane, December 29, 1825, Carr-Lane Papers, Mo.H.S.

22. Motz, *True Sisterhood*, 5. William Carr Lane to Mary Lane, April 17, 1819; William Carr Lane to his daughters, September 13, 1834, Carr-Lane Papers, Mo.H.S.

23. Faragher, *Daniel Boone*, 109–10, 281, 286.

24. Schroeder and Schultz-Geisberg, *Hold Dear*, 140–41, 134.

25. William Carr Lane to Mary Lane, September 1834, Carr-Lane Papers, Mo.H.S.

26. "The Evils of Reserve in Marriage," *St. Louis Enquirer*, December 18, 1824.

27. This was a common problem for evangelical women. See Sara Jones's struggle with her husband in Lyerly, *Southern Mind*, 185–68.

28. For a fascinating account of Harriet Livermore and women preachers, see Brekus, *Strangers and Pilgrims*, 1–3, 18–19, 210–11, 232–34, 247–48.

29. See, for example, Sarah von Phul to her sister, April 30, 1820, Von Phul Papers, Mo.H.S.

30. William Carr Lane to Mary Lane, May 1, 1819; Mary Lane to William Carr Lane, December 4, 1826; William Carr Lane to Mary Lane, January 11, 1831, Carr-Lane Papers, Mo.H.S.; Ravenswaay, *St. Louis*, 208.

31. Cyprian Clamorgan, *The Colored Aristocracy of St. Louis*, ed. and with intro. by Julie Winch (Columbia, Mo., 1999), 5; Barbara Fields, *Slavery and Freedom on*

the Middle Ground: Maryland during the Nineteenth Century (New Haven, 1985), 2; Greene et al., *Heritage*, 64.

32. This was common among free blacks. See James Oliver Horton, "Freedom's Yoke: Gender Conventions among Antebellum Free Blacks," *Feminist Studies*, vol. 12 (1986), 51–76, 61–62; Corbett, *In Her Place*, 6, 9; Greene et al., *Heritage*, 64; Clamorgan, *Aristocracy*, 10.

33. Clamorgan, *Aristocracy*, 16–17, 48, 59–60, 62, accused free black women of conspicuous consumption. In this he prefigured *The Black Bourgeoisie* (New York, 1957), in which E. Franklin Frazier argues that black middle-class women, in particular, pushed their husbands to acquire more and more to assert a status that constantly eluded them. Clamorgan, *Aristocracy*, 26–27.

34. Clamorgan, *Aristocracy*, 71, 72, 75, 76, 81. Unfortunately I could find no further identifications for these fascinating housemates.

35. This matches the Hortons' finding that southern female heads of families tended to be older than their northern counterparts and that this was the result of the death of a spouse (James O. Horton and Lois E. Horton, *In Hope of Liberty: Culture, Community, and Protest among Northern Free Blacks, 1700–1860* [New York, 1997–98]). For discussions of the West African extended family structure, see Niara Sudarska, "African American Families and Family Values," in *Black Families*, ed. Harriet Pipes MacAdoo (Thousand Oaks, Calif., 1992), 14–16; Niara Sudarska, *The Strength of Our Mothers: African American Women and Families, Essays and Speeches* (Trenton, N.J., 1996), 79–86; Clamorgan, *Aristocracy*, 75.

36. Clamorgan, *Aristocracy*, 54, 84; Horton, "Freedom's Yoke," 67, shows that this unconventional kind of life was not unusual among free blacks. *St. Louis Directory* for 1838–39; see Horton, "Freedom's Yoke," 56–58, for black men's expectations of their wives. See Ira Berlin, *Slaves Without Masters: The Free Negro in the Antebellum South* (New York, 1974), 246–47, for a discussion of some of the reasons why free blacks accumulated property. The 1830s initiated a two-decade-long period of growing prosperity for St. Louis and rising values for land (Primm, *Lion*, 137–39). James Thomas, *From Tennessee Slave to St. Louis Entrepreneur: The Autobiography of James Thomas*, ed. Loren Schweniger (Columbia, Mo., 1984), 102; Clamorgan, *Aristocracy*, 16.

37. Horton, "Freedom's Yoke," 55–58.

38. Clamorgan, *Aristocracy*, 47. Historians of free blacks Judy Day and M. James Kedro, "Free Blacks in St. Louis: Antebellum Conditions, Emancipation, and the Postwar Era," *Missouri Historical Society Bulletin*, vol. 30 (1974), 121, 124; Morris, *Southern Slavery*, 348, argues that whites did not enforce the literacy ban; see Linda Perkins, "Black Women and Racial 'Uplift' Prior to Emancipation," in *Black Woman Cross-Culturally*, 317–33, on the extensive antebellum activities of African American women for education and abolition.

39. Day and Kedro, "Free Blacks," 122; Hunter, "Slavery in St. Louis," 252; Francis and Emmet Williams, *Centenary Methodist Church of St. Louis, 1829–1939* (St. Louis, 1939), 6. Horton and Horton, *Liberty*, 14; Carla Peterson, *"Doers of the*

Word": African American Women Speakers and Writers in the North (1830–1880) (New York, 1995), 10; Richard Carwardine, " 'Antinomians,' and 'Arminians': Methodists and the Market Revolution," in *Market Revolution*, 294; Elizabeth Rauh Bethel, *The Roots of African-American Identity* (New York, 1997), 214, 10; Clamorgan, *Aristocracy*, 50; Horton and Horton, *Liberty*, 151; Horton, "Freedom's Yoke," 68; David O. Shipley, ed., *History of Black Baptists in Missouri* (Kansas City, Mo., 1976), 22–25.

40. Bethel, *African-American Identity*, 122; David Walker, *Appeal to the Coloured Citizens of the World* (New York, 1969); Ravenswaay, *St. Louis*, 281–95; Primm, *Lion*, 182–85.

41. Hunter Lloyd, "Slavery in St. Louis, 1804–1860," *Missouri Historical Society Bulletin*, vol. 30 (1974), 262; Primm, *Lion*, 186–87; Keckley, *Behind the Scenes*, 49.

42. Harry L. Watson, "Slavery and Development in a Dual Economy: The South and the Market Revolution," in *Market Revolution*, 51. White, *Ar'n't I*, 104; see also Marie Jenkins Schwartz, *Born in Bondage: Growing up Enslaved in the Antebellum South* (Cambridge., Mass., 2000), 176–205, for an extended discussion of slave courtship and marriage; see also Wilma King, " 'Rais Your Children up Rite': Parental Guidance and Child Rearing Practices Among Slaves in the Nineteenth-Century South," in *Working Toward Freedom: Slave Society and Domestic Economy in the American South*, ed. Larry Hudson (Rochester, N.Y., 1994), 153. Sharon Ann Holt, "Symbol, Memory, and Service: Resistance and Family Formation in Nineteenth-century African America," in *Working Toward Freedom*, 195–96. White, *Ar'n't I*, 96–97; Schwartz, *Born in Bondage*, 191; Jones, *Labor of Love*, 33–35; Stevenson, *Black and White*, 238–39; Schwartz, *Born in Bondage*, 176; Stevenson, *Black and White*, 231–32.

43. Schwartz, *Born in Bondage*, 200–201.

44. Hunter, "Slavery in St. Louis," 252. See Amy Dru Stanley, " 'The Right to Possess All the Faculties That God Has Given': Possessive Individualism, Slave Women, and Abolitionist Thought," in *Moral Problems in American Life*, 132–143. Stanley argues that abolitionist thought for black women meant bodily integrity, a radical interpretation of possessive individualism.

45. Schwartz, *Born in Bondage*, 5, 13, 157–58; Stevenson, *Black and White*, 235, writes of the challenges of matrifocal living and slavery's effect of encouraging black women to internalize ideals of "self-protection, self-determination and self-reliance."

46. Poole and Slawson, *Perry Co., Mo.*, 81.

47. Sibley, Journal, Lindenwood College Collection, Mo.H.S. *St. Louis Enquirer*, December 1, 1823; "Negroes for Sale or Hire," *Enquirer*, May 31, 1823; Scarpino, "Slavery in Callaway County," 270.

48. VanderVelde and Subramanian, "Mrs. Dred Scott," 1038–40, 1074–78, 1075.

49. VanderVelde and Subramanian, "Mrs. Dred Scott," 1085–87. See Finkelman, *Dred Scott*, for the whole case; see also Ravenswaay, *St. Louis*, 405–11; Primm, *Lion*, 240–42.

50. On exogamy and marriage between slaves on different plantations, see Steven-

son, *Black and White*, 229–31. These counties included Callaway, Boone, Howard, Cooper, Lafayette, Saline, and Clay. Jones, *Labor of Love*, 33–35; White, *Ar'n't I*, 98–106.

51. Davis, *Neglected Stories*, 38.

17. ST. LOUIS MARRIAGES: VIEWS FROM THE OUTSIDE

1. On violence, see Jenny Bourne Wahl, *The Bondsmen's Burden: An Economic Analysis of the Common Law of Southern Slavery* (New York, 1998), 132: "All in all, the punishments for white-on-white assaults were virtually nonexistent." See Lewis, "Motherhood and the Construction of the Male Citizen."

2. Anderson, *Social and Economic Basis*, 27; Dunlop, *Sixty Miles*, 143–74.

3. Bryan and Rose, *Pioneer Families*, 27, 108, 106, 101. From Mary Rolandson's narrative onward, there were plenty of accounts of captivity and warfare to read. Ravenswaay, *St. Louis*, 227. Duncan, *Baptists*, 79–82, 46–47, 219. Sarah von Phul to Henry von Phul, June 21, 1814, Von Phul Papers, Mo.H.S. Bale, "Packet," 163.

4. Gregory Dowd, *A Spirited Resistance: The North American Indian Struggle for Unity 1745–1815* (Baltimore, 1992); on Tecumseh, see R. David Edmunds, *The Shawnee Prophet* (Lincoln, Neb., 1983), 117–42; Joel Martin, *The Sacred Revolt, The Muskogees' Struggle for a New World* (Boston, 1991), 2; William Mc-Gloughlin, *Cherokee Resistance in the New Republic* (Chapel Hill, N.C., 1986); Jill Norgren, *The Cherokee Cases: The Confrontations of Law and Politics* (New York, 1996); Theda Perdue and Michael D. Green, *The Cherokee Removal: A Brief History with Documents* (New York, 1995); James W. Covington, *The Seminoles of Florida* (Gainesville, Fla., 1993); on the Mashpee of Massachusetts, see Jack Campisi, *The Mashpee Indians: Tribe on Trial* (Syracuse, N.Y., 1991), 13, 103; Gratiot, "Narrative," 268; Bryan and Rose, *Pioneer Families*, 195; Black Hawk, *Black Hawk, an Autobiography*, ed. Donald Jackson (Urbana, Ill., 1990).

5. For example, "Indian News," *St. Louis Free Press*, July 3, 1833; "The President and the Indians," *Free Press*, June 27, 1833; "Address to Black Hawk," *Free Press*, August 3, 1833; "The Cherokees," *St. Louis Beacon*, January 30, 1830; "The Shock of War," July 21, 1819, *St. Louis Enquirer*; "Treaty with the Kickapoo Indians," *Enquirer*, December 8, 1819; "Civilization of the Indians," *Enquirer*, February 16, 1820; "The Osage Mission," *Enquirer*, June 24, 1820; "Politics—Indians," *Beacon*, November 4, 1830. McCandless, *Missouri*, vol. 2, 54–55. For a missionary's diary of such incidents, see William Graves, *The First Protestant Osage Missions, 1820–1837* (Oswego, Kan., 1949), 51. Willard Rollings, *The Osage: An Ethnohistorical Study of Hegemony on the Prairie-Plains* (Columbia, Mo., 1992), 269–71.

6. Rollings, *Osage*, 279–81; McCandless, *Missouri*, vol. 2, 55–56.

7. Faragher, *Daniel Boone*, 313.

8. *St. Louis Beacon*, June 27, 1831. Frederick Jackson Turner, *The Significance of*

the Frontier in American History (1920, Tucson, 1992), 15. See, for example, *St. Louis Enquirer*, September 15, 1819; *Missouri Argus*, June 5, 1835.

9. "Politics-Indians," *St. Louis Beacon*, November 4, 1830. "Our Indian Affairs," "communicated" from *The Galenian*, Galena, Illinois, ran in the *St. Louis Beacon*, August 4, 1832; *Beacon*, August 26, 1830.

10. See Faragher, *Daniel Boone*, for incidents in the lives of the various members of the Boone family.

11. McCandless, *Missouri*, 118. Paul Cochrane, *History of St. Charles, Montgomery and Warren Counties, Mo.* (St. Louis, 1969 reprint), 165. Susan Branson, *Those Fiery Frenchified Dames: Women and Political Culture in Early National Philadelphia* (Philadelphia, 2001), 83–85. In the eighteenth century, Branson writes, "Some militia presentations were elaborate affairs that included processions, picnics, and toasts. Men and women frequently drank toasts *together* [emphasis in the original] after the ceremonies" (85). In 1837 Miss Wales did not drink toasts after the ceremonies with Richard Gentry et al., since women had been excused from toast drinking in Missouri.

12. *St. Louis Republican*, June 10, 1836, May 21, 1836; *Missouri Argus*, July 16, 1838. See Julie Roy Jeffrey, *Frontier Women: The Trans-Mississippi West, 1840–1880*, rev. ed. (New York, 1996), for the argument that women rarely found much common ground with Indians. Glenda Riley argues that white women had friendlier attitudes toward Indians than men (*Women and Indians on the Frontier, 1825–1915* [Albuquerque, 1984]. See also Annette Kolodny, *The Land Before Her: Fantasy and Experience of the American Frontiers, 1630–1860* (Chapel Hill, N.C., 1984), 11.

13. Jennifer M. Spear, " 'They Need Wives': Metissage and the Regulation of Sexuality in French Louisiana, 1699, 1730," in *Sex, Love, Race: Crossing Boundaries in North American History*, ed. Martha Hodes (New York, 1999), 35–59. William E. Foley and C. David Rice, *The First Chouteaus: River Barons of Early St. Louis* (Urbana, New York, Ill., 1983), 45. Tanis C. Thorne, "For the Good of Her People," in *Midwestern Women, Work Community, and Leadership at the Crossroads*, ed. Lucy Eldersveld Murphy and Wendy Hamand Venet (Bloomington, Ind., 1997), 110, 113.

14. See, for example, Victoire Gratiot to Isabelle Gratiot de Mun, May 18, 1821, De Mun Papers, Mo.H.S. "Chouteaus" was a word for friendly Europeans, not members of the Chouteau extended family. Adele Gratiot, "Mrs. Adele P. Gratiot's Narrative," *Report and Collections of the State Historical Society of Wisconsin, for the Years 1883, 1884, and 1885* (Madison, Wis., 1888), vol. 10, 269.

15. Jules de Mun to Isabelle de Mun, June 24–August 13, 1816; years later she was still terrified: Isabelle de Mun to Jules de Mun, June 1, 1832, De Mun Papers, Mo.H.S.

16. *Missouri Argus*, June 5, 1835; Kolodny, *Land Before Her*, 84; Timothy Flint, *Recollections of the Last Ten Years Passed in Occasional Residences and Journeyings in the Valley of the Mississippi* (Boston, 1826), 45; see also Bryan and Rose, *Pioneer Families*, 27.

17. Schroeder and Schulz-Geisberg, *Hold Dear*, 82. George Catlin, *North American Indians*, ed. and with intro. Peter Matthiessen (New York, 1989), 3; Nancy K. Anderson, " 'Curious Historical Data': Art History and Western American Art," in *Discovered Lands, Invented Pasts* (New Haven, 1992), 7; Lora Romero, "Vanishing Americans: Gender, Empire, and New Historicism," in *The Culture of Sentiment*, 115. For discussions of aspects of this phenomenon, see Bernard Sheehan, *Seeds of Extinction: Jeffersonian Philanthropy and the American Indian* (New York, 1974); Roy Harvey Pearce, *Savagism and Civilization: A Study of the Indian and the American Mind* (1953, Berkeley, Calif., 1988); Richard Slotkin's *Regeneration Through Violence: The Mythology of the American Frontier, 1600–1860* and *The Fatal Environment: The Myth of the Frontier in the Age of Industrialization, 1800–1890* (1973, Middletown, Conn., 1985). "Our Indian Affairs," *St. Louis Beacon*, August 4, 1832; Baym, *American Women Writers*, 158.

18. Kate L. Gregg, *The Road to Santa Fe: The Journal and Diaries of George Champlin Sibley* (Santa Fe, 1952), 9–14, 25–26. George Sibley to Mary Sibley, 1811 (Box No. 5, 12–14); George Sibley, Diary, vol. 10, 1818–1843, Letter to William Clark (1819?), Lindenwood College Collection, Mo.H.S.

19. George Sibley, Diary, vol. 10, 1818–1843, 15; George Sibley to Samuel Sibley, May 6, 1815, Lindenwood College Collection, Mo.H.S. Graves, *Osage Mission*, 31–32. Rollings, *Osage*, 11, 13, 41–42; Victor Tixier, *Travels on the Osage Prairies*, ed. John F. McDermott (Norman, Okla., 1940), 182–83. George Sibley to Dr. Belcher, October 27, 1827, Lindenwood College Collection, Mo.H.S. Graves, *Osage Mission*, 46, 130, 170. Ibid., 17, 23–24, 66. Ibid., 123; Samuels, *Culture of Sentiment*, 15.

20. See Appleby, *Inheriting*, 3; Mahoney, *Provincial*, 84–85. For the difference the Revolution made or did not make to American enterprise, see Appleby, *Inheriting*, and Jon Butler, *Becoming America: The Revolution Before 1776* (Cambridge, Mass., 2000).

21. See Appleby, *Inheriting*, 43–55; Charles Sellers, *The Market Revolution: Jacksonian America, 1815–1846* (New York, 1991), 47; Foley, *History of Missouri*, vol. 1, 119, 170; McCandless, *Missouri*, vol. 2, 10–13; Primm, *Lion*, 118–22. See also Foley, *Missouri*, 170–74; Richard E. Ellis, "The Market Revolution and the Transformation of American Politics, 1801–1837," in *Market Revolution*, 163; Wade, *Urban Frontier*, 173, 200–202; Primm, *Lion*, 123.

22. William Carr Lane to Mary Lane, September 16, 1819, Carr-Lane Papers, Mo.H.S.

23. *Missouri Argus*, December 16, 1836. See Mary Douglas, *The World of Goods: Toward an Anthropology of Consumption* (New York, 1996), 24, for culturally taming the results of inequality; Mary Louise Kete, *Sentimental Collaborations: Mourning and Middle-Class Identity in Nineteenth-Century America* (Durham, N.C., 2000), 35.

24. Mott, *Observations*, 15, 16; Lydia Sigourney criticized Indian removal for profit (Kete, *Sentimental Collaborations*, 123–24).

25. See, for example, *St. Louis Enquirer*, August 30, 1820; *St. Louis Free Press*, June 13, 1833.

26. Lockridge, *On the Sources*, 118.

27. For the goods proliferating in St. Louis, see Ravenswaay, *St. Louis*, 219–27, and Primm, *Lion*, 138–40. For a discussion of gender and urban household consumption in the 1850s, see Blumin, *Middle Class*, 185–189; in provincial Massachusetts, see Kelly, *New England Fashion*, 214–41; Mott, *Observations*, 217, 234, 236.

28. Sister Susan to Mrs. Cuthbert, October 7, 1836, Mo.H.S. For what Jeanne Boydston has called the pastoralization of women's work and its disappearance from consciousness, see *Home and Work*, 142–63.

29. See Francis Wayland's popular *The Elements of Political Economy* (New York, 1837) and Daniel Horowitz, *The Morality of Spending: Attitudes Toward the Consumer Society in America, 1875–1940* (Baltimore, 1985), 1–12. Corbett, *In Her Place*, 32–33; Wade, *Urban Frontier*, 109. Sarah Mason to Henry von Phul, July 20, 1825, Von Phul Papers, Mo.H.S. See Leora Auslander, "The Gendering of Consumer Practice in Nineteenth-Century France," in *The Sex of Things: Gender and Consumption in Historical Perspective*, ed. Victoria de Grazia (Berkeley, Calif., 1996), 82–85, on the middle-class wife's obligations in postrevolutionary France. Sarah Mason to her sister, April 30, 1820; Sarah Mason to Rosalie von Phul, June 12, 183?, Von Phul Papers, Mo.H.S.

30. Sarah von Phul Mason to Rosalie von Phul, April 30, 1820, Von Phul Papers, Mo.H.S.

31. See David Lavender for a romantic history of the Bent family: *Bent's Fort* (Omaha, Neb., 1954). W. C. Carr to Dorcas Carr, December 21, 1830, Carr Papers, Mo.H.S.

32. Sibley, Journal, Lindenwood College Collection, Mo.H.S.; Auslander, "Gendering of Consumer Practices," 84; see also Dunlop, *Sixty Miles*, on comfort, which she says women in the West neither defined nor had, 33–34, 171–72. See Gillian Brown, *Domestic Individualism: Imagining Self in Nineteenth-Century America* (Berkeley, Calif., 1990), 45–53.

33. *Missouri Argus*, May 22, 1835; William C. David, *Three Roads to the Alamo: The Lives and Fortunes of David Crockett, James Bowie, and William Barrett Travis* (New York, 1998), 395–96. "English Factory Labor," *St. Louis Free Press*, June 20, 1833; "Slaves in the South, & White Laborers of the North," *Free Press*, October 3, 1833; Primm, *Lion*, 174–75. See Eric Foner, "Free Labor and Nineteenth-Century Political Ideology," in *Market Revolution*, 105–6.

34. Thorne, "For the Good of Her People," 95–113. For Osage cosmology, see Garrick Bailey, *The Osage and the Invisible World from the Works of Francis La Fleche* (Norman, Okla., 1995). On some of these movements, see Dowd, *Spirited Resistance*; Martin, *Sacred Revolt*; McCloughlin, *Cherokee Renascence*; and James Mooney's classic on the Sioux, *The Ghost Dance*, reprinted in 1996 by the JG Press. The priests and Osages in large numbers began in 1898 to shift to the peyote religion, a transition that was largely complete by 1910 (Bailey, *Osage*, 18).

35. *St. Louis Enquirer*, April 17, 1838; St. Louis Board of Education Proceedings, no. 1, part 1, April 18, 1833–April 24, 1843, Mo.H.S.

36. Wall and Kurner, *Hardship and Hope*, 39; Lucy Eldersveld Murphy, "Journeywoman Milliner, Emily Austin, Migration, and Women's Work in the Nineteenth-Century Midwest," in *Midwestern Women*, 50, 54.

37. Wade, *Urban Frontier*, 169–70. See Alan Taylor, *Liberty Men and Great Proprietors: The Revolutionary Settlement on the Maine Frontier, 1769–1820* (Chapel Hill, N.C., 1990), 8; Christopher Clark, *Roots of Rural Capitalism: Western Massachusetts, 1780–1860* (Ithaca, N.Y., 1990), 323; Sellers, *Market Revolution*, 5–10; Farragher, *Sugar Creek*, 181–90; Stephen Aron, *How the West Was Lost: The Transformation of Kentucky from Daniel Boone to Henry Clay* (Baltimore, 1996), 122–23; Brekus, *Strangers and Pilgrims*, 234–43.

38. George C. Sibley to Rufus Easton, September 10, 1821, from Fort Osage, Lindenwood College Collection, Mo.H.S. See Corbett, *In Her Place*, 40–41; Rollings, *Osage*, 22, 59, 223, 227 n. 29, 259, 262. Mary Sibley to Russella, February 26, 1831, Lindenwood College Collection, Mo.H.S.

39. McCandless, *Missouri*, vol. 2, 120. Marlene Stein Wortman, ed., *Women in the American Law*, vol. 1, *From Colonial Times to the New Deal* (New York, 1985), 118.

40. Corbett, *In Her Place*, 1–17; see also Traer, *Marriage and Family*, 85, 138, for the changes the French Revolution made in civil law.

41. Elizabeth R. Varon, *We Mean to Be Counted: White Women and Politics in Antebellum Virginia* (Chapel Hill, N.C., 1998), 72, 82–83. For an especially violent election celebration narrated by Sarah von Phul, see Sarah Mason to Henry von Phul, August 6, 1825, Von Phul Papers, Mo.H.S.; Primm, *Lion*, 125. See Mahoney, *Provincial Lives*, 62–63; see Boynton Merrill, Jr., *Jefferson's Nephews: A Frontier Tragedy* (Lexington, Ky., 1987), 151–62. Varon, *We Mean to Be Counted*, 1–40, on women in Whig politics. See also Mary Ryan, *Women in Public: Between Banners and Ballots, 1825–1880* (Baltimore, 1990), particularly 3–18.

42. Ravenswaay, *St. Louis*, 261–64; Primm, *Lion*, 141; *Missouri Argus*, July 10, 1835.

43. Ravenswaay, *St. Louis*, 201; Nettie Beauregard, "De Mun Family in America," *Mo.H.S. Collections*, vol. 5 (1927), 329; De Pestre de Mun to Isabelle de Mun, June 3, 1817, De Mun Papers, Mo.H.S.; Lewis Linn to Elizabeth Linn, June 14, 1834, Lewis F. Linn Papers, Mo.H.S.; Van Ravenswaay, *St. Louis*, 147–48; William Carr Lane to Mary Lane, May 1, 1819, Carr-Lane Papers, Mo.H.S.; Ravenswaay, *St. Louis*, 208.

44. See Joanne Freeman on nationwide dueling: *Affairs of Honor: National Politics in the New Republic* (New Haven, 2001); Nathaniel Ewing to William Lane, October 1, 1827, Carr-Lane Papers, Mo.H.S.; Ravenswaay, *St. Louis*, 199–202. *Acts of the Second General Assembly of the State of Missouri Passed at the First Session Begun and Held at the Town of St. Charles* (St. Charles, 1823), 53–56; *The Revised Statutes of the State of Missouri Revised and Digested by the Eighth General Assembly During the Years 1834–1835* (St. Louis, 1835), 201–4.

45. See Catherine Allgor, *Parlor Politics, in Which the Ladies of Washington Help Build a City and a Government* (Richmond, Va., 2000), for a discussion of how the climate changed in the wake of the snubbing of Margaret Eaton; see also Reynolds, *Civil Tongues*.

46. Ravenswaay, *St. Louis*, 209. W. C. Carr to Dorcas Carr, December 21, 1830, Carr Papers, Mo.H.S.

47. Anthony Rotundo has argued that after the 1820s there emerged a type based on Daniel Boone and Davy Crockett, the "masculine primitive," which recognized physical bravery, charisma, and powerful instincts as proper and admirable male traits. It clearly applied to Andrew Jackson. Ed Hatton, "He Murdered Her Because He Loved Her," in *Over the Threshold: Intimate Violence in Early America*, eds. Christine Daniels and Michael V. Kennedy (New York, 1999), 114; E. Anthony Rotundo, "Learning About Manhood: Gender Ideals and the Middle Class Family in 19th-Century America," in *Manliness and Morality: Middle Class Masculinity in Britain and America, 1840–1900*, eds. J. A. Mangan and James Walvin (Manchester, U.K., 1987). For an account of the Eaton affair, see John F. Marszalek, *The Petticoat Affair: Manners, Mutiny, and Sex in Andrew Jackson's White House* (New York, 1997), 45–105. See also Jane Pease and William Pease, *Ladies, Women, and Wenches* (Chapel Hill, N.C., 1990), 138. For the implications for other reform movements, see Lori Ginzberg, *Women and the Work of Benevolence: Morality, Politics, and Class in the Nineteenth Century United States* (New Haven, 1990), 11–35. For Carr's full story, see William C. Carr to Dorcas Bent Carr, December 17, 1830, Carr Papers, Mo.H.S.; Primm, *Lion*, 97–99. Lavender, *Bent's Fort*, 22–25, 176, 187–88, 226.

48. Ravenswaay, *St. Louis*, 276–93; Primm, *Lion*, 182–85.

49. Ginzberg, *Women and the Work*, 69; Varon, *Counted*, 72, 80, 83. Sibley, Journal, Lindenwood College Collection, Mo.H.S. See also Annie M. Boylan, *The Sunday School: The Formation of an American Institution, 1790–1880* (New Haven, 1988).

50. Sibley, Journal, Lindenwood College Collection, Mo.H.S.

51. Ibid.; Mary Sibley to her sister, Russella, February 26, 1831, Lindenwood College Collection, Mo.H.S.

52. Archibald Gamble to Mary Sibley, February 28, 1844, Lindenwood College Collection, Mo.H.S.; Bale, "Packet," 164. On toleration, see George von Phul to John Breckenridge, December 31, 1818, Von Phul Papers, Mo.H.S.; William Carr Lane to his daughters, probably 1836, Carr-Lane Papers, Mo.H.S.

53. Sarah Ward to Anna Maria von Phul, July 21, 1823, Von Phul Papers, Mo.H.S.

54. "Constitution of the Female Benevolent Society," *St. Louis Enquirer*, February 16, 1825; Ravenswaay, *St. Louis*, 245. To compare Missouri with the rest of the South, see Cynthia Kierner, *Beyond the Household: Women's Place in the Early South, 1700–1835* (Ithaca, N.Y., 1998), 190–201. See also Amy Dru Stanley, *From Bondage to Contract: Wage Labor, Marriage, and the Market in the Age of Slave Emancipation* (New York, 1998), 98–137, on attitudes toward

poverty. See Ginzberg, *Women and the Work*; Nancy Hewitt, *Women's Activism and Social Change: Rochester, New York, 1822–1872* (Ithaca, N.Y., 1984); and Mary Ryan, *The Cradle of the Middle Class: The Family in Oneida County, New York, 1790–1865* (New York, 1981), on women's reform. See also Carolyn J. Lawes, *Women and Reform in a New England Community, 1815–1860* (Lexington, Ky., 2000), for reform in Worcester, Massachusetts.

55. See Ginzberg, *Women and the Work*, 36–66, on the various ways Protestant organizations hired, paid salaries, incorporated, etc. St. Louis women were no exception. For a discussion of Catholic sisters' work in this era see, Carol Coburn and Martha Smith, *Spirited Lives: How Nuns Shaped Catholic Culture and American Life, 1836–1920* (Chapel Hill, N.C., 1999), 1–52. See also Callan, *Sacred Heart* and *Duchesne*. For example, Ann Lucas Hunt gave more than a million dollars to various Catholic institutions (Corbett, *In Her Place*, 58).

56. Corbett, *In Her Place*, 79.

57. See Timothy Hacsi, *Second Home: Orphan Asylums and Poor Families* (Cambridge, Mass., 1997), 22, on the relation of epidemics to founding orphan asylums; see Corbett, *In Her Place*, 43. On this outbreak, see Ravenswaay, *St. Louis*, 269–73, and Primm, *Lion*, 163. St. Louis Protestant Orphan Asylum, By-laws Article 1, Mo.H.S. Ginzberg, *Women and the Work*, 1; Hacsi, *Second*, 78; Hewitt, *Women's Activism*, 40, identifies elite benevolent, evangelical women, and radical women working together in Rochester. St. Louis seems not to have had a radical wing. See Bellows, *Benevolence*, 32–38.

58. Ravenswaay, *St. Louis*, 148. See David J. Rothman, *The Discovery of the Asylum: Social Order and Disorder in the New Republic* (Boston, 1971), 170–79, for Jacksonian thinking on poverty and familial incapacity; Hacsi, *Second*, 9, 15.

59. Douglas, *World of Goods*, 24.

60. See Grossberg, *Governing*, 263–67, for apprenticing; Rothman, *Asylum*, 30–56, on colonial treatment of the poor. St. Louis Protestant Orphan Asylum Record Book, 1834–1852, January 7, 1835, Mo.H.S. For this philosophy writ large, see Marilyn Irvin Holt, *The Orphan Trains: Placing Out in America* (Lincoln, Neb., 1992); Carson, Donald, and Ryce, "Household Encounters," 86. On half orphans see Hacsi, *Second*, 115; St. Louis Asylum, vol. 1, Article 12, Mo.H.S.; Rothman, *Asylum*, 221–22.

61. Hacsi, *Second*, 57–61; Grossberg, *Governing*, 266; Foley, *Missouri*, 220–23, 266. An almshouse went up in St. Louis in 1827; a man entering lost the right to vote. Rothman, *Asylum*, 220.

62. St. Louis Protestant Orphan Asylum Record Book, 1834–1852, Mo.H.S.

63. Callan, *Sacred Heart*, 205, 199, 203, 207.

64. Bellows, *Benevolence*, 34–44: the Episcopalians founded another orphan society in 1843, chartered by the Missouri legislature in 1845, set up precisely the way the Protestant asylum had been, with the exception that men could be members (Corbett, *In Her Place*, 66).

65. Nancy Cott, *Public Vows: A History of Marriage and the Nation* (Cambridge, Mass., 2000), 17–19. For Hume and sociability, see *Moral Prejudices*, particu-

larly chapters 4 and 5; for an indictment of Adam Smith on sympathy, see Agnew, *Worlds Apart*, 174–75.

66. Douglas, *World of Goods*, 48–66, 91.

67. Mary Sibley's journal confirms this, and Mott specified it (*Observations*, 49–50).

68. Sibley, Journal, Lindenwood College Collection, Mo.H.S.

69. Concord Baptist Church Record Books, 1832–1846, March 1843, vol. 1 for 1838, Mo.H.S. There were twenty-six white men, six black men, fifty-nine white women, and four black women. Methodist women also outnumbered men (Lyerly, *Southern Mind*, 100).

70. Cedar Creek Baptist Church Record, Mo.H.S.; Bethel Baptist Church at Cape Girardeau, March 31, 1821, Mo.H.S. The Providence Baptist Church, June 10, 1837, September 9, 1837, Rambo Papers, Mo.H.S.

71. Sarah Mason to Rosalie von Phul, September 1, 1837, Von Phul Papers, Mo.H.S.; Hemphill, *Bowing*, ch. 7, particularly 151–52; John Kasson, *Rudeness and Civility: Manners in Nineteenth Century Urban America* (New York, 1990), 44–45.

72. George Ewing to William Lane, June 21, 1824; William Carr Lane to Mary Lane, January 17, 1821, Carr-Lane Papers, Mo.H.S.

73. Lewis Linn to Elizabeth Linn, January 19, 1841, Lewis F. Linn Papers, Mo.H.S.; Jane Ann Linn, Scrapbook, 1834; James H. Rolfe to Elizabeth Linn, December 28, 1845, Lewis F. Linn Papers, Mo.H.S. See also letters of Ann Biddle to her cousin on getting him an appointment in the army (no date, no date, and one dated St. Louis, November 5, 1832), Mullanphy Papers, Mo.H.S.; Ravenswaay, *St. Louis*, 265–67; Osofsky, ed., *Puttin' on Ole Massa*, 186.

74. Sarah Mason to Henry von Phul, August 6, 1825, Von Phul Papers, Mo.H.S.; see also Sarah Ward to Anna Maria von Phul, July 21, 1823, Von Phul Papers.

75. James H. Reefe to Mrs. Elizabeth Linn, December 28, 1845, Lewis F. Linn Papers, Mo.H.S.

18. MOTHERS AND MORALS

1. Mott, *Observations*, 9; see also Cott, *Public Vows*, 21–22; Stanley, *From Bondage to Contract*, 260; One advice book put the matter bluntly: "Religion is just what a woman needs. Without it she is ever restless or unhappy, ever wishing to be relieved from duty or from home" (*Young Lady's*, 343). See Ryan, *Cradle of the Middle Class*, 60–104, on the revivals and women's participation. Bennett, *Strictures*, 95; Barbara Epstein, *The Politics of Domesticity: Women, Evangelism, and Temperance in Nineteenth-Century America* (Middletown, Conn., 1981), 63; Lewis, "Mother's Love: The Construction of an Emotion in Nineteenth-Century America," in *Mothers and Motherhood: Readings in American History*, ed. Rima D. Apple and Janet Golden (Columbus, Ohio, 1997), 52–71; Bloch, "American Feminine Ideals," 101–26. See also Ryan, *Cradle of the Middle Class*.

2. Mott, *Observations*, 8. Child, *Mother's Book*, 2–3, 4, 6–9; Bennett, *Strictures*, 41.

3. Mott, *Observations*, 13; see Richard Brodhead's extraordinary "Sparing the Rod, Discipline and Fiction in Antebellum America," in *Cultures of Letters: Scenes of Reading and Writing in Nineteenth-Century America* (Chicago, 1993); Lewis, "Mother's Love," 58–59; Mott, *Observations*, 25, 75.

4. Lewis, "Mother's Love," 60–61; on the withdrawal of love, see Greven, *Protestant Temperament*, 49–55; Bernard Wishy, *The Child and the Republic* (Philadelphia, 1968), 42–47.

5. Berquin, *L'Ami*, 2–3.

6. Jules de Mun to Isabelle de Mun, Feb. 1, 1815; Jules de Mun to Isabelle Gratiot de Mun, July 16, 1816, De Mun Papers, Mo.H.S.

7. See, for example, Julie de Mun to Jules de Mun, February 20, 1832, on bodily description, De Mun Papers, Mo.H.S.; Dunlop, *Sixty Miles*, 159–61. See, for example, Cotton Mather, *Cares about the Nursery* (Boston, 1702), urging women to use the milk bottles God gave them; see Perry, "Colonizing the Breast," 204–38. No one in nineteenth-century St. Louis wrote like Landon Carter criticizing the use of breast-feeding as a means of contraception (see Part II, Chapter 5); *Young Lady's*, 187; Child, *Mother's Book*, 4.

8. Jules de Mun to Isabelle Gratiot de Mun, July 21, 1816, Rivierre des Kansas, De Mun Papers, Mo.H.S. See also Mme Duchesne's disgust for spoiling parents: Callan, *Duchesne*, 15–53.

9. Child, *Mother's Book*, 41, 42; Ravenswaay, *St. Louis*, 114; Lewis F. Linn to his daughter Jane, 1834, Lewis F. Linn Papers, Mo.H.S. For another example, see William Carr Lane to Anne Lane, December 20, 1830, Carr-Lane Papers, Mo.H.S.

10. *Young Lady's*, 187.

11. On changes in family size and style, see Coontz, *Private Life*, 185–99; see also Greven, *Protestant Temperament*, 25–27; Lewis, "Mother's Love," 54–55; Bloch, "Moral Mother," 117.

12. See Gilligan, *In a Different Voice*; for a synopsis of the position, see "In a Different Voice," in *Psychology of Women*. Gilligan's original study was designed to correct the male bias in Kohlberg's *Essays in Moral Development*.

13. Jane Pease and William Pease, *Ladies, Women, and Wenches: Choice and Constraint in Antebellum Charleston and Boston* (Chapel Hill, N.C., 1990), 28; Mott, *Observations*, 60–61, 40. Horowitz, *Spending*, 1–2, 11–12, quotes, Francis Wayland on fears that the poor would be idle and drink.

14. Victoire Gratiot to Isabelle Gratiot de Mun, May 18, 1821, De Mun Papers, Mo.H.S. Mahoney, *Provincial Lives*, 42–45.

15. Cece de Mun Depestre to Isabelle de Mun, April 19, 1817, De Mun Papers, Mo.H.S.

16. Mott, *Observations*, 73; Child, *Mother's Book*, 161–69; Bennett, *Strictures*, 41.

17. See Appleby, *Inheriting*, 121–28; *History of St. Charles*, 302; Bryan and Rose, *Pioneer Families*, 187; Wall and Korner, *Hardship and Hope*, 28–47; quote, 44.

18. Faragher, *Daniel Boone*, 311; Methodists and Baptists each had about twenty-

seven hundred congregations in 1820; Carwardine, " 'Antinomians' and 'Armini-ans,' " 290; Bryan and Rose, *Pioneer Families*, 418; Duncan, *Baptists*, 824; Faragher, *Daniel Boone*, 311. Ann Ewing to Mary Lane, October 26, 1822; Ann Ewing to Mary Lane, October 7, 1822; Nathaniel Ewing to William Ewing, October 17, 1822; Ann Ewing to Mary Lane, June 1, 1824; Nathaniel Ewing to William Lane, August 8, 1825, Carr-Lane Papers, Mo.H.S.; Greene et al., *Heritage*, 25, 62–64.

19. Jane Mullanphy Chambers to Bryan Mullanphy, February 13, 1827, Mullanphy Papers, Mo.H.S. See also Dorcas Bent Carr's plea to her stepson: Dorcas Bent Carr to Dabney Carr, January 7, 1850, Carr Papers, Mo.H.S. This was an unfinished letter, which either was never sent or was a copy of a letter that she did send.

20. Faragher, *Daniel Boone*, 220–23.

21. Grossberg, *Governing*, 3.

22. Tadman, *Speculators*, 98–102; William G. Eliot, *The Story of Archer Alexander, from Slavery to Freedom* (1885), reprint (Westport, Conn., 1970), 82.

23. John W. Blassingame, *Slave Testimony: Two Centuries of Letters, Speeches, Interviews, and Autobiographies* (Baton Rouge, La., 1977), 286–87; Johnson, *Soul by Soul*, 7; Blassingame, *Slave Testimony*, 210–11; Primm, *Lion*, 186–87.

24. See King, *Stolen Childhood*, on slave children growing up; see also Stevenson, *Black and White*, especially chapters 7 and 8, for conditions of child raising in the antebellum Upper South; see as well Marie Jenkins Schwartz, " 'At Noon, Oh How I Ran': Breastfeeding and Weaning on Plantation and Farm in Antebellum Virginia and Alabama," in *Discovering the Women in Slavery, Emancipating Perspectives on the American Past*, ed. Patricia Morton (Athens, Ga., 1996), 141–187; see Johnson, *Soul by Soul*, 22, on the constant fear of being separated; Schwartz, "At Noon," 242–43, 251. For the death of Matile Jackson's little brother, see Andrews, *Six Women's*, 12; see Jones, *Labor of Love*, 21; Primm, *Lion*, 187. George Morton's bill of sale, June 31, 1837, Mullanphy Papers, Mo.H.S.

25. See Nell Painter's evocative "Soul Murder and Slavery: Toward a Fully Loaded Cost Accounting," in *U.S. History as Women's History*, ed. Linda Kerber, Alice Kessler-Harris, and Kathryn Kish Sklan (Chapel Hill, N.C., 1995), 125–46; Yetman, ed., *Voices from Slavery*, 154–55. See Jones, *Labor of Love*, 13.

26. Keckley, *Behind the Scenes*, 9; VanderVelde and Subramanian, "Mrs. Dred Scott," 1072; James Horton, "Freedom's Yoke," 54, says men initiated most political actions for slaves, but that women slaves initiated court suits. In St. Louis, women initiated numerous suits. Petition of Jenny, "A Free Woman of Color," St. Louis Circuit Court, XXI–XXIII, May 9, 1825, Mo.H.S.; "Jenny v. Ephriam Musick and others," St. Louis Circuit Court, XXI–XXIII, June 1825, Mo.H.S. For an account of this story, see Finkelman, *Dred Scott* and VanderVelde and Subramanian, "Mrs. Dred Scott," 1032–1122. "Marguerite v. Pierre Chouteau, Sieur," St. Louis Circuit Court Records, November 30, 1836, Mo.H.S.; see also a good summary of this complex case in Corbett, *In Her Place*, 27–8.

27. Osofsky, *Puttin' on Ole Massa*, 179–209. There are several versions of William

Wells Brown's narrative. The one I have paraphrased is the first and claims fewer emblematic connections and occurrences in his development than later ones (Joyce Carol Oates, "The Wind Done Gone," *New York Review of Books*, June 21, 2001), 65.

28. For abolitionist literature on the violation of marriage in slavery, see Stanley, *Bondage to Contract*, 24–25, n. 50, n. 51.

29. Lewis, "Mother's Love"; Wishy, *Child and the Republic*, 28, 32; Ann Douglas, *Feminization of American Culture* (New York, 1977), mounted an important attack on the implications of this development. Many writers since, including Jane Tomkins (*Sensational Designs* [New York, 1985]) and Mary Kelly (*Private Woman, Public Stage* [New York, 1984]), have defended sentimental culture. More recently writers have analyzed its functions in negotiating a place within the expanding American economy; see Samuels, *The Culture of Sentiment*, and Kete, *Sentimental Collaborations*. Wishy, *Child*, 11–20.

30. Kete, *Sentimental Collaborations*, 1–49.

31. Margaret Marsh, "Motherhood Denied: Women and Infertility in Historical Perspective," in *Mothers and Motherhood*, 221; Sylvia D. Hoffert, *Private Matters: American Attitudes Toward Childbearing and Infant Nurture in the Urban North, 1800–1860* (Urbana, Ill., 1989), 80; Coontz, *Private Life*, 124–25.

32. Frederick Julius Gustorf, *The Uncorrupted Heart: Journal and Letters of F. J. Gustorf, 1800–1845* (Columbia, Mo., 1969), 36. As Gustorf wrote, "One German called them [American women] 'Calomel Faces,' which is very appropriate when you consider how much of this poison they consume, on advice of the American doctors, from childhood to the grave." See Saxton, *Louisa May*, 253; Judith Walzer Leavitt, "Under the Shadow of Maternity: American Women's Responses to Death and Debility Fears in Nineteenth-Century Childbirth," *Feminist Studies*, vol. 12 (1986), 135; Ekberg, *Colonial Ste. Genevieve*, 239–67; see also Wade, *Urban Frontier*, 96–99, 297–302; Foley, *Missouri*, vol. 1, 215–20. Leavitt, "Shadow," 36; Gary Laderman, *The Sacred Remains: American Attitudes Toward Death, 1799–1883* (New Haven, 1996), 24.

33. Wade, *Urban Frontier*, 299. See Charles Rosenberg, *The Cholera Years: The United States in 1832, 1849 and 1866* (Chicago, 1962), 55–64; Ravenswaay, *St. Louis*, 269–73.

34. See Silas Wright, Jr., to Elizabeth Linn, June 6, 1836; Lewis Linn to Elizabeth Linn, June 7, June 8, 1836, Lewis F. Linn Papers, Mo.H.S., for the belief that men were emotionally frailer than women in the face of death.

35. Marsh, "Motherhood Denied," 221; Leavitt "Shadow," 133, says the decline was caused by the active seeking of birth control; Brodie, *Contraception*, 4–5, agrees. McMillen, *Motherhood*, 182–83; Wyatt-Brown, *Southern Honour*, 205; Clinton, *Plantation Mistress*, 152–53; see also Lewis and Lockeridge, "Sally Has Been Sick," 5, contesting this view; Laurel Thatcher Ulrich, "'The Living Mother of a Living Child,'" in *Mothers and Motherhood*, 175–97; McMillen, *Motherhood*, 182–83; and Leavitt, *Brought to Bed*, 36–63. Foley, *Missouri*, vol. 7, 220–24. Bryan and Rose, *Pioneer Families*, XV. Leavitt, "Shadow," 132,

gives detailed examples of women's medical problems. (see Mary Holyoke). D'Emilio and Freedman, *Intimate Matters*, 57–66. Bryan and Rose, *Pioneer Families*, 77–78. The only reliable contraception methods in the 1830s were abstention and withdrawal (Brodie, *Contraception*, 57–86).

36. For a discussion of the replacement of midwives with doctors, see Catherine M. Scholten, *Childbearing in American Society, 1650–1850* (New York, 1985), 336–49; McMillen, *Motherhood*, 18–19, 68–72.

37. Hoffert, *Private Matters*, 67–68, 91–92.

38. Charles Gratiot to Isabelle Gratiot de Mun, March 28, 1814; Cece de Mun DePestre to Isabelle de Mun, April 19, 1817, De Mun Papers, Mo.H.S.

39. Maria von Phul to Henry von Phul, February 11, 1818, Von Phul Papers, Mo.H.S.; Isabelle de Mun to Jules de Mun, March 20, 1813[?], De Mun Papers, Mo.H.S.; William Lane to his mother, December 13, 1820, Sarah Ewing to Mary Lane, June 1, 1824, Carr-Lane Papers, Mo.H.S. Leavitt, "Shadow," 131–32, argues that childbirth's dangers promoted a kind of feminist response in women to form support groups and be active in their own care.

40. For a variety of birth experiences, see Bryan and Rose, *Pioneer Families*, 101, 303–4; Adele Gratiot to Isabelle de Mun, May 18, 1821, De Mun Papers, Mo.H.S.; Maria von Phul to Rosalie Saugrin von Phul, May 22, [?], Von Phul Papers, Mo.H.S.; William Lane to his mother, December 13, 1820; Sarah Ewing and Rachel Jenckes to Mary Lane, May 6, 1822; Sarah Law to Mary Lane, November 28, 182?; Sarah Ewing and Harriet Farrington to Mary Lane, September 13, 1827; Sarah Ewing and Rachel Jenckes to Mary Lane, May 6, 1822; Sarah Law to Mary Lane, November 28, 18??, Carr-Lane Papers, Mo.H.S.

41. Mary Lane to Sarah Law, no date, Carr-Lane Papers, Mo.H.S.

42. Elizabeth Kane to Elizabeth Linn, June 28, 1836, Lewis F. Linn Papers, Mo.H.S.

43. Schroeder and Schultz-Geisberg, *Hold Dear*, 111–12.

44. Brown, *Consent of the Governed*, 52.

45. Sarah von Phul Mason to Rosalie Saugrin von Phul, April 30, 1820, Von Phul Papers, Mo.H.S.

46. Anna Maria von Phul to Rosalie Saugrin von Phul, May 12, 1819; George von Phul to John Breckenridge, January 27 [?], Von Phul Papers, Mo.H.S. For her anxious, maternal years, see Sarah Mason to Henry von Phul, January 13, 1824; Sarah Mason to Henry and Rosalie von Phul, June 5, 1824?, Von Phul Papers, Mo.H.S.

47. Cece de Mun DePestre to Isabelle de Mun, March 12, 1837, De Mun Papers, Mo.H.S.; Schroeder and Shultz-Geisberg, *Hold Dear*, 139.

48. Stevenson, *Black and White*, 248–49; on childbirth and health, see White, *Ar'n't I*, 82–90, 101–9; see King, *Stolen Childhood*, 4–6, 150, on slave pregnancy and diminished African American fertility after the Civil War; Jones, *Labor of Love*, 19.

49. Dorcas Carr to Dabney Carr, January 1850; Henrietta S. Young to Dorcas Carr, March 11, 1857, Carr Papers, Mo.H.S. See Wahl, *Bondsman's Burden*, 49–76, on liability for hired slaves.

19. RACE, MORALITY, AND MOURNING

1. *St. Louis Free Press*, August 22, 1833; *St. Louis Enquirer*, March 31, 1821; ibid., September 1, 1822.

2. Revivalist minister Charles Finney said, "There is no need of young converts having . . . doubts as to their conversion. . . . A real Christian has no need to doubt," quoted in Thomas Cole, *The Journey of Life: A Cultural History of Aging in America* (New York 1992), 81. Elizabeth Hopkins to George Sibley, March 8, 1814, Lindenwood College Collection, Mo.H.S.

3. Kete, *Sentimental Collaborations*, 53. *St. Louis Enquirer*, June 7, 1824; Ravenswaay, *St. Louis*, 252–53. *St. Louis Beacon*, December 31, 1831; Ravenswaay, *St. Louis*, 143.

4. "The Mother's Last Prayer; or George Vining, A Narrative of Fact," No. 354. The American Tract Society, Lindenwood College Collection, Mo.H.S.; Cole, *Journey of Life*, 102–5, 138; Wishy, *Child*, 18.

5. Laderman, *Sacred Remains*, 29–30; see Douglas, *Feminization*, 200–226, for "consolation literature" and the development of romantic cemeteries. Robert Bishop and Jacqueline M. Atkins, *Folk Art in American Life* (New York, 1995), 45.

6. Douglas, *Feminization*, 201–2, 371 n. 6, has written of women and ministers' "inflating the importance of death" in this period to flatter themselves as they presided over the rituals surrounding it. I am not sure that the importance of death can be inflated although it can be trivialized; see Kelly, *New England Fashion*, 142–43, on how the "emphasis on sentiment and sensibility extended beyond female believers to reshape Protestantism itself."

7. Lyerly, *Southern Mind*, 28, 130; Mary Sibley, Journal, Lindenwood College Collection Papers, Mo.H.S.

8. For Thomas Cole on the differences between Puritan and evangelical conversion, see *Journey of Life*, 77–81. Mary Ryan has called the deathbed a "makeshift pulpit" (*Cradle of the Middle Class*, 87); see Lenore Davidoff and Catherine Hall, *Family Fortunes: Men and Women of the English Middle Class, 1780–1850* (Chicago, 1987), 117, on British evangelicals.

9. Lyerly, *Southern Mind*, 42–46. See Stowe, *Intimacy*, on courtship and the novel for this point. D. W. Winnicott, *Holding and Interpretation: Fragment of an Analysis* (1972, New York, 1986), 188–89, 192, writes about the notion of holding a weakened person in a safe, uncoercive embrace that enables him or her to experience himself without fear of disintegration.

10. All the quotes are from Sibley's Journal. See Kete, *Sentimental Collaborations*, 31–58, on mourning in antebellum America.

11. See Carroll Smith-Rosenberg, "The Female World of Love and Ritual," *A Heritage of Her Own*, 311–42, for the special friendships between women in this period. See Gillian Brown, *Domestic Individualism*, 33, on death in *Uncle Tom's Cabin*.

12. Hampsten, *Read This*, 135.

13. Maria von Phul to Rosalie Saugrain von Phul, May 22, ?, Von Phul Papers, Mo.H.S.; *Worlds Apart*, 187; see also Kete, *Sentimental Collaborations*, 35.

14. Ironically, it is often now true in movies and television where African Americans and Native Americans frequently represent the voice of simple virtues uncorrupted by commerce and false values.

15. Stevenson, *Black and White*, 171; Sobel, *World They Made*; Harriette Pipes McAdoo, *Black Families*, 57; Sterling Stuckey, *Slave Culture, Nationalist Theory and the Foundations of Black America* (New York, 1987), 14–17; Albert Raboteau, *Slave Religion: The "Invisible Institution" in the Antebellum South* (New York, 1978), 44–45; Gomez, *Exchanging*, 275–77.

16. Horton and Horton, *Liberty*, 127; see also Sobel, *World They Made*, 221. In eighteenth-century Virginia blacks and whites sometimes were buried next to each other.

17. *St. Louis Republican*, June 16, 1845, September 6, 1845, June 12, 1845, August 1, 1845, May 1845, June 23, 1845, November 17, 1845, May 6, 1845; *St. Louis Beacon*, September 16, 1830; Wahl, *Bondsman's Burden*, 32.

INDEX

Printed in the USA
CPSIA information can be obtained
at www.ICGtesting.com
LVHW091128150724
785511LV00001B/24